BRANDS AND BRAND MANAGEMENT

Contemporary Research Perspectives

D0082048

Marketing and Consumer Psychology Series

BRANDS AND BRAND MANAGEMENT

Contemporary Research Perspectives

Barbara Loken, Rohini Ahluwalia
and Michael J. Houston

Routledge
Taylor & Francis Group
New York   London

Psychology Press
Taylor & Francis Group
270 Madison Avenue
New York, NY 10016

Psychology Press
Taylor & Francis Group
27 Church Road
Hove, East Sussex BN3 2FA

© 2010 by Taylor and Francis Group, LLC
Psychology Press is an imprint of Taylor & Francis Group, an Informa business

Printed in the United States of America on acid-free paper
10 9 8 7 6 5 4 3 2 1

International Standard Book Number: 978-1-84169-759-8 (Hardback)

Library of Congress Cataloging-in-Publication Data

Brands and brand management : contemporary research perspectives / editors, Barbara Loken, Rohini Ahluwalia, Michael J. Houston.
    p. cm. -- (Marketing and consumer psychology series)
    Includes bibliographical references and index.
    ISBN 978-1-84169-759-8 (hardcover : alk. paper)
    1. Branding (Marketing) 2. Brand name products--Management. I. Loken, Barbara. II. Ahluwalia, Rohini, 1966- III. Houston, Michael J.

HF5415.1255.B73 2010
658.8'27--dc22
                                                            2009040020

Visit the Taylor & Francis Web site at
http://www.taylorandfrancis.com

and the Psychology Press Web site at
http://www.psypress.com

To our families for their support, insights, honesty, and good cheer.

And to the doctoral students, beginning with participants

in a 1986 consumer behavior seminar, who inspired

research on brands over the years

Contents

Section III Cultural, Sociological, and Global Branding Perspectives

Section IV New Directions in Measurement of Brand Equity

Section V   Protecting Brands

Series Foreword

The Marketing and Consumer Psychology book series was founded with a goal of providing a link between theory, research, and practice and an explicit recognition that academics and practitioners have much of value to learn from one another. The processes and modes of learning are often unique for different constituents of the marketing enterprise. The basic researcher prefers carefully controlled studies and uses research methods developed and enhanced by many disciplines. The practitioner faces immediate, constant, and long-term pressures for high levels of performance and creativity while desiring to learn more about the basic nature of brands and their roles in consumers' lives. Loken, Ahluwalia, and Houston's book provides a nice balance of the reflective luxury of academic perspectives on brands (especially the psychological aspects underlying brands) and their management along with a clear recognition of the challenges and demands faced by contemporary practitioners. Well-accomplished chapter authors provide succinct reviews of the current state of knowledge of various aspects of brands. The authors also provide an agenda for future research and areas of collaboration between academics and practitioners. This book will be of interest to graduate students and faculty in marketing, psychology, and communication, as well as practitioners and policy makers.

Curtis P. Haugtvedt
The Ohio State University
Marketing and Consumer Psychology book series editor

Foreword
Modern Branding Challenges

Introduction

Although some may question their importance, brands and branding have endured for literally centuries—and are likely to continue to thrive for many years to come—because of their fundamental purpose. At their best, brands allow consumers to reduce risk, simplify decision-making, and achieve greater satisfaction in their lives. To consumers, strong brands make their lives a little—or sometimes even a lot—better.

That is the good news. The bad news is that managing strong brands is as difficult as ever. Marketers now are having to cope with a wide variety of complex challenges: more diverse and enlightened consumers, heightened competition, rapidly changing technology, and environmental threats, to name a few. The marketing environment always changes, but the pace of change seems to have accelerated with the turn of the century. The rules of the branding game are different now. What worked 10 or 20 years ago might not work as well today, and almost certainly will not work as well 10 or 20 years from now.

There are a number of areas where marketers are rethinking—and sometimes fundamentally changing—their branding policies and practices. Here are six key ones that represent important branding priorities in the years to come.

Six Branding Priorities

Engage in participation marketing, recognize what consumers know and don't know about brands, and what they want and don't want from them.

Much has been made of the newly empowered consumer—in charge, setting the direction of the brand, and playing a much bigger role in how it is marketed. There is no question that consumers are more actively involved in the fortunes of brands than ever before. But the reality is, *only some of the consumers* want to get involved with *some of the brands* they use and, even then, only *some of the time.*

Largely due to the Internet, consumers can choose to become more involved than ever with a brand, communicating with the company and other consumers about their likes and dislikes about the brand and even how it is marketed. No question, some consumers will choose to become engaged at a deeper level with a brand, and marketers must do everything they can to encourage them to do so. But, regardless, many consumers will choose not to do so, and understanding how to best market a brand given such diversity in consumer backgrounds and interests is crucial.

Moreover, consumers often have difficult-to-express, undefined, ambiguous, or conflicting preferences. As a result, consumers may need guidance and assistance in even forming and conveying their preferences. In that regard, "participation marketing" may be a more appropriate concept for marketers to employ because marketers and consumers need to work together to find out how the firm can best satisfy consumer goals, given consumer knowledge and interests, and what they are willing to put into and hope to get out of the brand.

Craft well-designed products and services that provide a full set of functional and psychological benefits.

An increasingly crucial component of the value propositions for many firms is the design of their products and services. Adept marketers at firms such as Apple, Nike, Ritz Carlton, Singapore Airlines, and Samsung are maximizing functional and aesthetic aspects of the design of their products and/or services. Product design is not only how a product works, but also how it looks, feels, or even sounds and smells. Service design similarly is a function of all sensory aspects that consumers encounter and experience with a brand.

With the right designs, a brand offers advantages in product and service performance and imagery that can create significant functional and psychological benefits. A well-designed product or service affects consumers rationally and emotionally, both in their heads and in their hearts. Developing better designed products and services, however, requires a clear, comprehensive, and up-to-date understanding of consumers and how they purchase and use products and services, and think and feel about brands.

Design considerations will increasingly drive the innovation pipeline in terms of both new, as well as improved, products and services. Competitive advantages and brand strength will thus come from having better designed products and services than competitors, providing a wider range of more compelling consumer benefits as a result.

Develop fully integrated channel and communication strategies that optimally blend their strengths and weaknesses.

The diversity of means to communicate about products and services and sell them to consumers has exploded in recent years. Major shifts in media viewing habits have emerged due to the fragmentation of TV viewership; the growing use of DVRs, video gaming, and Internet broadband; the rise of mobile phones as an ubiquitous tool; the explosion of online blogs and social communities; and the greater importance of events, experience, and buzz marketing. These developments have affected how companies communicate about and distribute their products and services.

Marketers are increasingly embracing traditional and nontraditional communications, and different types of personal and mass media. It is hard to imagine a modern communication program that does not attempt to skillfully combine some form of (1) online, interactive communications, (2) "real world," experiential communications, and (3) traditional, mass media communications. Such combinations help marketers inform, entertain, persuade, and engage consumers and initiate ongoing conversations and dialogues. Marketers are also combining "push" and "pull" in their distribution strategies to maximize coverage and impact, selling directly via the mail, the Internet, telephones and cell phones, and company stores, while also selling indirectly via different types of wholesalers and retailers.

Design and implement a brand architecture strategy that maximizes long-term growth across product offerings, consumer and customer segments, and geographical markets.

For long-term financial success, the successful launch of new products and services and entry into new markets and market segments is of paramount importance. Brand growth requires a well-thought-out and implemented brand architecture strategy that defines: (1) the potential of a brand, (2) the types of product and service extensions that allow a brand to achieve that potential, and (3) the brand elements employed and positioning and images conveyed about all the different offerings for a brand in different markets and to different consumers.

A good brand architecture helps define brand boundaries in terms of what products or services the brand represents, what benefits it supplies, and what needs it satisfies. A good brand architecture provides "guardrails" as to appropriate and inappropriate line and category extensions. It clarifies the brand to consumers and motivates them in terms of which are the right versions of the product or service for them.

Given that the vast majority of new products are extensions and the vast majority of new products fail, the implication is clear: too many extensions fail. Why? Extensions are not creating sufficient relevance and differentiation in their product or service categories. An increasingly competitive marketplace will be even more unforgiving to poorly positioned and marketed extensions. Marketers must be rigorous and disciplined in their analysis and development of brand extensions to increase the likelihood of success. Understanding the relevance of the brand promise and how it should best be translated and adapted to different products and markets is of fundamental importance.

Embrace corporate social responsibility, and express a corporate point-of-view on societal, environmental, and community issues.

In part due to the heightened media coverage of business, there is greater transparency and awareness of companies, the words they use and actions they take, both inside and outside the company. Of greater concern to many consumers these days, especially younger ones, is whether a company is doing "good things" in terms of all aspects of society and the environment and all facets of employee and consumer lives.

Marketers must proactively embrace socially responsible and ethically and morally proper behavior at all times. Marketers need to find "win-win" solutions with cause marketing programs and other activities that allow them to enhance the welfare of consumers while still running their businesses profitably. If designed and implemented properly, cause marketing programs can accomplish a number of objectives for a brand: building brand awareness; enhancing brand image; establishing brand credibility; evoking brand feelings; creating a sense of brand community; and eliciting brand engagement.

Achieve greater accountability for brand investments and deeper understanding of the power of brands.

Heightened by tough financial times, marketers increasingly have had to do "more with less" across their marketing budgets and justify more persuasively every expenditure they do make. One challenge to achieving that goal is the broad and varied effects that any marketing activity may have on a brand: it may increase the breadth or depth of brand awareness; establish or strengthen performance-related or imagery-related brand associations; elicit positive judgments or feelings; create stronger ties or bonds with the brand; and initiate brand-related actions such as search, word-of-mouth, purchase, and so on. Moreover, in many, if not most cases, multiple effects will result from any one marketing activity.

But branding has broader effects than even these. Marketing effects on branding can be interpreted from a variety of perspectives. Notably, branding can be interpreted from economic, psychological, and sociological viewpoints. Regardless of the perspective adopted, however, fundamentally, marketing effects help create equity and value for the brand. In particular, the stronger the brand, the more power brand marketers have with consumers, distributors, and retailers. Extracting proper price premiums that reflect the power of the brand—and not over- or underpricing—is of paramount importance to marketers.

Conclusions

Recognizing the substantial intangible value of brands, branding is likely to remain a top priority for organizations of all kinds. Successful branding in the 21st century, however, requires new areas of emphasis and new skills. Six priority areas are:

1. Actively engaging in participation marketing
2. Crafting well-designed products and services
3. Developing fully integrated channel and communication strategies
4. Designing and implementing a robust brand architecture strategy
5. Embracing corporate social responsibility and expressing a corporate viewpoint on societal, environmental and community issues
6. Achieving greater accountability for brand investments and deeper understanding of the power of brands

Obviously, each area is complex and challenging and deserves greater analysis and discussion. Given this complexity, it is critical that (1) detailed, rich models are put forth to aid interpretation and planning, and (2) comprehensive, robust measures are employed to help trace any and all branding effects.

Fortunately, the branding area continues to receive intense research attention. This volume reflects the work of arguably the most talented collection of brand researchers at any top business school in the world, as well as the contributions of other leading branding thought leaders from other business schools or organizations. It offers perspectives and insights that will be vital to successful brand management in the future.

Specifically, it addresses branding topics that have been of enduring interest (brand extensions and brand alliances), as well as topics that have become increasingly more important in recent years (corporate social responsibility and brand emotions). It provides alternative perspectives on brands and their meaning, measurement, management, and protection. Collectively, these chapters significantly advance our understanding of the modern art and science of branding, tackling old problems and addressing new challenges in important ways.

Kevin Lane Keller
Dartmouth College

Preface

Branding practices have shifted greatly over the past two decades. In the 1980s and 1990s companies were increasing their understanding of the key attributes and benefits represented by their brands, experimenting with the use of brand extensions to leverage their brands, experimenting with brand alliances to provide competitive advantages in new categories, and attempting to determine how to measure their brands' equity. But not until recently have companies had multiple brand equity indices from which to choose. Similarly, not until recently have complex brand architectures become commonplace. Instead of experimenting with brand extension introductions companies now often manage multiple sub-branded products in multiple product categories.

The practice of branding has evolved in these and many other ways over the years. In the context of these changes, it is more important than ever to take stock of what the accumulated scientific research informs us about enduring scientific principles underlying the branding phenomenon, which can provide guidance in dealing with these changes. It is also an important time to review the new and emerging scientific insights in the literature related to factors that are likely to become even more consequential in the years to come. In contrast to topical branding practices, which often become quickly out of date, the science of branding provides knowledge-building, general principles about brands, and a broader understanding of the types of consumer, company, and contextual factors that influence brand perceptions, brand evaluations, and brand choice.

It is the science of brands that we address in this volume. Scientific research on brands has been conducted for many decades, and during the prior two decades we have witnessed a surge in research as the topics of leveraging brands, global, cultural, and social issues in branding, measurement of brand equity, and brand protection have brought renewed interest from both marketing professionals and marketing academic researchers. This surge has been driven, in part, by a wider scope of theoretical perspectives on branding topics, as theoretical guidance from cognitive psychology, social psychology, cross-cultural and cultural psychology, sociology, and economics has been provided. Also, resources for researchers and practitioners on brands and brand management have shown tremendous growth over the past decade, as witnessed by a growth in courses on brand management, proliferation of books and cases on brands, and growth in academic research on branding. Most books about brands and brand management focus on common-sense strategies of branding, based on best-of-practice and selected case studies, or focus on specialty topics of branding, such as brand relationships or brand identity. However, very few resources are available that meaningfully integrate the rich and vast body of scientific research and theories that have accumulated in the field, relating to both traditional and contemporary topics of branding.

In contrast to other books on brands, chapters in this volume focus on empirical research findings, models, and interdisciplinary theories that help us understand both traditional and contemporary branding topics. Importantly, we have among our chapter authors many of the world's leading experts in the science of branding, known both nationally and internationally for their reputations in their domains of brand research. While brand research sometimes uncovers findings that seem obvious, other research findings are not so obvious, and it is the undertaking of discerning the when and why of a particular finding that is fundamental to scholarly research on brands.

The Book's Audience

The audiences for this book fall primarily into three groups. First, the book is designed for scholarly researchers, who have need for reviews and compilations of relevant research findings on traditional and contemporary branding topics. The book is an aid to both doctoral students and faculty conducting research on the topics covered in the book. Second, the book is relevant for managers, analysts, and executives with a special interest in understanding theories and research underlying brand management. Third, the book should appeal to all graduate students, faculty, and marketing professionals with an interest in research findings about brands and an interest in deepening their understanding of how consumers view brands. Marketing professionals may also find the sidebars useful for understanding applications of branding principles.

Acknowledgments

We wish to thank Psychology Press and particularly Curtis Haugtvedt and Anne Duffy for their support of this volume and for advice and suggestions at each stage of the book-building process. Their comments and careful reading of the chapters are greatly appreciated. We wish to thank Rebecca D. Monro and Letta Wren Page for contributing their writing skills to the industry sidebars that are included in many chapters. Their extensive efforts with the Institute for Research in Marketing at the Carlson School of Management and their contacts with leading industry experts were important for identifying examples that demonstrate some of the research conclusions from this volume. We also thank Bob Ruekert and Jungkeun Kim for their efforts in categorizing the recent literature in the branding area, Hakkyun Kim for his literature search, and Brendan Meier for his help in formatting chapters. Finally, we are especially grateful to chapter authors for their willingness to contribute their insights and expertise in branding to this volume. Their empirical research and theoretical contributions in branding over the past 20 years have made this volume possible.

Barbara Loken
Rohini Ahluwalia
Michael J. Houston
Editors

The Editors

Barbara Loken is professor of marketing at the Carlson School, University of Minnesota. She is a recognized expert in the fields of branding and consumer psychology. She received her Ph.D. in social psychology at the University of Illinois and is currently both a professor in the marketing department and an adjunct professor in the psychology department at the University of Minnesota. She has published extensively on branding topics in leading marketing and consumer psychology journals. She has served as associate editor for the premier consumer marketing journal, *Journal of Consumer Research*, has served on the editorial boards of leading consumer marketing journals, and has received national media attention for her research.

Rohini Ahluwalia is professor of marketing at the Carlson School of Management, University of Minnesota. She received her Ph.D. from the Ohio State University. She is a well-known expert in the consumer psychology of persuasion, including branding and advertising issues. Her work has been published in leading scholarly journals, received research recognition (for instance, American Marketing Association's John A. Howard Best Dissertation award), and reported in several national and international media outlets such as National Public Radio, *New York Times*, *CBS News*, *Smart Money Russia*, and *Economic Times* (India). She currently serves as an associate editor for the *Journal of Consumer Research*, and has been named to the editorial review boards of several other leading marketing journals.

Michael J. Houston is Ecolab-Pierson M. Grieve Chair in International Marketing at the Carlson School of Management, University of Minnesota. He received his Ph.D. from the University of Illinois. He is a former editor of the *Journal of Marketing Research* and has served on the editorial boards of other leading marketing journals. He has published extensively in the area of consumer behavior. His current research focuses on cultural effects on consumer behavior, especially in the area of branding.

Contributors

Rohini Ahluwalia
Department of Marketing
Carlson School of Management
University of Minnesota

Stephen Baird
Trademark and Brand
    Management Group
Winthrop and Weinstine, P.A.

Antoine Bechara
Department of Psychology
College of Letters, Arts, and
    Sciences
University of Southern California

Chi-Yue Chiu
Department of Psychology
College of Liberal Arts and
    Sciences
University of Illinois at Urbana-
    Champaign

Xavier Dreze
Department of Marketing
Wharton School of Business
University of Pennsylvania

Tulin Erdem
Department of Marketing
Leonard N. Stern School of
    Business
New York University

Anne Fries
Faculty of Management,
    Economics, and Social Sciences
University of Cologne

Zeynep Gurhan-Canli
College of Administrative Sciences
    and Economics
Koc University

Michael J. Houston
Department of Marketing
Carlson School of Management
University of Minnesota

Deborah Roedder John
Department of Marketing
Carlson School of Management
University of Minnesota

Christopher Joiner
Department of Marketing
School of Management
George Mason University

Andrew Kaikati
Department of Marketing
Carlson School of Management
University of Minnesota

Hean Tat Keh
Department of Marketing
Guanghua School of Management
Peking University
Beijing, China

Jonathan Lee
Department of Marketing
College of Business
    Administration
California State University

Barbara Loken
Department of Marketing
Carlson School of Management
University of Minnesota

Deborah J. MacInnis
Department of Marketing
Marshall School of Business
University of Southern California

Albert M. Muniz, Jr.
Department of Marketing
Kellstadt Graduate School of
    Business
DePaul University

Thomas C. O'Guinn
Department of Marketing
Wisconsin School of Business
University of Wisconsin

C. Whan Park
Department of Marketing
Marshall School of Business
University of Southern California

Akshay Rao
Department of Marketing
Carlson School of Management
University of Minnesota

Baba Shiv
Department of Marketing
Graduate School of Business
Stanford University

Joffre Swait
Department of Marketing
School of Business
University of Alberta
and
Advantis, Inc.

Carlos Torelli
Department of Marketing
Carlson School of Management
University of Minnesota

Section I

Overview

1

On the Science of Branding: An Introduction

Barbara Loken, Rohini Ahluwalia, and Michael J. Houston
University of Minnesota

Chapters in this volume are based on the scientific literature of branding, covering both traditional and contemporary topics. Bringing together nationally and internationally-known branding experts helps us integrate and synthesize the scientific literature so that we better understand the major takeaways and insights relating to different topics of branding and where we are headed next. We have learned a tremendous amount, as these chapters will show. The field of branding has progressed from simple demonstrations of the importance of brands and brand names to a richer understanding of the mechanisms underlying consumers' responses to brands and the contexts in which different findings are likely to emerge. Further, chapters in this volume represent multidisciplinary perspectives, including economic (e.g., brand utility models), psychological (e.g., brand extension findings), measurement (e.g., indices of brand equity), and sociological (e.g., analyzing brands at a societal level) perspectives. Chapter authors have also highlighted contemporary issues of importance to both brand researchers and marketing professionals in the years to come.

Content of the Book

The book is divided into four sections.

Section I of the book includes topics relevant to building and leveraging brands, including brand extensions, brand alliances, brand loyalty, and corporate social responsibility:

- *Brand extensions* account for 80% of new product introductions (Keller, 2008; Simms, 2005) and are well recognized as the most frequently used product strategy for leveraging brands. Perhaps for this reason, academic research on brand extensions has far outnumbered all other research articles on branding during the past two decades (Ruekert and Kim, 2009). Brand extensions can provide companies with innovative design features, new benefits for products and services, and competitive advantages. They are the building blocks for designing a company's brand architecture. Chapter 2 on brand extensions, authored by Loken, Joiner, and Houston, reviews this prolific prior literature and highlights extension strategies that have been found to be most and least successful for brands. Research on subbrands and research on cross-cultural differences in brand extension evaluation offer looks at important issues to consider for brand architectures to be strong across different global markets.

- The topic of *brand alliances* is increasingly relevant for practitioners and researchers as alliances between brands become more commonplace in all aspects of marketing, but particularly marketing communications. In Chapter 3 by Rao, theoretical approaches that have informed research on the effectiveness of brand alliances and contexts in which they are successful are discussed. An organizing framework is proposed for identifying factors that influence brand alliances and relevant research is reviewed. In Rao's chapter, the potential benefits and costs to brand architecture from brand alliances can be discerned from previous research and the author's look to the future.

- *Brand loyalty* has been regarded as one of the most important topics for CEOs today (Dunn and Davis, 2004), and managing customer loyalty has become increasingly important for marketing professionals. Chapter 4 on brand loyalty, authored by Ahluwalia and Kaikati, synthesizes this literature and enlightens us about recent developments and important findings relating to different paths that can be used for building consumers' loyalty to brands. These findings are relevant to several branding initiatives that companies have, such as understanding factors that drive how consumers evaluate and respond to brands. As Ahluwalia and Kaikati illustrate, the relative role of performance, emotional connections, and switching inducements can vary in the formation of consumers' loyalty toward a brand, depending upon characteristics of the marketplace, product, firm, and consumer.

- Pairing of brands with social issues is described in Chapter 5 on *corporate social responsibility* by Gürhan-Canli and Fries. Research on corporate social responsibility (CSR) and branding has increased significantly in recent years, as this chapter shows, concomitant with the trend of companies to pursue these associations as part of their leveraging strategies to build brand trust and customer commitment. Gürhan-Canli and Fries summarize research on branding and CSR, covering major influential factors to consider in developing a CSR strategy. Some of these factors include consumer characteristics such as familiarity with and affinity for a cause, the fit between a brand and its CSR activities, and the company's trustworthiness and its perceived commitment to a CSR cause as revealed by financial contributions or duration of the cause-brand relationship. Collectively, these factors and others offer a useful framework within which to develop and/or enhance a CSR strategy that benefits one or more brands of a company.

Section II of this volume addresses contemporary perspectives on cultural and social aspects of branding. Theory and research on these topics have been increasing rapidly in recent years as marketers analyze brands from a global perspective and increasingly use nontraditional marketing techniques to understand their brands.

- Chapter 6 by Torelli, Keh, and Chiu analyzes research and theory on the *cultural symbolism of brands* in multicultural markets, and proposes a framework for understanding the effects of cultural symbolism on brand perceptions. Brands sometimes achieve "iconic" status, both nationally and internationally, and this chapter reflects on research that addresses the cultural symbolism of brands. These considerations have implications for the role of culture in marketing initiatives, such as the design of new product and services and the nature of brand communications.
- Chapter 7 by O'Guinn and Muniz develops a broad model of the *social brand*, which enables a more expansive view of influences on brand meanings. Drawing on a sociological perspective, the authors illustrate how brand meanings develop beyond the influence of marketing. Both consumer forces such as brand communities and institutional forces such as governments heavily impact brand meaning. The authors provide rich examples of these types of influences. The relevance of these forces is increasingly important in nontraditional marketing communications, such as understanding online social communities and their implications for brands.

Section III of this volume addresses the important topic of *brand equity* and provides perspectives from three researchers with significant expertise in this area. Brand equity is one of the core assets of companies (Lev, 2005).

- Chapter 8 by Park, MacInnis, Dreze, and Lee presents a new measure of brand equity, termed *Marksure (marketing, surplus, and efficiency)*, which considers consumers' relationships with their brands and companies' investments in developing these relationships. The authors provide theoretical rationales underlying components of the model as well as examples of how this interesting measure might be used by marketing professionals.

- Chapter 9 by Shiv and Bechara examines brand equity from the perspective of *customer value proposition* (CVP), an emerging area of interest in marketing. The authors propose that understanding consumers' emotions toward a brand is essential for creating committed consumers and increasing CVP, and as a result, creating a competitive advantage for a brand. Advances in neuroscience and the ability to track brand emotion are also discussed in this chapter. The power of the heart or emotions in influencing consumer decision making and brand choices is clearly elucidated by Shiv and Bechara. These authors present a framework for brand value that factors in the role of functional as well as emotional benefits.

- Chapter 10 by Erdem and Swait provides a significant review of *quantitative utility models of brand equity*. These models are based on the assumption that brands provide utility or value to consumers, and this value may affect any or all stages of consumers' decision making, such as formation of brand perceptions, information search, and brand choice. The authors provide an integrative framework of brand equity based on utility maximization and discrete choice modeling. These models can incorporate marketing initiatives that evaluate a brand's performance based on brand features, as well as initiatives relating to price, promotion, and distribution activities.

Section IV of this volume addresses the topic of brand protection.

- Research on *brand dilution* and the harmful impact that failed or inconsistent brand extensions potentially have on the parent brand have been important topics in the brand literature. Chapter 11 by Loken and John extends the reach of brand dilution to review the *external sources of brand dilution*, such as negative publicity, consumer blogging, and trademark dilution. *Internal sources of brand dilution*, including harmful effects due to brand promotions, brand distribution, and brand extensions, are also reviewed.

- Finally, the essential topic of *legal protection of brands and trademarks* is described in Chapter 12 by Baird, an attorney with specialized expertise in trademark law. The chapter reviews the components of a brand that may be trademarked as well as the legal definitions of trademark confusion and trademark dilution. The relevance of understanding trademarks in forming brands is not only important for protecting brands but also for building and leveraging them. Marketers must be mindful of legal considerations in developing both traditional and online trademarks for any elements of a brand including brand name, sensory features, or new product design features.

Social Media and a Look to the Future

Nontraditional media are the wave of the future for marketing practitioners. With this in mind, topics described in this volume have strong relevance for understanding the effectiveness of building brands online. While research in the past has generally relied on traditional forms of marketing (e.g., persuasive appeals rather than participative marketing approaches), many of the findings also have cross-over appeal to nontraditional settings. Research on consumer-brand connections and emotional ties is described in chapters by Alhuwalia and Kaikati (Chapter 4), Park, MacInnis, Dreze, and Lee (Chapter 8), and Shiv and Bechara (Chapter 9). Further, Torelli, Heu, and Chiu (Chapter 6) describe the importance of culture in creating brand meaning. Research that understands the roles of brand loyalty, consumer-brand connections, and emotions in fostering social communities that form online or through nontraditional media is an important area for future research. These connections can also serve to differentiate a brand.

Brand communities, consumer collectives, and consumer tribes, described by O'Guinn and Muniz (Chapter 7), are certainly some of the means by which participation marketing could emerge to satisfy needs of consumers. These consumer aggregates, as well as governments, trade organizations, and other forces in contemporary society, participate in the co-creation of brands. Marketers encourage consumers' participation with the brand through loyalty programs and emotional bonds (Chapter 4), but may go further in encouraging consumers to formulate their own goals for the brand.

O'Guinn and Muniz (Chapter 7) and Loken and John (Chapter 11) demonstrate how consumers and other social forces can lead to changes in a brand and even brand dilution outside the control of the marketer. Research on participation marketing and recent marketing techniques for engaging consumers through social communities, social media, or similar interactions is at a nascent stage. Conditions under which consumers can participate in the branding process in order to best satisfy their needs and goals is a largely unexplored area of research. Future research might also tell us whether distant brand extensions are more readily accepted when consumers have requested or participated in the brand extension concept.

Younger (and increasingly, older) consumers' preoccupation with Facebook, Twitter, and other social media has heightened the interests of practitioners and has allowed marketers access to consumers on a one-to-one basis without the interface of traditional media. Online videos and downloads of television shows, movies, and other videos provide consumers more choice in the types of online sources they wish to use, and consequently the types of advertising they are willing to receive. The vast online arena for consumer knowledge about brands is a priority for marketers and should be a fruitful area for future research.

References

Dunn, M., & Davis, S. (2004). Creating the brand-driven business: It's the CEO who must lead the way. *Handbook of Business Strategy, 5*, 243–248.

Keller, K.L. (2008). *Strategic brand management: Building, measuring, and managing brand equity* (3rd ed.). Upper Saddle River, NJ: Pearson Education Inc.

Lev, B. (2005). *Intangibles: Management, measurement, and reporting.* Vancouver: University of British Columbia Press.

Ruekert, R.W., & Kim, J. (2009). The development of the field of brand management research: A review of research from 1987 to 2006. Working paper.

Simms, J. (2005). Where are all the new ideas? *Marketing (UK), December 18,* 34–36.

Section II

Managing and Leveraging Brands

2

Leveraging a Brand Through Brand Extension:
A Review of Two Decades of Research*

Barbara Loken
University of Minnesota

Christopher Joiner
George Mason University

Michael J. Houston
University of Minnesota

In this chapter, we review 20 years of research on family brands, particularly as it pertains to brand extensions and the conditions under which brand extensions are likely to succeed. Companies rely on brand extensions as low-cost, low-risk leveraging strategies to reach new consumer segments, meet changing consumer needs, respond to competitors' extensions, and increase shelf space in a tough retail environment. Brand extensions can also revitalize brands and introduce innovation, thereby boosting usage occasions for a brand, increasing first-mover advantages in certain product categories, and increasing consumers' perceptions of a brand as youthful and innovative. In this chapter we address academic research pertaining to brand extensions and the factors that improve their chances for success.

What Is a Brand Extension?

We begin by defining a *brand extension*, as well as enumerate many of the types of brand extensions that exist in the marketplace. We define

* The authors wish to thank Tim Heath and Sanjay Puligadda for their careful reading of this chapter and their thoughtful comments and suggestions. The first author wishes to thank the Institute for Research in Marketing for providing funding for producing this chapter.

brand extension as a product or service introduced in the marketplace that includes an existing brand's name. For example, Tide to Go instant stain remover is an extension of the Tide brand name. The term *line extension* refers to a particular type of brand extension, a variant of an existing product within the same product category. For example, extending from Diet Coke to No Caffeine Diet Coke would be an example of a line extension.*

We define a *sub-brand extension* as one in which the parent brand name is assigned to the brand extension along with another name created by the company. For example, Toyota Camry, Canon PowerShot, and Courtyard by Marriott are all sub-branded extensions that include both the parent brand name (Toyota, Canon, Marriott) and another created name (Camry, PowerShot, Courtyard). The added name serves to differentiate the product from others of the parent brand. While there are many variants of sub-branded extensions, a common one is an *endorser brand extension* such as Polo by Ralph Lauren, Cottenelle by Kleenex, or Courtyard by Marriott, which assigns a stronger role to the sub-branded name through the use of "by" or "from" or endorsement by font and type size on product packaging. With endorser and many sub-brands in general, a goal of many companies is to establish a differentiated brand name (Polo, Cottenelle, Courtyard) under the parent brand name (Ralph Lauren, Kleenex, Marriott) which over time (as consumers learn about the endorsed brand) is recognizable without the parent.

We define *co-branded extensions* as extensions that pair two established brand names, such as the Eddie Bower edition of Ford Explorer or Pillsbury Cinnabon rolls, and in which *both* brands are included in the name of the extension. Co-branded extensions, like sub-branded extensions, can include endorser relationships, such as Campbell's V8 soups, in which both brands are established (in this case, they are from the same company, but usually they are not). Co-branded extensions are sometimes referred to as *composite brands* or one form of *brand alliance*.[†] Research on brand alliances is reviewed elsewhere (Rao, this volume).

The term *family brand* is an overarching name given to brands or lines within a category (e.g., Toyota includes Camry and RAV4 as sub-brands and LE and LX as models or variations of one or more lines), and the *parent*

---

* The distinction between a line and a brand extension is not always apparent. For example, a bag of Hershey's miniature chocolate with almond candy bars may be viewed as a line extension of the regular Hershey's chocolate bars, and yet with sufficient variation in target market or packaging, it could represent a brand extension. While the literature sometimes makes a distinction between line and brand extension, for the purposes of brevity in this chapter we often group them and refer to both as brand extensions.

† Some brand alliances do not name both brands, such as distributor's brands (e.g., Sears Roadhandler Tires are made by Michelin but are not indicated as such), and are not included in our definition since consumers may be unaware of such alliances.

brand name, such as Toyota, is the brand name that links all the individual products of the brand. The larger network of brands and sub-brands built by a company is often referred to as a *house of brands, brand hierarchy,* or *brand architecture*. These terms are used to describe the multiple ways in which parent brand names can be used with sub-brands and co-brands to extend to new product categories, new consumer markets, and new situational uses for brands.

Most brand extensions succeed in part because of consumers' familiarity with the parent brand name. Consumers trust that a new brand extension will fulfill the brand's promise and they expect a brand extension to be consistent with the parent brand's core associations. For example, a Coke extension might be expected to be "great tasting," "cola-flavored," and "carbonated." The brand associations that are held most strongly by consumers, for a given situation or for a targeted group of consumers, are *core associations* about the brand, and may include brand image attributes, prototypical products of the brand, the brand's logo, trademarked color combinations, sonic brand tones, CSR initiatives, and/or other prominent elements of a brand. Consumers expect that a new brand extension will include some (although perhaps not all) of these core associations. In addition, however, some brand extensions play a new role in the family, broadening out the brand's image associations in favorable ways and taking risks by changing one or more core brand associations. For example, the Curves International fitness club chain successfully broadened its brand concept of female-only fitness centers to include food products. The company's line of brand extensions, including breakfast cereals and bars, introduced an entirely new set of associations to the Curve's core brand (e.g., "reducing calories to lose weight").

In this chapter, we examine two scenarios involving brand extensions. First, we examine brand extensions that stretch associations that are familiar to consumers and consistent with consumers' expectations for the brand. Most of the existing academic research examines factors leading to success or failure of new brand extensions in the context of brand names and associations that are familiar to consumers. Unless otherwise specified, we use the term brand extension to refer to extensions without a sub-brand or co-brand name attached to them. We review the research findings concerning factors that heighten success of these brand extensions. Second, less frequently researched, but nevertheless increasingly important for the development of brand portfolios, are brand stretches, which function to broaden the brand's core associations and strengths but also have the advantage of retaining at least some of the brand's core strengths. Some of these brand stretches are innovations in product categories to which they extend (e.g., Westin Heavenly Beds). In these instances, the parent brand is often paired with a new sub-branded extension (e.g., Apple's iPhone) or co-branded extension (e.g., Pillsbury Cinnabon rolls or

Radisson's Select Comfort Sleep Number bed) that identifies an innovation or feature that is either unique to the brand or unique to the product category in which the extension occurs. The distinctiveness of the sub-branding or co-branding label, as well as the association with the core brand, can have significant competitive advantages for the brand.

In the sections that follow, we discuss relevant research findings on success or failure of brand extensions. We begin with a discussion of three brand factors (brand strength, brand extension consistency, and information prominence or accessibility) that have been found in academic research to increase acceptance of brand extensions. Next, we examine some of the brand extension strategies that have been researched relevant to product, pricing, distribution, promotion, and competitive strategies, and evaluate their effectiveness. A number of marketing strategies have been found to increase acceptance of a brand extension even when other conditions, such as the brand extension's fit, are not favorable, and these are examined as well. We then turn to a discussion of brand stretches that depart significantly from the brand's original categories and brand extension innovations, both of which are increasingly common in the marketplace. Sub-brand and co-brand names used on brand extensions have been found to reduce risk, but they have other advantages for brand extensions that are also discussed. With a focus on the nature of self-construal and the attendant differences in processing, we then examine the effects of culture on the evaluation of brand extensions. Finally, we address future research needs for brand extensions. Theoretical perspectives on branding research are covered elsewhere (Loken, 2006; Loken, Joiner, & Peck, 2002; Loken, Barsalou, & Joiner, 2008).

Brand Extensions That Extend Familiar Brand Associations

Research on brand extensions has identified three key factors that influence whether a new brand extension introduced in the marketplace is evaluated favorably or not. A brand extension is more likely to be accepted (1) when consumers feel commitment, trust, and/or liking for the parent brand or have had experience using the parent brand, (2) when the extension is consistent with the core brand image or product associations of the parent brand, and (3) when the focus of the information about the brand extension (which could include associations about the parent brand, the product category of the extension, the distinctive features of the brand extension, or other foci) includes favorable relevant information. We discuss each of these factors in turn (other useful reviews of the brand extension literature can be found in Bridges, Keller, & Sood, 2000; Czellar,

2003; Keller, 2002a, Loken et al., 2008; and Völckner & Sattler, 2006). Parent brand information has low impact on extension success under some conditions (e.g., when it is not accessible to consumers), and these conditions are addressed as well.

Parent Brand Commitment, Trust, Liking, and Experience

Not surprisingly, brand extensions are more likely to be accepted from high-quality brands (Aaker & Keller, 1990; Randall, Ulrich, & Reibstein, 1998), well-liked brands (Rangaswamy, Burke, & Oliva, 1993), and from stronger brands with higher market share (Reddy, Holak, & Bhat, 1994; Smith & Park, 1992) than from brands that are average in rating, are less well liked, and have lower market shares. Consumers' feelings of trust and commitment toward a parent brand have also been found to increase acceptance of brand extensions (Park & Kim, 2002; see also Kirmani, Sood, & Bridges, 1999; Völckner & Sattler, 2006). Brands that are rated highly on esteem and that are prominent in the marketplace, such as Coca-Cola, Hershey's, and Campbell's, have also been found to create positive stock market reaction when introducing brand extensions (Lane & Jacobson, 1995).

Other research describes specific marketing conditions that favor strong brands, and findings depend to some extent on whether brand strength derives from *knowledge* or *familiarity* with the brand or from prior *experiences* with the brand's products. When consumers have low knowledge of the brand extension's product category, and the extended product is one that requires trial in order to evaluate it (e.g., cold remedies or other experience goods), trust in the brand name becomes even more important. Smith and Park (1992), for example, found that a brand extension's market share and the brand's advertising efficiency were greater when consumers were familiar with the parent brand but unfamiliar with the extension category. Furthermore, effects of a parent brand on a brand extension's market share and advertising efficiency are greatest at the time of the extension's introduction, when beliefs about the brand extension are most unfamiliar or most malleable; importantly, the effects decrease over time (Smith & Park, 1992). Consumers also rely more on a strong parent brand when the brand extension is introduced in a product category that has only a few competitors (Smith & Park, 1992). On the other hand, if a brand's dominance in the extension category is unclear or questionable (Kim, 2006; see also Herr, Farquhar, & Fazio, 1996), evaluations of the extension are more likely to be influenced by factors other than the parent brand name.

Research on prior experience with a brand yields more mixed findings, but tends to suggest that prior positive experience with a parent brand increases acceptance of a new brand extension (Kim & Sullivan, 1998; Swaminathan, 2003; Swaminathan, Fox, & Reddy, 2001; Völckner

& Sattler, 2006). Furthermore, consumers' experiences with an intervening extension increases purchase rates of a subsequent brand extension (Swaminathan, 2003). On the other hand, the role of parent brand experiences reduces significantly after consumers try the brand extension. Prior experiences with the parent brand can increase expectations for the brand extension and if the extension's performance is not matched, consumers may show even lower rates of repurchase than non-experienced consumers (cf. Swaminathan et al., 2001).

Brand Extension Consistency

A second factor that influences brand extension acceptance is the *consistency*, fit, or similarity between elements of the brand extension and elements of the parent brand. When the relationship between the parent brand and the brand extension is perceived to be high, attitudes toward the parent brand and beliefs about the brand's core associations will be more likely to transfer to the new brand extension. An abundance of research findings support the consistency effect. For example, extensions are more likely to be accepted when they occur in a product category that is perceived as similar to or a good fit with the parent brand categories (Aaker & Keller, 1990; Boush et al., 1987; Boush & Loken, 1991; Herr et al., 1996; Völckner & Sattler, 2006). Consistency with respect to a core brand association also enhances acceptance of a brand extension, such as the brand Coach extending on the "prestige" image attribute, the brand Calvin Klein extending on an "edgy" image attribute (Bhat & Reddy, 2001; Park, Milberg, & Lawson, 1991), or a brand extending on a brand usage goal (Martin & Stewart, 2001), such as Reebok cotton spandex athletic apparel. In fact, brand image consistency has been found, at times, to be more important than product category consistency in achieving brand extension success. Park et al. (1991) found that a brand extension that maintained a prestige brand image of a symbolic product (e.g., perfume) led to even greater extension acceptance than a brand extension that moved to a similar product category. Broniarcyzk and Alba (1994) found that the relevance of the core brand associations to the new product category was more important than the similarity of the extension and brand product categories. For example, a Timex alarm system, for which "reliability" is relevant, may be perceived more favorably than a Timex bracelet, which appears similar to a watch but for which Timex associations are less relevant.

The consistency effect is widespread although it tends to vary with certain consumer groups and with expertise. For example, Zhang and Sood (2002) found that children ages 11–12 based extension evaluations more on surface cues (such as the brand's name or linguistic features like rhyming names, Coca-Cola Gola iced tea or Wrigley's Higley toffee) and less on deep cues (such as similarity in product categories of parent brand and extension). Adults, in contrast, used the consistency rule more often, evaluating near extensions (e.g., Coca-Cola iced tea) more favorably than far extensions (e.g., Coca-Cola toffee). When the children were cued to make similarity judgments prior to evaluation, this knowledge prompted them to behave more like adults, evaluating near extensions more favorably than far extensions. Muthukrishnan and Weitz (1991) found that both experts and novices used a consistency rule in judgments of brand extensions, but experts based their judgments on more complex cues. That is, experts (more than novices) transferred associations from the parent brand to the extension when fit between them was based on complex attributes (e.g., the fit between a computer and a camera relied on technological competencies). Novices, on the other hand, transferred associations based on surface similarities between the parent brand and the extension categories (e.g., the fit between camera and film). Finally, Puligadda, Ross, and Grewal (2008) found that consumers who tended to be generally receptive to brand information, or more *brand centric*, were more likely to rely on brand image consistency in evaluating extensions than consumers who were not brand centric.

Information Prominence and Accessibility

The third factor that influences brand extension acceptance is information in the marketing environment that is *prominent* or of sufficient intensity to capture consumers' attention and thought. The associations in memory that are most *accessible* to consumers are the ones most likely to influence judgments of a new brand extension. Information that is prominent (from the point of view of the marketer) or accessible (from the point of view of the consumer) determines both the focus of attention and consumers' interpretation of brand information (and this could include information about the brand's image attributes, information about the brand's existing products, and/or information about the new extension and new extension category).

One way in which accessibility becomes important is in determining whether information that consumers bring to mind reinforces similarities between the parent brand and the brand extension or highlights differences between them. Depending on which information is accessible or selectively attended to about the brand (e.g., the brand image attributes or the product categories of the brand) or about the brand extension (e.g., the product category of the extension, relation-to-category information, or unique, *individuating* information about the extension), the transfer of beliefs and affect from the brand to brand extension can vary. For example, a consumer who recently attended an engaging athletic event sponsored by Coke will have different information accessible about Coke than a consumer who recently tried the Coke extension Coke Blak. These different cognitions for different consumers, or for the same consumer on different occasions, have implications for the interpretation of new information. Information that is currently accessible (to the consumer) or prominent (in the marketing environment) about the brand serves as the backdrop for evaluating a new extension. Researchers have shown, for example, that providing information unique to the extension (e.g., Klink & Smith, 2001) or increasing people's knowledge of the product category of the extension (e.g., McCarthy, Heath, & Milberg, 2001) increases the prominence of extension information and reduces the importance of brand name. Therefore, a poor fitting extension might be partially overcome by providing more product information about the extension itself. The importance of prominence or accessibility of information in affecting judgments has been found in a variety of research in consumer psychology, and its importance in branding has been widely established (e.g., Ahluwalia & Gurhan-Canli, 2000; Boush, 1993; Bridges et al., 2000; Loken, 2006; Loken et al., 2008; Pryor & Brodie, 1998; Shine, Park, & Wyer, 2007, Van Osselaer & Alba, 2003).

Strategic Brand Decision Making

Building brands through consistency is not only supported by academic research; it makes intuitive sense as a marketing goal. Consumers are less confused about what the brand represents and are able to predict performance for each of the brand's products when consistency is maintained. Further, study results make clear that the connection between a parent brand and a brand extension needs to be perceived as a good fit from the consumer's, rather than the marketer's, perspective. When marketers desire to extend their brands to moderately dissimilar categories to reach new consumers, encourage new usage occasions, or introduce new product benefits, a connection to the parent brand may need to be communicated clearly to the consumer. Prior research indicates that consumers probably engage in more thought when evaluating moderately inconsistent brand extensions (relative to consistent extensions) and require more time to evaluate them (Boush & Loken, 1991; Lane, 2000). Searching for a connection between the parent brand and the brand extension may be the reason, and marketing strategies can facilitate achieving resolution of inconsistencies.

In this section, we review research findings that apply the three principles described above (brand strength, brand consistency, and information prominence) to understanding product, price, distribution, promotion, and competitive strategy decisions with respect to brand extensions. We focus on findings that improve or reduce acceptance rates of brand extensions.

Product Branding Strategies

As noted earlier, creating brand extensions that are consistent with the brand's core promise, either by extending into similar and compatible product categories, extending along attributes that are consistent with the parent brand, or extending based on consumers' goals for using and purchasing the brand, increases the success of the brand extension (Aaker & Keller, 1990; Bottomley & Holden, 2001; Boush & Loken, 1991; Broniarczyk & Alba, 1994; Park et al., 1991). In addition to this general consistency strategy, several product development strategies, such as (1) increasing brand breadth, (2) maintaining quality consistency, (3) logical sequencing of brand extension introductions, and (4) generating brand extension synergies have been studied in the context of brand extensions.

The first strategy found to impact brand extension success or failure is increasing the *broadness* of the brand (Boush & Loken, 1991; Dacin & Smith, 1994; Meyvis & Janiszewski, 2004). Boush and Loken (1991) found that a brand that includes products in diverse product categories (e.g., Healthy Choice) has certain advantages over narrow brands that include products in only one product category (e.g., Campbell's) in extending to new categories. Narrow brands have advantages over broad categories in introducing a line extension within the same category of expertise (e.g., a new soup) but have disadvantages in moving to a moderately different product category (e.g., spaghetti sauce or frozen vegetables).

One rationale behind the broadness findings is that narrow brands trigger from consumers' memories the product category as a core brand association and consumers selectively attend to this information (Meyvis & Janiszewski, 2004). For example, consumers selectively attend to and consider "cola beverage" when evaluating a Pepsi brand extension, and selectively attend to and consider "soup" when evaluating a Campbell's brand extension. As a result, when consumers evaluate a new Pepsi cola beverage, or a new Campbell's soup, these line extensions are compatible with the consumers' accessible product category associations, but extensions to different product categories, such as Crystal Pepsi (a clear-colored beverage) or Campbell's spaghetti sauce (which fared less well than Prego spaghetti sauce), are not viewed as compatible. Herr et al. (1996) found, too, that when a strong brand is linked to a particular product category, this product category association deters consumers' tendencies to transfer beliefs and affect about the brand to a brand extension in a distant product category. When consumers think about an extension of a broad brand, in contrast, the brand associations that are prominent are more likely to include nonproduct-category associations, such as "exclusive" in the case of the Ralph Lauren brand, or "healthy meal" in the case of the Healthy Choice brand (cf. Park et al., 1991). As a result, an extension into a moderately different product category is more likely to be perceived as consistent with the brand. Rangaswamy et al. (1993), too, found that when two brands were preferred equally, but one was associated with brand image attributes (and not physical attributes of the product category), it was more successful in extending to distant extensions than the other brand that was linked to both brand image and physical attributes of the product categories. The authors argue, for example, that Oscar Mayer may have difficulty extending to cheese, chips, and other nonmeat product categories, since the name is closely associated with meat products.

Another product development factor found to increase extension success is quality consistency of products of the brand. Not surprisingly, brands that are consistently high in quality (and particularly ones with a high number of products in their portfolio) have been found to be more successful in extending than brands with high quality variation (Dacin & Smith, 1994). Consumers infer that a brand successful in making consistently high quality products is likely to make another one. A product strategy that has been found to increase perceived brand quality and expertise is introducing multiple versions of a brand, within a brand line, such as multiple flavors of chocolate (Berger, Draganska, & Simonson 2007). On the other hand, a product strategy that can reduce quality perceptions and hamper future success is extending vertically downward on a quality dimension. Jun, Mazundar, and Raj (1999) found that when the parent brand's product category was at a higher technological level than a brand extension (e.g., Motorola moving from high-end workstations to desktop computers), the extension was judged more favorably than when the parent brand's product category was at a lower technological level than the extension (e.g., Canon moving from 35 mm cameras to camcorders). Experts, however, more than novices, valued upward technological extensions (Jun et al., 1999), and a vertical move upward was rated more favorably when the move was to a similar category (from cameras to camcorders) than when the move was to a dissimilar category (from televisions to computers).

A third product strategy found to increase brand extension success is the logical sequencing of extensions. When multiple brand extensions are introduced sequentially under a well-liked brand name, success of a brand extension in a moderately different product category can be improved if the ordering of the extension introductions progresses from the greatest fit to the lowest fit category. Dawar and Anderson (1994) found that acceptance of a distant brand extension (e.g., Cheerios salty snack mix) was better achieved when first introducing a moderately-consistent brand extension (Cheerios milk and cereal bars) than either by not introducing it or by introducing a poor-fitting intermediate extension. Introducing extensions in a sequential manner allows the consumer's perceptions of the brand category to expand gradually such that inconsistent extensions are viewed as a better fit for the parent category and thus more likely to be accepted. Ralph Lauren is an example of a brand that extended successfully from clothing to bedding to home furnishings, rather than directly from clothing to home furnishings. Keller and Aaker (1992) found that an unsuccessful intervening extension can make subsequent extensions difficult for a high quality parent brand. But a successful extension has a positive effect on subsequent extensions for an average-quality parent brand. Swaminathan (2003), using scanner panel data, found that having experience with both the parent brand (e.g., Tide) and an intervening extension (e.g., Tide dishwashing liquid) increased purchases of a subsequent brand extension (e.g., Tide stain removal), especially among those with more to gain from the experience. Having more than one experience with the intervening extension also increased purchases. While these studies show that sequencing brand extension introductions from most to least consistent, and promoting trial of intervening extensions, can be a successful strategy for increasing brand extension acceptance, company expertise also needs to be considered. Moving from clothing to sunglasses may be perceived by consumers as easier than moving from sunglasses to clothing. The *latent brand equity* of a brand allows it to move from a more to a less technologically advanced category more easily than the reverse.

A fourth product extension strategy found to increase extension acceptance is the simultaneous introduction of multiple brand extensions that have a synergistic effect (Shine et al., 2007). Research indicates that when two extensions were complementary (e.g., a digital camera and a digital photo printer), the synergies between the new product uses outweighed the importance of parent brand-extension similarity.

Pricing Brand Strategies

Several pricing decisions that affect acceptance of a brand extension have been examined in academic research, including (1) price premiums and extension fit, and (2) step-up and step-down pricing. The first issue is whether brand extensions from highly valued parent brands can command price premiums. A price premium is the amount consumers are willing to pay for a product as compared to another product with the same set of benefits (cf. Aaker, 1991). Researchers (DelVecchio & Smith, 2007) found that a high fit between the parent brand and the brand extension category increased the price premium, but only when social and financial risk associated with the extension product category was high. In other words, a high fit extension eased the uncertainty associated with a high-risk extension. Whether a strong, liked brand can command a price premium is important in several contexts, such as in determining licensing fees for a brand (e.g., Ralph Lauren; Curves

EXTENDING A STRONG, NARROW BRAND SUCCESSFULLY

General Mills believes that the key to Cheerios' extension success is that the brand builds on established strength and continues to innovate to increase its value to consumers. "Because Cheerios is our strongest cereal brand equity and the category leader, it is a powerful platform for brand extensions," says Vivian Callaway, Senior Vice President, Center for Learning and Experimentation at General Mills. "Cheerios has incredible brand equity. This cereal is so well known and so trusted that new additions to the brand have an automatic credibility on the shelves.

"When the parent brand is strong," Callaway notes, "the trust and experience will transfer to the rest of the brand." Conversely, if your brand is running low on equity, extension may not be the best marketplace strategy — best to step back and shore up equity rather than run the risk of a wary reception from shoppers.

General Mills first introduced Cheerios (as Cheeri Oats) in 1941 and has been building on the brand's name ever since, particularly in the last 30 years. Consumers have welcomed the cereal's fortification with vitamins and minerals, clinical studies on the heart-health benefits of oats and new varieties and flavors. Most people in America have an experience and, indeed, a relationship with Cheerios—the little O's are often babies' first solid food. Whether the yellow-box brand, Multi-grain or Honey Nut, billions of people have tasted and trusted Cheerios. While, like many famous brands, Cheerios carry a story, General Mills' consistent spot at the top of the pack speaks most powerfully for the value of trust the brand holds in the cereal aisle.

But Cheerios is also a brand that was formerly connected to only one category—cereal—and still has that strong connection to the category. So how does a company stretch a strong, but narrow brand such as Kleenex, Campbell's, or Cheerios? A brand that is stretched too far too quickly can jeopardize its equity. Appropriate sequencing of line and brand extensions can broaden a brand gradually and increase its ability to leverage to new categories.

Cheerios is an example of a narrow brand that gradually introduced new line extensions successfully and more recently is expanding to new categories such as breakfast bars. "General Mills has introduced at least 12 Cheerios brand extensions since the advent of Honey Nut in 1979," concludes Callaway. "Combined, these extensions account for a significant share of the market—7.6 in 2008, up .9 over year ago, with a total dollar share of 12.9, a full point higher

than just a year ago." Stretching a strong, trusted, brand thought-
fully and gradually has added to the Cheerios brand promise and
"turned the Cheerios franchise into a true mega brand."

R.D.M. & L.W.P.

International) that uses needed manufacturing skills or channel ties of
another brand (e.g., Sherwin Williams; General Mills) to extend its own
brand to a new product category (e.g., Ralph Lauren house paint; Curves
breakfast cereal and bars).

A second pricing issue examined in academic research is whether a
brand extension that is a vertical step-up or step-down in price from the
parent brand is likely to be accepted. Research suggests that consumers
often evaluate a step-down pricing strategy negatively (Kirmani et al.,
1999; Kim, Lavack, & Smith, 2001; see also Randall et al., 1998). However,
extension fit and ownership qualify this effect. One set of studies examined whether distant brand extensions would yield more or less acceptance when they were priced high. Taylor and Bearden (2002) found that
raising the price of a dissimilar brand extension increased consumers' ratings of the extension, which they argued reflected consumers' high price-
high quality inferences for dissimilar but not for similar extensions. They
argue that when low cost positioning strategies are used for dissimilar
extensions, consumers infer that the extension is low in quality (rather
than high in value) and may show lower acceptance rates. Kim et al. (2001),
too, found that using graphical and linguistic distancing techniques that
differentiated the parent brand from the extension were harmful to brand
extensions when the price point was a step downward, since they probably indicated a lower quality difference.

Research also suggests that owners differ from nonowners in their
acceptance of step-up and step-down pricing. Kirmani et al. (1999) found
that owners (versus non-owners) of a brand (e.g., Acura) were more accept-
ing of both upward and downward price extensions as long as the brand
was a non-prestige brand. When the brand was a prestige brand (e.g.,
American Express or BMW), owners were more likely than non-owners
to accept upward price extensions (e.g., American Express platinum card)
but not downward stretches of prestige brands (e.g., a new entry-level
BMW for $11,990). Downward stretches violated owners' desires for brand
exclusivity, and therefore sub-branding strategies (e.g., Ultra by BMW)
were preferred.

Finally, it seems reasonable to assume that consumers will expect the
price of a brand extension to be consistent with the parent brand pricing
strategy. For example, Harley-Davidson is viewed as a premium brand

in motorcycles; if they were to extend to automobiles consumers might expect these automobiles to command a premium price while simultaneously factoring in that motorcycles are less pricey than automobiles (Jun, MacInnis, & Park, 2004).

Distribution Branding Strategies

The retail environment is an important context in which brand extensions are exposed to consumers. Manufacturers carefully select retail locations that best reinforce their brand's image (Joachimsthaler & Aaker, 1997) and that maintain consistency between a brand's image and the retailer. A brand extension that appears in a "provocative, edgy" retail outlet may be viewed as a poor fit with a parent brand that has a "sincere, wholesome" image. Similarly, a brand extension of a high-status brand that appears in a discount store may be perceived negatively. As described earlier, brand owners of prestige brands often wish to maintain brand exclusivity. They may negatively view lower-priced brand extensions of Coach or other designers sold in outlet malls, whereas non-owners of the brand may view the lower-priced extensions as a way to achieve designer-brand status. Placing different versions of a brand in different retail outlets (e.g., Charmin Basic in Walmart and Charmin Ultra in high-end grocery stores) is a strategy sometimes used, with the assumption that different consumers are exposed to each of the brand variants. (However, see Loken & John, Chapter 11, this volume, for concerns about brand dilution in retail locations.)

Manufacturers have control over their choices of distribution channels and retail locations, but they have less control over the way in which their products are displayed in stores. The category in which a brand extension is displayed (e.g., in the context of other products of the brand versus in the context of other brands in the category) may affect brand extension perceptions. More research is needed to determine whether retail displays and assortments that are inconsistent with the brand's image, or that increase the prominence of the brand's other products or competitor brands, reduce acceptance of brand extensions.

Another consumer factor with implications for retail and distribution that has been researched relates to consumer mood or affective states. The effects of consumers' moods and other affective states on brand extension acceptance has relevance to retailing decisions as these states are sometimes triggered by a retail environment. Research has found that consumers who were in a positive mood tended to show increased acceptance of brand extensions (e.g., Nike basketball nets) that were moderately different from the well-liked parent brand. This effect seemed to occur because being in a positive mood enhanced consumers' similarity ratings of the brand extension and the parent brand when consumers considered the fit of the extension prior to judgment (Barone, 2005; Barone & Miniard, 2002; Barone, Miniard, & Romeo, 2000; Yeung & Wyer, 2005) or served as an affective heuristic in lower involvement situations (Barone, 2005). The same effects did not occur for disliked brands or for extensions that were extremely inconsistent with the parent brand (Barone & Miniard, 2002; Barone et al., 2000). Consumers' favorable feelings about the parent brand may also come from other elements of the retail environment in which extension information is evaluated. For example, retailing environments sometimes encourage trial and favorable, engaging experiences may increase positive affect and subsequent product acceptance. Research finds that consumers' feelings of involvement in the product category in which a new brand extension is introduced, or involvement that resolves ambiguities or inconsistencies between the parent brand and the brand extension, increases consumers' evaluations and likelihood of purchasing the new brand extension (Hansen & Hem, 2004; Maoz & Tybout, 2002).

Promotional Brand Strategies

Increasingly, research on brand extensions has turned to understanding the effects of promotional strategies in enhancing acceptance of inconsistent brand extensions. Early research found that strong advertising and promotional support improved the success of extensions (Reddy et al., 1994; see, also, Völckner & Sattler, 2006). More recent research has attempted to understand how advertising works to improve an extension's success. Research has examined increasing fit through (1) ad repetition, (2) advertising message, and (3) changing the prominence of the parent brand name in marketing communications. In short, research findings suggest that promotions, advertising, and other product information that increase consumers' perceptions of brand extension fit (to the parent brand) increase consumers' acceptance of the extension (cf. Bottomley & Holden, 2001; Lane, 2000; Martin & Stewart, 2001). One advertising technique that enhances fit is simply repeated exposures to brand extension information (Klink & Smith, 2001; Lane, 2000). For example, research by Lane (2000) suggests that repeated exposure to information that links an extension positively to a brand directs the focus of attention and increases positive thoughts about the brand extension. With an increased number of exposures (five versus one) more positive thoughts about the extension were triggered, even when the exposure information included brand associations not strongly related to the brand. Klink and Smith (2001) found, too, that multiple exposures (three versus one) increased consumers' ratings of a moderately dissimilar extension, even, in this case, when only the brand name and extension product category information were provided. Other research (Lehmann, Stuart, Johar, & Thozhur, 2007) has found that being able to visualize the brand extension is important and can predict choice behavior. However, linkages between a brand and brand extension will not always be credible if the brand extension is too far a stretch. Lane (2000) found that when a brand extension (product category) was extremely dissimilar from the brand, even multiple exposures did not increase acceptance of the extension. It seems reasonable to assume, then, that consumers will rate brand extensions more favorably when ad repetition enables consumers to establish a connection between the parent brand and the brand extension on their own, or when the ad explicitly makes a connection and the connection is a credible one.

Van Osselaer and Alba (2003) show how prominent associations of a parent brand affect brand extension acceptance. While we tend to think that brands should always position themselves along key image attributes, when positioned attributes are not relevant to a new brand extension, these positioning effects can hamper acceptance of the extension. Instead, a positioning strategy that focuses on overall brand name (rather than brand attribute) prominence may be more advantageous. Thus, extension products may be rated as less acceptable when certain of the brand's product associations that are prominent are not relevant to those extension products (Van Osselaer & Alba, 2003). Broniarczyk and Gershoff (2003) found that if a brand extends on a trivial attribute (e.g., pro-vitamin ingredients in shampoo), and this information is prominent to consumers, future extensions in different product categories will be rated less positively, especially if the brand is a lower-tier brand. The prominence of the trivial attribute may decrease perceived fit of the brand to other product categories and lead to lower extendibility.

Reducing the prominence of parent brand information can sometimes work to the marketer's advantage. McCarthy et al. (2001) found that when consumers were provided with significant amounts of new product information relating to a new brand extension, it mattered little whether the new product was named after an existing brand (i.e., a brand extension) or not. Furthermore, the abundance of new product information reduced the importance of brand extension fit (see also Klink & Smith, 2001). In such cases, marketers may desire to create new brand names (e.g., the Swiffer name instead of a Mr. Clean extension). When new product information is amply provided to consumers, creating a new brand name (instead of using a brand extension) may have long-term advantages in product positioning and brand architecture.

Competitive Strategies

Recent research by Oakley, Duhachek, Balachander, and Sriram (2008) demonstrates that the process by which brand extensions are introduced into a new category (e.g., Clorox, Lysol, and Mr. Clean into the cleaning wipes category) is a dynamic one such that brand extensions are evaluated in the context of entrants in the category. The absence or presence of other brands in the extension product category (i.e., whether the extension is a pioneer or a follower in the category) can influence consumers' reactions to the brand extension. Pioneer extensions are more likely to be evaluated singularly (without reference to a comparison brand) and yield favorable evaluations if the parent brand is liked; a follower extension, in contrast, is compared to other brands already in the category (e.g., the pioneer).

Finally, Kumar (2005) examined competitor responses to brand extensions in the context of *counter-extensions*. When one brand introduces a brand extension (e.g., Redenbacher's, a popcorn brand, introducing a corn crisp extension) in a product category dominated by a second brand (Bugles), a counter-extension is a (retaliatory) move made by the second brand (Bugles) into the first brand's category (e.g., Bugles popcorn). The initial move broadens the consumer's perception of the category (popcorn and corn crisps increase in perceived similarity), and the counter-extension can benefit from this change. Counter-extensions were also found to be rated more favorably (hurting the first brand more) when the initial extension was solo-branded (Redenbacher's corn crisps) than when it was co-branded (e.g., Redenbacher's Jays or Jays Redenbacher's corn crisps). A co-branded extension enables consumers to separate the Redenbacher brand from the brand extension and, more importantly, the category perceptions remain narrowly defined (popcorn, corn crisps); as a result, consumers respond less favorably to a retaliatory move on the part of the competitor brand.

While consistency is one of the tenets of brand extension strategies, exceptions to the rule are prevalent. As indicated in the Redenbacher example, and as discussed next, when a brand extension is a significant departure for the brand with respect to product category expertise, consumer franchise, or brand usage context, a sub-branding strategy is often advisable. When brand extensions represent unique or innovative extensions, strong connections with some of the brand's core associations may not be warranted.

Brand Extensions That Are Innovative

Although much of the focus of both research and practice has pertained to consistency between the parent brand and new extensions, there are reasons why companies may want to use their brand extensions to signal a break from the parent brand (cf. Aaker, 2007). In these situations inconsistency may be viewed favorably, with companies wanting to extend along different, innovative attributes, and to call attention to these differences. While the brand manufacturer may in some cases create new opportunities by using a new brand name (e.g., Lexus) that is different from the existing parent brand (e.g., Toyota), in other cases the manufacturer may find a brand extension strategy beneficial even in casting a wide net that significantly stretches the brand. The following sections illustrate some of the reasons why marketers may want to introduce brand extensions that are inconsistent with the parent brand, including situations in which (1) the brand needs to be revitalized, (2) the target consumer prefers novelty and/or risk, (3) the brand stretching will broaden the brand and create long-range opportunities, or (4) the brand has potential first-mover advantages in a new product category.

Brand Revitalization

Older brands can become stodgy and require a complete change in positioning (e.g., youthful associations) to brighten and revitalize the brand. While these newer associations may be inconsistent with the older stodgy image, they can represent a positive change. When a brand is not strongly liked, research finds that inconsistent extensions are sometimes preferred to consistent ones (e.g., Boush et al., 1987; Brown & Dacin, 1997; cf. Kim, 2006; Wänke, Bless, & Schwartz, 1998).

Further, certain types of brands are more likely to require continual updating and innovation. For example, inconsistent extensions of *experiential* brands may be valued by the consumer for their uniqueness and innovativeness. Researchers (Sood & Dreze, 2006) have found that for certain experiential extensions, such as movie sequels (e.g., High School Musical 3), experiential attributes are likely to satiate, with consumers preferring to experience novelty in the brand extension. Dissimilarity is preferred to similarity for such experiential brand extensions (Sood & Dreze, 1996). When consumers satiate on a product, they tend to prefer an alternative with different attributes on a subsequent occasion (Lattin & McAlister, 1985; McAlister, 1982). Further, information about a brand extension that is innovative or unique (e.g., a Timex bicycle with a unique gear system) may be highlighted through promotions, and this information, rather than a parent brand connection, may be a strong determinant of extension success (Klink & Smith, 2001).

Consumers Who Prefer Novelty and Risk

Certain types of consumers may find inconsistent brand extensions more pleasing than consistent extensions. Consumers who are less risk-averse (either chronically or situationally) or who place more emphasis on hedonic (versus functional) values have been found to rate inconsistent extensions more favorably than consistent extensions (cf. Yeo & Park, 2006), perhaps because they interpret the extensions as more "adventurous." Also, consumers who are high in an innovativeness trait tend to be less sensitive to risk and are more likely to accept moderately different brand extensions (Klink & Smith, 2001; Völckner & Sattler, 2006). It seems likely that marketers who are selling products to consumers typically seen as less risk-averse and more attuned to hedonic values may have more latitude with inconsistent brand extensions.

Increasing Brand Breadth

As described previously, a broad brand carries the advantages of being able to extend into a wider range of categories with greater acceptance (Boush & Loken, 1991; Meyvis & Janiszewski, 2004). A brand manufacturer that has continued to use a narrow brand strategy over many years (e.g., Kleenex) may find it increasingly difficult over time to add the same product offerings as competitors (e.g., Scott). The narrowness of the brand category, over time, becomes more strongly etched in consumers' perceptions of the brand. Since inconsistent brand extensions are evaluated more positively for broad (than narrow) brands (Boush & Loken, 1991; Sheinin & Schmitt, 1994), stretching a narrow brand early on in the life of the brand can have advantages if done successfully, and can present more long-range opportunities in new product categories. Since older narrow brands, such as Campbell's, face greater challenges, increased brand breadth may be attempted sometimes through sub-branding, co-branding, and endorser relationships (e.g., Campbell's V8 soups). Further, if the quality of extensions that are introduced remains constant, consumers' confidence in their evaluations of the brand extensions increases (Dacin & Smith, 1994).

Establishing a First-Mover Advantage

Research on order-of-entry effects in the marketplace indicates that the pioneer holds enduring general advantages over later entrants (Carpenter & Nakamoto, 1989; Oakley et al., 2008). Brand extensions are often a viable option for introducing a new pioneering product. Line extensions of strong brands entering early in a product sub-category have been found to be more successful than extensions entering later (Reddy et al., 1994). Brand extensions that are inconsistent with the parent brand tend to be more positively evaluated when they enter the new product market as a pioneer rather than as a follower (Oakley et al., 2008).

Research has found numerous strategies for which introducing inconsistent brand extensions may be warranted (see, also, Loken & John, Chapter 11, this volume, for a discussion of risks to the parent brand in introducing inconsistent brand extensions). The most common strategy shown to be effective in introducing inconsistent brand extensions is sub-branding.

Sub-Brand Strategies

How should a company proceed if it decides that its brand extension should signal some form of differentiation or innovation, whether a brand revitalization, an experiential attribute innovation, or a first-mover in a new product category? More generally, how should a brand manufacturer introduce a quite distant brand extension? The most commonly recommended strategy, based on prior research, is a *sub-branding* strategy (see, also, Aaker, 2007). The new sub-brand name can range in prominence, relative to the existing brand name, from greater in importance than the parent brand name (e.g., Apple's iPod or iPhone) to less than or equally important as the parent brand name (e.g., Samsung DuoCam camcorders). The sub-branding strategy can also differ in whether the parent brand name serves as a modifier (e.g., Courtyard by Marriott) or not (Hallmark Shoebox greeting cards). While research on the range of sub-brand naming strategies is limited, an ample number of studies, some already discussed, demonstrate that the parent brand's use of sub-brands not only protects the parent brand from failed or inconsistent brand extensions (Kirmani et al., 1999; Milberg, Park, & McCarthy, 1997), but also may confer benefits to the brand extension (Sood & Dreze, 2006). Research shows that if a sub-branding strategy is used for a brand extension that is inconsistent with the parent brand (e.g., a photocopier "Caliber by Timex"), evaluation of the brand extension increases relative to using a direct strategy (a photocopier "by Timex") in which only the parent brand name appears on the extension. This subcategory helps insulate the original parent brand associations from changes due to an inconsistent brand extension (Milberg et al., 1997), and also helps the consumer understand that the extension is differentiated from the parent.

Desai and Keller (2002) found that the sub-branding of an ingredient (e.g., Tide with EverFresh scented bath soap) increased extension acceptance in the long run as compared to a strategy of co-branding with a familiar brand name (e.g., Tide with Irish Spring scented bath soap), as long as the brand extension was not a good fit for the brand. Janiszewski and Van Osselaer (2000) found that co-branding with another familiar brand name increased expectations of the extension's quality. In such cases, marketers should ensure that consumers' experiences with the extension meet their expectations. Further, if an ingredient brand is co-branded with other known brands as well (e.g., Intel co-branding with many computer brands), its value to a co-branded alliance may diminish (Janiszewski & Van Osselear, 2000). For these reasons, sub-branding extensions are often preferred to co-branded extensions. Sub-branded ingredients may have other advantages as well. Carpenter, Glazer, and Nakamoto (1994) found that naming an attribute that a competitor did not name increased brand preference (see also Brown & Carpenter, 2000). Aaker (2007) argues, too, that innovative branded ingredients, features, and subcategories (e.g., Westin's Heavenly beds) can strengthen brand extension positioning and may decrease the likelihood that competitors can take over the innovative ingredient or feature. Analogous to other sub-branding strategies, a branded ingredient can serve to differentiate the extension from the brand. This area of brand extension strategy calls out for future investigation. By combining existing and new brand names on a brand extension, sub-branding often provides marketers with an entirely new set of strategic branding options.

Finally, companies are increasingly using sub-branding strategies to denote their cause and social marketing efforts. For example, General Mills' use of Yoplait's "Save Lids to Save Lives" cause marketing campaign, or their pairing of breakfast cereals with their "Boxtops for Education" social programs, are examples of the use of novel sub-branding strategies. While research exists concerning brand partnerships between brands and charity organizations (see Gürhan-Canli & Fries, Chapter 5, this volume), less is known about sub-branding strategies that combine a well-established brand and a socially relevant sub-brand.

Cultural Factors in Brand Extension Evaluation

In our global economy, marketers are increasingly cognizant that products distributed and sold to consumers in other cultures may be perceived differently from products sold locally. American brands are increasingly present in other countries, and understanding differences between cultures in acceptance of brand extensions has therefore become important. Also, consumers in many cultures are increasingly bi-cultural, resulting from the increased Westernization of many traditionally Eastern cultures, the increased cultural diversity within the United States and many European countries, and increased availability of products globally. Depending on the context in which brand information is received by a bi-cultural consumer, a particular cultural view (e.g., relational or independent; Eastern or Western) may be more accessible. The effects of culture on the acceptance of a brand extension potentially have implications for the extension strategy that is pursued, how the extension is promoted and distributed, and how innovative it can be. A growing body of research has examined culture and its effects on the acceptance of a brand extension. This research has focused primarily on differences in Eastern and Western cultures.

The major focus driving the research has been on differences in self-view among cultures. Members of Eastern cultures are characterized as having an interdependent view of self. They base their identity on roles and relationships and view themselves in the context of, and inseparable from, important others. Members of Western cultures possess an independent self-view, focusing on personal attributes that distinguish them from others. The consequences of these different views of self on how individuals process information (Markus and Kitayama, 1991) permeates the research on culture and brand extension evaluations.

The earliest to examine cultural effects on brand extension acceptance appear to be Han and Schmitt (1997). Comparing Hong Kong consumers to U.S. consumers, they found that the perceived fit of an extension is more important to U.S. consumers, while characteristics of the company (e.g., size) offering the extension is more important to Hong Kong consumers when the fit of the extension is low. They attribute these findings to the collectivist versus individualist nature of the cultures. The collectivist consumers of Hong Kong are willing to consider the characteristics of companies as a basis for trusting a low-fit extension, while the individualistic U.S. consumers rely on their judgment abilities to assess the fit. This finding represents an early indication that the stretch available for a brand extension may be greater in collectivist cultures.

Further evidence that acceptance of brand extensions without strong fit may be stronger in collectivist cultures stems from the work of Ng and Houston (2006). Drawing on the view that individuals with an independent self-construal engage in a more abstract form of thinking and focus more on trait attributes in their judgments of objects or events, requiring them to abstract and generalize across contexts, Ng and Houston (2006) suggest that independents are more likely to form judgments about a brand that apply across categories in which the brand operates. Individuals with an interdependent self-construal focus more on context and are more likely to engage in concrete thinking. Consequently, they are more inclined to think about the brand in different contexts. In free-association measures they found that independents are more likely to retrieve brand associations that are global beliefs (e.g., Sony is high quality) about a brand that are applied to different product categories in which the brand operates. Interdependents, on the other hand, retrieve more exemplars of the brand (e.g., Sony televisions). Furthermore, independents tend to group together brands that share the same global associations, while interdependents group together brands that tend to be used together in the same usage occasion. Therefore, interdependents are more favorable toward extensions that may be used in the same usage occasion as existing products of the brand than independents, while independents are more favorable toward extensions falling in the same product category.

Monga and John (2007) examined evaluations of brand extensions between Easterners and Westerners and proposed that the holistic style of processing of Easterners yields more favorable evaluations of brand extensions than the analytic style of Westerners. Holistic processing results in greater attention to the field, thus allowing more opportunity for connections to be made between the extension and the parent brand. The analytic style of Westerners focuses them on whether the same attributes transfer from one category to another, resulting in more favorable evaluations for extensions fitting closely with the category of the parent brand. Their findings show that Easterners indeed evaluate brand extensions more favorably, especially as they depart further from the parent category. Cultural differences in evaluations do not occur for extensions with a strong fit to the parent brand.

In somewhat similar research, Ahluwalia (2008) also found that the relational processing style of individuals with an interdependent self-construal allowed them to consider a wider array of relationships between distant brand extensions and the parent brand. The taxonomic processing of low interdependents focuses primarily on category and attribute bases of similarity, thereby limiting the scope of relationships they consider. More positive evaluations of brand extensions occur on the part of high interdependents when considering brand extensions that represent a stretch from the parent brand. However, this effect is only realized when high interdependents are motivated to elaborate or think about a moderately inconsistent extension, allowing them to find a suitable connection between the parent brand and the extension. Under low motivation conditions or with an extremely inconsistent extension, suitable connections remain elusive, regardless of the level of interdependency in the self.

The above findings collectively suggest that brand extensions may be more positively evaluated in Eastern cultures where an interdependent self-construal is chronic. Furthermore, a wider scope of possible extensions would seem to be available. The collective findings summarized above were generated through either comparisons of cross-national samples from Eastern and Western cultures or through comparisons of samples primed to temporarily elicit an interdependent or independent self-view. The priming methodology is based on the view that individuals possess both types of self, and primes can make one temporarily more dominant than the other. Using priming methods, research can be conducted within one country but generate findings that reflect what might be expected in a different culture, thereby controlling for other cross-national differences.

In somewhat of a departure from cross-cultural research focused on self-construal as the key source of cultural effects, Merz, Alden, Hoyer, and Desai (2008) invoke some of Hofstede's (2001) cultural dimensions as a basis for understanding cross-cultural differences in the potential success of brand extensions. Specifically, they consider power distance, uncertainty avoidance, and individualism-collectivism as cultural dimensions that moderate the determinants of brand extension evaluations. While not offering empirical findings, they suggest a large number of propositions involving the three cultural dimensions. For example, cultures high in power distance will attach more importance to perceived similarity between the parent and the extension when evaluating the extension than cultures low in power distance. They propose a similar effect when considering uncertainty avoidance as a cultural dimension. Too numerous to mention here, these propositions are offered as a framework to guide future research.

Conclusions and Future Research

Since 1980, when brand extensions began to proliferate, the marketplace has changed remarkably. Consumers have been bombarded with hundreds of new brand extensions each year. No doubt they are also becoming increasingly aware and savvy about brands and have expectations and norms about how brands *should* extend into new categories. Many well-known brands have stretched to very new and different categories in the past two decades (e.g., clothing to accessories, perfume, and house wares; sedans to SUVs, minivans, and crossover vehicles). As a result of these stretches, brand extensions that would have appeared distant in 1980 or 1990 probably seem less distant in 2009. Results on brand extension consistency highlight the importance of considering consistency from the point of view of the consumer, not the marketer. Brand extension strategies that consumers perceive as extending brands to similar product categories, or extending along core brand associations that are consistent with the parent brand associations, are more likely to be successful than those in which categories or associations are perceived as inconsistent. Further, elements of the brand and the brand extension that are consistent can be made prominent to the consumer (if they are not already prominent) through product, pricing, promotion, and distribution decisions.

Numerous alternative brand extension strategies that may potentially affect introduction of a brand extension were reviewed. Research on product brand strategies shows that brand extension acceptance increases when brand breadth is high, when quality consistency in extensions is maintained, and when brand extensions are introduced either in a logical sequence from most to least similar or are introduced simultaneously with complementary synergies. Research on pricing strategies indicates that brand extensions are more likely to be accepted by brand owners when they are a step up rather than a step down in pricing, that price premiums increase when extending into categories of high social or financial risk, and that pricing an extension high can signal quality to the consumer. Research suggests, too, that brand extension success may increase when the retail environment triggers a positive mood. Brand extension acceptance may also be higher for introductions in countries that foster relational or Eastern thought styles. Research on promotional strategies suggests that when the brand extension is not a strong fit to the parent brand, promotional strategies and advertising repetition can be useful for making consumers aware of a credible connection (if one exists) between the parent brand and the brand extension. Research on competitive context suggests that brand extension success increases for first-movers in a category, and increases when the consumer does not already have loyalty to incumbent brands in the extension product category.

Sub-branding strategies have been shown to be useful in differentiating extensions of a brand. They can be useful for introducing brand extensions that are not a good fit for the parent brand but that seek to address other needs, such as brand revitalization, increased product breadth, first-mover advantages in new categories, experiential brands, and for consumers who prefer novelty and risk.

We also see that culture, as characterized by independent versus interdependent self-construals, may influence how far a brand extension can stretch. The relational, context-driven processing style of interdependents compared to the abstract, taxonomic style of independents appears to allow greater acceptance of extensions that are at least moderately inconsistent with the parent brand.

As we have reviewed research and practice related to brand extension strategies, we have touched on a number of areas that seem to provide tremendous opportunities for future development and investigation. As both companies and consumers become increasingly familiar with brand extensions and ever-expanding family brands, research needs to continue to examine extensions dynamically and the conditions under which sub-brands are beneficial. Research is also needed on whether some branding strategies are more useful than others for grouping and naming sub-brands. Research on sequential and simultaneous introductions of extensions, the impact of multiple exposures to promotions for the extension over time, and consideration of the order-of-entry effects on extension evaluations are all examples of this type of research.

However, there is much more that can be done. For example, research could examine whether fit judgments change over time and how these changes influence an extension's evaluation as it moves from a "new" product to a more established product. It would also be useful to know how these changes are influenced by the presence or absence of subsequent extension introductions. Additionally, research can consider how changes to the parent brand's core associations over time influence both the parent brand and also subsequent brand extensions.

Future brand extension research would benefit from further investigation into the context in which an extension is introduced—specifically in terms of competing brands. Competition may be relevant both in the parent brand's core product categories, but also in the extension category. The presence or absence of direct competitors, the accessibility of this competitive information, and the role of situational contexts in influencing this competitive set are all viable future research topics.

Another contextual variable worth examining is the role of the retail setting on brand extension judgments. Additional research is needed to determine whether retail displays and assortments inconsistent with the brand's image, or that increase either the prominence of the brand's other products or competitor brands, influence acceptance of brand extensions. This needs to be considered in traditional bricks-and-mortar settings as well as in online retail settings where display options are extensive and potentially influential. As sub-brands increase in popularity, multiple questions about how they should be displayed (e.g., individual, in groupings) in online retail settings might be addressed. There has been some interesting initial research that has considered the role of product design in influencing brand perceptions (Kreuzbauer & Malter, 2005). A potential contribution of this research is to investigate the role that product form and design (e.g., packaging, graphics, colors) can play in brand extension strategy. Marketers typically go through a great deal of time and effort in designing their brand extensions to include some resemblance to the other products in the family brand and yet much of the research done on brand extensions fails to take this into account, often using simple, visually limited stimuli. To what extent can different design concepts influence the acceptability of brand extensions?

Although there have been some recent studies that have begun to look into it, future research must continue to examine brand extensions and cross-cultural issues (Ahlluwalia, 2008; Bottomley & Holden, 2001; Merz et al., 2008; Monga & John, 2007; Ng & Houston, 2006). Global brands and attempts at standardized international communication efforts suggest that marketers would benefit from a more rigorous approach to determining how and when cross-cultural issues impact brand extension strategies.

Finally, the application of brand extension strategies to social marketing (such as health or environmental marketing) has been virtually ignored in the academic research community. As researchers try to bring a number of relevant concepts from the commercial world to the non-profit world by considering where there are similarities and differences between practices in each, brand extensions strategies may be increasingly considered. For example, can successful not-for-profit brands (e.g., Smithsonian) extend to other activities, causes, or products (e.g., furniture)? Do the same factors that drive the acceptance of extensions in commercial products influence extensions of brands in nonprofit marketing contexts? Nonprofit marketers are likely to be just as interested in leveraging their brands to further pursue their objectives as traditional marketers. The use of sub-brands in cause marketing and other corporate social responsibility initiatives is also a topic open for research.

Over the past 20 years, a great deal of progress has been made in understanding family brands, brand extensions, and the conditions under which brand extensions are likely to succeed. Given the interest of both practitioners and academics in this topic, we can expect this to continue to be a significant area of knowledge development in the future.

References

Aaker, D.A. (1991). *Managing brand equity.* New York: The Free Press.

Aaker, D.A. (2007). Innovation: Brand it or lose it. *California Management Review, 50* (1), 8–24.

Aaker, D.A., & Keller, K.L. (1990). Consumer evaluations of brand extensions. *Journal of Marketing, 54* (January), 27–41.

Ahluwalia, R. (2008). How far can a brand stretch? Understanding the role of self-construal. *Journal of Marketing Research, 45* (June), 337–350.

Ahluwalia, R., & Gürhan-Canli, Z. (2000). The effects of extensions on the family brand name: An accessibility-diagnosticity perspective. *Journal of Consumer Research, 27* (3), 371–382.

Barone, M.J. (2005). The interactive effects of mood and involvement on brand extension evaluations. *Journal of Consumer Psychology, 15* (3), 263–270.

Barone, M.J., & Miniard, P.W. (2002). Mood and brand extension judgments: Asymmetric effects for desirable versus undesirable brands. *Journal of Consumer Psychology, 12* (4), 283–290.

Barone, M.J., Miniard, P.W., & Romeo, J. (2000). The influence of positive mood on brand extension evaluations. *Journal of Consumer Research, 26* (March), 387–402.

Berger, J., Draganska, M., & Simonson, I. (2007). The influence of product variety on brand perception and choice. *Marketing Science, 26* (July–August), 460–472.

Bhat, S., & Reddy, S.K. (2001). The impact of parental brand attribute associations and affect on brand extension evaluation. *Journal of Business Research, 53* (3), 111–122.

Bottomley, P., & Holden, S.L.S. (2001). Do we really know how consumers evaluate brand extensions? Empirical generalizations based on secondary analysis of eight studies, *Journal of Marketing Research, 38,* 494–500.

Boush. D., Shipp, S., Loken, B., Gencturk, E., Crockett, S., Kennedy, E., Minshall, B., Misurell, D., Rockford, L., & Strobel, J. (1987). Affect generalization to similar and dissimilar brand extensions. *Psychology and Marketing, 4* (3), 225–237.

Boush D.M. (1993). How advertising slogans can prime evaluations of brand extension evaluation. *Psychology & Marketing, 4* (3), 67–78.

Boush, D.M., & Loken, B. (1991). A process-tracing study of brand extension evaluation. *Journal of Marketing Research, 28* (1), 16–28.

Bridges, S., Keller, K., & Sood, S. (2000). Communication strategies for brand extensions: Enhancing perceived fit by establishing explanatory links. *Journal of Advertising, 29* (4), 1–11.

Broniarczyk, S.M., & Alba, J.W. (1994). The importance of the brand in brand extension. *Journal of Marketing Research, 31* (May), 214–218.

Broniarczyk, S.M., & Gershoff, A.D. (2003). The reciprocal effects of brand equity and trivial attributes. *Journal of Marketing Research, 40,* 161–175.

Brown, C.L., & Carpenter, G.S. (2000). Why is the trivial important? A reasons-based account for the effects of trivial attributes on choice. *Journal of Consumer Research, 26* (March), 372–385.

Brown, T. J., & Dacin, P.A. (1997). The company and the product: Corporate associations and consumer product responses. *Journal of Marketing, 6,* 68–84.

Carpenter, G.S., Glazer, R., & Nakamoto, K. (1994). Meaningful brands from meaningless differentiation: The dependence on irrelevant attributes. *Journal of Marketing Research, 31* (August), 339–350.

Carpenter, G.S., & Nakamoto, K. (1989). Consumer preference formation and pioneering advantage. Journal of Marketing Research, 26(August), 285-298.

Czellar, S. (2003). Consumer attitude toward brand extension: An integrative model and research propositions. *International Journal of Research in Marketing, 20,* 97–115.

Dacin, P.A., & Smith, D.C. (1994). The effect of brand portfolio characteristics on consumer evaluations of brand extensions. *Journal of Marketing Research, 31* (May), 229–242.

Dawar, N., & Anderson, P.F. (1994). The effects of order and direction on multiple brand extensions. *Journal of Business Research, 30* (2), 119–129.

DelVecchio, D., & Smith, D.C. (2007). Brand extension price premiums: The effects of perceived fit and extension product category risk. *Journal of the Academy of Marketing Science, 33* (2), 184–196.

Desai, K.K., & Keller, K.L. (2002). The effects of ingredient branding strategies on host brand extendibility. *Journal of Marketing, 66* (1), 73–93.

Fedorikhin A., Park, C.W., & Thomson, M. (2008). Beyond fit and attitude: The effect of emotional attachment on consumer responses to brand extensions. Journal of Consumer Psychology, 18(4), 281-291.

Han, J.K., & Schmitt, B.H. (1997). Product-category dynamics and corporate identity in brand extensions. *Journal of International Marketing, 5* (1), 77–92.

Hansen, H., & Hem, L.E. (2004). Brand extension evaluations: Effects of affective commitment, involvement, price consciousness and preference for bundling in the extension category. *Advances in Consumer Research, 31,* 375–381.

Herr, P.M., Farquhar, P.H., & Fazio, R.H. (1996). The impact of dominance and relatedness on brand extensions. *Journal of Consumer Psychology, 5,* 135–159.

Hofstede, G. (2001). *Culture's consequences: Comparing values, behaviors, institutions, and organizations across nations.* Thousand Oaks, CA: Sage.

Janiszewski, C., & Van Osselear, S.M.J. (2000). A connectionist model of brand-quality associations. *Journal of Marketing Research, 37* (3), 331–350.

Joachimsthaler, E., & Aaker, D.A. (1997). Building brands without mass media. *Harvard Business Review, 75* (January–February), 39–50.

Jun, S.Y., MacInnis, D.J., & Park, C.W. (2004). Price perceptions in brand extensions: Formation and impact on brand extension evaluation. *Advances in Consumer Research, 31,* 137–142.

Jun, S.Y., Mazumdar, T., & Raj, S.P. (1999). Effects of technology hierarchy brand extension evaluations. *Journal of Business Research, 46* (1), 31–43.

Keller, K.L. (2002a). *Branding and Brand Equity.* Cambridge, MA: Marketing Science Institute.

Keller, K.L. (2002b), Branding and brand management. In B. Weitz & R. Wensley (Eds.), *Handbook of marketing.* London: Sage.

Keller, K.L., & Aaker, D.A. (1992). The effects of sequential introduction of brand extensions. *Journal of Marketing Research, 29,* 35–50.

Kim, B.D., & Sullivan, M.W. (1998). The effect of parent brand experience on line extension trial and repeat purchase. *Marketing Letters,* 181–193.

Kim, C.K., Lavack, A.M., & Smith, M. (2001). Consumer evaluation of vertical brand extensions and core brands. *Journal of Business Research, 52,* 211–222.

Kim, H.M. (2006). Evaluations of moderately typical products: The role of within-versus cross-manufacturer comparisons. *Journal of Consumer Psychology, 16* (1), 70–78.

Kirmani, A., Sood, S., & Bridges, S. (1999). The ownership effect in consumer responses to brand line stretches. *Journal of Marketing, 63,* 88–101.

Klink, R.R., & Smith, D.C. (2001). Threats to the external validity of brand extension research. *Journal of Marketing Research, 38* (3), 326–336.

Kreuzbauer, R., & Malter, A.J. (2005). Embodied cognition and new product design: Changing product form to influence brand categorization. *Journal of Product Innovation Management, 22* (March), 165–176.

Kumar, P. (2005). The impact of cobranding on customer evaluation of brand counterextensions. *Journal of Marketing, 69,* 1–18.

Lane, V. (2000). The impact of ad repetition and ad content on consumer perceptions of incongruent extensions. *Journal of Marketing, 64* (2), 80–92.

Lane, V.R., & Jacobsen, R. (1995). Stock market reactions to brand extension announcements: The effects of brand attitude and familiarity. *Journal of Marketing, 59* (1), 63–77.

Lattin, J.M., & McAlister, L. (1985). Using a variety-seeking model to identify substitute and complementary relationships among competing products. *Journal of Marketing Research, 22* (August), 330–339.

Lehmann, D.R., Stuart, J.A., Johar, G.V., & Thozhur, A. (2007). Spontaneous visualization and concept evaluation. *Journal of the Academy of Marketing Science, 35* (3), 309–316.

Loken, B. (2006) Consumer psychology: Categorization, inferences, affect, and persuasion. *Annual Review of Psychology, 57,* 453–485.

Loken, B., Barsalou, L., & Joiner, C. (2008). Concepts and categorization in consumer psychology. In C.P. Haugtvedt, P. Herr, & Frank Kardes (Eds.), *Handbook of consumer psychology*, Mahwah, NJ: Lawrence Erlbaum Associates, Inc.

Loken, B., Joiner, C., & Peck, J. (2002). Category attitude measures: Exemplars as inputs. *Journal of Consumer Psychology, 12* (2), 149–161.

Markus, H.R., & Kitayama, S. (1991). Culture and the self: Implications for cognition, emotion and motivation. *Psychological Review, 98* (2), 224–253.

Martin, I., & Stewart, D. (2001). The dimensionality of measures of product similarity under goal-congruent and goal-incongruent conditions. *Journal of Marketing Research, 38* (November), 471–484.

Maoz, E., & Tybout, A.M. (2002).The moderating role of involvement and differentiation in the evaluation of brand extensions. *Journal of Consumer Psychology, 12* (2), 119–132.

McAlister, L. (1982). A dynamic attribute satiation model of variety-seeking behavior. *Journal of Consumer Research, 9* (September), 141–150.

McCarthy, M.S., Heath, T.B., & Milberg, S.J. (2001). New brands versus brand extensions, attitudes versus choice: Experimental evidence for theory and practice. *Marketing Letters, 12* (1), 75–90.

Merz, M.A., Alden, D.L., Hoyer, W.D., & Desai, K.K. (2008). Brand extension research: A cross-cultural perspective. *Review of Marketing Research, 4,* 92–122.

Meyvis, T., & Janiszewski, C. (2004). When are broader brands stronger brands? An accessibility perspective on the success of brand extensions. *Journal of Consumer Research, 31* (2), 346–357.

Milberg, S.J., Park, C.W., & McCarthy, M.S. (1997). Managing negative feedback effects associated with brand extensions: The impact of alternative branding strategies. *Journal of Consumer Psychology, 6,* 119–140.

Monga, A.B., & John, D.R. (2007). Cultural differences in brand extension evaluation: The influence of analytic versus holistic thinking. *Journal of Consumer Research, 33* (4), 529–536.

Muthukrishnan, A.V., & Weitz, B.A. (1991). The role of product knowledge in the evaluation of brand extensions. *Advances in Consumer Research, 18,* 407–413.

Ng, S., & Houston, M.J. (2006). Exemplars or beliefs? The impact of self-view on the nature and relative influence of brand associations. *Journal of Consumer Research, 32* (4), 519–529.

Oakley, J.L., Duhachek, A., Balachander, S., & Sriram, S. (2008). Order of entry and the moderating role of comparison brands in brand extension evaluation. *Journal of Consumer Research 34* (5), 706–712.

Park, C. W., Milberg, S., & Lawson, R. (1991). Evaluation of brand extensions: The role of product feature similarity and brand concept consistency. *Journal of Consumer Research, 18* (September), 185–193.

Park, J.W., & Kim, K.H. (2002). Acceptance of brand extensions: Interactive influences of product category similarity, typicality of claimed benefits, and brand relationship quality. *Advances in Consumer Research, 29,* 190–198.

Pryor, K., & Brodie, R.J. (1998). How advertising slogans can prime evaluations of brand extensions: Further empirical results. *Journal of Product and Brand Management, 7* (6), 497–508.

Puligadda, S., Ross, W.T., & Grewel, R. (2008). Individual differences in orientation towards brands: The role of brand centricity. Working paper, Miami University, Oxford, Ohio.

Randall, T., Ulrich, K., & Reibstein, D. (1998). Brand equity and vertical product line extent. *Marketing Science, 17* (4), 356–379.

Rangaswamy, A., Burke, R.R., & Oliva, T.A. (1993). Brand equity and the extendibility of brand names. *International Journal of Research in Marketing, 10* (1), 61–75.

Reddy, S.K., Holak, S.L., & Bhat, S. (1994). To extend or not to extend: Success determinants of line extensions. *Journal of Marketing Research, 31* (May), 243–262.

Sheinin, D.A., & Schmitt, B.H. (1994). Extending brands with new product concepts: The role of category attribute congruity, brand affect, and brand breadth. *Journal of Business Research, 31* (1), 1–10.

Shine, B.C., Park, J., & Wyer, R.S. Jr. (2007). Brand synergy effects in multiple brand extensions. *Journal of Marketing Research, 44* (November), 663–670.

Smith, D.C., & Park, C.W. (1992). The effects of brand extensions on market share and advertising efficiency. *Journal of Marketing Research, 29* (3), 296–313.

Sood, S., & Dreze, X. (2006). Brand extensions of experiential goods: Movie sequel evaluations. *Journal of Consumer Research, 33* (3), 352–360.

Swaminathan, V. (2003). Sequential brand extensions and brand choice behavior. *Journal of Business Research, 56*, 431–442.

Swaminathan, V., Fox, R.J., & Reddy, S.K. (2001). The impact of brand extension introduction on choice. *Journal of Marketing, 65*, 1–15.

Taylor, V., & Bearden, W.O. (2002). The effects of price on brand extension evaluation: The moderating role of extension similarity. *Journal of Academy of Marketing Science, 30* (2), 131–140.

Van Osselaer, S.J., & Alba, J.W. (2003). Locus of equity and brand extension. *Journal of Consumer Research, 29* (4), 539–550.

Völckner, F., & Sattler, H. (2006). Drivers of brand extension success. *Journal of Marketing, 70* (2), 18–34.

Wänke, M., Bless, H., & Schwarz, N. (1998). Context effects in product line extensions: Context is not destiny. *Journal of Consumer Psychology, 7*, 299–322.

Yeo, J., & Park, J. (2006). Effects of parent-extension similarity and self regulatory focus on evaluations of brand extensions. *Journal of Consumer Psychology, 16* (3), 272–282.

Yeung, C., & Wyer, R.S. Jr. (2005). Does loving a brand mean loving its products? The role of brand-elicited affect in brand extension evaluations. *Journal of Marketing Research, 42* (November), 495–506.

Zhang, S., & Sood, S. (2002). Deep and surface cues: Brand extension evaluations by children and adults. *Journal of Consumer Research, 29* (1), 129–141.

3

Brand Alliances

Akshay Rao
University of Minnesota

Introduction

Dell computers are equipped with Intel processors, while Sun computers are powered by AMD processors. Some Visa credit cards issued by U.S. Bank also feature the Northwest Airlines brand name. Fisher Price sells toys that are plastic replicas of McDonald's products.

In these and many other instances, consumers encounter a product that explicitly or implicitly features two or more brand names. In some instances, the brand names are visibly identified and therefore they convey information about the presence of an additional important attribute that enhances product performance. Thus, a computer that is Intel powered presumably elicits favorable reactions from a consumer, because the Intel powered computer engenders perceptions of speed and performance. In other instances, the multiple brand names may provide relatively little information of value to the consumer. For example, information about the issuing bank associated with a credit card likely has little bearing on a consumer's decision to use that card.

In light of the plethora of such illustrations of products and services featuring multiple brands, of the range of circumstances in which such multiple brands are featured on a product, and of the seeming arbitrariness of the decision to feature multiple brands on a product, the topic of such *brand alliances* is one that has begun to attract the interest of marketing academics trained in a variety of disciplines. Some who are trained as economists approach the topic from the perspective of the firm and attempt to identify the conditions under which firms choose to ally themselves with other firms, based on assumptions and theories about how consumers employ brand information in their choice decisions. Meanwhile, psychologists and social psychologists examine the conditions under which consumers may react favorably to brand alliances, relative to conditions under which consumers may not react favorably to brand alliances. Yet other behaviorally oriented researchers are interested in the strategic consequences of brand alliances. It is my goal in this chapter to describe these various theoretical perspectives that inform the recent research on the topic of brand alliances, identify issues that have emerged and been resolved thanks to the research that has been conducted, and reflect on the several remaining questions that would benefit from further research scrutiny.

Organizing Framework

There are many ways in which to skin the proverbial cat when integrating the literature on brand alliances. Since my review of the work is selective, and is designed to make a specific set of points, I have taken the liberty of organizing the literature according to the factors displayed in Figure 3.1. As will become evident by and by, this organizing framework is parsimonious and has utility, since it readily incorporates several of the important concepts from various literature on the topic.

I focus on three broad categories of factors. The first factor pertains to elements that exist prior to an alliance. Most brands possess a host of properties that predate the formation of an alliance. Indeed, it is these very properties that make them attractive as alliance partners. These properties include (but are not limited to) brand *reputation*, consumer *attitudes toward the brand*, brand *image,* and *personality*. In addition, consumers whom a brand alliance eventually addresses possess certain relevant properties, such as the degree to which they exhibit "self-complexity" (i.e., they have complex rather than simple personalities (Monga & Lau-Gesk, 2007))* and their familiarity with the brand. The second factor encapsulates the evaluation of the alliance *per se*, both as a static entity (i.e., consumer reactions to a proposed or actual alliance between two brands) as well as a dynamic one (in which brand allies sometimes behave or misbehave in an unanticipated fashion, and this (mis)behavior impacts consumer perceptions). The third factor captures post-alliance consequences. Favorable attitudes toward the alliance as well as the individual brands that form the alliance as a consequence of

---

* As I elaborate upon later, brand properties interact with consumer factors such as the consumer's "self-complexity." However, in the interest of parsimony, I have not created a separate category that captures individual differences among consumers.

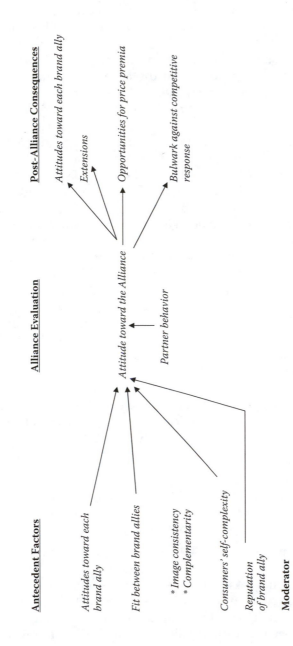

FIGURE 3.1   An Organizing Framework.

the formation of the alliance is a desirable outcome, as is the ability to charge premium prices. Further, the alliance may provide an opportunity for extensions to new markets (a desirable outcome) and may result in competitive responses due to the extensions (a potentially undesirable outcome).

Before I turn to the substance of this chapter, it would be useful to clarify some issues of terminology. In the academic literature as well as in the popular press, a variety of terms have been used to describe the phenomenon of two or more brands being featured on a product. *Co-branding* is a term that is widely used in the business press to describe numerous versions of the phenomenon, including when a credit card features the network brand (e.g., Visa or MasterCard) and an affiliate (such as an airline or hotel chain [Leuthesser, Kohli, & Suri, 2003]). *Composite branding* is another term that has been employed to describe the same phenomenon (Park, Jun, & Shocker, 1996). *Ingredient branding* refers to the circumstance in which a component or element of a complex *host* product is also identified (e.g., Intel inside a Compaq PC; Venkatesh & Mahajan, 1997). *Joint branding* is yet another term that has appeared in this literature (Rao & Ruekert, 1994). I prefer the term *brand alliance* (Rao & Ruekert, 1994) because it conveys a sense that that there is semipermanence to the relationship, that there is a strategic element to the decision to feature multiple brands, and the term ties nicely into an extant literature on strategic alliances from which research on this topic can borrow. Simonin and Ruth (1998) employ our terminology as well when they describe brand alliances to "... involve the short- or long-term association or combination of two or more individual brands, products, and/ or other distinctive proprietary assets. These brands or products can be represented physically ... or symbolically ... by the association of brand names, logos or other proprietary assets" (pp. 20–21).

Theoretical Perspectives and Evidence

Broadly speaking, there are two theoretical perspectives that have been brought to bear on the topic of brand alliances. The first draws upon "information economics" to identify the conditions under which a brand alliance is desirable so as to convince consumers that the unobservable quality of the product is high. The second literature stream draws upon "behavioral" perspectives (principally cognitive and social psychology based) to identify how consumers react to various combinations of brand names that differ on theoretically defensible dimensions.

Information Economics

The field of information economics deals principally with problems of "information asymmetry," the examination of which yielded the 2001 Nobel Prize in Economics to George Akerlof, Joe Stiglitz, and Michael Spence. The chief issue examined in this literature is how markets function when one party to a transaction knows more about an important element of the transaction relative to the other party. Akerlof (1970) famously employed the illustration of a used car that might be a "lemon" to analyze markets comprising sellers wishing to sell their used cars and buyers who may be skeptical about the used car owner's claims about the car's unobservable quality. Buyers rationally believe that the owner has more private (negative) information about the quality of the car— whether it has been in a wreck, how frequently it has been driven under adverse circumstances, whether it has ever had an oil leak, and the like. This belief leads to a tendency on the part of buyers to offer less than the asking price for a used car, which then results in only low quality used cars being available for sale.*

This intuition turns out to be extremely powerful from a marketing standpoint. For one thing, it identifies a role for brand names to assure skeptical buyers that used cars and other products whose quality is *unobservable* are in fact as good as their sellers claim. If the product fails, consumers can potentially punish the brand name associated with the product that did not live up to its promise. They can suspend repeat purchase, they can engage in negative word-of-mouth, they can boycott other products sold under the same brand name, and, under the appropriate circumstances, they can sue the offending brand. In effect, a brand's investment in its "reputation" as well as its future profits would be at risk. Because firms selling branded products recognize these possibilities, they often have incentives not to fail their customers.

If brand names can serve to assure consumers about the unobservable quality of a product by identifying the seller and making the seller vulnerable to punishment, the brand name serves as a *signal* of

---

* It turns out that there are two kinds of information asymmetry problems: adverse selection problems are problems in which one party (the seller) has private information about product quality, but it can not change quality (i.e., quality is "exogenous"); moral hazard problems are problems in which one party (the seller) has private information about product quality and it can change quality from one transaction to the next (i.e., quality is endogenous).

unobservable quality.* Such signals are useful devices in markets where buyers are uncertain about product quality because, to the extent that consumers can inflict economic damage on the seller, it limits the seller's tendency to shade on quality (Kirmani & Rao, 2000). However, not all brand names can serve as signals. For a brand name to successfully signal, it is critical that the brand name be perceived to be *vulnerable to consumer sanction* (Rao, Qu, & Ruekert, 1999).† If consumers don't believe that they can harm a brand if it shades on quality, then any claims the brand makes about unobservable quality are not credible because, if the claim turns out to be false, there is no damage that the consumer can inflict on the brand name.

This is an important and seemingly counter-intuitive insight from the academic literature in marketing. It turns out that the signaling property of a brand name, which is a valuable property, is contingent on a *weakness* of the brand, its vulnerability to consumer sanction. Conversely, a strong brand that is *not* vulnerable to consumer sanction cannot successfully signal, because it has nothing (or little) to lose, if it should shade on quality.

Implications for the Formation of Brand Alliances

Based on this (unconscionably) brief review of the information economics literature and its pertinence to the signaling value of brand names, it follows that a brand name that is unable to signal its unobservable quality (perhaps because it is a new brand that does not have a reputation, and therefore has little to lose) is at a singular disadvantage in a marketplace populated by

---

* When the seller's problem is to communicate credibly to the marketplace that its product is truly of high quality, engaging in an action that is costly or potentially costly can make the claim credible, if the marketplace is assured that the costs associated with the action will be forfeited when the firm's quality claim turns out to be false. Such costly actions are called signals. The signal derives its credibility from the belief that only high-quality firms would incur such costs because they are confident that once their true high quality is revealed, the firm will recover signaling costs incurred in the initial period from repeat sales (Spence, 1973). For the signal to be successful, it should be the strategy of choice for the high-quality seller alone, and the low-quality seller should prefer not to signal because, if it falsely claims that its product is of high quality (by incurring the cost of a signal), once its claim is discovered to be false, the cost associated with the signal will be irrevocably lost (Kirmani & Rao, 2000). Signals are a good way to solve adverse selection problems, while incentives (such as price and wage premia) are a good way to solve moral hazard problems (Rao & Monroe, 1996). These theoretical subtleties are not particularly germane to the points I make in this chapter so I do not discuss them further here.

† One can think of this vulnerability to consumer sanction as an economic asset that is at stake. I will (loosely) refer to this economic asset as the brand's reputation. I use the term "reputation" not in its colloquial sense but rather as the monetary value of the brand that will be forfeited should it renege on its quality-related promise.

skeptical consumers who care about unobservable quality. How then can a new brand that lacks a reputation signal its unobservable quality?

In early work on the topic (Rao & Ruekert, 1994), we addressed this issue. When a brand lacks reputation, it can spend resources to build (make) its reputation or it can rent (buy) a reputation from another reputable brand. That is, a reputationless brand can form an alliance with a reputable brand that serves as an "endorser" of the reputationless brand's unobservable product quality. A textbook example of this reputation renting is the case of NutraSweet.

NutraSweet, a branded version of aspartame (an artificial sweetener), was introduced into the market as an alternative to saccharin. Saccharin had received bad press because, when consumed in sufficient quantities, it had been implicated as a carcinogen in laboratory rats. As a consequence, NutraSweet faced similar health-related concerns when it was launched. These concerns are a typical manifestation of unobservable quality. Consumers were concerned about the long-term negative effects of consuming a sugar substitute, and any claim that NutraSweet might have made that it was not in fact a long-term health hazard would not have been credible since NutraSweet lacked a reputation. If the product turned out to be harmful, NutraSweet (a single-product firm) would likely no longer be in existence and therefore, NutraSweet could not credibly offer its future profits as a hostage to enhance the credibility of its claim about unobservable quality.

The eventual success of NutraSweet is attributable in large measure to its implicit endorsement by other reputable brands such as Coca-Cola and Pepsi, which featured it as an ingredient in its Diet formulations. That is, when Coke and Pepsi and hundreds of other products (that seemingly had independently verified NutraSweet's health and safety claims) featured NutraSweetened products, they implicitly conveyed to the market that, should the product turn out to be harmful, consumers would have the opportunity to harm them (the brand allies). Consequently, a brand that is itself invulnerable to consumer sanction might be able to signal its unobservable quality if it forms an alliance with a brand that *is* vulnerable to consumer sanction. In exchange for staking its reputation, the reputable brand ally presumably derives some economic benefit—a royalty payment, access to unaddressed profitable markets, access to proprietary technology and the like (Rao & Ruekert, 1994), a topic to which I will return below.

Evidence

The most direct evidence on the signaling value of brand alliances comes from experimental work I conducted with colleagues at the University of Minnesota (Rao, Qu, & Ruekert, 1999). In that research we examined the ability of a brand ally to credibly signal unobservable quality when the original brand was an unknown brand. To accomplish this, we explicitly manipulated the reputation of the brand ally. In the first condition, we "endowed" a *fictitious* brand ally with the property of vulnerability to consumer sanction. Respondents were informed via the experimental stimulus (an independent industry analyst's opinion) that a failure to deliver on the unobservable claim could result in damage to the brand ally's future profits. In the second condition, respondents were informed that a failure to deliver on the unobservable claim was unlikely to harm the brand ally. In a replication of this design, we similarly manipulated the vulnerability of a *real* brand ally to consumer sanction. The results indicated that, whenever the brand ally was perceived to be vulnerable to consumer sanction, the credibility of the claim about unobservable quality increased. That is, when an unknown brand was allied with another unknown brand that was believed to be vulnerable to harm, the alliance's claims about unobservable product performance were deemed to be relatively more believable. Further, when the unknown brand was paired with a well-known brand (Sony) that was experimentally manipulated either to be vulnerable to consumer sanction or immune to consumer sanction, the same effect was observed. (Predictably, there was a main effect due to the use of the well-known and respected Sony brand name.) When Sony was deemed to be immune to harm, perceptions about unobservable product quality were *lower* than when Sony was deemed to be vulnerable to consumer sanction.

Summary

The theoretical perspective of information economics and the relatively sparse empirical literature allows some tentative conclusions to be drawn about the manner in which consumers might draw or be persuaded to draw inferences about brand alliances.

Economically rational consumers ought to realize that firms recognize that brands are valuable assets. When firms offer such assets as a "hostage" in the marketplace, the accompanying claims about unobservable quality are likely true, otherwise the firm is likely to forfeit its hostage, which would be an economically irrational action on the part of the firm.

The empirical evidence further indicates that consumers do not spontaneously generate these theories about the firm's rationality (and, implicitly, the rationality of other consumers). They need to be alerted to these arguments in the experimental stimuli, and only then do they behave like economically rational agents. The obvious implication is that firms wishing to employ brand alliances as signals of unobservable quality need to vigorously communicate the underlying signaling rationale to consumers, otherwise consumers will not interpret the brand alliance signal as intended.

We now turn to an examination of an alternative perspective on brand alliances that draws from behavioral theories that are not premised on economically rational, utility-maximizing consumers.

Behavioral Research

The central premise in the psychology- and social-psychology-oriented literature in marketing on the role of brands in a cluttered marketplace is that brands serve as a "cue" that prompts a memory trace or "schema" that then generates feelings, emotions, moods, affect, preferences, and a host of other psychological reactions. To the extent that a brand generates *positive* psychological reactions, it is a valuable marketing asset. Advertising, the price charged, channels of distribution employed, and the attributes of the product itself are designed to act in concert to generate *strong, favorable,* and *unique* brand associations (Keller, 2008). These associations can result in a brand image that reflects the brand's benefits, the brand's personality, the brand's values, and other image elements that play a role in brand preference and usage.

An individual brand that has an independent image often faces difficulties when allying with another brand that has its own independent image. Existing attitudes toward the two brands and the degree to which they "fit" consumer segments addressed by the two brands, and post-alliance behavior by the brands, are some of the factors that have consequences for consumers' evaluations and subsequent strategy.

Brand Attitudes

Simonin and Ruth (1998) propose and test a series of hypotheses regarding the role of consumer attitudes toward individual brand allies and their subsequent attitude toward the alliance. They further examine the role of "perceived" fit or consistency between the brand images of the brand allies and the moderating role of consumer familiarity with the brand.

While their findings that brands that elicit favorable attitudes are likely to be evaluated more favorably in an alliance and that (generally) the effect is more pronounced for familiar brands are not particularly surprising,[*] the additional finding that *fit* matters is important. Note that, in the information economics literature discussed above, the notion of image consistency or fit was irrelevant. In principle, if a brand had a reputation at risk, it was a good potential ally from a signaling standpoint. That is, Eddie Bauer and Ford could enter into an alliance purely because of the signaling value of the brand names. However, the behavioral research provides an additional nuance regarding consumer perceptions of image consistency

---

[*] However, the reverse findings would have been noteworthy.

BRAND FIT AND ALLIANCE SUCCESS

With thousands of patents to its credit and a product presence in over 200 countries, 3M is a global powerhouse. The 3M brand is its most valuable corporate asset. The company's brand framework has two major roles, lending authority with the 3M name and differentiation with strategic brand alliances including brands like Scotch™, Scotchgard™, and Filtrete™.

A powerful brand asset requires careful stewardship, particularly in selecting potential partners for ingredient branding. "Ingredient brand strategies represent great opportunities for 3M, but can also bring significant risk when poorly managed," says Dean Adams, 3M's former director of corporate brand management, who recently retired after 34 years with the Minnesota-based firm. He adds, "You need business leadership to drive successful ingredient brand strategies. That requires creating supportive business plans, finding good partners, and communicating in the marketplace." When the branded ingredient is a clear product differentiator and the host brand has a natural fit, a winning partnership that complements both brands can emerge.

For Adams, Scotchgard™ is one of 3M's ingredient brand stars. The brand has been licensed in many categories successfully. "Bissell's carpet cleaner with Scotchgard™ protector, for example, plays to the strengths of both brands." Adams explains, "Bissell had its own brand of detergent and added Scotchgard™ chemistry to offer protection from soiling after cleaning. The combined product is differentiated from competitors, increases the value for the end user, and is great business for both companies."

If the branded ingredients are not perceived to be a natural fit, however, consumers might not trust the product offering. Careful attention must be paid to communicating the key messages of the ingredient and host brand to avoid customer confusion. "When 3M licensed Scotchgard™ to Essilor, the world's largest eyeglass lens manufacturer, 3M and Essilor worked together with LensCrafters, the largest U.S. eyewear retailer, to create a retail demonstration kit. LensCrafters' sales people used it to show shoppers how the Scotchgard™ keeps products looking newer longer and adds value," he says. By reinforcing the brand fit, 3M and LensCrafters created a buyer favorite with their superior lenses. "Top marketing teams support brand alliances by reinforcing each partner brand and what they bring to the table," says Adams.

R.D.M. & L.W.P.

that is relevant to brand alliances. This literature suggests that Marlboro and the Mayo Clinic (both extremely successful and reputable brands) would not represent a successful brand alliance because of the inconsistency in their images.

Consumers

More recently, Monga and Lau-Gesk (2007) examined how alliances comprising brands with different personalities might be perceived. Drawing upon Jennifer Aaker's (1997) pioneering work, they argue that "[c]onsumers imbue brands with human personality traits" (p. 390). They then propose that people with complex personalities prefer brand alliances, because brand alliances are more complex than a single brand. They design and execute a series of ingenious experiments to test this core idea that the fit between personality and the stimulus leads to preference. They then extend their argument to implicate consumers' cultural orientations. They manipulate independent versus interdependent self-construals, and also examine differences between Caucasian and Hispanic subjects to assess whether these segments of consumers naturally vary in the degree to which they introspect (potentially about "self-complexity") and observe that, indeed, respondents who are more independent (and thus more "self-reflective") tend to prefer complexity, and thus view brand alliances more favorably.*

The fundamental finding from this research pertains not to a property of the brand, but to a property of the consumer. Those who introspect and recognize their own "self-complexity" respond more favorably to brand alliances, which are more complex than a single brand by definition. Engendering self-complexity may be stimulus driven (through priming processes in an ad) or may naturally occur in some populations more than others.

Brand Behavior

Votolato and Unnava (2006) ask and answer an important question that has implications for alliance management. While Simonin and Ruth established that favorably evaluated alliances had unsurprising favorable impacts on the individual brand allies, Votolato and Unnava ask what happens when an alliance partner unexpectedly engages in a questionable action. Does this "negative" action have predictable negative effects

---

* This is a particularly laudable theoretical development because of the recent emerging literature on the need to generalize behavioral theories beyond traditional Caucasian and North American settings, since respondents in other cultures tend to display remarkably different behavior and do so for theoretically plausible reasons (Aaker & Lee, 2001; Briley, Morris, & Simonson, 2000; Chen, Ng, & Rao, 2005; Hong & Chiu, 2001).

on the other brand ally? If so, does the nature of the negative action (an action that reflects *incompetence* versus an action that reflects a *moral failure*) matter?

The results are instructive. First, it was observed that the brand ally's incompetence impacted attitudes toward the "host" brand more so than moral failure. However, when the brand ally was a person (a spokesperson), that person's moral failures had a greater impact on host brand evaluations than that person's incompetence. (Additionally, the host brand's culpability in the negative action—incompetence or moral failure—played an important role in evaluations.) As the authors note "... the negative spillover should occur from a partner to its host *only* when the negative information is consistent with the relation type ..." (p. 200, emphasis added).

The implications of these findings are provocative. Seemingly, in a brand alliance involving two corporate entities, competence is a relatively more important attribute, presumably because it is under that corporate entity's control. Firms are expected to be *capable* of performing tasks correctly, but expectations regarding ethical and/or moral behavior are less strong. Conversely, in a brand alliance involving a corporate entity and a person, adhering to moral norms is seemingly more important, again presumably because *that virtue* is under that entity's (the person's) control. People are apparently expected to do the right thing more so than they are expected to do things right.*

Consequences

Successful brand alliances accomplish many things. They potentially enhance attitudes toward the original component brands as my previous discussion of Simonin and Ruth (1998) indicates. Further, they (a) provide opportunities for the brands to extend into new markets (Desai & Keller, 2002), (b) enhance consumers' willingness to pay (Venkatesh & Mahajan, 1997), and (c) potentially provide a bulwark against competitive incursions into core markets (Kumar, 2005). Let me elaborate.

Desai and Keller make a persuasive argument that a brand that offers a new attribute or feature would be well advised to do so employing an ingredient brand ally that has substantial brand equity associated with that feature. Such a strategy will be more effective than offering a new feature under only the existing brand's name because, in the multiple brand setting, one brand "... may be able to borrow some of the equity ..." of the

---

* This implication raises some legitimate conceptual concerns regarding popular press articles (e.g., Peters, 1997) that suggest that individuals should brand themselves much like products do. A person may be qualitatively different from an inanimate object, from a branding standpoint.

other brand (p. 77). This is particularly true when the extension is associated with a new attribute (as opposed to being a mere "slot filler"). In other words, Sony with Dolby surround sound is more effective than just Sony with surround sound. Or, Tide with Irish Spring scent is preferable to Tide with its own EverFresh scent.

Venkatesh and Mahajan offer a mathematical model as well as empirical evidence to conclude that, when elements of a brand alliance are not incongruous (in their case the fit of the brands (PC and chip) was based on their complementarity) it is feasible to generate relatively high prices when two well-known brands are allied. In their particular instance, a Compaq PC with an Intel chip dominated all other combinations in terms of optimal prices and revenue units.*

Finally, Kumar examines the competitive response associated with a brand alliance's extension into a new market. He argues that when a brand extends into a new market by itself, it strengthens "... customer perception of the similarity and fit between the parent and extension categories and [therefore] enhances customer evaluations of a counter-extension. However, a [brand alliance-based] extension merely inherits select attributes from each partner brand and leaves the perceptions of similarity between a parent category and the extension category relatively unchanged" (p. 1). Over four studies, he finds support for the essential claim that the absence of a brand ally facilitates consumers' transfer of similarity perceptions across categories, while the presence of a brand ally allows consumers to invoke rival theories (such as attributing extension success to the presence of the brand ally), thus making it *less* feasible for a rival in the extension category to respond with a counter-extension.

Summary

Based on this selective review of some of the important behaviorally oriented papers on the topic, several insights emerge. Brand alliances need to be based on some consumer-driven notion of fit (be it image based or complementarity driven) for them to be successful, and the success of the alliance can feed the success of the original brand allies. Additionally, should the ally engage in negative behavior (demonstrate incompetence or violate a moral norm), the other brand may suffer. This has potential implications for ally selection that transcend static issues of current brand equity, and requires an examination of the future behavior of brand managers. Finally, the economic and strategic consequences of brand alliances

---

* Strictly speaking, the Venkatesh and Mahajan model is not easily classified as "behavioral." However, the reliance on a prospect theory-based functional form to describe their data suggests that the underlying argument draws more from behavioral decision theory than from information economics.

are noteworthy. Successful alliances have implications for future extensions, for profitability, and for shoring up current markets.

I now turn to the final section of this chapter, in which I describe some managerial implications of the extant research and raise questions for future research that would benefit from rigorous research scrutiny.

Implications and Applications

As the preceding review should suggest, there are some interesting insights that are beginning to emerge regarding the antecedents to the formation of brand alliances, issues that are germane to the management of brand alliances, and the potential implications of brand alliances. Nevertheless, there clearly is a lot of work to be done. In this section, I attempt to lay out an agenda for future research on topics that I think are important in this area, either because they are theoretically interesting, managerially consequential, or both. In the discussion that follows, rather than employ a discipline-based template (e.g., economics versus psychology), I focus on substantive elements of brand alliances. The presumption is that multiple disciplinary perspectives can be brought to bear on the knotty problems that remain.

Issues Related to the Formation and Management of Brand Alliances

Firms and brands contemplating brand alliances do so for a variety of reasons: access to proprietary technology (Sony and Dolby), access to new geographic markets (Northwest Airlines and KLM, or 3M and Birla) access to new customer segments (Discover Card and HSBC), access to new channels (Cheerios and Nestle), and quality signaling (NutraSweet and Coca-Cola). The underlying impetus is generally monetary, either in the short, medium, or long term. For instance, short-run promotions featuring Bacardi Rum and Coca-Cola are relatively simple, tactical decisions, while long-run technologically based alliances such as between Compaq and Intel are quite a bit more complex strategic decisions. How then should firms analyze the alliance formation decision? A simple cost-benefit approach would emphasize the following factors.

Benefits

Each partner must assess the economic benefits of alliance formation based on their assessment of (a) the size of the economic pie that will be available,* (b) whether the size of the pie will remain static, expand, or shrink over time, and (c) whether the focal partner's share of the pie is attractive and equitable, given other opportunities for alliance formation. While this decision is an economic one, it also implicates a multitude of managerial judgments about economic issues. Risk and uncertainty about the future are germane to judgments about whether the size of the pie will change. Successes or failures at forming prior alliances will likely influence judgments about the likely success of prospective alliances (Monga & Rao, 2006). Further, the manner in which options are framed will likely influence judgments. Managers may view prospective outcomes as losses relative to one reference point (e.g., a fair outcome) or they might view prospective outcomes as a gain relative to some other reference point (e.g., the current state of wealth). This suggests that the topic of brand alliance formation and the possible managerial biases involved in evaluating prospective alliances is ripe for examination employing a behavioral decision theory template. Loss aversion, asymmetries in risk preferences due to the framing of the decision problem, and successes or failures in prior attempts at alliance formation ought to play a role in how managers approach the current decision, and these are topics that have received considerable scrutiny in the literature that incorporates the prospect theory value function in managerial decision making.

Costs

Most brand alliances involve some direct cost to one or both partners. Generally, the partner with the greater equity or reputation will "extract" a royalty payment (e.g., Sunkist received royalties of $10.3 million by licensing its name to soda, candy, and vitamin manufacturers [Rao & Ruekert, 1994]) from the brand ally, unless it (a) anticipates substantial incremental revenue from the alliance that makes the potential royalty payment pale in comparison or (b) fears that another strong brand ally may be under consideration. These factors may therefore play a role in the relatively weak brand ally's negotiation, as it emphasizes the gains to be had from the alliance, as well as the availability of alternative brand allies.

In addition to direct costs, however, there are numerous indirect and relatively "soft" costs that managers need to consider. In particular, alliance partner behavior with regard to postcontractual fulfillment of unanticipated and ill-defined obligations is a topic that can be addressed using the tenets of transactions cost analysis (Williamson, 1981). Managers entering a brand alliance need to protect their interests including the brand's

---

* Key parameters of the pie are the size of the prospective consumer segment (i.e., new buyers, or buyers who are persuaded due to the quality signal) and their willingness to pay (Rao & Ruekert, 1994).

reputation and image, arguably their most precious corporate asset. Protecting brand assets against opportunism on the part of the brand ally requires anticipating potentially damaging opportunistic behavior and installing safeguards. Such safeguards can be based on the accurate monitoring of ally behavior and the specification of contractually enforceable consequences following the violation of *ex ante* agreements. The types of safeguards that brand allies employ and how they vary across different settings is an area that is potentially of significant theoretical and substantive interest. For instance, in international brand alliances, where recourse to legal redress may be difficult and extraordinarily expensive, are there efficient market-based safeguards that can be employed to assure adherence to pre-contractual commitments?

Finally, independent of the actions of brand allies, a brand manager may consider the long-term impact of an alliance on the original brand's equity. It is possible that a brand may lose its original identity when it is allied with a powerful brand ally. This might lead some brands to seek brand allies with no or limited brand equity. Such alliances with neutral brands are commonplace in the payment card business, where some brands (such as PULSE) are attractive to other brands (such as Discover or Visa) because the neutral brand's image is unlikely to interfere with that of the high-equity brand. Yet, other than Rao et al. (1999), there is limited work on brand alliances involving brands with no image.

Issues Related to Consumer Perceptions of Brand Alliances

Perhaps the most interesting and fruitful area for future research on consumer perceptions of brand alliances lies in the area of "fit." This notion of fit is a rather slippery concept since it lies in the eyes of the beholder. It is predicated on the notion that two brands in an alliance must "hang together" in some coherent fashion. Yet, what makes two entities cohere remains puzzling in many instances. For instance, it is true that Mercedes Benz and Coca-Cola are highly regarded in their respective industries, but intuitively they seem not to be appropriate natural allies. However, if that is true, it is unclear why Coach and Lexus (relatively disparate, but high-quality brands) are natural allies. It can be argued that, at some abstract level, Coach and Lexus belong together, but it is unclear why the same argument does not work for Coke and Mercedes.

The most promising theoretical approach to analyzing consumer perceptions of brand alliances is categorization theory (Barsalou, 1992). People sort objects into natural (e.g., whales and elephants both belong to the same category of mammals) or *ad hoc* (e.g., ants and sandwiches belong to the same category of "things found at a picnic") categories. To the extent that brands can be naturally or artificially categorized together, the ability to generate a perception of fit increases.

Another dimension of fit that future research might address is the degree to which the brand's "narrative" is consistent with that of its ally. Recent popular press treatments of the general topic of branding (e.g., Hanlon, 2006) suggest that, among other properties, successful brands generate a narrative in consumers' minds. For instance, many iconic brands have a "creation story" that generates consumer empathy. HP's creation story involves two engineers working in a garage, while Nike's creation story involves an athlete using a waffle iron to improve the fit of the sole of his shoe. To the extent that these creation stories (and associated narratives) are instrumental in generating consumer affect, when brands form an alliance, the creation stories need to be consistent as well. For obvious reasons, the Ben and Jerry's brand likely will not be an appropriate ally for the Fox News brand, because their creation stories conflict in terms of the values they represent.

Finally, in light of the recent work on differences in brand extensibility in different cultures (Ng & Houston, 2006) and the temptation to form alliances rather than engage in "go-it-alone" strategies when entering foreign markets, it would be worthwhile to examine theoretically justifiable differences in perceptions of brand alliances across independent and interdependent cultures employing bicultural subjects (Chen et al., 2005; Monga & Lau-Gesk, 2007).

Issues Related to the Strategic Consequences of Brand Alliances

Following the formation of a successful alliance, the original brands may wish to extend into new markets. To what extent does the original brand become diluted due its alliance with another brand? Does this dilution limit its ability to act as an independent agent? Conversely, does a successful alliance enhance the original brand's equity and thus increase its ability to enter new markets? It would be worthwhile to generate a set of contingent variables that specify the conditions under which a brand ally's equity is either diluted or enhanced due to the formation of an alliance. Factors such as the relative strengths of the partner brands and the strengths of their associated images might play a role in the degree to which one brand might lose its identity once the alliance is formed. The loss of a brand's identity following the formation of an alliance might influence its ability to charge a premium price, to form new alliances, and to extend into new markets.

Conclusion

The topic of brand alliances is a rich area for research in marketing because it can draw from multiple theoretical perspectives to offer new insights on an issue that is of considerable practical significance. Whether it be in payment cards or in the airline business, whether consumers are highly involved automobile shoppers or relatively uninvolved grocery product shoppers, whether the product is new or an existing product, in service contexts that are rife with moral hazard problems or product contexts where adverse selection is more of an issue, the role of one or more brand names in communicating product quality and influencing consumer choice is paramount. The questions that have been posed and addressed in this chapter offer a preliminary perspective that should serve as a fillip to more rigorous research on the broad set of issues surrounding the antecedents to, the management of, and the consequences of brand alliances.

References

Aaker, J. (1997). Dimensions of brand personality. *Journal of Marketing Research, 34* (August), 347–356.

Aaker, J., & Lee A.Y. (2001). "I" seek pleasures and "we" avoid pains: The role of self-regulatory goals in information processing and persuasion. *Journal of Consumer Research, 28* (1), 33–49.

Akerlof, G. (1970). The market for "lemons": Quality and the market mechanism. *Quarterly Journal of Economics, 84* (August), 488–500.

Barsalou, L.W. (1992). *Cognitive psychology: An overview for cognitive scientists.* Hillsdale, NJ: Lawrence Erlbaum Associates.

Briley, D., Morris, M.W., & Simonson, I. (2000). Reasons as carriers of culture: Dynamic versus dispositional models of cultural influence on decision making. *Journal of Consumer Research, 27* (September), 157–178.

Chen, H., Ng, S., & Rao, A.R. (2005). Cultural differences in consumer impatience. *Journal of Marketing Research, 42* (August), 291–301.

Desai, K.K., & Keller, K.L. (2002). The effects of ingredient branding strategies on host brand extendibility. *Journal of Marketing, 66* (January), 73–93.

Hanlon, P. (2006). *Primal branding.* New York: Free Press.

Hong, Y., & Chiu, C. (2001). Toward a paradigm shift: From cross-cultural differences in social cognition to social-cognitive mediation of cultural differences. *Social Cognition, 19* (3), 181–196.

Keller, K.L. (2008). *Strategic brand management: Building, measuring and managing brand equity.* Upper Saddle River, NJ: Pearson Prentice Hall.

Kirmani, A., & Rao, A.R. (2000). No pain, no gain: A critical review of the literature on signaling unobservable product quality. *Journal of Marketing,* (April),
66–79.

Kumar, P. (2005). The impact of cobranding on customer evaluation of brand counterextensions. *Journal of Marketing, 69* (July), 1–18.

Leuthesser, L., Kohli, C., & Suri, R. (2003). 2 + 2 = 5? A framework for using co-
branding to leverage a brand, *Brand Management, 11* (1), September, 35–47.

Monga, A.B., & Lau-Gesk, L. (2007). Blending co-brand personalities: An examination of the complex self. *Journal of Marketing Research, 44* (August), 389–400.

Monga, A. & Rao, A.R. (2006). Domain based asymmetry in expectations of the
future. *Organizational Behavior and Human Decision Processes, 100* (May),
35–46.

Ng, S., & Houston, M.J. (2006). Exemplars or beliefs? The impact of self-view on
the nature and relative influence of brand associations. *Journal of Consumer
Research, 32* (March), 519–529.

Park, C.W., Jun, S.Y., & Shocker, A.D. (1996). Composite branding alliances: An
investigation of extension and feedback effects. *Journal of Marketing Research,
33* (November), 453–466.

Peters, T. (1997). The brand called you. *Fast Company,* August. Retrieved April
3, 2008 from http://www.fastcompany.com/magazine/10/brandyou.
html?page=0%2C0.

Rao, A.R., Lu, Q., & Ruekert, R.W. (1999). Signaling unobservable quality through
a brand ally. *Journal of Marketing Research, 36* (2), 258–268.

Rao, A.R., & Monroe, K.B. (1996). Causes and consequences of price premiums.
Journal of Business (October), 511–536.

Rao, A.R., & Ruekert, R.W. (1994). Brand alliances as signals of product quality.
Sloan Management Review (Fall), 87–97.

Simonin, B.L., & Ruth, J. (1998). Is a company known by the company it keeps?
Assessing the spillover effects of brand alliances on consumer brand attitudes. *Journal of Marketing Research, 35* (February), 30–42.

Spence, M. (1973). Job market signaling. *Quarterly Journal of Economics, 87,* 355–74.

Venkatesh, R., & Mahajan, V. (1997). Products with branded components: An
approach for premium pricing and partner selection. *Marketing Science, 16*
(2), 146–165.

Votolato, N.L., & Unnava, H.R. (2006). Spillover of negative information on brand
alliances. *Journal of Consumer Psychology, 16* (2), 196–202.

Williamson, O. (1981). The economics of organization: The transaction cost
approach. *American Journal of Sociology, 87,* 548.

4

Traveling the Paths to Brand Loyalty

Rohini Ahluwalia
University of Minnesota

Andrew M. Kaikati
University of Minnesota

Brand and customer loyalty have recently been termed the "holy grail" of marketing (e.g., Shugan, 2005). They represent not only the most desired goal but also the most challenging one for chief executive officers today. In fact, managing loyalty effectively has been identified as one of the biggest challenges facing chief executive officers (Dunn & Davis, 2004). The shift in focus from customer acquisition to loyalty and retention is not surprising, given the several favorable outcomes closely associated with brand loyalty. In fact, evidence from the field suggests that even small changes in loyalty and retention (e.g., 5%) can result in large changes in profitability (e.g., 25%–100%; Reichheld, Markey, & Hopton, 2000). For instance, when analyzing field data from the recall of two brands owned by the same company (Kraft), Cleeren, Dekimpe, and Nelson (2008) uncovered dramatic differences in the ability of the strong versus weak loyalty brand to recover after a 5-month recall period. The higher loyalty brand was able to reach 70% of its precrisis sales level within a quarter of its reintroduction; the weaker loyalty brand, however, faced a much tougher recovery, unable to reach even half of its precrisis sales level after one quarter.

Despite the perceived importance of and top-management's emphasis on brand loyalty, it is widely reported to be declining (e.g., Kapferer, 2005). An issue of critical importance in the contemporary marketplace, therefore, is to understand how a brand can travel the road from brand liking to brand loyalty. An impressive body of literature has developed recently on this topic, in several subfields of marketing, ranging from customer satisfaction/dissatisfaction, to customer relationship management, consumer behavior, and choice modeling; however, attempts to organize the extant findings from these different streams into an integrative and meaningful framework have been scarce. Our chapter endeavors to bridge this gap.

However, before discussing the different paths to brand loyalty in detail, we will attempt to provide a clearer and better understanding of the destination itself (i.e., brand loyalty): what it is and how it works.

Brand Loyalty

There are several definitions of brand loyalty in the marketing literature. Some scholars have focused on behavioral loyalty, which equates loyalty with repeat purchase behavior and similar overt measures such as share of wallet, proportion of purchase, and purchase sequence (Cunningham, 1966; Kahn, Kalwani, & Morrison, 1986). It is, however, believed that behavioral loyalty alone offers too simplistic a view of the loyalty construct and does not capture the multidimensionality and richness associated with it (Jacoby & Chestnut, 1978; Jacoby & Kyner, 1973; Keller, 2007). For instance, a consumer may make several repeat purchases of a particular brand simply because it happens to be conveniently located in the store, and not because s/he feels any particular sense of loyalty or even preference toward it. In fact, loyalty based solely on repeat purchase behavior has been termed as "spurious" loyalty (Day, 1969; Dick & Basu, 1994). Instead, the concept of attitudinal loyalty or the psychological attachment or commitment of the consumer to the brand has been discussed with regard to understanding "true" loyalty (e.g., Ahluwalia, Unnava, & Burnkrant, 2001; Jacoby & Chestnut, 1978; Jacoby & Kyner, 1973; Keller, 2007). Increasingly, researchers are defining loyalty as "stickiness to the brand," which is a combination of attitudinal commitment and overt loyalty behaviors (Dick & Basu, 1994; Jacoby & Kyner, 1973; Odin, Odin, & Valette-Florence, 1999; Oliver, 1997).

We argue that adopting an information-processing perspective for understanding brand loyalty can allow not only for a clearer appreciation of the relationship between its two components—i.e., commitment and repeat purchase behavior—but also a deeper explanation of the "mechanism" underlying loyalty and how it results in the several valuable outcomes reported to accompany it (e.g., increased profitability, favorable word-of-mouth, ability to charge higher prices, and easier recovery from crises; Ahluwalia, Burnkrant, & Unnava, 2000; Cleeren et al., 2008; Dick & Basu, 1994; O'Brien & Jones, 1995; Reichheld et al., 2000). Specifically, it can be argued that the formation of loyalty (or commitment) induces one simple yet profound and far-reaching change in the way people process information about brands: they begin engaging in defensive processing (Ahluwalia, 2002; Ahluwalia et al., 2001); this important change induces repeat purchase behavior and has the potential to lead to the favorable outcomes associated with loyalty.

Defensive processing, which is triggered by a motivation to protect or defend existing attitudes toward favorite brands, implies a significant change, and at times, even a reversal of the natural information processing tendencies of people (e.g., Ahluwalia, 2002; Ahluwalia et al., 2000; Chaiken, Giner-Sorolla, & Chen, 1996). For instance, although there is a natural tendency of individuals to give more weight to negative as compared to positive information about brands (e.g., Herr, Kardes, & Kim, 1991; Mizerski, 1982), given the higher perceived diagnosticity of the former, this negativity effect is known to be eliminated, and at times even reversed, for brands and political candidates that consumers are committed to (e.g., Ahluwalia, 2002; Ahluwalia et al., 2001; Klein & Ahluwalia, 2005). Similarly, although consumers typically exhibit a greater spillover (extent to which information about a particular attribute changes beliefs relating to other attributes) of negative (as compared to positive) information about one attribute to other related attributes, loyal consumers are known to demonstrate exactly the opposite pattern of effects (Ahluwalia et al., 2001). Specifically, loyal consumers tend to isolate the impact of negative information about their preferred brand to the attribute affected by the negative news (i.e., the target attribute), minimizing its impact by not allowing it to spillover to the entire brand representation. In contrast, in the face of a natural tendency to isolate the effect of positive brand-related information to the target attribute (given its lower perceived diagnosticity), committed consumers spillover or generalize the impact of positive information to other related attributes, enhancing its effect on the brand representation (Ahluwalia et al., 2001).

Stated simply, the defensive processing of brand-related information by loyal customers leads them to exhibit, as compared to their nonloyal counterparts, (a) lowered attention as well as higher resistance to positive information about and from competitor brands, such as advertising, switching inducements (e.g., price discounts), and publicity (Choi & Ahluwalia, 2006; Dick & Basu, 1994; Klein & Ahluwalia, 2005; Kiel & Layton, 1981), reducing their likelihood of being persuaded by the competition; and (b) greater resistance to negative information about the preferred brand, enabling it to recover more easily from negative crises that can have potentially devastating consequences for revenue, profitability, and market share (Ahluwalia, 2002; Ahluwalia et al., 2000; Dawar & Pillutla, 2000). In other words, defensive processing induced by loyalty is likely to restrain committed customers from succumbing to switching inducements (positive information about competition, negative information about the target brand), leading to repeat purchase behavior. This, from an information processing perspective, is the mechanism underlying brand loyalty and is likely to result in many of the market-place outcomes noted to accompany loyalty, such as increased market share (Assael, 1998), higher profitability (e.g., O'Brien & Jones, 1995), premium prices (Dick & Basu, 1994), and stronger resilience against crises (Ahluwalia et al., 2000; Cleeren et al., 2008).

It is important to note that biased processing of brand-related information commences as soon as a consumer develops liking for a brand, even if preferences are weak at that point, and continues to develop from weaker consistency-based biases (e.g., attenuation of the negativity effect) to the stronger defensive processing (e.g., reversal of the negativity effect), as preferences become stronger and brand loyalty develops (e.g., Ahluwalia, 2002). For instance, even though formation of weak preferences can lead to some level of information distortion (e.g., Carlson & Pearo, 2004; Russo, Meloy, & Medvec, 1998), reduced spillover of negative information (Ahluwalia et al., 2001), and resistance of small competitor discounts (Choi & Ahluwalia, 2006); the processes invoked by higher levels of commitment are most likely to result in inattention to competitive alternatives (Jacobson, Waldron, & Moore, 1980; Kiel & Layton, 1981; Miller, 1997), complete curtailment of negative but enhanced spillover of positive information (Ahluwalia et al., 2001), and increased resistance to larger competitor discounts (Choi & Ahluwalia, 2006). The stronger mechanisms that accompany defensive processing have been most closely linked with the consequential outcomes that managers are most concerned about (e.g., Ahluwalia, 2002; Cleeren et al., 2008; Dick & Basu, 1994), motivating the need for brands to travel the path from brand liking to brand loyalty.

The Three Paths to Brand Loyalty

A review of the literature reveals three major factors leading to loyalty: performance, connections, and incentives. The performance set of factors is based on consumers' experience with the brand. Positive and consistent performance is known to result in the development of brand trust, leading to experience-based loyalty. The second set of factors focus on the development of a connection between the brand and consumer, which typically tends to be affect laden and hence enables the development of affective loyalty. The third path focuses on economic incentives (e.g., loyalty programs) that are likely to create switching barriers that enhance customer retention, inducing economic or behavioral loyalty. We will discuss each of these paths in more detail next.

The Performance Path

The consumer's experience with the brand's performance over time (e.g., its benefits, functionality, and value as experienced and/or perceived, as well as recovery efforts during service failures) leads to the development of brand trust (Chaudhuri & Holbrook, 2001; Yim, Tse, & Chan, 2008) and is also reflected in the level of satisfaction with the brand (Oliver, 1999; Verhoef, 2003). Satisfaction with the brand typically reflects the mean valence or extremity of the consumer's past experiences with the brand. Brand trust, on the other hand, is based on the strength of brand-related beliefs. It represents the degree of certainty or confidence with which consumers hold their beliefs about the brand, based on their past experiences with it —the more consistent their favorable experiences with the brand, the higher their level of brand trust.

Both brand trust and satisfaction have been independently linked to brand loyalty (Chaudhuri & Holbrook, 2001; Verhoef, 2003; Yim et al., 2008), with some researchers suggesting that higher satisfaction often implies high levels of loyalty (e.g., Heilman, Bowman, & Wright, 2000). However, recent research has revealed that although loyal consumers are most typically satisfied, satisfaction does not universally translate into loyalty (e.g., Oliver, 1999), and more than 60% of customers who switch to another brand, report themselves as being "satisfied" (e.g., Chandrashekaran, Rotte, Tax, & Grewal, 2007; Jones & Sasser, 1995; Keiningham & Vavra, 2001; Reichheld, 1993). In fact, a meta-analysis of customer satisfaction research reports that satisfaction explains less than 25% of the variance in repeat purchase (Szymanski & Henard, 2001).

Given the debate relating to the relationship between a brand's performance and consumer loyalty, we will next attempt to identify factors that are likely to determine when a brand's performance is likely to convert into brand loyalty. A systematic review of the literature suggests four such factors: (a) the *consistency* of brand performance, (b) *level* of brand performance, (c) customer characteristics, and (d) marketplace characteristics. We discuss the findings related to each of these factors next.

Certainty or Consistency of Brand Performance

Past research suggests that satisfaction (or mean valence of consumer's past experiences with the brand) is more likely to translate into loyalty when that satisfaction level is based on consistent performance or is associated with high levels of certainty, characterized by low variability in past experiences. For instance, Chandrashekaran et al.'s (2007) analysis of data from an ongoing customer satisfaction tracking study conducted by a large U.S.-based service organization (as well as in a conceptual replication in a business-to-consumer context) uncovered that satisfaction converts into loyalty only when there is a low level of uncertainty (or higher level of brand trust) around that satisfaction rating. The translation from satisfaction to loyalty was lowered by approximately 60% on average in their data when the same satisfaction was more weakly held (i.e., characterized by high uncertainty or low level of brand trust). The level of uncertainty was determined in their research by the extent of current and prior experience, as well as service recovery actions undertaken by the company. Importantly, the authors found that even one service failure induced a significant amount of uncertainty (lowered brand trust), indicating the critical role that consistency of favorable brand experiences plays in the conversion of performance-based factors into brand loyalty.

Findings from several studies support the notion that brand trust is a significant predictor of brand loyalty (e.g., Chaudhuri & Holbrook, 2001; Yim et al., 2008) because it creates valued exchange relationships, especially in vulnerable and uncertain environments (Morgan & Hunt, 1994).

Level of Brand Performance

The concept of exceeding the expectations of the consumer or the notion of "delight" and positive emotion (Jones & Sasser, 1995; Rust & Oliver, 2000) have also been considered in relation to building loyalty. However, some researchers have questioned whether simply delighting the consumer can help build long-term loyalty (e.g., Hart & Johnson, 1999; Iacobucci, Grayson, & Ostrom, 1994). Recent research by Chitturi, Raghunathan, and Mahajan (2008) provides deeper insights into this issue.

Specifically, Chitturi et al. (2008) find that exceeding expectations on utilitarian attributes is only likely to increase satisfaction without influencing loyalty, but that exceeding on the hedonic attributes, which results in "delight," can indeed lead to generation of greater amounts of positive word of mouth and enhance repeat purchase intentions. They find support for their hypotheses in three studies conducted with cell phones, laptop computers, and cars. Their research demonstrates that products that meet or exceed customers' utilitarian needs (e.g., antilock brakes and stability features in an automobile) generate prevention-type emotions, such as confidence and security, which lead to enhanced satisfaction. On the other hand, products that meet or exceed customers' hedonic wants (e.g., cars with panoramic sunroofs, six speaker audio systems) can generate more promotion-oriented emotions, such as cheerfulness and excitement, which enhance customer delight. Most importantly, their research reveals that customer delight (as opposed to customer satisfaction) enhances customer loyalty by improving both word-of-mouth and repurchase intentions. It is, however, important to note that delight from hedonic features is typically likely to be evoked and become meaningful for consumer decisions after the consumer's functional needs have already been satisfied.

Customer Characteristics

Consumers who rate high on uncertainty avoidance are known to give more weight than their low uncertainty avoidant counterparts to the brand's performance, in forming their loyalty to a brand (e.g., Erdem & Swait, 1999; 2004). Additionally, Cooil, Keiningham, Aksoy, and Hsu (2007) find that the relationship between satisfaction and loyalty (as assessed by share of wallet) is moderated both by demographic and situational characteristics. They find that consumers who have higher levels of income and larger volumes of money-out business are more responsive to higher satisfaction levels, demonstrating a stronger link between their satisfaction with the product's performance and their loyalty.

Marketplace Characteristics

Several research studies provide an interesting insight into how the drivers of brand loyalty differ across the stages of the product life cycle and market competition, providing a very dynamic view of drivers of loyalty. For instance, Heilman et al. (2000) examine how brand preferences evolve for consumers who are new to established product categories (disposable diapers and towels). They find little evidence of brand loyalty early in consumers' experiences, but as consumers gather more information and as perceived risk subsides, they buy the brands they prefer, and loyalty develops. Importantly, they find that loyalty is shaped to a great extent by the product experience, as consumers tend to gravitate toward brands that provide them with the greatest utility or best performance. In other words, their research suggests that initial loyalties of consumers who are new to a category tend to be formed on the basis of their experience with the brand's performance.

As consumers get better acquainted with brands, though, and their level of experience with the industry and its offerings increases, the role of brand performance in driving brand loyalty tends to diminish (especially if brand quality is relatively high and most brands perform well, i.e., in mature markets), and shifts toward other drivers of loyalty (such as their relationship with or connections to the brand, or other rewards offered by brands). Several studies reveal that the effect of satisfaction on loyalty is likely to be attenuated when other factors such as relational elements and switching costs come into the picture (Lemon, White, & Winer, 2002; Oliver, 1999; Rust, Lemon, & Zeithaml, 2004). A longitudinal study of cellular phone customers by Johnson, Hermann, and Huber (2006) provides further interesting insights in this regard. Their research demonstrates how loyalty intentions evolve from being purely performance based (as assessed by perceived value) early in the diffusion process to being brand and relationship based as the market evolves. They find that perceived value has a positive direct effect on loyalty intentions, but that this effect decreases over time. Specifically, perceptions of overall value drive loyalty intentions early in the diffusion process. As the market grows and customer experience accumulates, other elements (e.g., affective aspects of the relationship and brand) come to drive loyalty intentions, clearly exceeding the direct positive influence of perceived value. Their findings suggest that early in the introduction and growth of an offering, managers should maintain a focus on improving value and demonstrating their performance advantages.

There is also some evidence to suggest that performance can have a strong influence on loyalty outcomes even in more mature industries (e.g., financial services, hair salons, fast food) to the extent that it leads to the generation of favorable affect and consumer-brand affection (e.g., Verhoef, 2003; Ying, Tse, & Chan, 2008). Specifically, these authors find that the effects of performance-based factors (such as satisfaction, value, and trust) on loyalty in these industries may be mediated by affective connections.

Summary

A review of the literature in this area suggests that a brand's high level of performance (on both dimensions—extremity as well as consistency) is a necessary but not sufficient condition for the formation of brand loyalty. Consumers tend to focus heavily on the functional aspects of a brand's performance when they are new to the product category, lack experience with the category, or perceive a high level of risk in the marketplace. Under these circumstances, their loyalty tends to be based heavily on their experience with the brand and its perceived performance (satisfaction and trust). However, as consumers' experience with the product category increases, markets mature, or even as the level of uncertainty in the marketplace drops, the brand's performance elements may become simply table stakes as their weight continues to decrease. At this point, other strategies (such as formation of affective connections and institution of switching costs) that offer the potential to distinguish the brand from competitors with somewhat similar levels of performance may be more likely to determine the consumer's level of loyalty to the brand. However, to the extent that the brand's performance itself can help in the formation of emotional connections with the brand (e.g., via customer service), it becomes more likely to result in loyalty formation. We discuss the affective and behavioral paths to brand loyalty next.

The Path of Consumer-Brand Connection

A second set of factors known to influence brand loyalty can be categorized as consumer-brand connections. Consumers can develop connections with brands because of the degree to which they can personally identify with a brand based on an identity and/or values overlap, or because of the association of the brand to similar others (e.g., intergenerational influence, brand communities), or even because of its relevance to the customer's situation. It is important to note, though, that although many of these connections may be related to the consumer's self-identity, they can also be driven simply by affective or emotional associations that a consumer has developed with the brand (e.g., brand's emotion-oriented communications that the consumer can connect with). As such, consumers are known to develop varying levels of relationships with brands, ranging from casual relationships (e.g., "flings") to committed relationships (e.g., "best friendships"; committed "partnerships") (Fournier, 1998). Stronger brand-consumer relationships have been shown to result in higher levels of brand loyalty, greater willingness to pay price premium and more positive word-of-mouth (Carroll & Ahuvia, 2006; Dick & Basu, 1994; Godes & Mayzlin, 2008; Thomson, MacInnis, & Park, 2005). Fournier (1998) suggests that the feelings linked to attachments lie at the core of all strong consumer-brand relationships, implying that strong consumer-brand connections are likely to be affect laden. Similarly, Jewell, and Unnava (2003) found that heavy users of a product category tended to have primarily affective brand associations, whereas light users had primarily cognitive associations to brands.

We categorize consumer-brand connections in terms of two distinct dimensions: (i) the degree of "fit," that is, the closeness or similarity between the brand and consumer (e.g., based on extent of overlap in values, self-identity, goals, etc.), and (ii) the intensity of affect or emotion that accompanies the connection (ranging from mild affection to passion and intense love). The two dimensions are not necessarily correlated. For instance, although it is possible for a consumer to have a high level of both fit and emotional association with a brand (e.g., iPod, Harley Davidson), high level of fit but weaker emotional associations (e.g., Sony, New Balance), as well as lower fit but strong emotional associations (e.g., Louis Vuitton, Porsche) are also likely.

Fit with Consumer

The fit dimension represents the extent of overlap between the consumer and the brand. Although overlap is typically assessed in relation to the consumer's self-concept (actual or ideal), it can also be based on the consumer's broader identity, which includes others who are strongly connected to the consumer's self-concept (e.g., loved ones, family members, groups). The similarity between consumer and the brand can be based on values, personality, shared interests, and goals.

Consumers are known to form strong relationships with brands that have values, personality associations, and goals congruent with their self-concept (Fournier, 1998; Sirgy, 1982), and use brands as a means of expressing their self-identity (e.g., Escalas & Bettman, 2005; Reed, 2004; Swaminathan, Stilley, & Ahluwalia, 2009). Brands that "fit" with their self-concept can not only give consumers a sense of comfort, closeness, and intimacy (Aaker, 1999; Swaminathan, Page, & Gürhan-Canli, 2007), but can also help them in signaling important attributes about themselves to others (Belk, 1988; Swaminathan et al., 2009; Wallendorf & Arnould, 1988). In this regard, although a "fit" with *actual* self-concept is most likely to generate a sense of comfort and intimacy with the brand, the brand's connections with the *ideal* self-concept are more likely to enhance its value for signaling to others.

By humanizing the brand, brand personality provides opportunities for building strong consumer-brand personality-based connections (e.g., Aaker, 1999). Swaminathan et al. (2009) provide an attachment theory perspective (Hazan & Shaver, 1994) for understanding the role of brand personality in the formation of consumer-brand connections for the signaling role. They find that consumers who have an anxious attachment style (negative view of self) are more likely to discriminate between brands based on the brand's personality than those who are less anxious about relationships. For the anxious attachment types, when the brand matches their ideal self-concept, brand attachment, purchase likelihood, and brand choice are enhanced. As such, these individuals tend to use the brand as a means for signaling their ideal self-concept to potential relational partners.

Consumers can also have a "values"-based connection with a brand (e.g., The Body Shop and environmentalism). In this regard, social and cause-related marketing as well as affinity marketing have the potential to influence consumer-brand connections and loyalty to the extent they clearly and strongly resonate with their consumers' values. Values associated with the brand (e.g., power, benevolence; Bardi & Schwartz, 2003; Schwartz, 1992; Torelli & Kaikati, 2009) can also help build bonds with consumers if these values are highly salient and important for their consumers. Indeed, Allen, Gupta, and Monnier (2008) found that when the values symbolized by a product's brand name were congruent with consumers' own personal value levels, the product was evaluated more favorably. For instance, participants who scored relatively high in excitement and enjoyment values had a more positive taste evaluation when told they had tasted Pepsi than when told they had tasted Woolworth-brand cola.

Consumer-brand connections can be formed not only on the basis of self-concept connection, but also on broader group-based identities associated to the self-concept. For instance, Swaminathan et al. (2007) examined consumer-brand relationships based on self-concept connections (e.g., with Mercedes), as well as connections to a group-level patriotic identity (e.g., country-of-origin connection with Ford) in a series of two studies. Their results reveal that, under independent self-construal, self-concept connection is more important; however, under interdependent self-construal, the brand's connection to the group level identity of country-of-origin becomes more important.

Similarly, consumers are also known to form connections with brands on the basis of other group level identities, such as families (e.g., intergenerational influence or within-family transmission of information and beliefs from one generation to the next (Childers & Rao, 1992; Moore, Wilkie, & Lutz, 2002), and also brand communities (e.g., Algesheimer, Dholakia, & Herrmann, 2005; Muniz & O'Guinn, 2001; Schouten, McAlexander, & Koening, 2007). As such, connections with these broader representations of the self, or self-relevant groups, can induce the formation of bonds, varying in their level of strength from the high fit and intimate connections that some brand communities can evoke (e.g., Harley Davidson) to the much looser level of fit represented by intergenerational influence in some product categories (e.g., private goods).

Emotional Intensity of the Connection

Consumers are known to develop emotional ties with brands which can range from mild affection to stronger emotional bonds such as "passion" and even "brand love" (Carroll & Ahuvia, 2006; Fournier, 1998; Thomson et al., 2005; Yim et al., 2008).

Emotional connections between consumers and brands can be formed in several ways. They can develop over time with increased quantity and quality of positive interactions and growing intimacy between the brand and consumer (e.g., Baldwin, Keelan, Fehr, Enns, & Koh-Rangarajoo, 1996; Thomson, 2006; Yim et al., 2008). In this regard, customer relationship management using databases that facilitate customized, responsive, regular interaction with valued customers may offer a strong potential for building emotional ties. Similarly, products and services that allow for repeated and customized interactions between the consumer and brand may enable the building of emotional ties (e.g., iPod, health clubs).

Consumer-brand emotional ties can also strengthen if the brand begins to play an important role in the consumer's life (e.g., as a relational partner or by fulfilling an important emotional need) (Fournier 1998). These types of emotional ties appear to be dependent upon consumer characteristics, as some consumers may be more likely to develop stronger and deeper relationships with brands than others.

Finally, brands also attempt to develop emotional ties with consumers by trying to arouse emotions in their communications (e.g., Cisco's "human network" advertising campaign) and/or service experience (e.g., through its service personnel and servicescape; Yim et al., 2008), that consumers can connect or identify with. As such, the arousal and generation of strong emotions in advertising is known to transfer over to the brand, becoming associated with it (e.g., Batra, & Ray, 1986; Holbrook & Batra, 1987; Holbrook & O'Shaughnessy, 1984). To the extent consumers can strongly identify or connect with the emotions being aroused by the brand, the consumer is likely to form an attachment or bond with the brand.

Some factors that have been known to influence the formation of consumer-brand connections include the product category, marketplace factors, and the ability of the brand to humanize itself. These are discussed next.

Product Category

Although building strong emotional connections is desirable, past research suggests that higher intensity emotional connections are easier to build in some product categories versus others. For instance, Carroll and Ahuvia (2006) report stronger levels of "brand love" for brands in product categories perceived as more hedonic (as compared with utilitarian) and for brands that offer more in terms of symbolic benefits. Similarly, Thomson et al. (2005) find some support for the notion that brands from higher involvement as well as more symbolic or hedonic categories (e.g., The Body Shop, Hermet Lang, BMW, Prada) tend to develop stronger emotional attachments than their low involvement or functional counterparts (e.g., AT&T, All, Ziploc).

Yim et al. (2008) find that the type of service (transactional or relational) tends to determine whether the development of customer-brand connections is likely to translate into commitment and repeat purchase behavior. Specifically, although transactional services and products, where variety may be valued (e.g., fast food restaurants, cereals), can effectively develop brand intimacy (fit), as well as emotional connections (e.g., passion and excitement), these connections are unlikely to translate into higher commitment levels. However, in the case of relational services (e.g., hair salon, health club) high levels of consumer-brand connections translate into higher levels of loyalty.

Marketplace Factors

The role of affective factors in general, and consumer-brand connections in particular, are likely to become more important in determining brand loyalty as markets mature, competition intensifies, and the marketplace risk decreases. As such, hedonic and emotional factors are likely to become more important than utilitarian (or performance-based factors) only after a "necessary" level of functional performance is met (Chitturi, Raghunathan, & Mahajan, 2007; Kivetz & Simonson, 2002). As Johnson et al. (2006) demonstrate in their longitudinal study of cell phone customers, loyalty intentions evolve from being purely value based early in the diffusion process to being brand and relationship based as the market evolves. More importantly, although the impact of the brand- and relationship-based factors on loyalty intentions was only small (and negative) in the first phase of their study, as the market grew to include a variety of competitors, the influence of brands and relationships on intentions became positive and eventually exceeded the direct, positive influence of perceived value. In this regard, many of the research studies that assess loyalty in mature categories (e.g., fast food, hair salons, and financial services) have demonstrated the strong impact of consumer-brand connections on loyalty intentions and outcomes (e.g., Chaudhuri & Holbrook, 2001; Verhoef, 2003; Yim et al., 2008).

Humanizing Brands

The more human-like a brand, or the more it is imbued with humanizing qualities, the easier it may be for consumers to form connections with it, since overlap in terms of values, personality, goals, and identities is more plausible to establish, as is the elicitation of emotions that consumers value and can relate to. It is not unusual for researchers to use the interpersonal relationship metaphor when attempting to understand the nature of relationships between consumers and brands (e.g., Fournier, 1998; Swaminathan et al., 2009; Thomson, 2006).

Brands can be humanized in many different ways, ranging from imbuing the brand with a distinct personality in all aspects of its communications (e.g., MTV and Coca-Cola as exciting, Hallmark as sincere, Nike as rugged; Aaker, 1997; Aaker, Fournier, & Brasel, 2004), associating it with celebrities whose personality it wants to signal (e.g., Accenture and Tiger Woods, BMW and James Bond; Escalas & Bettman, 2008; Till, 1998), anthromorphizing the brand (e.g., the Mac versus PC characters developed by Apple, the Verizon guy; Aggarwal & McGill, 2007), and the use of human brands (e.g., Thompson, 2006), both real (e.g., Martha Stewart) and fictitious (e.g., Betty Crocker).

Summary

Consumer-brand connections are typically affect laden and can be defined in terms of the (a) extent of fit between brand and consumer's self-concept and (b) intensity of the emotion accompanying the connection. These dimensions reveal the various avenues open to companies for forging connections between their brands and consumers. Consumer-brand connections can become an extremely important driver of brand loyalty, as markets mature, competition intensifies, and brands are perceived as relatively similar in their performance. More importantly, as compared to the incentives route that we discuss next, consumer-brand connections are more likely to lead to "true" versus "spurious" loyalty. Although consumer-brand connections may be easier to form in some product categories (e.g., hedonic, lower involvement, symbolic, relational) than others (e.g., functional and lower involvement), humanizing the brand (e.g., by developing a brand personality or using human representations and celebrities) offers a potential avenue for enabling such connections in a wider range of product categories. We expect this path to brand loyalty to become even more important in the future as competition continues to intensify in the global marketplace. We also noticed that despite its high strategic value, this path has received relatively scant research attention compared to the other two (performance, and incentives) discussed in this chapter. This area offers many potential avenues for interested researchers, ranging from a better understanding of the different dimensions of consumer-brand connections, to factors influencing the effectiveness of these connections (e.g., in determining loyalty) and their interactions with the other strategic paths to loyalty (performance and incentives).

The Path Paved With Incentives

In this section we will focus on a discussion of loyalty programs that offer consumers incentives to engage in repeated purchase of the brand. A "loyalty program" is defined as a program that allows consumers to accumulate rewards (such as price discounts, free goods, or even special recognition) when they make repeated purchases with a firm. Such a program is intended to foster customer loyalty over time. Loyalty programs can enhance consumers' perceptions of the value of what a firm has to offer (Bolton, Kannan, & Bramlett, 2000; Yi & Jeon, 2003), and can hence be instrumental in customer relationship initiation and retention (Sirdeshmukh, Singh, & Sabol, 2002; Woodruff, 1997). Enhanced value perception is a necessary condition to a loyalty program's success (O'Brien & Jones, 1995). In essence, loyalty programs can compensate for a lack of affective connections and reduce customer defection by raising switching costs. Past research indicates that competitive switching barriers benefit the firm and can result in higher prices in the marketplace (Kim, Shi, & Srinivasan, 2001), especially in the context of high variety-seeking products and services (Zhang, Krishna, & Dhar, 2000). Additionally, giving free rewards can also increase the customer's sense of recognition and importance and thereby deepen his or her relationship with the firm (Bitner, 1995; Gwinner, Gremler, & Bitner, 1998). Further, it can offer other psychological benefits such as the opportunity to indulge in guilt-free luxuries (Kivetz & Simonson, 2002).

LOYALTY MARKETING LEADS TO INCREASED CUSTOMER RETENTION AND SPEND, AS WELL AS MEASURABLE MARKETING RESULTS

Loyalty programs are almost everywhere consumers are. From frequent flyer programs to punch cards at coffee shops, these programs continue to be one of the most important—and cost-effective—ways to retain customers. Their ability to drive business performance and increase revenue and profit are just a few of the reasons that loyalty programs have made the list of the top 10 CEO priorities for 10 years running.

"For smart marketers, a loyalty program allows firms to gather information to power the entire business. It is one of the best investments a company can make—in tough times and in good times—because it offers resilience to a business," says Mike Kust, Chief Marketing Officer for Carlson Marketing, a global leader in marketing services and part of the Carlson family of companies. Carlson provides hotel, restaurant, travel, and marketing services for clients including Radisson and TGI Fridays. It was built on the success of its Gold Bond Stamps loyalty program.

As the programs have evolved with the market, they have become more sophisticated and varied, expanding to include online auctions, access to exclusive benefits, and tiered promotions. For instance, a frequent flier may choose to redeem his or her miles to play a round of golf with Tiger Woods at Pebble Beach. These innovations represent a much different way to use the loyalty currency to engage and keep customers. For loyalty programs, innovation and alignment with customers' needs are essential.

"Today, more than ever, businesses need to retain their best customers and get a measurable return for their marketing dollars. Loyalty programs are a tried and true way to do both. It is 7 to 10 times more costly to attract a new customer than to retain an existing one," says Kust. "In fact, data from some of our clients' programs demonstrate that customers involved in loyalty programs stay with the brand 50% longer and significantly outspend non-members."

"At its heart, a loyalty program is an example of measurable marketing. Core loyalty marketing is a value exchange. It's a relationship based on reciprocity," says Kust. "Customers earn currency for their engagement with the brand. In turn, the firm can generate behavioral data that help to target a segment of one. It increases knowledge of customers and enhances a company's ability to treat each customer uniquely at every touchpoint."

> The continual evolution of loyalty programs will prove indispensable to companies in an increasingly crowded marketplace. As new options emerge that leverage digital and mobile technology, loyal customers will benefit, too. The migration from points and prizes to timely information, more relevant offers and one-of-a-kind experiences should cause consumers to smile.
>
> **R.D.M. & L.W.P.**

Loyalty programs have become rampant in the recent years. A few years ago, more than half of U.S. adults were enrolled in at least one loyalty program (Kivetz & Simonson, 2003); the level of participation continues to grow at a fast pace. From 2000 to 2006, total loyalty program enrollments in the United States increased 35.5% to 1.5 billion (Ferguson & Hlavinka, 2007; cf. Liu & Yang, 2009). With the growing prevalence of loyalty programs in many industries, some researchers are beginning to question the value of loyalty programs and wonder if they only represent the necessary cost of doing business in some industries without providing a clear return on investment (e.g., Ferguson & Hlavinka, 2007; Liu & Yang, 2009; Dowling, 2002; Shugan, 2005). For example, Dowling (2002) suggests that loyalty programs do not necessarily foster loyalty, are not cost effective, and that the proliferation of loyalty programs is a "me-too" scheme. The findings with relation to the outcomes of loyalty programs (customer retention, share of wallet, market share, price premium) are mixed (e.g., Bolton et al., 2000; Leenheer, van Heerde, Bijmolt, T.H.A., & Smidts, 2003; Liu, 2007; Magi, 2003; Sharp & Sharp, 1997; Shugan, 2005; Verhoef, 2003), fueling the controversy related to their effectiveness. Our discussion of loyalty programs will, therefore, focus on the identification of factors that influence the performance of loyalty programs and can help the manager enhance the effectiveness of such programs.

Reward Characteristics

Rewards in a loyalty program can be categorized along several dimensions: They can be immediate (rewards given for every visit, e.g., membership program which gives 20% discount on every purchase or an instant scratch) or delayed (rewards given for every nth visit/purchase, e.g., free item after eight purchases or a frequent buyer program); direct (directly support value proposition of the product, e.g., free sandwich after eight sandwich purchases, airline frequent flyer) or indirect (unrelated to the given product, e.g., free movie ticket after eight sandwich purchases, frequent buyer club); hard (concrete or tangible benefits, e.g., free ticket) or soft (intangible benefits such as special recognition, upgrading) (Dowling & Uncles, 1997; Yi & Jeon, 2003).

Direct rewards are known to be preferable over and more likely to result in loyalty outcomes than indirect rewards, especially in high involvement situations (Yi & Jeon, 2003). Keh and Lee (2006), using the context of two services (banks and restaurants), find that although direct rewards generally tend to create more loyalty than indirect rewards, these results can differ based upon the time horizon of the reward (immediate or delayed) as well as the satisfaction level of the customer. For satisfied customers, the advantage of direct rewards emerges when they are delayed, but this was not observed in the case of immediate rewards. However, for customers with lower levels of satisfaction, direct (versus indirect) rewards had greater potential to enhance loyalty when offered for immediate redemption, but not in the delay condition. Although delayed rewards may be better at enhancing long-term relationships and in high involvement settings, some research suggests that immediate rewards may be more powerful under conditions of low involvement due to a desire for instant gratification (Dowling & Uncles, 1997). Yi and Jeon (2003) find in the context of their experiments, that in low-involvement situations, immediate rewards (e.g., an instant scratch card with 10% probability of winning) are more effective than delayed rewards (e.g., rewards to customer for every tenth visit) in producing program loyalty and brand loyalty.

Roehm, Pullins, and Roehm (2002) demonstrate the important role that the choice of incentive plays in determining the success of a loyalty program in building brand loyalty. Their findings suggest that incentives that overlap with the brand's associations (termed as "cue-compatible" incentives) prompt rehearsal of the favorable associations, enhancing their accessibility. This enhanced accessibility helps boost post-program loyalty. For example, if core Slice associations include the concept "refreshing," a newsletter offering refreshing recipes would be cue compatible and enhance the accessibility of the favorable "refreshing" associations, whereas one with little relationship to this theme or to other Slice associations would be cue incompatible and could interfere with brand associations. Importantly, when the incentives introduced new associations that interfered with the accessibility of the existing favorable brand associations, decrements in post-program loyalty were observed. Their research also suggests that incentives that are concrete or tangible could undermine post-program loyalty, especially if they induce elaboration of the incentive at the expense of the brand (which might be more likely with indirect rewards). As such, it can be argued that the more attractive, unusual, or elaboration-generating the tangible incentive, the higher its interference effects are likely to be.

Consumers' Related Factors

Lal and Bell (2003) and Liu (2007) examine the moderating effect of consumers' usage levels on the effectiveness of loyalty programs. Contrary to the traditional wisdom that loyalty programs serve as a defense mechanism mainly for heavy buyers, these studies find that loyalty programs instead lead to the biggest increase in spending and purchase frequency among light buyers.

Lal and Bell (2003) examine data from a grocery store chain that offered rewards such as free product (hams and turkeys) and discount coupons based on total accumulated spending levels. The authors found that the promotions had the least impact on the shopping behavior of the chain's "best customers" (identified by high previous spending levels). The program, however, reached profitability due to its impact on "cherry pickers" (i.e., customers who did not previously have high spending levels at the grocery chain). Their findings suggest that offering tangible promotions such as free goods and discounts may be beneficial for attracting the price-sensitive cherry pickers, but it is possible that value-added services may be better suited for the less price-sensitive shoppers who are already high spenders and less likely to be influenced by price-related incentives.

Liu (2007) examines the impact of a loyalty program on consumers' purchase behavior in a convenience store franchise over a 2-year period. The results suggest that the loyalty program's effect on behavior was contingent on consumers' initial usage levels. Consumers who were heavy buyers at the beginning of the program were most likely to claim the rewards they earned and thus benefited the most from the program. However, their spending levels and exclusive loyalty to the store did not increase over time. In contrast, the loyalty program had positive effects on both light and moderate buyers' purchase frequencies and transaction sizes, and it made these consumers more loyal to the store. Interestingly, consumers who started with low usage levels changed their behavior as much as or more than moderate and heavy buyers, contradicting the commonly held belief that light buyers are less-than-ideal targets for loyalty programs and that they will not perceive much value in the program (Dowling & Uncles, 1997; O'Brien & Jones, 1995). The loyalty program did not initially appear very attractive to light buyers. However, these consumers diversified their purchases and branched into the firm's other service areas. By claiming a higher portion of rewards, they also gradually invested more efforts into the program, allowing them to benefit more from the loyalty program, further motivating them to spend more and patronize the store more exclusively.

Another consumer-related factor, future orientation, has received some support in the literature. Loyalty programs have been found to be more appealing to consumers who do not heavily discount future benefits (e.g., Kopalle & Neslin, 2003). This is not surprising given that most loyalty programs do reward consumers in the future. Similarly, Lewis (2004) notes that for a loyalty program to be effective, it must "motivate customers to view purchases as a sequence of related decisions rather than as independent transactions." In other words, if a consumer performs the appropriate sequence of activities over time, he or she will be rewarded in the future.

Firm Characteristics

Past research has reported that high share brands have a significantly larger share of loyalty than low share brands, a phenomenon termed as the double jeopardy effect (Ehrenberg, Goodhardt, & Barwise, 1990; Fader & Schmittlein, 1993). Thus, low-market share brands are at a disadvantage to high-market share brands in two ways. In addition to having fewer customers, those few customers who *do* purchase the low-market share brand do so less frequently than do consumers of the high-market share brand. Double jeopardy is known to occur even for brands that are functionally substitutable and indistinguishable in blind product tests.

This phenomenon is driven mostly by brand awareness. Consumers who are familiar with both the high- and low-market share brands tend to switch between them, while the consumers who are aware of only the high-market share brand will tend to purchase that brand consistently. Ehrenberg et al. (1990) suggest that in order to overcome double jeopardy, managers of a low-market share brand should aim to increase the number of buyers (e.g., attract new buyers) rather than try to increase the purchase frequency of existing buyers.

Consistent with these findings, two studies reported by Liu and Yang (2009) also reveal that only loyalty programs associated with high-share, but not low-share, firms demonstrate sales lifts. This occurs because high-share firms tend to possess complementary product and customer resources (e.g., a larger customer base, more diverse product portfolio, wider distribution channels, and better ability to partner with other companies) that enhance the effectiveness of its loyalty program as compared to firms with smaller market shares.

These findings together suggest that loyalty programs are likely to be a more effective strategy for high-share (as compared to low-share) brands because not only do the high-share brands have more potential for loyalty development (Ehrenberg et al., 1990), but they also have more complementary resources to make the loyalty program more effective (Liu & Yang, 2009).

Marketplace Characteristics

Past research suggests that the effectiveness of loyalty programs is likely to be lowered in highly competitive markets where: (a) the marketplace is crowded with several loyalty programs (e.g., Dowling & Uncles, 1997; Magi, 2003; Shugan, 2005) and/or (b) the market for the product category is saturated and does not offer any potential for expansion (e.g., Dowling & Uncles, 1997; Liu & Yang, 2009). Based on findings from the British grocery market, where market shares of competing firms have remained stable despite use of loyalty programs, Dowling and Uncles (1997) argued that a loyalty program is unlikely to alter customer behavior fundamentally, especially in established competitive markets.

Interestingly, recent research by Liu and Yang (2009) reveals that the ineffectiveness of loyalty programs due to the crowding effect (i.e., factor [a] above) is contingent on the expandability of the product category (i.e., factor [b]). They find that market crowding by loyalty programs has a negative effect under low category expandability, but its effect disappears under high category expandability. In other words, if market demand is flexible, either because the industry is in the growth stage of the life cycle or because demand can be stolen from related industries or stimulated from consumers, crowding will be less of an issue, and loyalty programs can still be a viable strategy for expanding the firm's business. In contrast, in a rigid market in which firms compete for a limited, fixed set of demand, offering more loyalty programs functions at best as a defense mechanism, resulting in limited incremental contribution to the brand's bottom line and a zero-sum game for the industry.

Summary

The path paved with incentives or loyalty programs can be an attractive one, especially for firms with a large market share; the complementary resources available to them are likely to enhance the effectiveness of their loyalty program, allowing them to confer "stickiness" to their already large market base. Notably, loyalty programs can be effective in increasing loyalty for not only the heavy users, but also light and medium users of the brand/service. Additionally, reward programs that increase the perceived value of the offering and create switching barriers can be most effective in generating loyalty in markets that are growing (e.g., growth stage of product life cycle) or have the potential to expand. However, as markets become saturated not only with loyalty programs, but also in terms of market growth and expansion, reward programs simply become a defensive strategy and are more appropriate only for large share brands. In such marketplace settings, consumer-brand connections (second path discussed in this chapter) may offer a more effective means of building "true" brand loyalty. Similarly, from a strategy perspective, small share and niche brands, instead of creating switching barriers, may benefit more from building consumer-brand connections, which are not only more difficult to imitate but also create greater differentiation and may be more likely to induce loyalty for these brands. Such a strategy can also allow them to grow their market share, thereby increasing their potential to implement an effective rewards program later.

From a tactics perspective, the type of incentive plays an important role in determining the effectiveness of the rewards program. Direct rewards, especially if delayed, are likely to be more effective in generating loyalty than are immediate and indirect rewards, especially for satisfied customers. Additionally, incentives and communications that are consistent with the brand's dominant favorable associations (e.g., attributes, image) and thereby reinforce them are also more likely to increase loyalty than incentives that are unrelated to them. Interestingly, highly attention-getting and unusual tangible rewards may actually undermine brand loyalty, since they focus the consumer's attention on the reward instead of the brand.

Although most of the literature has tended to focus on the economic benefits of loyalty programs, some researchers have also uncovered their potential to establish affective connections with consumers. In this regard, reward programs, combined with efficient data mining, provide a huge potential for one-to-one marketing, and customized interactions with consumers. These types of interactions can be helpful in building emotional connections between the brand and consumer, and would benefit from additional research in the future.

Conclusion

Loyalty is an important destination for most companies. Although typically assessed in terms of repeat purchase behavior and share of wallet, "true" loyalty is accompanied by a commitment toward the brand. This commitment or psychological attachment could be based on the consumer's experience with the brand, affect, or connections formed between the consumer and brand, or even its perceived value to the consumer. The defensive processing induced by loyalty or commitment (lowered attention and increased resistance to favorable information about competitors, and increased resistance to unfavorable information about the preferred brand) enables the consumer to resist switching inducements, exhibiting repeat purchases of the target brand. Notably, similar patterns of defensive information processing have emerged in the literature, irrespective of the basis of the consumer's commitment (e.g., Ahluwalia et al., 2000).

How can a brand work its way toward loyalty? A review of the literature suggests three potential paths. Specific findings relating to circumstances under which each path is most likely to be effective are outlined above in the sections corresponding to the paths. Overall, the performance path is a crucial place to begin the journey. As such, it is a prerequisite to the formation of loyalty. It appears to be most influential during consumers' initial experiences with the brand and product category, especially in the formation of early loyalty. It also appears to play an important role for developing loyalty when markets have higher levels of uncertainty and consumers don't have a lot of information about the product category. It is, in effect, a necessary, although not always sufficient, condition for building brand loyalty. During the market growth and maturity phases, it is possible that its role may diminish compared to other paths that may gain in importance during these phases (connections and incentives). In particular, the incentives path (loyalty programs) appears to be a useful one for companies that are operating in markets that offer growth opportunities, particularly if the company has a high market share. In mature markets, differentiation becomes important for building and sustaining loyalty in the face of brands that seemingly imitate each, perform at competitive levels, and tend to saturate the market with loyalty programs as well as markets that don't provide avenues for growth. The consumer-brand connection route offers a path for differentiating the brand under such circumstances. This path may also be more appropriate for companies that have smaller market shares. Our chapter outlines several strategies for building consumer-brand connections, as well as limitations to their formation. However, more research in the area of consumer-brand connections and how and when they impact brand loyalty would be desirable.

The role of product category also promises to play an important role in understanding which path(s) to loyalty may be most appropriate for a company. For instance, product categories associated with symbolic or hedonic consumption may offer a greater potential for building consumer-brand connections. The traditional single-brand loyalty has been difficult to find for some product categories (e.g., variety seeking). In these categories, multibrand loyalty instead of exclusive loyalty may be the best that a company can hope to build. Future research should also attempt to identify other product-category-related factors that impact loyalty formation and outcomes. Additionally, the dynamics and synergies between the different paths to loyalty formation would also benefit from further research.

References

Aaker, J. (1997). Dimensions of brand personality. *Journal of Marketing Research, 34,* 347–357.

Aaker, J. (1999). Brand personality: A path to differentiation. In R. Morgan (Ed.), *Brands Face the Future*. New York: Research International, 13–21.

Aaker, J., Fournier, S., & Brasel, S.A. (2004). When good brands do bad. *Journal of Consumer Research, 31,* 1–16.

Aggarwal, P., & McGill, A.L. (2007). Is that car smiling at me? Schema congruity as a basis for evaluating anthropomorphized products. *Journal of Consumer Research, 34,* 468–479.

Ahluwalia, R. (2002). How prevalent is the negativity effect in consumer environments? *Journal of Consumer Research, 29,* 270–279.

Ahluwalia, R., Burnkrant, R.E., & Unnava, H.R. (2000). Consumer response to publicity: The moderating role of commitment. *Journal of Marketing Research, 37,* 203–214.

Ahluwalia, R., Unnava, H.R., & Burnkrant, R.E. (2001). The moderating role of commitment on the spillover effect of marketing communications. *Journal of Marketing Research, 38,* 458–470.

Algesheimer, R., Dholakia, U.M., & Herrmann, A. (2005). The social influence of brand community: Evidence from European car clubs. *Journal of Marketing, 69,* 19–34.

Allen, M.W., Gupta, R., & Monnier, A. (2008). The interactive effect of cultural symbols and human values on taste evaluation. *Journal of Consumer Research, 35,* 294–308.

Assael, H. (1998). *Consumer behavior and marketing action* (6th ed.). Cincinnati, OH: South Western College Publishing.

Baldwin, M.W., Keelan, J.P.R., Fehr, B., Enns, V., & Koh-Rangarajoo, E. (1996). Social-cognitive conceptualization of attachment working models: Availability and accessibility effects. *Journal of Personality and Social Psychology, 71,* 94–109.

Bardi, A., & Schwartz, S.H. (2003). Values and behavior: Strength and structure of relations. *Personality and Social Psychology Bulletin, 29,* 1207–1220.

Batra, R., & Ray, M.L. (1986). Affective responses mediating acceptance of advertising. *Journal of Consumer Research, 13,* 234–249.

Belk, R.W. (1988). Possessions and the extended self. *Journal of Consumer Research, 15,* 139–168.

Bitner, M.J. (1995). Relationship marketing: It's all about promises. *Journal of the Academy of Marketing Science, 23,* 246–251.

Bolton, R.N., Kannan, P.K., & Bramlett, M.D. (2000). Implications of loyalty program membership and service experiences for customer retention and value. *Journal of the Academy of Marketing Science, 28,* 95–108.

Carlson, K.A., & Pearo, L.K. (2004). Limiting predecisional distortion by prior valuation of attribute components. *Organizational Behavior and Human Decision Processes, 1,* 48–59.

Carroll, B.A., & Ahuvia, A.C. (2006). Some antecedents and outcomes of brand love. *Marketing Letters, 17,* 79–89.

Chaiken, S., Giner-Sorolla, R., & Chen, S. (1996). Beyond accuracy: Defense and impression motives in heuristic and systematic information processing. In P. M. Gollwitzer & J. A. Bargh (Eds.), *The psychology of action: Linking cognition and motivation to behavior.* New York: Guilford, 553–578.

Chandrashekaran, M., Rotte, K., Tax, S.S., & Grewal, R. (2007). Satisfaction strength and customer loyalty. *Journal of Marketing Research, 44,* 153–163.

Chaudhuri, A., & Holbrook, M.B. (2001). The chain of effects from brand trust and brand affect to brand performance: The role of brand loyalty. *Journal of Marketing, 65,* 81–93.

Childers, T.L., & Rao, A.R. (1992). The influence of familial and peer-based reference groups on consumer decisions. *Journal of Consumer Research, 19,* 198–211.

Chitturi, R., Raghunathan, R., & Mahajan, V. (2007). Form versus function: How the intensities of specific emotions evoked in functional versus hedonic trade-offs mediate product preferences. *Journal of Marketing Research, 44,* 702–714.

Chitturi, R., Raghunathan, R., & Mahajan, V. (2008). Delight by design: The role of hedonic versus utilitarian benefits. *Journal of Marketing, 72,* 48–63.

Choi, B., & Ahluwalia, R. (2006). The role of consumer inferences about price discounts in influencing switching behavior. In C. Pechmann & L. Price (Eds.), *Advances in consumer research* (Vol. 33, pp. 252–253). Provo, UT: Association for Consumer Research.

Cleeren, K., Dekimpe, M.G., & Helsen, K. (2008). Weathering product-harm crises. *Journal of the Academy of Marketing Science, 36,* 262–270.

Cooil, B., Keiningham, T.L., Aksoy, L., & Hsu, M. (2007). A longitudinal analysis of customer satisfaction and share of wallet: Investigating the moderating effect of customer characteristics. *Journal of Marketing, 71,* 67–83.

Cunningham, S.M. (1966). Brand loyalty: What, where, how much? *Harvard Business Review, 34,* 116–128.

Dawar, N., & Pillutla, N.N. (2000). Impact of product-harm crises on brand equity: The moderating role of consumer expectations. *Journal of Marketing Research, 37,* 215–226.

Day, G.S. (1969). A two-dimensional concept of brand loyalty. *Journal of Advertising Research, 9,* 29–35.

Dick, A.S., & Basu, K. (1994). Customer loyalty: Toward an integrated conceptual framework. *Journal of the Academy of Marketing Science, 22,* 99–113.

Dowling, G.R. (2002). Customer relationship management: In B2C markets, often less is more. *California Management Review, 44,* 87–104.

Dowling. G.R., & Uncles, M. (1997). Do customer loyalty programs really work? *Sloan Management Review, 38,* 71–82.

Dunn, M., & Davis, S. (2004). Creating the brand-driven business: It's the CEO who must lead the way. *Handbook of Business Strategy, 5,* 243–248.

Ehrenberg, A.S.C., Goodhardt, G.J., & Barwise, T.P. (1990). Double jeopardy revisited. *Journal of Marketing, 54,* 82–91.

Erdem, T., & Swait, J. (1999). Brand equity as a signaling phenomenon. *Journal of Consumer Psychology, 7,* 131–157.

Erdem, T., & Swait, J. (2004). Brand credibility, brand consideration, and choice. *Journal of Consumer Research, 31,* 191–198.

Escalas, J.E., & Bettman, J.R. (2005). Self-construal, reference groups, and brand meaning. *Journal of Consumer Research, 32*, 378–389.

Escalas, J.E., & Bettman, J.R. (2008). Connecting with celebrities: Celebrity endorsement, brand meaning, and self-brand connections. Working paper.

Fader, P.S., & Schmittlein, D.C. (1993). Excess behavioral loyalty for high-share brands: Deviations from the Dirichlet model for repeat purchasing. *Journal of Marketing Research, 30*, 478–493.

Ferguson, R., & Hlavinka, K. (2007). *Quo Vadis: Sizing Up the U.S. Loyalty Marketing Industry*. Milford, OH: Colloquy.

Fournier, S. (1998). Consumers and their brands: Developing relationship theory in consumer research. *Journal of Consumer Research, 24*, 343–373.

Godes, D., & Mayzlin, D. (2008). Firm-created word-of-mouth communication: Evidence from a field test. *Marketing Science*, forthcoming.

Gwinner, K.P., Gremler, D.D., & Bitner, M.J. (1998). Relational benefits in services industries: The customer's perspective. *Journal of the Academy of Marketing Science, 26*, 101–114.

Hart, C.W., & Johnson, M.D. (1999). Growing the trust relationship. *Marketing Management, 8*, 8–19.

Hazan, C., & Shaver, P.R. (1994). Attachment as an organizational framework for research on close relationships. *Psychological Inquiry, 5*, 1–22.

Heilman, C.M., Bowman, D., & Wright, G.P. (2000). The evolution of brand preferences and choice behaviors of consumers new to a market. *Journal of Marketing Research, 37*, 139–155.

Herr, P.M., Kardes, F.R., & Kim, J. (1991). Effects of word-of-mouth and product-attribute information on persuasion: An accessibility-diagnosticity perspective. *Journal of Consumer Research, 17*, 454–462.

Holbrook, M.B., & O'Shaughnessy, J. (1984). The role of emotion in advertising. *Psychology and Marketing, 1*, 45–64.

Holbrook, M.B., & Batra, R. (1987). Assessing the role of emotions as mediators of consumer responses to advertising. *Journal of Consumer Research, 14*, 404–420.

Iacobucci, D., Grayson, K., & Ostrom, A. (1994). The calculus of service quality and customer satisfaction: Theoretical and empirical differentiation and integration. In T.A. Swartz, D.H. Bowen, & S.W. Brown (Eds.), *Advances in services marketing and management* (Vol. 3, pp. 1–67). Greenwich, CT: JAI Press.

Jacobson, N.S., Waldron, H., & Moore, D. (1980). Toward a behavioral profile of marital distress. *Journal of Consulting and Clinical Psychology, 48*, 696–703.

Jacoby, J., & Chestnut, R.W. (1978). *Brand loyalty measurement and management*. New York: Wiley.

Jacoby, J., & Kyner, D.B. (1973). Brand loyalty versus repeat purchase behavior. *Journal of Marketing Research, 10*, 1–9.

Jewell, R.D., & Unnava, H.R. (2003). When competitive interference can be beneficial. *Journal of Consumer Research, 30*, 283–291.

Johnson, M.D., Hermann, A., & Huber, F. (2006). The evolution of loyalty intentions. *Journal of Marketing, 70*, 122–132.

Jones, T.O., & Sasser, W.E., Jr. (1995). Why satisfied consumers defect. *Harvard Business Review, 73*, 88–99.

Kahn, B.E., Kalwani, M.U., & Morrison, D.G. (1986). Measuring variety seeking and reinforcement behaviors using panel data. *Journal of Marketing Research, 23*, 89–100.

Kapferer, J. (2005). The roots of brand loyalty decline: An international comparison. *Ivey Business Journal Online, March–April*, 1–6.

Keh, H.T., & Lee, Y.H. (2006). Do reward programs build loyalty for services? The moderating effect of satisfaction on type and timing of rewards. *Journal of Retailing, 82*, 127–136.

Keiningham, T.L., & Vavra, T.G. (2001). *The customer delight principle: Exceeding customers' expectations for bottom-line success.* Chicago, IL: American Marketing Association.

Keller, K.L. (2007). *Strategic brand management: Building, measuring, and managing brand equity* (3rd ed.). Upper Saddle River, NJ: Prentice Hall.

Kiel, G.C., & Layton, R.A. (1981). Dimensions of consumer information seeking behavior. *Journal of Marketing Research, 18*, 233–239.

Kim, B.D., Shi, M., & Srinivasan, K. (2001). Reward programs and tacit collusion. *Marketing Science, 20*, 99–120.

Kivetz, R., & Simonson, I. (2002). Earning the right to indulge: Effort as a determinant of customer preferences toward frequency program rewards. *Journal of Marketing Research, 39*, 155–170.

Kivetz, R., & Simonson, I. (2003). The idiosyncratic fit heuristic: Effort advantage as a determinant of consumer response to loyalty programs. *Journal of Marketing Research, 40*, 454–467.

Klein, J.G., & Ahluwalia, R. (2005). Negativity in the evaluation of political candidates. *Journal of Marketing, 69*, 131–142.

Kopalle, P.K., & Neslin, S.A. (2003). The economic viability of frequency reward programs in a strategic competitive environment. *Review of Marketing Science, 1*, 1–39.

Lal, R., & Bell, D.E. (2003). The impact of frequent shopper programs in grocery retailing. *Quantitative Marketing and Economics, 1*, 179–202.

Leenheer, J., van Heerde, H.J., Bijmolt, T.H.A., & Smidts, A. (2007). Do loyalty programs really enhance behavioral loyalty? An empirical analysis accounting for self-selecting members. *International Journal of Research in Marketing, 24*, 31–48.

Lemon, K.N., White, T.B., & Winer, R.S. (2002). Dynamic customer relationship management: Incorporating future considerations into the service retention decision. *Journal of Marketing, 66*, 1–14.

Lewis, M. (2004). The influence of loyalty programs and short-term promotions on customer retention. *Journal of Marketing Research, 41*, 281–292.

Liu, Y. (2007). The long-term impact of loyalty programs on consumer purchase behavior and loyalty. *Journal of Marketing, 71*, 19–35.

Liu, Y., & Yang, R. (2009). Competing loyalty programs: Impact of market saturation, market share, and category expandability. *Journal of Marketing, 73*, 93–108.

Magi, A.W. (2003). Share of wallet in retailing: The effects of customer satisfaction, loyalty cards and shopper characteristics. *Journal of Retailing, 79*, 97–106.

Miller, R.S. (1997). Inattentive and contented: Relationship commitment and attention to alternatives. *Journal of Personality and Social Psychology, 73*, 758–766.

Mizerski, R.W. (1982). An attribution explanation for the disproportionate influence of unfavorable information. *Journal of Consumer Research, 9,* 301–310.

Moore, E.S., Wilkie, W.L., & Lutz, R.J. (2002). Passing the torch: Intergenerational influence as a source of brand equity. *Journal of Marketing, 66,* 17–37.

Morgan, R.M., & Hunt, S.D. (1994). The commitment-trust theory of relationship marketing. *Journal of Marketing, 58,* 20–38.

Muniz, A.M., Jr., & O'Guinn, T.C. (2001). Brand community. *Journal of Consumer Research, 27,* 412–432.

O'Brien, L., & Jones, C. (1995). Do rewards really create loyalty? *Long Range Planning, 4,* 130.

Odin, Y., Odin, N., & Valette-Florence, P. (2001). Conceptual and operational aspects of brand loyalty: An empirical investigation. *Journal of Business Research, 53,* 75–84.

Oliver, R.L. (1997). *Satisfaction: A behavioral perspective on the consumer.* New York: McGraw-Hill.

Oliver, R.L. (1999). Whence customer loyalty? *Journal of Marketing, 63,* 33–44.

Reed II, A. (2004). Activating the self-importance of consumer selves: Exploring identity salience effects on judgments. *Journal of Consumer Research, 31,* 286–295.

Reichheld, F.F. (1993). Loyalty-based management. *Harvard Business Review, 71,* 64–73.

Reichheld, F.F., Markey, R.G., Jr., & Hopton, C. (2000). The loyalty effect: The relationship between loyalty and profits. *European Business Journal, 12,* 134–139.

Roehm, M.L., Pullins, E.B., & Roehm, H.A., Jr. (2002). Designing loyalty-building programs for packaged goods brands. *Journal of Marketing Research, 39,* 202–213.

Russo, J.E., Meloy, M.G., & Medvec, V.H. (1998). Predecisional distortion of product information. *Journal of Marketing Research, 35,* 438–452.

Rust, R.T., Lemon, K.N., & Zeithaml, V.A. (2004). Return on marketing: Using customer equity to focus marketing strategy. *Journal of Marketing, 68,* 109–127.

Rust, R.T., & Oliver, R.L. (2000). Should we delight the customer? *Journal of the Academy of Marketing Science, 28,* 86–94.

Schouten, J.W., McAlexander, J.H., & Koening, H.F. (2007). Transcendent customer experience and brand community. *Journal of the Academy of Marketing Science, 35,* 357–68.

Schwartz, S.H. (1992). Universals in the content and structure of values: Theoretical advances and empirical tests in 20 countries. *Advances in Experimental Social Psychology, 25,* 1–65.

Sharp, B. & Sharp, A. (1997). Loyalty programs and their impact on repeat-purchase loyalty patterns. *International Journal of Research in Marketing, 14,* 473–486.

Shugan, S.M. (2005). Brand loyalty programs: Are they shams? *Marketing Science, 24,* 185–193.

Sirdeshmukh, D., Singh, J., & Sabol, B. (2002). Consumer trust, value, and loyalty in relational exchanges. *Journal of Marketing, 66,* 15–37.

Sirgy, M.J. (1982). Self-concept in consumer behavior: A critical review. *Journal of Consumer Research, 9,* 287–300.

Swaminathan, V., Page, K.L., & Gürhan-Canli, Z. (2007). "My" brand or "our" brand: The effects of brand relationship dimensions and self-construal on brand evaluations. *Journal of Consumer Research, 34,* 248–259.

Swaminathan, V., Stilley, K.M., & Ahluwalia, R. (2009). When brand personality matters: The moderating roles of attachment styles. *Journal of Consumer Research,* forthcoming.

Szymanski, D.M., & Henard, D.H. (2001). Customer satisfaction: A meta-analysis of the empirical evidence. *Journal of the Academy of Marketing Science, 29,* 16–35.

Thomson, M. (2006). Human brands: Investigating antecedents to consumers' strong attachments to celebrities. *Journal of Marketing, 70,* 104–119.

Thomson, M., MacInnis, D.J., & Park, C.W. (2005). The ties that bind: Measuring the strength of consumers' emotional attachments to brands. *Journal of Consumer Psychology, 15,* 77–91.

Till, B.D. (1998). Using celebrity endorsers effectively: Lessons from associative learning. *Journal of Product and Brand Management, 7,* 400–409.

Torelli, C.J., & Kaikati, A.M. (2009). Values as predictors of judgments and behaviors: The role of abstract and concrete mindsets. *Journal of Personality and Social Psychology, 96,* 231–247.

Verhoef, P.C. (2003). Understanding the effect of customer relationship management efforts on customer retention and customer share development. *Journal of Marketing, 67,* 30–45.

Wallendorf, M., & Arnould, E.J. (1988). "My favorite things:" A cross-cultural inquiry into object attachment, possessiveness, and social linkage. *Journal of Consumer Research, 14,* 4, 531–547.

Woodruff, R.B. (1997). Customer value: The next source for competitive advantage. *Journal of the Academy of Marketing Science, 25,* 139–153.

Yi, Y., & Jeon, H. (2003). Effects of loyalty programs on value perception, program loyalty, and brand loyalty. *Journal of the Academy of Marketing Science, 31,* 229–240.

Yim, C.K.B., Tse, D.K., & Chan, K.W. (2008). Strengthening customer loyalty through intimacy and passion. *Journal of Marketing Research, 45,* 741–756.

Zhang, Z.J., Krishna, A., & Dhar, S.K. (2000). The optimal choice of promotion vehicles: Front-loaded or rear-loaded incentives? *Management Science, 46,* 348–362.

5

Branding and Corporate Social Responsibility (CSR)*

Zeynep Gürhan-Canli
Koç University

Anne Fries
University of Cologne

Branding is about creating and delivering a promise to target consumers. This promise can be about functional satisfaction, experiential enrichment, or aspirational fulfillment (Kapferer, 2004; Keller, 2008). Increasingly, brands are promising that they care not only about their customers but also about their employees, the environment, and humanity at large. Exxon Mobil's recent advertising campaign attempts to position it as an environmentally sensitive company. PUR cares about water safety in developing countries, and companies such as Ben & Jerry's and The Body Shop have even positioned their whole corporate strategy on CSR, committing to be fully socially responsible brands. As these examples indicate, CSR refers to a company's "status and activities with respect to its perceived societal obligations" (Brown & Dacin, 1997, p. 68).

Corporations behaving in socially responsible ways do not transgress the law. In addition, they try to make a positive impact by voluntarily contributing to various social and environmental causes. These initiatives are thought to help build brand equity by enhancing brand awareness and image and by creating a sense of community (Hoeffler & Keller, 2002). Du, Bhattacharya, and Sen (2007a, p. 687) suggest that "a CSR initiative could build consumer trust as it signals that the company is serious about bettering social welfare (the benevolence dimension of trust) and is competent in effecting positive social change (the credibility dimension of trust)."

* The authors would like to thank Karen Gedenk, Franziska Volckner, and an anonymous reviewer for their valuable comments.

Such institutional initiatives are no longer considered an afterthought or trade-off but are strategic actions that help corporations to achieve support from the communities in which they operate (Handelman & Arnold, 1999). This view has been echoed in the management literature indicating that the strategic use of CSR policy is positively related to reputation (Fombrun, 1996). Researchers now convincingly argue that the issue is not whether a corporation should be socially responsible (Smith, 2003), the issue is how to conduct these initiatives to have maximum impact on the constituents (Keller & Lehmann, 2006).

CSR activities affect a variety of outcomes, including a corporation's image, company evaluations, product evaluations, purchase intentions, and the company's market value (Luo & Bhattacharya, 2006). It is important to acknowledge, however, that the impact of CSR activities goes beyond the traditional marketing context. Specifically, CSR is used by companies for the recruitment and retention of talented human resources (Greening & Turban, 2000). CSR activities have an impact on the target cause/issue, nonprofit organization, and the society (see Bhattacharya & Korschun, 2008, and Lichtenstein, Drumwright, & Braig, 2004, on these issues). In this chapter, we will review the academic literature on CSR as it relates to branding-related outcomes.

CSR activities for brand-building purposes include, but are not limited to, sponsorships and philanthropic initiatives, cause-related marketing, advocacy advertising, and employee participation in supported programs. Sponsorships and philanthropic initiatives are direct donations by the companies to support a certain cause such as donations to schools or sponsorships of cultural activities. Cause-related marketing is characterized by a company's product linked to a certain cause. The company makes a donation to the specified cause each time a consumer purchases the product (Varadarajan & Menon, 1988). Advocacy advertising means an advertising message tries to influence a consumer's behavior. An example would be a company calling on the consumer to exercise more in order to prevent a cardiovascular disease (Menod & Kahn, 2003). Employee participation in supported programs generally means employee involvement in social activities (Bhattacharya & Sen, 2004).

Although all these activities vary in terms of the level of commitment expected from the corporation, they are all voluntary activities. The voluntary nature of these activities paves the way for brand-building purposes. Companies hope that consumers will take these activities at face value and attribute positive characteristics to the company resulting in favorable evaluations, acquisition of new customers, and increased loyalty. Our review, however, suggests that favorable evaluations depend on several factors.

Some of these factors (e.g., communication) are design variables that companies can influence. Others (e.g., some consumer characteristics) may not be controlled by companies. We grouped these factors under four major categories. These categories are consumer characteristics, company characteristics and actions, company—CSR fit, and accessibility of other corporate and brand associations. Consumer characteristics include consumers' familiarity and affinity with the cause and their personal characteristics. Company characteristics and actions comprise a company's prior reputation, design elements of CSR activities (i.e., elements a company can influence when engaging in CSR), and the communication of CSR initiatives. The third category deals with the fit between a company and its CSR activities. The fourth category is about the process by which CSR associations influence product and company evaluations when other associations such as corporate ability or product attribute information are also accessible.

Figure 5.1 gives an overview of the effects of the different variables involved. The input variables are consumer characteristics, company characteristics and actions, and company—CSR fit. They affect output variables and their effects are usually mediated by consumer skepticism. The relationship between the input and the various output variables is moderated by the fourth category, namely, the accessibility of other corporate and brand associations.

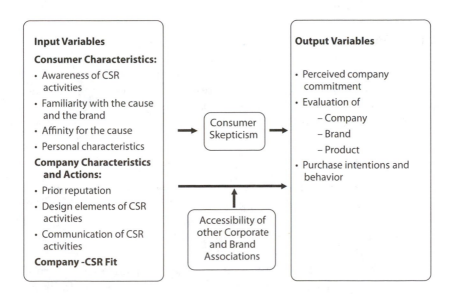

FIGURE 5.1
Effect of CSR on branding-related outcomes.

Consumer Characteristics

Awareness

Consumers' awareness of a company's CSR activities is a basic prerequisite for CSR to have any influence on brand-related outcomes. Several CSR initiatives are unnoticed and thus do not have any influence on corporate or brand image (Bhattacharya & Sen, 2004).

Familiarity

Once awareness is secured, consumers' degree of familiarity with the cause and the brand can moderate the effect of CSR on brand and cause evaluations. Lafferty, Goldsmith, and Hult (2004) and Lafferty and Goldsmith (2005) investigate how familiarity with the cause and the brand affect the impact of the cause—brand alliance on attitudes toward the cause and the brand involved. They base their reasoning on attitude accessibility theory stating that consumers anchor on the most easily accessible information. Consequently, if consumers are familiar with a brand and have a positive brand attitude before the brand gets involved in CSR, they will adjust their attitudes toward the cause based on their brand attitude. Thus, a low familiarity cause profits from the positive brand attitude. If the familiarity toward the cause is already high, there will be no attitude change toward the cause. In terms of brand attitudes, findings have been mixed. Whereas Lafferty and Goldsmith (2005) find that attitudes toward brands are greater after the alliance for both low and high familiar causes, Lafferty et al. (2004) find that attitudinal effects on brands are much higher for familiar (vs. unfamiliar) causes. For new brands, the authors suggest cooperation with the most favorable causes because of the overall positive effect of a cause—brand alliance on brand attitudes.

Affinity for the Cause

Consumers' affinity for the CSR activity plays a major role in evaluations and choice (Arora & Henderson, 2007; Basil & Herr, 2006; Drumwright, 1996; Lafferty et al., 2004; Sen & Bhattacharya, 2001) and consequently, managers have to carefully think about the choice of a suitable cause for their social activities.

In general, research has shown that prior positive attitudes toward the cause have a significant effect on the success of cause—brand alliances and the brand (Arora & Henderson, 2007; Basil & Herr, 2006; Lafferty et al., 2004). For example, Arora and Henderson (2007) investigated the effect of CSR on brand attitudes and purchase likelihood, and indeed find that higher cause affinity has a positive effect on these two dependent variables. They use cause affinity to explain heterogeneity in the sample and find that consumers who have a higher (vs. lower) cause affinity are more concerned about promotions with a social dimension.

Sen and Bhattacharya (2001) show that changes in company evaluation due to CSR activities are greater for consumers who are more supportive of a CSR domain. These authors also demonstrate that a company's CSR effort increases consumers' perceptions of the congruence between the characteristics of the company and the consumers, particularly in areas where consumers are more supportive. Increased level of congruence then leads to higher company evaluations due to consumer–company identification. Consumer–company identification is quite important from a branding perspective. By creating a strong identification through CSR, companies can create a dedicated customer base.

Personal Characteristics

Consumers' evaluations of CSR initiatives also vary as a function of their personal characteristics. Youn and Kim (2008) investigated the effects of psychographic and demographic factors on willingness to support cause-related marketing campaigns. For general charitable causes, external locus of control (i.e., lower self-efficacy), public self-consciousness, higher interpersonal trust, higher advertising skepticism, healthy eating, environmental responsibility, religiosity, stronger social networks, and previous prosocial behaviors are positively related with supporting cause-related marketing campaigns. Among several demographic factors included in the model, only age was significant in predicting intentions to support. Younger people are more supportive of brands associated with charitable causes. Basil and Weber (2006) investigated the extent to which personality traits affect the perception of companies' social activities and consumers' purchase behavior. They find that consumers who are driven by certain values are more susceptive to corporate social behavior than consumers who are low in this disposition. Consumers who are concerned about their appearances (i.e., those who are concerned about what others think of them) are also more likely to support a company engaging in CSR. They do so because purchasing from companies involved with CSR is recognized as a socially appropriate behavior. In contrast to the findings of Youn and Kim (2008), Basil and Weber (2006) find that women and older consumers are more supportive of CSR. Thus, extant research is not conclusive regarding the effect of demographic factors on the effect of CSR on branding.

Mohr, Webb, and Harris (2001) identified four groups of consumers with respect to their evaluations of CSR initiatives. Some consumers believe that companies should not engage in any activity beyond providing a high-quality product, making a profit, and treating employees well. These consumers (identified as pre-contemplators) base their purchase decisions on standard economic criteria and do not consider CSR when choosing products. Another group of consumers, contemplators, evaluate CSR initiatives favorably, but they either do not know much about CSR records of companies or believe that such initiatives have limited impact. Consequently, their purchase decisions are rarely based on CSR. In contrast, another group of consumers (identified as maintainers) base their purchase decisions predominantly on CSR. They search for information about companies' CSR activities and would like to influence corporate behavior by rewarding companies with good CSR records. Finally, consumers in the last group, the action group, have strong and favorable views about CSR. However, CSR is not a major factor in purchase decisions because they either find it difficult to learn about such initiatives or are skeptical about these efforts.

Consumer skepticism about CSR initiatives can be due to their dispositional skepticism or be raised due to situational factors (Forehand & Grier, 2003). Dispositional skepticism is an individual's tendency to be suspicious of others' motives in general, not only the motives of corporations. Skepticism can also be triggered situationally as a function of company and brand characteristics, characteristics of the cause, and the interaction of these factors (Barone, Miyazaki & Taylor, 2000; Drumwright, 1996; Ellen, Webb, & Mohr, 2006). Skeptic consumers infer egoistic, self-centered motives, or stakeholder-centered motives, leading to negative consumer responses (Ellen et al., 2006). Companies engaging in CSR should convey that they are driven by values. They can also convey that their self-centered motives are strategic as opposed to egoistic.

Company Characteristics and Actions

Prior Reputation of the Company

In general, consumers are less skeptical of CSR initiatives when a trustworthy (vs. untrustworthy) company engages in these initiatives. For example, Osterhus (1997) finds that trust in the company and attributions of consumer responsibility should be activated to increase the effectiveness of pro-social positioning strategies such as energy conservation. Similarly, Du, Bhattacharya, and Sen (2007a) find that trust mediates the relation between a company's CSR initiative and consumers' brand evaluations. Strahilevitz (2003) shows that the more ethical a company is perceived to be initially, the more likely it is to be judged as having altruistic motives for engaging in CSR. Klein and Dawar (2004) demonstrate that trustworthy companies with positive CSR records are less likely to be blamed if a product-harm crisis takes place. The locus of the crisis is perceived as external (vs. internal) and the crisis event is perceived as unstable (vs. stable) and uncontrollable (vs. controllable) when a company's prior CSR record is positive (vs. negative). Yoon, Gürhan-Canli, and Schwarz. (2006) show that consumers are quite skeptical about CSR activities and that these activities can backfire if a company supports causes in an area in which it has a bad reputation (e.g., cigarette manufacturers providing funds for cancer research). Consequently, a company needs to carefully choose the type of CSR activity it engages in.

Design Elements of CSR Activities

Consumer skepticism is an important issue companies have to deal with when engaging in CSR activities. Companies can control for it by carefully designing their CSR activities. The different design elements need to convey serious commitment. Design elements include the amount of financial contributions to a cause, how CSR activities are framed, the duration of the cause—brand relationship, geographical proximity of the cause, the positioning of the company in terms of CSR, and whether the brand is a pioneer in CSR efforts. Consumers can infer the level of company commitment to the cause considering these different types of information.

Findings concerning the amount of financial contributions are mixed Whereas Dahl and Lavack (1995) and Holmes and Kilbane (1993) find that consumers perceive the cause—brand alliance to be more beneficial when donations are larger, Ellen, Mohr, and Webb. (2000) and Arora and Henderson (2007) did not find any evidence of the effect of the amount of donation on brand-related outcomes. Ellen et al. (2000) vary the level of commitment by describing the low level simply as collecting donations from the consumers and the high level as collecting donations from the consumers first and then in a second step matching these donations. The authors hypothesize that the matching of donations would convey a greater commitment of the company. However, they do not find any variation as a function of the type of donation. Arora and Henderson (2007) vary the magnitude of donation in the context of cause promotions. Specifically, they have three treatment conditions with donations of 15, 30, and 45 cents made to a charitable organization when consumers purchase water. They also do not find any significant effect of the magnitude of the donation amount on consumer responses.

Strahilevitz (1999) investigated whether consumers prefer a brand tied to a donation over a brand on price promotion or over a brand featured at a lower regular price. She finds that consumers' willingness to pay more for a charity-linked brand depends on several variables, such as product type (i.e., hedonic vs. utilitarian products) and donation magnitude. As for donation magnitude, consumers are more likely to choose a brand offering a donation over a brand offering an equivalently lower price when the donation and price difference are relatively small than when they are relatively large.

Companies can make a monetary or nonmonetary donation (e.g., goods they manufacture) to a specific social cause or they can tie these kinds of donations to the sales level as in cause-related marketing. Dean (2003/2004) finds that firms using unconditional (vs. conditional) donations are perceived as less self-focused. However, brand evaluations are not affected by the type of the donation.

In the context of conditional donations, Grau, Garretson, and Pirsch (2007) investigated whether the amount of a donation to a social cause relative to the price of the product plays a role in consumer evaluations of the appropriateness of the amount donated to the cause. They find that respondents care about the relation between the product's price and the amount donated. Small donations relative to the price are considered to be inappropriate and promote consumer skepticism.

Conditional donations can be framed explicitly or implicitly using donation quantifiers (Grau et al., 2007). Companies can use exact, calculable, estimated, or abstract donation quantifiers. By using exact quantifiers, a company communicates the exact amount of the donation made if the target product is purchased by the customer (e.g., 5 cents are donated each time a bottle of water with a price 89 cents is purchased). With calculable quantifiers, consumers are given information (e.g., the percentage of the product price donated to the cause) so that they can calculate the donation themselves. Estimable quantifiers do not present much information about the donation mechanism. Consumers are informed about one piece of information needed to calculate the actual donation amount, but with their limited knowledge, they will not be able to calculate the exact amount donated (e.g., 5% of the profit from the proceeds would be donated to a cause). Because consumers are unlikely to know the exact margin, they are unable to tell how much is actually donated to the cause. Abstract quantifiers reveal even less information about the company's contribution. They state that an amount will be donated, but whether it is a certain percentage of the price or the profit, for example, remains unclear. Considering the different frames of conditional donations, perceived commitment is highest if a company uses exact quantifiers and lowest if it uses abstract quantifiers. Grau et al. (2007) investigated which of these quantifiers influenced consumer trust the most. Not surprisingly, they find that consumers prefer more tangible information regarding donations. Providing more (vs. less) details is perceived as trustworthier and demonstrates a greater commitment of the company.

The duration of a company's involvement with the cause is another variable that influences perceived commitment (Drumwright, 1996). The longer the relationship the more committed the company is perceived to be. Grau et al. (2007) examine the effects of the duration of cause–brand cooperation together with consumer effort on consumer responses. In the example they used, consumers had to turn in yogurt lids in order to trigger a donation. The lids can be sent in only until a certain date. The authors investigate whether this deadline decreases consumer procrastination or incites the consumers to scrutinize the company's commitment to raise money for the cause. They find that consumers do not judge deadlines to be generally negative as long as they are reasonably set. Consumers seem to understand that a company has to introduce a deadline for operational procedures. Consumers also seem to understand that the company has to place a limit on the total amount it will donate to the cause (Grau et al., 2007). The donation cap does not affect perceived company commitment.

Companies can choose to support local, regional, or national causes. Research on prosocial behavior has shown that being close to the recipient of a donation increases the likelihood of engaging in some form of prosocial behavior (Burnett & Wood, 1988). Consequently, consumers may have more favorable attitudes toward companies supporting local causes than companies supporting national or international causes. Ross, Stutts, and Patterson (1991) and Grau and Folse (2007) find that consumers are more likely to support causes that have a local or regional focus than a national or international focus. However, Ross, Patterson, and Stutts (1992) find that consumers' attitudes toward cause-related marketing initiatives do not vary for local or national causes. These contradicting findings require further research.

A brand that positions itself on CSR by integrating its CSR strategy with its core business strategy displays the most commitment and consequently is more likely to capture consumers' loyalty (Du, Bhattacharya, & Sen, 2007b). Thus, CSR positioning becomes a competitive advantage since the brand is able to differentiate itself from competitors. When CSR activities are implemented correctly, they influence consumers' awareness positively and this awareness may spill over positively to consumers' beliefs about the brand's performance in product-specific dimensions. Du et al. (2007b) find that consumers have higher levels of CSR awareness, higher intrinsic attributions and lower extrinsic attributions (i.e., lower image motives), and more favorable CSR beliefs for a brand positioned on CSR than for the competitors' brands. Furthermore, the authors show that higher brand loyalty is clearly an advantage of CSR brands. Finally, being perceived as a pioneer in CSR positioning is another important factor in the context of CSR positioning (Bhattacharya & Sen, 2004). Consumers perceive companies as more committed if they are pioneers in CSR versus if they are using CSR as an add-on.

Communication of CSR Activities

Communicating about one's CSR activities is a crucial factor that companies have to consider. On the one hand, managers do not want to advertise at all about their CSR efforts because consumers' skepticism about company motives would elevate under intense advertising. For example, Apple—with iPod Nano, iPod Shuffle, and iTunes Gift Card (PRODUCT) RED™ supporting the Global Fund—does not advertise CSR initiatives. On the other hand, it is necessary to communicate CSR efforts to consumers in order to improve brand-related outcomes. Clear and credible communication can enhance consumers' attitudes toward a company embracing CSR. Additionally, a company can increase the consumers' perception of fit between a company and a social cause by using a communication that highlights how the company and the cause are related (Simmons & Becker-Olsen, 2006).

Although communication about CSR is an important issue, relatively little research addresses how communication can be used to increase the effectiveness of CSR initiatives with respect to brand-related outcomes. Specifically, extant research examined the effect of three communication-related factors on consumer evaluations (Forehand & Grier, 2003; Simmons & Becker-Olsen, 2006; Yoon et al., 2006). These factors are message source, message content, and the amount spent on advertising relative to the amount spent on the cause itself.

When companies decide to communicate their CSR initiatives to consumers, they can do so using company sources (e.g., advertising, company Web sites) or using third parties (e.g., public relations, partnering with charitable organization or other beneficiaries). All else being equal, it is more advantageous to communicate CSR initiatives through third parties as opposed to company sources. Simmons and Becker-Olsen (2006) show that communication through the sponsored nonprofit can be particularly beneficial for low-fit sponsorships. Yoon et al. (2006) find that the source through which consumers learn about CSR affects perceived sincerity of company motives. Third party (i.e., neutral) sources are perceived as unbiased sources. When consumers learn about CSR activities through such unbiased sources they attribute more sincere, other-centered motives to company actions and thus evaluate the companies more favorably.

In terms of message content, Forehand and Grier (2003) examine the effect of expressing company intent on consumer skepticism and company evaluations. In their experiment, there were two levels of stated motive: (1) public-serving motives, and (2) public-serving and firm-serving motives. They find that firm-serving attributions lead to a decrease in company evaluations only when they are inconsistent with the firm's expressed motive. Specifically, company evaluations were lowest when firm-serving motives were salient and the company expressed public-serving motives.

Consumers seem to penalize companies when they infer that companies are not sincerely motivated to help out. Menon and Kahn (2003) show that cause promotions result in more favorable CSR ratings than advocacy advertising. Cause promotions promise a donation to a charity contingent on the purchase of a product. In advocacy advertising, companies try to raise awareness about social issues. Menon and Kahn (2003) find that consumers elaborate on advocacy advertising more than they do on cause promotions because advocacy advertising is perceived as more unusual than cause promotions. Increased elaboration leads consumers to think more about motives behind these CSR initiatives and results in less favorable CSR ratings for companies involved in advocacy advertising (vs. cause promotions).

Another factor that affects perceived sincerity is the ratio of CSR contributions and CSR-related advertising. Consumers infer insincere motives when they learn that a company spends more on advertising that features CSR than on CSR activities. Consumers evaluate companies more favorably when companies spend more on CSR activities than on advertising that features CSR (Yoon et al., 2006). For example, Avon, a company famous for supporting breast cancer causes, was criticized because about 40% of the donor contribution went into advertising, marketing, administration, and logistic costs, and not to the charities. Currently, Avon claims that 100% of proceeds are donated to the charities (Benson, 2006).

Company–CSR Fit

Extensive research investigated the moderating effect of fit between a company and the CSR activity on evaluations, intentions, and choice. Generally speaking, fit indicates a good match between the type of social performance a company exhibits and the company's characteristics (Brammer & Pavelin, 2006). The company's characteristics comprise the company's mission; products; brand image and positioning; manufacturing; technologies; target market; and relationships with stakeholders such as employees, consumers, and community (Brammer & Pavelin, 2006; Ellen et al., 2000; Simmons & Becker-Olsen, 2006; Varadarajan & Menon, 1988). In sum, the company's characteristics include all business activities.

Fit is not strictly a CSR issue, but it is of interest in several research streams in branding such as brand extensions, comarketing alliances, sponsorships, and brand alliances. In general, perceived fit leads to a positive effect on consumer attitude toward the company or the brand unless consumers are exposed to negative information about the brand or the new extension (e.g., Aaker & Keller, 1990; Keller & Lehmann, 2006).

Extant research on the effect of company–CSR fit has produced mixed results. Some researchers suggest that high fit should lead to a positive effect on consumer evaluations and purchase intentions (Basil & Herr, 2006; Lafferty et al., 2004; Pracejus & Olsen, 2004). In contrast, others find that high fit increases the salience of branding benefits for the company and may raise consumers' skepticism about company motives (Ellen et al., 2000; Forehand & Grier, 2003; Yoon et al., 2006). There is also some evidence indicating no effect of fit (Lafferty, 2007) or that the effect of fit varies as a function of other variables (Barone, Norman, & Miyazaki, 2007; Menon & Kahn, 2003; Nan & Heo, 2007).

Lafferty et al. (2004) find a positive effect of attitude toward a cause–brand alliance on postexposure attitudes toward the cause and the brand. Two of the antecedents of the cause–brand alliance are fit components: brand–name fit and product–category fit. Brand–name fit means how logical consumers perceive the cause–brand pairing to be (e.g., women's cosmetics brand and breast cancer research). Analogously, product–category fit means the logical fit of the two product categories involved (e.g., fiber cereal and cancer research). They find that perceptions of brand–name fit are positively related to attitudes toward the cause–brand attitude. Product–category fit, however, does not seem to play a role.

Basil and Herr (2006) also show that fit has a positive impact on attitude toward both the cause–brand alliance and the change in attitude toward the company due to the cause–brand alliance. Additionally, high fit leads to perceptions of a stronger relationship between the company and the charity involved. The effect of fit on company–cause attitude is partially mediated by perceptions of relationship strength. One can conclude that fit partially influences the attitude toward a cause–brand alliance by strengthening perceptions of the relationship between the firm and the charity. The authors also investigate the effect of fit on judgmental as opposed to affective assessment of cause–company alliances and find that fit influences judgments of appropriateness or propriety more strongly than judgments of positive affect.

When comparing common price promotions with promotions that have a social component, fit also plays a role. Arora and Henderson (2007) find that promotions with a self component (i.e., price promotions) are generally more effective than those promotions with a social component (i.e., promotions related to a social cause). The level of fit between the company and the cause, however, moderates this finding. Consumers, who perceive the level of fit to be higher, favor promotions with a social component. Pracejus and Olsen (2004) use a choice-based conjoint analysis to examine how consumers' willingness to pay varies as a function of fit. The authors find that a high-fit charity can result in 5 to 10 times the value of donation to a low-fit charity. They find a similar effect for market share as well.

Previous research also examined psychological processes underlying the positive effect of fit. Consumers generate fewer thoughts that are focused on company motives when they evaluate CSR activities that have high (vs. low) fit. These thoughts are more favorable and as a consequence lead to more positive attitudes toward the company (Becker-Olsen, Cudmore, & Hill, 2006; Simmons & Becker-Olsen, 2006). Additionally, companies are judged to be more credible and thus purchase intentions increase (Becker-Olsen et al., 2006; Simmons & Becker-Olsen, 2006).

There are also some studies that did not find an effect of fit. For example, Lafferty (2007) does not find support for her hypothesis that a better fitting cause has a more positive effect on attitudes toward the company. Besides fit, she examined the direct effect of corporate credibility on brand attitude. This variable might have diminished the importance of fit. Nan and Heo (2007) do not find that a high fit leads to more favorable attitudes. Interestingly, they find an interaction of cause–brand fit with brand consciousness. That is, the impact of the level of brand–cause fit on attitudes toward the brand and the advertisement is more pronounced for individuals with high (vs. low) brand consciousness. Brand–cause fit does not have an impact on either ad or brand evaluations for consumers who had low brand consciousness. Barone et al. (2007) show that when company motivations are positive for engaging in CSR (e.g., company does not expect to benefit from the sponsorship of a charitable organization), fit has a positive impact on evaluations. Fit has no effect on evaluations when company motivations are perceived to be negative. They also find that if consumer attitudes toward the cause are relatively high, fit has no impact on consumer evaluations. If consumer attitudes toward the cause are low, fit has a positive impact on evaluations.

Menon and Kahn (2003) examine the effect of fit as a function of two types of philanthropic messages: first, cause promotions that promise a donation when a purchase is made, and second, advocacy advertising of social issues that are sponsored by brands. The authors find that the impact of fit between the sponsor and the social issue depends on the consumers' focus (i.e., whether they focus on the sponsor or the social issue). Low fit is perceived as more appropriate if the focus is on the social issue or on the message such as in advocacy advertising. High fit is more appropriate if the focus is on the purchase of a brand such as in cause promotions.

High fit has a negative effect when branding benefits for the company are salient. In this situation, CSR activities may raise consumers' skepticism about company motives and thus CSR activities are not only ineffective but may actually harm the company. Yoon et al. (2006) and Forehand and Grier (2003) find that CSR activities that have high versus low fit resulted in perceptions of lower sincerity and perceived sincerity mediated the effect of fit on consumer evaluations. In a retailing context,

Ellen et al. (2000) find a positive effect of low fit on the evaluations of CSR activities. If the donation is incongruent, rather than congruent with the company's core business, consumers evaluate a CSR offer more positively. Although their finding is not very strong, it suggests that high fit would not necessarily be beneficial for branding purposes in the context of CSR.

Accessibility of Other Corporate and Brand Associations

A growing body of literature has investigated the process by which CSR associations influence product and company evaluations and intentions to purchase when other associations such as corporate ability, brand, or product information are also accessible (Arora & Henderson, 2007; Berens, van Riel, & van Bruggen, 2005; Biehal & Sheinin, 2007; Brown & Dacin, 1997; Folkes & Kamins, 1999; Gürhan-Canli & Batra, 2004; Sen & Bhattacharya, 2001). In this section, we summarize some of the major findings from these studies.

1. CSR associations have more influence when other associations are relatively less accessible. For example, Arora and Henderson (2007) find that CSR associations influence product quality perceptions when consumers are unfamiliar with the brand. Berens et al. (2005) demonstrate that the dominance of corporate brand affects accessibility of corporate ability associations. When the corporate brand is not dominant and accessibility of corporate ability associations decreases, CSR influences product evaluations under low diagnosticity threshold (i.e., low involvement) or when consumers perceive CSR associations as more diagnostic (i.e., when the fit is high). In the context of other accessible associations, CSR influences product evaluations under limited conditions such as when product quality is low and when consumers care about the supported cause highly (Sen & Bhattacharya, 2001).

2. CSR associations influence product evaluations indirectly through their effect on corporate evaluations. In contrast, corporate ability associations also have a direct influence on product evaluations (Brown & Dacin, 1997). CSR associations may have a direct influence on product evaluations when CSR domain is relevant for inferring corporate ability (e.g., CSR initiatives focusing on well-being of employees; Sen & Bhattacharya, 2001).

3. Corporate evaluations (including those based on CSR) can be used as an evaluative context to judge new products. Superior

corporate images may lead to mediocre product ratings due to contrast effects (Brown & Dacin, 1997; Sen & Bhattacharya, 2001).

4. Some consumers may perceive a trade-off between corporate ability and CSR. That is, they may believe that companies are pursuing CSR at the expense of improving corporate ability. CSR initiatives may hurt company evaluations if consumers have such beliefs (Sen & Bhattacharya, 2001).

5. Product attribute information is more diagnostic than positive CSR information in forming company evaluations (Folkes & Kamins, 1999; Gürhan-Canli & Batra, 2004). In contrast, negative CSR information is more diagnostic than product attribute information (Folkes & Kamins, 1999). In general, consumers are more sensitive to negative versus positive CSR information (Sen & Bhattacharya, 2001).

6. CSR messages work best for an umbrella brand when many products are dissimilarly positioned and when the objective is to maintain a portfolio of brands with different positioning (Biehal & Sheinin, 2007).

Conclusion

We have identified four categories that influence consumers' perceptions of CSR and company evaluations. These categories are consumer characteristics, company characteristics and actions, company–CSR fit, and accessibility of other corporate and brand associations. Our review suggests that companies should attempt to reduce consumers' skepticism regarding their CSR efforts if they would like to reap any branding benefits. Untrustworthy companies can change their image only if consumers attribute sincere motives to CSR activities. This requires that companies should choose their CSR initiatives carefully in terms of fit, demonstrate their commitment, and be cautious in communicating these initiatives to their customers.

Our review also identified several mixed findings in the literature. Future research is required to address these mixed findings and identify other variables that may affect consumer skepticism. For example, an interesting avenue for further research is investigating whether brands having the same partner or supporting similar causes influences consumer responses. Additionally, future research can investigate the extent to which core brand associations are diluted due to newly created CSR associations. More research is also needed to understand when and how to communicate CSR initiatives to consumers.

It is also important to investigate how to get customers involved with CSR in order to reduce their skepticism. Skepticism can be raised not only about company motives but also about product performance. Consumers may assume that a product advocating green consumption would perform poorly or be expensive. Research can address how to increase awareness about CSR without too much advertising. Examining long-term effects of CSR initiatives is also important from a branding perspective (Simmons & Becker-Olsen, 2006). We hope that this chapter will be useful to stimulate further research in this important area.

References

Aaker, D. A., & Keller, K. L. (1990). Consumer evaluations of brand extensions. *Journal of Marketing, 54*, 27–41.

Arora, N., & Henderson, T. (2007). Embedded premium promotion: Why it works and how to make it more effective. *Marketing Science, 26*, 514–531.

Barone, M. J., Miyazaki, A. D., & Taylor, K. A. (2000). The influence of cause-related marketing on consumer choice: Does one good turn deserve another? *Journal of the Academy of Marketing Science, 28*, 248–262.

Barone, M. J., Norman, A. T., & Miyazaki, A. D. (2007). Consumer response to retailer use of cause-related marketing: Is more fit better? *Journal of Retailing, 83*, 437–445.

Basil, D. Z., & Herr, P. M. (2006). Attitudinal balance and cause-related marketing: An empirical application of balance theory. *Journal of Consumer Psychology, 16*, 391–403.

Basil, D. Z., & Weber, D. (2006). Values motivation and concern for appearances: the effect of personality traits on responses to corporate social responsibility. *International Journal of Nonprofit & Voluntary Sector Marketing, 11*, 61–72.

Becker-Olsen, K. L., Cudmore, B. A., & Hill, R. P. (2006). The impact of perceived corporate social responsibility on consumer behavior. *Journal of Business Research, 59*, 46–53.

Benson, H. (2006, October 22). Pinklash. *San Francisco Chronicle,*2p, D-1.

Berens, G., van Riel, C. B. M., & van Bruggen, G. H. (2005). Corporate associations and consumer product responses: The moderating role of corporate brand dominance. *Journal of Marketing, 69*, 35–48.

Bhattacharya, C. B., & Korschun, D. (2008). Stakeholder marketing: Beyond the four Ps and the customer. *Journal of Public Policy and Marketing, 27*, 113–116.

Bhattacharya, C. B., & Sen, S. (2004). Doing better at doing good: When, why, and how consumers respond to corporate social initiatives. *California Management Review, 47*, 9–24.

Biehal, G. J., & Sheinin, D. A. (2007). The influence of corporate messages on the product portfolio. *Journal of Marketing, 71,* 12–25.

Brammer, S. J., & Pavelin, S. (2006). Corporate reputation and social performance: The importance of fit. *Journal of Management Studies, 43,* 435–455.

Brown, T. J., & Dacin, P. A. (1997). The company and the product: Corporate associations and consumer product responses. *Journal of Marketing, 61,* 68–84.

Burnett, J. J., & Wood, Van R. (1988). A proposed model of the donation decision process. *Research in Consumer Behavior, 3,* 1–47.

Dahl, D. W., & Lavack, A M. (1995). Cause-related marketing: impact of size corporate donation and size of cause-related promotion on consumer perceptions and participation. *AMA Winter Educators' Conference Proceedings, 6,* 476–481.

Dean, D. H. (2003/2004). Consumer perception of corporate donations. *Journal of Advertising, 32,* 91–102.

Drumwright, M. E. (1996). Company advertising with a social dimension: The role of noneconomic criteria. *Journal of Marketing, 60,* 71–87.

Du, S., Bhattacharya, C. B., & Sen, S. (2007a). Convergence of interests-cultivating consumer trust through corporate social initiatives. *Advances in Consumer Research, 34,* 678–687.

Du, S., Bhattacharya, C. B., & Sen, S. (2007b). Reaping relational rewards from corporate social responsibility: The role of competitive positioning. *International Journal of Research in Marketing, 24,* 224–241.

Ellen, P. S., Mohr, L. A., & Webb, D. J. (2000). Charitable programs and the retailer: Do they mix? *Journal of Retailing, 76,* 393–406.

Ellen, P. S., Webb, D. J., & Mohr, L. A. (2006). Building corporate associations: Consumer attributions for corporate socially responsible programs. *Journal of the Academy of Marketing Science, 34,* 147–157.

Folkes, V. S., & Kamins, M. A. (1999). Effects of information about firms' ethical and unethical actions on consumers' attitudes. *Journal of Consumer Psychology, 8,* 243–259.

Fombrun, C. J. & Van Riel, C. (1997). The reputational landscape. *Corporate Reputation Review, 1,* 5–13.

Forehand, M. R., & Grier, S. (2003). When is honesty the best policy? The effect of stated company intent on consumer skepticism. *Journal of Consumer Psychology, 13,* 349–356.

Grau, S. L., & Folse, J. A. (2007). Cause-relate mMarketing. *Journal of Advertising, 36,* 19–33.

Grau, S. L., Garretson, J. A., & Pirsch, J. (2007). Cause-related marketing: An exploratory study of campaign donation structures issues. *Journal of Nonprofit & Public Sector Marketing, 18,* 69–91.

Greening, D. W., & Turban, D. B. (2000). Corporate social performance as a competitive advantage in attracting a quality workforce. *Business and Society, 39,* 254–280.

Gürhan-Canli, Z., & Batra, R. (2004). When corporate image affects product evaluations: The moderating role of perceived risk. *Journal of Marketing Research, 41,* 197–205.

Handelman, J. M., & Arnold, S. J. (1999). The role of marketing actions with a social dimension: Appeals to the institutional environment. *Journal of Marketing, 63,* 33–48.

Hoeffler, S., & Keller, K. L. (2002). Building brand equity through societal marketing. *Journal of Public Policy and Marketing, 21,* 78–89.

Holmes, J., & Kilbane, C. J. (1993). Cause-related marketing Selected effects of price and charitable donations. *Journal of Nonprofit & Public Sector Marketing, 1,* 67–83.

Kapferer, J. N. (2004) *The new strategic brand management Creating and sustaining brand equity long term,* (2nd ed)., London and Sterling, VA: Kogan Page.

Keller, K. L. (2008) *Strategic brand management Building, measuring, and managing brand equity* (3rd. ed.). Upper Saddle River, NJ: Prentice Hall.

Keller, K. L., & Lehmann, D. R. (2006). Brands and branding: Research findings and future priorities. *Marketing Science, 25,* 740–759.

Klein, G., & Dawar, N. (2004). Corporate social responsibility and consumer attributions and brand evaluations in a product–harm crisis. *International Journal of Research in Marketing, 21,* 203–217.

Lafferty, B. A. (2007). The relevance of fit in a cause–brand alliance when consumers evaluate corporate credibility. *Journal of Business Research, 60,* 447–453.

Lafferty, B. A., & Goldsmith, R. E. (2005). Cause—brand alliances: Does the cause help the brand or does the brand help the cause? *Journal of Business Research, 58,* 423–429.

Lafferty, B. A., Goldsmith, R. E., & Hult, G. T. M. (2004). The impact of the alliance on the partners: A look at cause—brand alliances. *Psychology & Marketing, 21,* 509–531.

Lichtenstein, D. R., Drumwright, M. E., & Braig, B. M. (2004). The effect of corporate social responsibility on customer donations to corporate-supported nonprofits. *Journal of Marketing, 68,* 16–32.

Luo, X., & Bhattacharya, C. B. (2006). Corporate social responsibility, customer satisfaction, and market value. *Journal of Marketing, 70,* 1–16.

Menon, S., & Kahn, B. E. (2003). Corporate sponsorships of philanthropic activities: When do they impact perception of sponsor brand? *Journal of Consumer Psychology, 13,* 316–327.

Mohr, L. A., Webb, D. J., & Harris, K. E. (2001). Do consumers expect companies to be socially responsible? The impact of corporate social responsibility on buying behavior. *The Journal of Consumer Affairs, 35,* 45–72.

Nan, X., & Heo, K. (2007). Consumer responses to corporate social responsibility (CSR) initiatives. *Journal of Advertising, 36,* 63–74.

Osterhus, T. L. (1997). Pro-social consumer influence strategies: When and how do they work? *Journal of Marketing, 61,* 16–29.

Pracejus, J. W., & Olsen, G. D. (2004). The role of brand/cause fit in the effectiveness of cause-related marketing campaigns. *Journal of Business Research, 57,* 635–640.

Ross, J. K., Patterson, L. T., & Stutts, M. A. (1992). Consumer perceptions of organizations that use cause-related marketing. *Journal of the Academy of Marketing Science, 20,* 93–97.

Ross, J. K., Stutts, M. A., & Patterson, L. (1991). Tactical considerations for the effective use of cause-related marketing. *The Journal of Applied Business Research, 7,* 58–65.

Sen, S., & Bhattacharya, C. B. (2001). Does doing good always lead to doing better? Consumer reactions to corporate social responsibility. *Journal of Marketing Research, 38,* 225–243.

Simmons, C. J., & Becker-Olsen, K. L. (2006). Achieving marketing objectives through social sponsorships. *Journal of Marketing, 70,* 154–169.

Smith, N. C. (2003). Corporate social responsibility: Whether or how? *California Management Review, 45,* 52–76.

Strahilevitz, M. (1999). The effects of product type and donation magnitude on willingness to pay more for a charity-linked brand. *Journal of Consumer Psychology, 8,* 215–241.

Strahilevitz, M. (2003). The effects of prior impressions of a firm's ethics on the success of a cause-related marketing campaign: Do the good look better while the bad look worse? *Journal of Nonprofit and Public Sector Marketing, 11,* 77–92.

Varadarajan, P. R., & Menon, A. (1988). Cause-related marketing: A coalignment of marketing strategy and corporate philanthropy. *Journal of Marketing, 52,* 58–74.

Yoon, Y., Gurhan-Canli, Z., & Schwarz, N. (2006). The effect of corporate social responsibility (CSR) activities on companies with bad reputations. *Journal of Consumer Psychology, 16,* 377–390.

Youn, S., & Kim, H. (2008). Antecedents of consumer attitudes toward cause-related marketing. *Journal of Advertising Research, 48,* 123–137.

Section III

Cultural, Sociological, and Global Branding Perspectives

6

Cultural Symbolism of Brands

Carlos J. Torelli
University of Minnesota

Hean Tat Keh
Peking University

Chi-Yue Chiu
*University of Illimois at Urbana-Champaign
and Nanyang Technological Universtiy*

This chapter discusses how studying the cultural symbolism of brands can help further develop models of brand management in multicultural markets. A framework is offered to better understand the impact of the cultural symbolism of brands on brand perceptions and the fulfillment of identity goals.

Brand Building in Multicultural Markets

One of the most difficult choices that multinational corporations face is deciding whether to standardize their communication strategy or to customize it to target consumers in different cultural settings (Laroche, Kirpalani, Pons, & Zhou, 2001). As new global markets emerge, and existing markets become increasingly segmented along ethnic or subcultural lines, the need for deepening self-brand connections with consumers who have different cultural values has never been more important (Shavitt, Lee, & Torelli, 2008). Companies that succeed at imbuing brands with symbolic meanings that resonate among these multicultural consumers would have a competitive edge in the complex markets of the twenty-first century. The ultimate goal is for companies to build brands that become symbols of culturally diverse groups. More specifically, companies need to build iconic brands with distinct, relevant associations that can create deep psychological bonds with multicultural consumers and lead to the highest possible level of brand identification (Keller 1993, 2001). Can brands be turned into symbols of culturally-diverse groups? If so, how can this be accomplished and maintained over time? In this chapter, we propose that these questions can be answered by focusing on the cultural symbolism of brands and on the relationship between the cultural values of consumers and the culturally relevant associations of brands.

Brand Symbolism and Consumer Identity

People buy products not only for what they do, but also for what the product means; thus brands can be symbols that become part of the individual identities of consumers (Levy, 1959). People use the symbolism in brands to communicate to others who they are or who they aspire to be. The social identity function of brands facilitates expressing to others one's central values and self-concept (Shavitt, 1990). Based on social identity theory (Tajfel and Turner 2001), the self can be conceptualized as comprising a personal identity and a group identity. Attachment to brands and products is conceptualized as reflecting consumers' desires to reinforce either type of identity depending on the product and the context (Kleine, Kleine, & Allen, 1995; Swaminathan, Page, & Gürhan-Canli, 2007). A consumer may feel attached to his Harley Davidson because it communicates to others a rugged personality (e.g., Aaker, 1999; Sirgy, 1982), whereas another consumer may like his Ford pick-up truck because it reinforces his national identity (Johansson, 1989; Shimp & Sharma, 1987).

Research on the role of brands in reinforcing desirable group identities has been studied from at least two perspectives. One line of reference group research (e.g., Bearden & Etzel, 1982; Childers & Rao, 1992; Escalas & Bettman, 2005; Park & Lessig, 1977) has focused on the influence that persons or groups of people have on consumers' decisions. A reference group is a social group that is important to a consumer and that is used for self-comparison purposes (Escalas & Bettman, 2003). This stream of research shows that group influences can be driven by consumers' desires to make informed decisions, to comply with the wishes of others, or to psychologically associate with the group (Bearden & Etzel, 1982). The usage of a brand associated with an in-group can strengthen the psychological bond with the group and consequently increase perceptions of belongingness to the group (Escalas & Bettman, 2003). Furthermore, desirable group identities are better signaled by means of distinctive product choices that can unmistakably communicate the identity (Berger & Heath, 2007). Overall, this stream of research informs us about the appropriation of brand meanings by consumers in order to distinctively communicate a desirable group identity to others.

Another line of reference group research focuses on the influence of national identity and brand country-of-origin on consumer decisions (e.g., Gürhan-Canli & Maheswaran, 2000; Leclerc, Schmitt, & Dubé, 1994; Maheswaran, 1994). This line of research shows that brands can sometimes be used to express one's national identity. In particular, ethnocentric consumers can be more likely to purchase domestic over foreign products, as a means of reinforcing their patriotic national identity (Shimp & Sharma, 1987). Country-of-origin information can be used to differentiate between in-group and out-group members and can lead to product decisions that enhance perceptions of connectedness with a group (Swaminathan et al., 2007).

Both lines of research provide us with a good perspective about how consumers use brand meanings to manage their personal and social identities. Consumers make brand choices to selectively communicate to others personal characteristics and/or desirable group identities. However, existing research has little to say about what makes a brand a group symbol. Besides a strong connection between a brand and its country-of-origin, little is known about the drivers of group symbolism for a brand. There is also limited insight on the mechanisms underlying the appropriation of brand meanings for fulfilling a desirable group identity. We address these issues next by focusing on the cultural symbolism of brands.

Cultural Symbolism of Brands and Iconic Brands

McCracken's (1986) model of meaning transfer states that brand meanings originate in the culturally constituted world and move into brands through several instruments such as advertising, the fashion system, and reference groups. In particular, reference groups shape brand meanings via the associations consumers hold regarding the groups of individuals who use the brand (Muniz & O'Guinn, 2001). These meanings can transfer to consumers, as consumers appropriate brand meanings for constructing their individual identities (Escalas & Bettman, 2005). As a result of this dynamic process of social verification, subjective brand meanings become an objective reality as the members of a particular group implicitly agree on the brand symbolism (see Krauss & Fussell, 1996).

Powerful brands that achieve dominant positions thanks to their high levels of group symbolism are frequently referred to as *iconic* brands. Holt (2004) defines an iconic brand as a consumer brand that carries "consensus expressions of particular values held dear by some members of a society" (p. 4). Iconic brands carry a heavy symbolic load for consumers, who frequently rely on them to communicate to others who they are or aspire to be. For these brands to become culturally influential their symbolic meanings should be widely and durably distributed in the culture (Sperber, 1996). Through the sharing of these meanings in an ongoing, dynamic process of social verification (Hardin & Higgins, 1996), they become a shared reality. It is precisely this shared understanding of the symbolic meaning of an iconic brand that facilitates the communication of ideals and aspirations to others through brand usage or consumption (see Fussell & Krauss, 1992; Krauss & Fussell, 1996). Repeated communications of these meanings would further facilitate embedding the brand in the culture (Sperber, 1996).

The present article adopts a broad definition of culture as shared elements that provide the standards for perceiving, believing, evaluating, communicating, and acting among those who share a language, a historical period, and a geographic location (Triandis, 1989, 1996). Culture is the lens through which individuals see and provide meanings to the phenomenal world. Groups of individuals who share the same standards form a cultural category or group. Within the group, there is ready comprehension of the rules and meanings that help organize the phenomenal world (see McCracken, 1986). Brands that are recognized as symbols of a cultural group should be strongly associated with abstract group meanings.

There is evidence that consumers attribute cultural significance to certain commercial brands (Aaker, Benet-Martinez, & Garolera, 2001). For example, some brands in the United States are associated with *ruggedness* (i.e., strength, masculinity, and toughness) and some brands in Japan are associated with *peacefulness*, and ruggedness and peacefulness are abstract dimensions characteristic of American and East Asian cultures, respectively. To the extent that these brands are associated with knowledge about the culture, they can reach an iconic status and act as cultural reminders (see Betsky, 1997; Ortner, 1973). Encountering such iconic brands can serve as subtle cultural primes that bring to mind culturally relevant concepts and identities. For instance, among Americans, subsequent to viewing an American cultural symbol, their awareness of American values (e.g., freedom, individuality) is enhanced. Similarly, the Chinese, after viewing a Chinese cultural symbol, spontaneously think of Chinese values (e.g., obedience) (Fu, Chiu, Morris, & Young, 2007; Hong, Morris, Chiu, & Benet-Martinez, 2000). By extension, for iconic brands loaded with cultural meanings, incidental exposure to these brands may spontaneously evoke its attendant cultural meanings (e.g., Marlboro can activate the value of rugged individualism in the U.S. culture).

Measuring the Cultural Symbolism of Brands

From the preceding discussion, we can identify three defining characteristics of a brand rich in cultural symbolism, or an iconic brand: (1) it symbolizes culturally relevant values, needs, and aspirations; (2) it is connected to diverse elements of cultural knowledge including values and other cultural icons; and (3) incidental exposure to an iconic brand can bring to mind its attendant cultural meanings. Since the degree of cultural symbolism is the result of an implicit agreement among group members about the extent to which the brand symbolizes abstract group characteristics, we cannot dissociate brand iconicity from the cultural group it symbolizes. In other words, we should study cultural symbolism from the perspective of the cultural group providing the standards for assigning meanings.

Distinctions among cultural groups can be established by dividing the human community using criteria that meaningfully capture differences in the phenomenal world, such as gender, age, class, occupation, or ethnicity (see McCracken, 1986). For instance, we can distinguish between Latinos and European Americans or between females and males based on distinguishable cultural realities. At a more abstract level, we can also distinguish among cultural groups by observing patterns of shared values, beliefs, and attitudes that are organized around a theme (i.e., cultural syndromes; Triandis, 1996). The constructs of *individualism* and *collectivism* represent the most broadly used cultural syndromes in cross-cultural research (Gudykunst & Ting-Toomey, 1988). In individualistic cultures, people value independence from others and subordinate the goals of their ingroups to their own personal goals. In collectivistic cultures, in contrast, individuals value interdependent relationships to others and subordinate their personal goals to those of their ingroups (Hofstede, 1980, 2001; Triandis, 1989).

Once we choose a cultural group, we can study the degree of cultural symbolism, for the group and from the group perspective, of a variety of brands. This will facilitate identifying brands with high levels of cultural symbolism and judged by group members to be iconic. Past research on brand iconicity has studied the socio-historical meanings of specific brands and identified some brands that symbolize consumers' abstract ideals (e.g., in North American society; Holt, 2003, 2004). Building upon existing work, this article takes a social-psychological approach and studies the degree of cultural symbolism of brands using a shared reality perspective (Hardin & Higgins, 1996). As indicated earlier, the cultural symbolism of brands emerges from an ongoing, dynamic process of social verification of abstract brand meanings. Implicit brand meanings shared by the group can be accurately articulated by group members, and can be measured by asking them to rate the extent to which fellow group members believe brands symbolize abstract group characteristics (see Fussell & Krauss, 1992).

Notice that cultural symbolism should be distinguished from strong country-of-origin connections (Gürhan-Canli & Maheswaran, 2000). Brand iconicity is conceptualized in relation to cultural categories extending beyond those established using nationality as a defining criterion. Studying the brands that are symbolic of the teenage culture in Western societies may render country-of-origin associations to be of little use. In addition, cultural symbolism emerges, at least in part, from associations with abstract group meanings such as values. A country-of-origin connection is a more concrete brand aspect that may not be enough to justify high levels of cultural symbolism. When using nationality as the defining cultural criterion, we are likely to find that iconic brands have strong country-of-origin connections. However, this would not be a sufficient condition to grant an iconic status. For instance, although most Americans would recognize Hallmark as an American brand, probably fewer Americans would consider it a symbol of American culture as outlined in this research.

Recently, Torelli, Chiu, and Keh (2008a) developed a seven-item scale to measure the cultural symbolism of brands. They assessed its reliability and validity among European American consumers, using nationality as the criterion for defining cultural categories. The items in the scale capture the abstract group meanings associated with the brand (e.g., "The brand embodies group values"), the cultural symbolism for the group (e.g., "The brand is an icon of the group's culture"), the degree of interconnectedness with other group-related icons (e.g., "A picture of the brand with an American flag makes a lot of sense," in the case of Americans as the cultural group), and the extent to which the brand can evoke the group identity ("The brand reminds me of my group identity").

The importance of cultural constructs for a cultural group can be determined by aggregating individual responses of group members (i.e., actual self-importance) or by assessing people's beliefs about the importance of the concept for the group (i.e., perceived cultural importance; Wan et al., 2007). The latter approach is congruent with the shared reality perspective of brand symbolism. However, the former approach is the one often used by (cross-) cultural researchers. Since the correspondence between what people commonly believe is important for the culture (perceived cultural importance) and the aggregation of individual importance ratings (actual self-importance) is often imperfect (Wan et al., 2007), we assessed the cultural symbolism of a variety of brands from both perspectives. We asked American participants to rate a variety of brands (more than 40) in terms of their symbolism for American culture using the newly developed seven-item scale. We used familiar brands chosen from a balanced mix of utilitarian and symbolic categories. No familiar brands with obvious associations with a foreign culture were included in the study (e.g., Toyota or Sony). This was done to provide a stronger test of the distinction between iconicity and country-of-origin connection. One group of participants rated brands from their personal perspective (i.e., their personal opinions about the cultural symbolism), whereas another group used the group perspective (i.e., how Americans in general would respond to the items). Participants also rated the brands in terms of involvement, familiarity, degree of country association (e.g., is it an American brand?), and indicated their level of attachment to the brands.

Results showed that the seven-item scale was reliable ($\alpha = .93$) and valid for discriminating among brands with different levels of cultural iconicity.

TABLE 6.1

Mean Iconicity Scores From Self Versus Group Perspectives

Brand	Iconicity Self-Perspective	Group Perspective
Ford	5.7	6.3
Coke	5.5	6.1
Nike	4.6	5.4
Budweiser	4.5	5.1
Cheerios	4.6	5.1
Miller	3.5	5.0
Kodak	3.6	4.4
New Balance	3.3	4.0
Dasani	3.7	3.8
Tombstone	3.2	3.8
Chicken of the sea	2.6	3.3

Note: Only a subset of brands is included.

As shown in Table 6.1, the American brands with the highest iconicity scores are brands widely regarded as American icons (e.g., Ford, Coke, and Nike). Brand iconicity was found to be partially correlated with, but distinct from, involvement ($r = .32$), familiarity ($r = .30$), degree of country association ($r = .49$), and brand attachment ($r = .33$).

There is similarity between the self- and group-perspective ratings of cultural symbolism for the different brands. Group-based scores are slightly higher than the self-based ones. This is not very surprising as the self-perspective ratings capture idiosyncratic opinions that may be expressed based on implicit comparisons with other group members and hence subject to more variability (e.g., I think Coke is more [less] iconic than my peers do, so I'll give it a higher [lower] rating; see Heine, Lehman, Peng, & Greenholtz, 2002 for a discussion). However, both ratings point to a similar order of brands in terms of levels of cultural symbolism. Ford, Coke, and Nike are brands with high levels of iconicity for Americans. The level of cultural symbolism for these brands is higher than that for Miller and Kodak, which could be regarded by many as American icons. The latter brands are higher in iconicity than Tombstone and Chicken of the Sea, which few considered symbolic of American culture.

These results illustrate how brand iconicity can be measured and used to discriminate among brands with different levels of cultural symbolism. Studying brand iconicity as the degree to which a brand symbolizes the values, needs, and aspirations of the members of a particular cultural group provide further insights on the symbolic meanings of brands. Brands high in iconicity have the power to connect diverse elements of cultural knowledge and can act as reminders of culturally relevant values and beliefs. The cultural symbolism embedded in brands also has the potential to help consumers manage their social identities. In the sections that follow, we illustrate how brand iconicity can be used to further develop existing models of brand management.

Iconic Brands as Cultural Primes in Globalized Markets

Iconic brands can act as cultural primes. Incidental exposure to an iconic brand can bring to mind its attendant cultural meanings. This can have consequences for the evaluation of brands in globalized markets. With the advancement of globalization, the marketplace is suffused with images of various iconic brands and products. Continued exposure to iconic products and brands can serve as a cognitive socialization process whereby different cultural values and beliefs are repeatedly activated in consumers' working memory. As Lau-Gesk (2003) points out, as the world becomes more culturally diverse and mobile, it is more common for consumers to possess knowledge about the symbols and values of multiple cultures.

Some recent studies provide evidence for the activation of cultural constructs upon processing information about brands with high levels of cultural symbolism (Torelli et al., 2008a; Torelli, Tam, Au, Chiu, & Keh, 2008c). In a study on European American consumers, we asked participants to write a story about the meaning of being an American, one that could convey to those unfamiliar with American culture the shared values and beliefs that are important to Americans, or the elements that define being a person of worth in American culture. As part of the task, participants were presented with three brands and asked to use them when writing their stories. One group of participants was presented with high iconicity brands (e.g., Coke), whereas another group was presented with low iconicity brands (e.g., Tombstone). After writing the story, participants were asked to indicate how easy it was for them to write the story and how well the story described to others the shared values and beliefs that are important to Americans. Results showed that when writing about their culture, participants were more fluent in idea generation when they could include in their story high iconicity brands than when they could not (as those in the low iconicity brand condition). This result was found in both self-reports of communicative fluency and the number of ideas included in the story. These findings suggest that iconic brands are carriers of core cultural values.

More direct evidence on the activation of culturally important values upon exposure to iconic brands is provided in a cued recall study (Torelli et al., 2008c). European American participants were exposed to values of high and low importance to Americans. After taking an unrelated survey for about half an hour later, participants were presented with a surprise cued recall task. They were shown images of brands high or low in

CULTURAL IDENTITIES AND VALUES
EMBODIED IN BRANDS

Why is "Ford Tough" American? Why do people drink, and identify with, Coke all over the world—not just in the United States? When a brand communicates ideals and aspirations to others it takes on cultural symbolism that becomes very important to both the product and the consumer.

"Brands can make people feel like they are part of a global, or local, community. Just as people go to museums to feel like they are part of a bigger world, brands can do the same thing," says Nathalie Wilson, Vice President of Brand at Minneapolis-based Yamamoto-Moss Mackenzie.

Additionally, brands allow consumers to communicate with other consumers. Products can convey that someone is an individual, or part of a specific group. Sporting a Harley Davidson label on your clothes makes one statement while the Nike logo imparts a very different message. Both of them suggest an identity—that the wearer belongs to a group who shares a certain set of ideals. This may happen regardless of whether the brand is being worn or bought in the country of origin or in another country.

Starbucks is a strong American brand that personifies independence, western society, and in many ways, affordable luxury. When Starbucks takes a store to different countries these western standards are communicated through the presence of the brand. In Asian countries Starbucks brings the cultural identity of independence, or autonomy. For those consumers, holding a Starbucks cup symbolizes status, individualism, or aspiration. But, like many other food chains such as McDonald's and Dairy Queen, Starbucks has learned that incorporating part of the local culture into the existing brand's menu can increase its success.

Cultures sometimes clash, with brands as the centerpiece. Starbucks has several outlets across China, some more successful than others. The Starbucks located in the Forbidden City in China eventually closed. The Forbidden City is a symbol of China's rich cultural heritage. The conflicting values of West and East, in a robustly traditional location, led to organized protests and criticisms, which may have accelerated the demise of Starbucks in that location. In other locations, such as Beijing and Guangdong, Starbucks introduced vegetable tofu rolls and Chinese-style mushroom and pepper sandwiches, which no doubt has communicated that the western brand can accommodate eastern tastes ... and perhaps eastern values?

"Understanding what the target audience is looking for—a collective or individual identity—is crucial to the success of a brand entering another culture," says Wilson. "When someone is looking for an identity, it is important that the brand personify the attitude and spirit the consumer desires."

Cultural identities and values are conveyed by iconic brands. As globalization increases, these values and identities will become increasingly apparent, and important.

R.D.M. & L.W.P.

iconicity as recall cues and asked to recall the values they had seen earlier. Participants recalled more culturally important values when the retrieval cues were iconic brands than when they were noniconic brands. Whether the retrieval cues were iconic or noniconic brands did not influence recall of culturally unimportant values.

The cultural priming effects of iconic brands can be particularly important for managers of global brands. In globalized markets, it is commonplace to see the coexistence of symbols of different cultural traditions in the same location or product (as in the cases of Starbucks in China's Forbidden City and Batman toys with a "Made in China" label). Globalization has also increased the tension between the creation of a homogeneous global culture and the attachment to the values, customs, and traditions of local cultures (Fu and Chiu, 2007). Such tension is also evident in the marketplace, where contrastive meanings provided by global and local brands and their cultural messages coexist and jointly shape people's cultural associations (Robertson, 1995). In some cases, the juxtaposition of cultural symbols can enhance the perceptibility of otherwise unnoticed cultural differences and reinforce the perception of cultural incompatibility.

Torelli et al. (2008c) provide evidence for culturally influenced judgments upon the juxtaposition of cultural symbols. In a study with European Americans, participants were presented with products that symbolize both ingroup and a foreign culture (as in the case of a China-made iconic U.S. product for Americans—e.g., "Chenxiao tennis shoes") and asked to evaluate them. Later, in an ostensibly unrelated task, they were presented with a measure of cultural perception and a measure of perceived incompatibility of cultures (Chiu, Mallorie, Keh, & Law, 2007). The cultural measure was designed to assess participants' expectation that another American would possess value preferences characteristic of American culture. The cultural incompatibility measure was based on past research findings on cultural differences in values and beliefs (see Chiu and Hong, 2006, 2007). Results showed that coexistence of symbols of the ingroup culture (iconic products of the United States) and a foreign culture (the products' Chinese origin) in commercial products strengthens the belief in the incompatibility of American and Chinese cultures. It also lowers evaluation of imported products that are icons of U.S. culture and reinforces the expectancy that Americans would not choose foreign (collectivist) values. These findings suggest that exposure to such products renders culture a salient organizing construct for perceiving culturally pertinent information. Such exposure also increases the perceiver's tendency to attribute stereotypic characteristics of the activated cultures to members of the respective culture and hence increases the perceptibility of cultural differences and cultural incompatibility.

Iconic Brands and Self-Identity

Iconic brands carry a heavy symbolic load for consumers, and they frequently rely on them for constructing their identities. As stated by Holt (2004), "consumers flock to brands that embody the ideals they admire, brands that help them express who they want to be" (pp. 3–4). Symbolic self-completion theory (Wicklund & Gollwitzer, 1981) posits that personal identities can be viewed as goals that individuals willfully pursue through self-symbolizing (i.e., emphasizing the characteristics of their identities). This theory further suggests that self-symbolizing efforts will be undertaken when the person cannot find adequate symbols for representing and anchoring their identities. Patronizing iconic brands can be a self-symbolizing strategy. By being a patron of iconic brands, one can emphasize his/her alignment with and adherence to the culture.

The degree to which a consumer identifies himself or herself with a member group can affect the formation of self-brand connections with a symbolic brand (Escalas & Bettman, 2003, 2005). An underlying assumption for the more favorable evaluations of iconic brands that symbolize culturally relevant values is the identification of the consumer with these values. Consumers' positive evaluations of iconic brands would be based on their instrumentality for fulfilling positively valued identities. Consumers may not value the cultural symbolism of an iconic brand, and may evaluate the brands less favorably, when they do not identify themselves with the culture. Accordingly, cultural identification should moderate the attitude toward an iconic brand.

Along this line, Torelli et al. (2008a) asked European American consumers to evaluate a diverse set of brands with varying degrees of cultural symbolism for Americans (e.g., Coke and Chicken of the Sea). They were also asked to complete a scale to measure identification with American culture (Wan et al., 2007). Results showed a positive and significant correlation between the evaluation of iconic brands and participants' level of identification with American culture ($r = .33$). The higher the level of identification with American culture, the more participants liked iconic brands.

Torelli et al. (2008a) also manipulated the need for self-symbolizing. Because people would engage in self-symbolizing when symbolic markers of their group identity are tarnished, it was expected that people would elevate their preferences for iconic brands over noniconic ones when they were reminded of a tarnished identity marker than when they were not. Furthermore, self-completion theory assumes symbolic markers of identities are potential substitutes for one another (Braun & Wicklund, 1989; Wicklund & Gollwitzer, 1981). Thus, consumers may engage in self-symbolizing by increasing their liking for brands high (versus low) in iconicity, even when they are reminded of a tarnished marker of an unrelated group identity. The participants were either reminded or not reminded of a recent ban on their university's mascot (a symbolic marker of their student identity) and subsequently asked to indicate their liking for brands high (versus low) in iconicity. Consistent with the symbolic self-completion theory, results showed that a ban on the symbolic marker of an important group identity increased the tendency to base brand preferences on brand iconicity.

The use of brands with high levels of cultural symbolism for managing consumers' self-identities may underlie recent trends in global advertising. Zhang (2009) shows that the responses to persuasive appeals by young Chinese consumers resemble those found among bicultural individuals (e.g., East Asians born and raised in the United States). This state of affairs may help explain why, in rapidly transitioning economies, Westernized appeals are increasingly common. For example, appeals to youth/modernity, individuality/independence, and technology are rather salient in Chinese advertisements (Zhang & Shavitt, 2003) as well as frequently employed by contemporary Taiwanese advertising agencies (Shao, Raymond, & Taylor, 1999).

In addition, consumers in developing countries tend to respond favorably to markedly Western products. For instance, in a study of Indian consumers (Batra, Ramaswamy, Alden, Steenkamp, & Ramachander, 2000), brands perceived as having a nonlocal (Western) country of origin were favored over brands perceived to be local. This effect was stronger for consumers with a greater admiration for the lifestyle in economically developed countries. These culturally incongruous findings are meaningful because they suggest the important role that advertising can play in reshaping cultural values in countries experiencing rapid economic growth (Zhang & Shavitt, 2003). Rather than reflecting existing cultural values, advertising content in those countries promotes new aspirational values, such as individuality and modernity, hence these new values become acceptable and desirable among consumers.

At the aggregate level, brands that symbolize culturally relevant values should enjoy relatively high levels of preference among members of the cultural group. However, individuals may differ in their liking for these culturally relevant brands as a function of their own level of identification with the culturally relevant values. Although most Americans would probably like Nike due to its culturally relevant associations with independence and freedom, American consumers who do not espouse these values as much as they may other values (e.g., helpfulness to others) may not find these brand associations to be particularly appealing. The flip side of this argument is that the same consumer instead may show favorable attitudes toward an icon of a foreign culture that symbolizes these values (e.g., a Chinese brand of herbal tea). Past research shows that consumers sometimes favor global (versus local) brands due to perceptions of higher quality and prestige (Steenkamp, Batra, & Alden, 2003). Beyond these positive associations, global brands associated with foreign values can also help consumers fulfill important self-identity goals. For example, a Chinese consumer may think about the individualist values characteristic of American culture when passing by a Starbucks outlet in downtown Beijing. If the consumer values a nonculturally nurtured independent self-identity, the activated cultural associations upon seeing the iconic American brand may increase purchase intention. In summary, brands that are iconic in a culture should be more likely to enjoy widespread favorability due to the match between the values associated with the brand and those that are important to the members of the culture. However, iconic brands that symbolize desirable values of a foreign culture can also appeal to local consumers for whom these values are important, even in the event of a contradiction with culturally nurtured values.

Existing models of brand equity (e.g., Keller, 1993) emphasize that creating favorable, strong, and unique brand associations in memory are key elements for building a strong brand. At the consumer level, forming a self-brand connection is a psychological manifestation of brand equity (Escalas & Bettman, 2003). The ultimate level of brand-building activity is frequently characterized by a deep psychological bond between the customer and the brand. The discussion in this chapter suggests that brands high in iconicity may be more likely to resonate with consumers who can rely on these brands to fulfill identity goals. The identity value of iconic brands can produce more favorable brand evaluations when consumers have a heightened need for self-symbolizing. This heightened need for self-symbolizing can be triggered not only by a threat to a symbolic marker of a group identity, but more generally by perceptions of unsatisfactory progress toward the fulfillment of a self-defining goal (Wicklund & Gollwitzer, 1981). For instance, consumers who are reminded of their lack of expertise in a self-defining domain (e.g., a freshman who knows little about his new college environment), their lack of status within a group (e.g., a recent college graduate in her first entry-level job), or their failure to successfully perform a self-defining task (e.g., a new assistant professor who receives a low student evaluation score) may elevate their evaluation of iconic brands as a means to repair their tarnished self-concept.

How Do Brands Become Cultural Symbols?

In the previous discussion, we have indicated that iconic brands symbolize abstract group meanings. A prerequisite for creating an iconic brand should then be establishing a brand image congruent with these abstract meanings. A common approach for studying abstract cultural representations is to focus on the values that are important for the members of a cultural group (e.g., cultural orientation; Triandis, 1995). Values are abstract representations about desirable end states that reflect what is important to us in our lives (Feather, 1990, 1995; Schwartz & Bilsky, 1987, 1990). Extensive research has established a theory and measurement of values in over 200 samples in more than 60 countries on every inhabited continent (Schwartz, 1992; Schwartz & Boehnke, 2004). In cross-cultural consumer behavior, the broad value dimensions of individualism (IND) or collectivism (COL) (Hofstede, 1980; Triandis, 1995) are the ones that have received more research attention (Shavitt et al., 2008). Individualism refers to the emphasis on the attainment of values that serve the individual (e.g., self-direction, power), whereas collectivism refers to the emphasis on values that serve the collective (e.g., concerns for the welfare of others, conformity) (Gardner, Gabriel, & Lee, 1999; Schwartz, 1990; Triandis, McCusker, & Hui 1990).

In different cultures, people endorse individualistic and collectivistic values to varying degrees. For instance, in North American cultures (e.g., the United States and Canada), the endorsement of individualistic values is more common than it is in East Asian cultures (e.g., China and Japan), whereas the opposite is true for the endorsement of collectivistic values (Triandis, 1995). One should then expect that brands with a more "individualistic" image should be more likely to reach an iconic status in the United States. In contrast, brands with a more "collectivistic" image should be more likely to reach an iconic status in China. This expectation is congruent with the notion that people should have more favorable attitudes toward brands that match their personal characteristics (Malhotra, 1988; Sirgy, 1982). It is also congruent with findings suggesting that North Americans (East Asians) have more favorable attitudes toward brands that highlight an individualistic (collectivistic) view of the self (Aaker & Schmitt, 2001; Han & Shavitt, 1994).

Brand practitioners could evaluate the progress toward the achievement of an iconic status for a target brand by monitoring the extent to which the brand image matches the values that are important in a focal culture. Unfortunately, existing measures of human-like brand representations (e.g., brand personality; Aaker, 1997) cannot be easily matched to the abstract values endorsed by diverse cultural groups. Recently, Torelli, Ozsomer, Carvalho, Keh, and Maehle (2008b) developed a scale to measure the values embodied by a brand or the brand values. The brand values scale captures the degree to which a brand is associated with the different values that are distinguishable by people in most cultures: power, achievement, hedonism, stimulation, self-direction, universalism, benevolence, tradition, conformity, and security.

As indicated earlier, since iconic brands symbolize the values and aspirations of the members of a particular cultural group, they should be associated with culturally important values. In other words, the higher the level of brand iconicity, the stronger should be the association between the brand and the values that are important in the focal culture. Recent evidence supports this prediction. Torelli et al. (2008a) asked European American participants to rate a variety of brands using the brand values scale. They computed the average "individualism" score for each brand by averaging the ratings of the values that serve the individual (power, achievement, hedonism, stimulation, and self-direction) and correlated it with the brand's average iconicity score. Results showed a positive and significant correlation between iconicity scores and the association with individualistic values. In other words, the higher the level of brand iconicity, the more the brand was associated with individualistic values. This finding supports the notion that associating a brand with the values that are important for the members of a particular cultural group may increase the likelihood of turning the brand into a cultural symbol.

Conclusions

As marketing efforts become increasingly globalized, it is imperative to understand the cultural significance of brands for multicultural consumers. As societies become more globalized, cultural boundaries also get blurred and new hybrids of cultural values will emerge. Branding activities aimed at establishing deep self-brand connections will require a thorough understanding of the cultural symbolism of brands. Existing models of brand equity (e.g., Keller, 1993) emphasize that the ultimate level of brand-building activity is frequently characterized by a deep psychological bond between the customer and the brand (Keh,

Pang, & Peng, 2008). A brand achieves the highest level of "resonance" when the consumer identifies deeply and feels in synch with the brand (Keller, 2001). The discussion in this chapter suggests that brands that achieve high levels of cultural symbolism may be more likely to resonate with consumers.

When launching a new brand in a foreign market, or when targeting a sub-cultural segment in an existing market, associating the brand with important cultural values would facilitate imbuing it with symbolic group meanings. In turn, this might lead to high levels of cultural symbolism for the group. To the extent that target culture(s) share the same important values (e.g., individualistic values), branding professionals may need to do little adjustments to their positioning strategies and still aim at achieving an iconic status in multiple markets. However, an established brand with a strong image that is incompatible with the values symbolized by a target culture may find it difficult to appeal to broader audiences unless it repositions itself. Aiming at becoming a cultural symbol in the target culture would require a departure from the current image in order to embody the values that are important in the target culture. Companies may be hesitant to adopt this strategy as it might lead to brand dilution in existing markets and to more challenging efforts when coordinating global marketing efforts. When the risk for dilution in existing markets outweigh the potential benefits (in terms of market share) from imbuing the brand in the new culture, branding practitioners may opt for being an important niche player in the target culture. For example, Harley Davidson is recognized for its consistent brand image of independence and freedom in every country it operates. Although Harley Davidson could be recognized as an iconic brand in America, and perhaps in some other countries that are culturally similar like Australia and Canada, it might be difficult for the brand to become a cultural symbol in collectivistic countries like Japan or China. In these latter countries, the brand might attempt to become a strong niche player by appealing to sub-cultural segments that endorse individualistic values (e.g., educated young individuals).

Although most of the discussion in this article refers to cultural groups defined in terms of nationality and ethnicity, we are not advocating that these are the only important variables for studying the cultural meanings of brands. As indicated earlier in the discussion, distinctions among cultural groups can be established by dividing the human community using any meaningful criteria such as gender, age, class, occupation, or ethnicity. To illustrate, a similar set of results should be obtained if one focuses on females in North America as the cultural group of interest. We anticipate that American women would perceive certain brands to capture better than others the abstract meanings of being a female in American society. Liking for these brands should be higher among women for whom the female identity is particularly important. The same predictions can be extrapolated to the study of brand preferences among Southerners, Latinos, or consumers from the Mountain West.

This chapter offers a framework to better understand the impact of the cultural meanings associated with consumer brands on brand perceptions and the fulfillment of identity goals. The discussions here illustrate the theoretical and practical significance of studying the cultural symbolism of brands for further developing models of brand management in local and global markets.

References

Aaker, J.L. (1997). Dimensions of brand personality. *Journal of Marketing Research, 34 (3)*, 347–356.

Aaker, J.L. (1999). The malleable self: The role of self-expression in persuasion. *Journal of Marketing Research, 36 (1)*, 45–57.

Aaker, J.L., Benet-Martinez, V., & Garolera, J. (2001). Consumption symbols as carriers of culture: A study of Japanese and Spanish brand personality constucts. *Journal of Personality and Social Psychology, 81 (3)*, 492–508.

Aaker, J.L., & Schmitt, B. (2001). Culture-dependent assimilation and differentiation of the self: Preferences for consumption symbols in the United States and China. *Journal of Cross-Cultural Psychology, 32 (5)*, 561–576.

Batra, R., Ramaswamy, V., Alden, D.L., Steenkamp, J.E.M., & Ramachander, S. (2000). Effects of brand local and nonlocal origin on consumer attitudes in developing countries. *Journal of Consumer Psychology, 9 (2)*, 83–95.

Bearden, W.O., & Etzel, M.J. (1982). Reference group influence on product and brand purchase decisions. *Journal of Consumer Research, 9 (2)*, 183–194.

Berger, J., & Heath, C. (2007). Where consumers diverge from others: Identity signaling and product domains. *Journal of Consumer Research, 34 (2)*, 121–134.

Betsky, A. (1997). *Icons: Magnets of meaning*. San Francisco: Chronicle Books.

Braun, O.L., & Wicklund, R.A. (1989). Psychological antecedents of conspicuous consumption. *Journal of Economic Psychology, 10 (2)*, 161–187.

Childers, T.L., & Rao, A.R. (1992). The influence of familial and peer-based reference groups on consumer decisions. *Journal of Consumer Research, 19 (2)*, 198–211.

Chiu, C., & Hong, Y. (2006). *Social psychology of culture*. New York: Psychology Press.

Chiu, C., & Hong, Y. (2007). Cultural processes: Basic principles. In T.E. Higgins & A.W. Kruglanski (Eds.), *Social psychology: Handbook of basic principles*. New York: Guilford Press, 785–806.

Chiu, C., Mallorie, L., Keh, H.T., & Law, W. (2007). Seeing culture in multicultural space: Joint presentation of cultures increases ingroup attribution of culture-typical characteristics. *Journal of Cross-Cultural Psychology*, forthcoming.

Escalas, J.E., & Bettman, J.R. (2003). You are what they eat: The influence of reference groups on consumers' connections to brands. *Journal of Consumer Psychology, 13 (3)*, 339–348.

Escalas, J.E., & Bettman, J.R. (2005). Self-construal, reference groups, and brand meaning. *Journal of Consumer Research, 32 (3),* 378–389.

Feather, N.T. (1990). Bridging the gap between values and actions: Recent applications of the expectancy-value model. In T.E. Higgins & R.M. Sorrentino (Eds.), *Handbook of motivation and cognition: Foundations of social behavior* (vol. 2). New York: Guilford Press, 151–192.

Feather, N.T. (1995). Values, valences, and choice: The influences of values on the perceived attractiveness and choice of alternatives. *Journal of Personality and Social Psychology, 68 (6),* 1135–1151.

Fu, H., & Chiu, C. (2007). Local culture's responses to globalization: Exemplary persons and their attendant values. *Journal of Cross-Cultural Psychology, 38,* 636–653.

Fu, H., Chiu, C., Morris, M.W., & Young, M. (2007). Spontaneous inferences from cultural cues: Varying responses of cultural insiders and outsiders. *Journal of Cross-Cultural Psychology, 38,* 58–75.

Fussell, S.R., & Krauss, R.M. (1992). Coordination of knowledge in communication: Effects of speakers' assumptions about what others know. *Journal of Personality and Social Psychology, 62 (3),* 378–391.

Gardner, W.L., Gabriel, S., & Lee, A.Y. (1999). "I" value freedom, but "we" value relationships: Self-construal priming mirrors cultural differences in judgment. *Psychological Science, 10 (4),* 321–326.

Gudykunst, W.B., & Ting-Toomey, S. (1988). *Culture and interpersonal communication.* Newbury Park, CA: Sage.

Gürhan-Canli, Z., & Maheswaran, D. (2000). Cultural variations in country of origin effects. *Journal of Marketing Research, 37 (3),* 309–317.

Han, S., & Shavitt, S. (1994). Persuasion and culture: Advertising appeals in individualistic and collectivistic societies. *Journal of Experimental Social Psychology, 30 (4),* 326–350.

Hardin, C.D., & Higgins, E.T. (1996). Shared reality: How social verification makes the subjective objective. In R.M Sorrentino & E.T. Higgins (Eds.), *Handbook of motivation and cognition* (vol. 3). New York: Guilford Press, 28–84.

Heine, S.J., Lehman, D.R., Peng, K., & Greenholtz, J. (2002). What's wrong with cross-cultural comparisons of subjective Likert scales? The reference-group effect. *Journal of Personality and Social Psychology, 82 (6),* 903–918.

Hofstede, G.H. (1980). *Culture's consequences: International differences in work-related values.* Newbury Park, CA: Sage.

Hofstede, G.H. (2001). *Culture's consequences: Comparing values, behaviors, institutions and organizations across nations.* Thousand Oaks, CA: Sage.

Holt, D.B. (2003). How to build an iconic brand. *Market Leader,* summer, 35–42.

Holt, D.B. (2004). *How brands become icons: The principles of cultural branding.* Cambridge, MA: Harvard Business School Press.

Hong, Y., Morris, M.W., Chiu, C., & Benet-Martinez, V. (2000). Multicultural minds: A dynamic constructivist approach to culture and cognition. *American Psychologist, 55 (7),* 709–720.

Johansson, J.K. (1989). Determinants and effects of the use of "made in" labels. *International Marketing Review, 6 (1),* 47–58.

Keh, H.T., Pang, J., & Peng, S. (2008). Can consumer-brand relationships be intimate, passionate and committed? Conceptualization and validation of brand love. Unpublished manuscript.

Keller, K.L. (1993). Conceptualizing, measuring, managing customer-based brand equity. *Journal of Marketing, 57 (1)*, 1–22.

Keller, K.L. (2001). Building customer-based brand equity. *Marketing Management, 10 (2)*, 14–19.

Kleine, S.S., Kleine, R.E., III, & Allen, C.T. (1995). How is a possession "me" or "not me"? Characterizing types and an antecedent of material possession attachment. *Journal of Consumer Research, 22 (3)*, 327–343.

Krauss, R.M., & Fussell, S.R. (1996). Social psychological models of interpersonal communication. In E.T. Higgins & A.W. Kruglanski (Eds.), *Social psychology: Handbook of basic principles*. New York: Guilford Press, 655–701.

Laroche, M., Kirpalani, V.H., Pons, F., & Zhou, L. (2001). A model of advertising standardization in multinational corporations. *Journal of International Business Studies, 32 (2)*, 249–266.

Lau-Gesk, L.G. (2003). Activating culture through persuasion appeals: An examination of the bicultural consumer. *Journal of Consumer Psychology, 13 (3)*, 301–315.

Leclerc, F., Schmitt, B.H., & Dubé, L. (1994). Foreign branding and its effects on product perceptions and attitudes. *Journal of Marketing Research, 31 (2)*, 263–270.

Maheswaran, D. (1994). Country of origin as a stereotype: Effects of consumer expertise and attribute strength on product evaluations. *Journal of Consumer Research, 21 (2)*, 354–365.

Malhotra, N.K. (1988). Self concept and product choice: An integrated perspective. *Journal of Economic Psychology, 9 (1)*, 1–28.

McCracken, G. (1986). Culture and consumption: A theoretical account of the structure and movement of the cultural meaning of consumer goods. *Journal of Consumer Research, 13 (1)*, 71–84.

Muniz, A.M., & O'Guinn, T.C. (2001). Brand community. *Journal of Consumer Research, 27 (4)*, 412–432.

Ortner, S.B. (1973). On key symbols. *American Anthropologist, 75 (5)*, 1338–1346.

Park, C.W., & Lessig, V.P. (1977). Students and housewives: Differences in susceptibility to reference group influence. *Journal of Consumer Research, 4 (2)*, 102–110.

Robertson, R. (1995). Glocalization: Time-space and homogeneity-heterogeneity. In M. Featherstone, S. Lash, & R. Robertson (Eds.), *Global modernities*. London: Sage, 25–44.

Schwartz, S.H. (1990). Individualism-collectivism: Critique and proposed refinements. *Journal of Cross-Cultural Psychology, 21 (2)*, 139–157.

Schwartz, S.H. (1992). Universals in the content and structure of values: Theoretical advances and empirical tests in 20 countries. In M.P. Zanna (Ed.), *Advances in experimental social psychology* (vol. 25). San Diego, CA: Academic Press, 1–65.

Schwartz, S.H., & Bilsky, W. (1987). Toward a universal psychological structure of human values. *Journal of Personality and Social Psychology, 53 (3)*, 550–562.

Schwartz, S.H., & Bilsky, W. (1990). Toward a theory of the universal content and structure of values: Extensions and cross-cultural replications. *Journal of Personality and Social Psychology, 58 (5)*, 878–891.

Schwartz, S.H., & Boehnke, K. (2004). Evaluating the structure of human values with confirmatory factor analysis. *Journal of Research in Personality, 38 (3)*, 230–255.

Shao, A.T., Raymond, M.A., & Taylor, C. (1999). Shifting advertising appeals in Taiwan. *Journal of Advertising Research, 39 (6),* 61–69.

Shavitt, S. (1990). The role of attitude objects in attitude functions. *Journal of Experimental Social Psychology, 26 (2),* 124–148.

Shavitt, S., Lee, A.Y., & Torelli, C.J. (2008). Cross-cultural issues in consumer behavior. In M. Wanke (Ed.), *Social psychology of consumer behavior.* Forthcoming.

Shimp, T.A., & Sharma, S. (1987). Consumer ethnocentrism: Construction and validation of the CETSCALE. *Journal of Marketing Research, 24 (3),* 280–289.

Sirgy, M.J. (1982). Self-concept in consumer behavior: A critical review. *Journal of Consumer Research, 9 (3),* 287–300.

Sperber, D. (1996). *Explaining culture: A naturalistic approach.* Massachusetts: Blackwell.

Steenkamp, J., Batra, R., & Alden, D.L. (2003). How perceived brand globalness creates brand value. *Journal of International Business Studies, 34 (1),* 53–65.

Swaminathan, V., Page, K.L., & Gürhan-Canli, Z. (2007). "My" brand or "our" brand: The effects of brand relationship dimensions and self-construal on brand evaluations. *Journal of Consumer Research, 34 (2),* 248–259.

Tajfel, H., & Turner, J. (2001). An integrative theory of intergroup conflict. In M.A. Hogg & D. Abrams (Eds.), *Intergroup relations: Essential readings.* New York: Psychology Press, 94–109.

Torelli, C.J., Chiu, C., & Keh, H.T. (2008a). Brand iconicity: A shared reality perspective. Unpublished manuscript.

Torelli, C.J., Ozsomer, A., Carvalho, S., Keh, H.T., & Maehle, N. (2008b). Consumer brand values: Cross-cultural implications for brand image decisions. Manuscript under review.

Torelli, C.J., Tam, K., Au, K.C., Chiu, C., & Keh, H.T. (2008c). Psychological reactions to foreign cultures in globalized economy: Effects of simultaneous activation of cultures. Manuscript under review.

Triandis, H.C. (1989). The self and social behavior in differing cultural contexts. *Psychological Review, 96 (3),* 506–520.

Triandis, H.C. (1995). *Individualism & collectivism.* Boulder, CO: Westview Press.

Triandis, H.C. (1996). The psychological measurement of cultural syndromes. *American Psychologist, 51 (4),* 407–415.

Triandis, H.C., McCusker, C., & Hui, C. (1990). Multimethod probes of individualism and collectivism. *Journal of Personality and Social Psychology, 59 (5),* 1006–1020.

Wan, C., Chiu, C., Tam, K., Lee, S., Lau, I., & Peng, S. (2007). Perceived cultural importance and actual self-importance of values in cultural identification. *Journal of Personality and Social Psychology, 92,* 337–354.

Wicklund, R.A., & Gollwitzer, P.M. (1981). Symbolic self-completion, attempted influence, and self-deprecation. *Basic and Applied Social Psychology, 2 (2),* 89–114.

Zhang, J. (2009). The effect of advertising appeals in activating self-construals: A case of "bicultural" Chinese generation X consumers. *Journal of Advertising 38,* 63–81.

Zhang, J., & Shavitt, S. (2003). Cultural values in advertisements to the Chinese X-generation: Promoting modernity and individualism. *Journal of Advertising, 32 (1),* 23–33.

7

Toward a Sociological Model of Brands

Thomas C. O'Guinn
University of Wisconsin–Madison

Albert M. Muniz, Jr.
DePaul University, Chicago

This chapter offers a basic social model of brands. It is a model with meaning creation at its center. Meaning defines brands, and people make meaning. People make meaning through social means: they make meaning through their interaction, through the institutions they have created and maintained, through accommodation and negotiation with marketers, through rumors, through politics, and often in reaction to a disruption in the social sphere. Brands are meaning. This is true even when that meaning is mundane. Meaning is the most powerful source of sustainable competitive differentiation.

Unlike the vast majority of the brand literature our model is not constrained by a singular focus on the marketer–consumer dyad. This single dyadic relationship, while certainly important, is also quite limiting. This dyadic thinking about brands is too sparse, too simple. Brands are created by interactions of multiple parties, institutions, publics, and social forces. Even the term *cocreation* belies the brand's true nature and is still mired in this fictive dyad. Nothing in the material world, the social world, or brand world is that simple, that isolated. Nothing in these worlds lends itself to such an obviously reductionist treatment. Thus, we reject the au courant cocreation term, not because it goes too far, but because it doesn't go far enough. Cocreation is in the messy reality of social life a critically constrained construct. While multiple social forces always had a hand in brand creation, current trends amplify their importance. For example, many feel that we have just witnessed the *prelude* to the consumers-as-creators phenomenon (Anderson, 2006; Shirky, 2008). Consumer-generated brand content and consumer (re)designed brands are common topics in the contemporary trade press and commonly observed in the lives of ordinary consumers. A sea change in mediated communications has clearly enabled multiple parties to play significant roles in the construction of the contemporary brand.

We also reject the necessity of a critical stance (cf. Holt, 2004; Thompson & Coskuner-Balli, 2007) to meaningfully theorize brands. The sine qua non of critical theory, critiquing market capitalism, while fashionable in the comfortable confines of trust-fund-baby parlor repartee (McCloskey, 2006), is neither necessary nor sufficient to understand basic social construction. Brands are social constructions under any political banner, within any political ideology. They can be easily theorized without the assumed requisite and entirely predictable critique. Part of the social construction of brands does, of course, rely upon economic relationships, their inequities, and other related social stratification. Again, this reality does not in and of itself necessitate a critical stance or a critical sociology. Such heavy, cumbersome, but often fashionable baggage can be, and typically is, an impediment to material understanding.

The theory of brands proposed here is based on essential sociology that predates the critical turn by decades. It draws on the idea of community, itself a construct in active use for well over a century. It requires no projection of personality, human–analog relationship, or summing of attitudes. Rather than corralled dyads, our theory of brands is based on the interplay of several essential social forces, institutions, consumers, and aggregations of consumers. This interplay yields social meaning; it yields brands.

Beyond Attitudes

Despite our sincere desire for comity, it is necessary to situate our formulation vis-à-vis the one that has dominated the (marketing) field for so very long: brands as a weighted sum of attributes/beliefs. While an over-reliance on attitude theory and measurement is the proximal problem, the underlying discipline of social psychology (as practiced in consumer research) is rarely very social, at least where brands are concerned. This is a significant problem. To be sure, social psychologists attempt (more or less and occasionally) to account for the influence of others on individual consumers' thoughts and judgments. But this is hardly the same as studying consumer behavior formed and enacted within and by collectives, collectives themselves shaped by social forces, institutions, and other collectives. Brands are socially constructed, socially maintained, and socially altered. So, how can a paradigm that is barely social itself do justice to something so thoroughly social?

Brand attitude work emerged just after WWII. Foundational to post–World War II psychology were promises of early attitude theorists that now seem outlandish (Schramm & Roberts, 1974). For example, psychologists

Cooper and Jahoda (1947) describe social psychology's giddy plan to rid the world of racial bigotry once and for all, really. Regrettably, this did not work out so well. In these halcyon days of psychological essentialism and exuberance, attitude theorists also planned to make short work of human-brand relationships (Martineau, 1957). Just as with racism, this proved a peskier problem than the nascent consumer psychologists imagined. Undaunted, these pioneers soon turned to multiattribute and other attitude models (Fishbein, 1963; Fishbein & Ajzen, 1975). This proved moderately capable of predicting other quasi-behavioral brand measures but still left many unsatisfied.

These days, and really for quite some time, brand managers have talked in terms of qualitative insights and brand meaning. The oft-repeated object lesson of the Coca-Cola Company's confusing attitude assessment of a product with the cultural meaning of a brand is now an MBA legend, as it should be (Hays, 2004; Pendergrast, 2000). Consistent with this is the high demand for consultants and brand experts from anthropology, communications, and sociology (Sunderland & Denny, 2007). On-site brand ethnographies are now more the norm than the exception in many industries. Clearly, there is a need for a meaning-centered social model of brands.

Community as Example

Several years ago, we became interested in applying the notion of community to consumption (Muniz & O'Guinn, 1995, 2001; O'Guinn & Muniz, 2000). Like a handful of others (Fischer, Bristor, & Gainer, 1996; Maffesoli, 1996; Schouten & McAlexander, 1995), we believed we were observing a form of community playing out in the marketplace. We were.

We did not, however, begin our *brand community* research as an ending point. Instead, we intended to use the community construct only as a concrete first example of where core sociological constructs could be applied to marketing and consumer behavior. It was our first example. We never dreamed it would take on the larger life it has. While we remain flattered by the attention, widespread "real world" use (see Figure 7.1), acceptance, and extensions of our brand community idea, we were merely offering an example. Now we wish to contribute to a wider vision and a greater project: a social theory of brands. Our idea of brand community is subsumed within this larger model.

First, what is a brand? A brand is *a vessel of popular meanings*. The reader will no doubt note that we use the term *popular* rather than *commercial* or

FIGURE 7.1
(See color insert.) This Swatch in-store display invokes brand community.

some other narrower mercantile construction. A visit to a contemporary thesaurus shows "popular" as a synonym for "commercial." This of course makes sense in that life inside a consumer culture has erased whatever distinction that once (if ever) existed between these terms. The popular is the commercial; popular culture is commercial culture, consumer culture. Just as the U.S. Supreme Court has acknowledged the struggle to keep political and (popular) commercial speech distinct, we cannot say that California Governor Arnold Schwarzenegger is not a brand or that Ben & Jerry's contains no political meaning.

The Social Model

The basic **components** of our model (see Figure 7.2) are the *marketer,* the *object,* the *individual consumer, consumer collectives,* and *institutions.* The essential **processes** are *accommodation, negotiation, mediated-cultivation, collective memory, polity, rumor,* and *disruption.*

We will walk though the model from left to right. The **marketer** is easily conceived. It is the agent who at one time was thought to own the brand, determine its meaning. While that was never really true, it is certainly not today. Marketers "create" the brand in the sense that they attempt to insert an initial form, message, packaging, position, and platform. The marketer launches the brand and tries to vest it with intended meanings in an attempt to bring about a desired consumer response. Although it probably need not be said again, we will: marketers neither own nor control the brand. They do not create the brand: society does. The marketer is but one part of this social universe.

Even the mighty marketer rarely if ever begins tabula rasa. Marketers are themselves products of social production. Tide is manufactured by Procter & Gamble. Procter & Gamble is itself socially formed by various stakeholders, partners, biases, traditions, cultures, social memory, laws, customs, and real and imagined competitors. Interested and vested others contribute to the birth and launch of brands. Marketers negotiate with engineers, creators, and holders of intellectual property, market researchers, competitors within and beyond the company, an "imagined" market

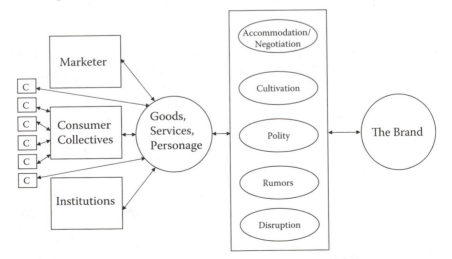

FIGURE 7.2
A social construction model of brands.

for the good or service, etc. For those who have had the opportunity to actually be involved in the launch of a brand you know quite well about all the backstage politics, expectations games, test market results, institutional memory and history, imagined target market, segment and profile, and on and on (Rothenberg, 1994; Stabiner, 1993). All of these processes, and more, are involved in the social production of the brand before it is ever launched. For an excellent discussion of how this played out in the development, introduction, and marketing of the Gatorade brand, see Rovell (2006).

The **object** is just that, the physical thing, the material, the actual good or service, the entity offered to a public.

The **consumer** is the individual actor in the model. This part of the model is where the vast majority of extant brand knowledge resides. It is where consumer research has labored and produced valuable knowledge about how individuals will "process" brand information, advertising and other brand communication, and make judgments and decisions. It is where psychologists have made their legitimate contributions.

Consumer collectives are groups of consumers. These may be face-to-face (such as local car clubs, bowling leagues, user groups). They may be computer mediated (such as on-line communities). They may, many times, exist as imagined (Anderson, 1983) collectives, collectives with a sense of "we-ness" or belonging not requiring any specific action or prescribed behavior, merely a feeling of collective, being a part of a group of like-minded and feeling others. This idea of imagined community was first used by sociologists (Anderson, 1983) to understand how nation states (a relatively new phenomenon in human history) came to be. How can hundreds of millions of people residing in nations covering hundreds or thousands of miles come to actually think of themselves as Americans, Germans, or French? How can people who never meet one another share such a strong sense of identity, something worth dying for? In a clearly more trivial sense, how can millions of users of a brand come to think of themselves as loyal Coke drinkers, Apple computer users, or Volvo types?

> People around the world are today connected to each other by brand-name consumer products as much as by anything else.—Roberto Goizueta, late C.E.O, The Coca-Cola Company (Pendergrast, 2000).

The idea of imagined community is useful here: in brands we sometimes see how admittedly small, but still meaningful, felt affiliations can yield imagined communities of their own, brand communities. Like the late Daniel Boorstin once said, "Nearly all the things we consume become thin, but not negligible bonds with thousands of other Americans." (Boorstin, 1961). Thin, but not negligible bonds: this is an enormously important idea to get across. It is this idea that takes the brand community notion away from those who wish to think of it as only applicable to the marginal consumer:

the interesting, but odd consumer. Here, Boorstin is not speaking of the marginal, but the ordinary, the mundane. So, too, are we when we speak of brand community members in this way. While "lead users" and the truly fanatical are important in their own right (Von Hippel, 1986), most members of brand communities are largely silent members who feel the small tug of these thin but not insignificant ties that bind consumers to their brands. In the mid-range are brands such as Tupperware (see Figure 7.3). Tupperware products were sold via Tupperware parties. A host would invite friends and neighbors to a party to learn about Tupperware products. These parties sold Tupperware but also developed and reinforced bonds among consumers in similar life circumstances.

Brand communities are but one example of consumer aggregations. Consumer tribes (Cova & Cova, 2002), subcultures of consumption (Schouten & McAlexander, 1995), and subcultural communities (Kates, 2004) are other examples. Brand communities, just like other forms of community, possess three defining characteristics: *consciousness of kind, evidence of rituals and traditions*, and a *sense of obligation to the community and its members*. Muniz and O'Guinn (2001) and others (Bagozzi & Dholakia, 2006;

FIGURE 7.3
(See color insert.) Tupperware cofounder Brownie Wise was the force behind one of the first popular brand communities.

Cova & Pace, 2006; Cova, Pace, & Park, 2007; Muniz & Schau, 2005) have extended, refined, and better-specified brand community. These researchers have noted specific dynamics, such as desired marginality and member legitimacy, and the use of specialized forms of brand creation, such as community activism and consumer-generated media content (Etgar, 2008; Muniz & Schau, 2007). While extant academic research has documented 50 or so brand communities, we have individually been contacted by, or otherwise been made aware of, a couple hundred other marketers' efforts to build and/or manage brand community (see Figure 7.4). These extend from major software brands to traditional CPG brands.

Institutions including, but not limited to, media, retailers, equity markets, government, and NGOs also play a role in brand creation. These institutions bring the weight of economics, norms, practice, sanctions, regulations, even law to the ongoing creation of brands. The media, for example, determine what raw materials and modes of meaning creation (e.g., television advertisements, Web pages, branded entertainment, and consumer-generated content) will be available. They determine, as institutions, what demographics can be reached during a certain day-part for a given cost per thousand of eyeballs delivered.

Institutions not only define the channels of communication opportunity, but also what is not possible, what audiences cannot be delivered for a certain brand for a given price (see Figure 7.5). Television is bought in the "up-fronts" in a highly institutionalized manner ... about $10 billion a year in the United States alone. The parameters of those institutions, their rules, their highly ritualized procedures, their lists of possible and impossible have a significant impact on what a brand comes to mean. The types of programs available are themselves a product of deeply embedded group

Scion Seeks Community in New Campaign

by Aaron Baar, Monday, Jul 28, 2008 5:00 AM ET

After five years of selling itself as a car that can reflect one's individuality, Scion is looking to celebrate its community of individual owners via a new marketing campaign that showcases how owners come together via their customized vehicles.

"Five years ago, when we started, we were all about personalization," Dawn Ahmed, corporate manager for Scion, tells *Marketing Daily*. "One of the things that surprised us was how quickly people took ownership of our brand and the passion they have for it."

FIGURE 7.4
The Scion brand has been developed in large part via community-building efforts.

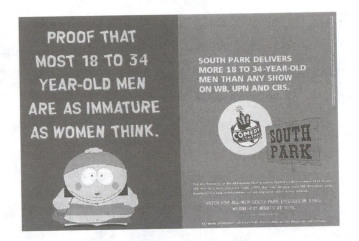

FIGURE 7.5
(See color insert.) Here, the producers of *South Park* appeal in the trade press to media buyers with the promise that their show can effectively deliver a valuable demographic.

and cultural processes. For example, the 2007–2008 television season witnessed a pronounced thematic shift, with networks moving way from longtime trusted genres featuring doctors, cops, and lawyers to shows featuring distinctly spiritual and supernatural themes. Most observers agreed that this shift represented a culturally driven desire for fantasy and escapism. As one network programming director noted, "The real world has become such a horrendous place that people are looking for magic to avoid the tragic" (Brill quoted in Elliott, 2007, p. 5). If you need further examples we suggest you pick up *Brandweek*, *Ad Age*, or even a newspaper. We have all but forgotten the production side of consumer research. Again, this is where the sociological approach, rich in a tradition of both production and consumption, can contribute.

The list of institutions goes on and on. Obviously retailers with their own rules, traditions, histories, trade organizations, lawyers, and lobbyists significantly participate in the creation of brands. The near-byzantine structure of retail space negotiation has an enormous impact on what a brand comes to signify through its display in public space or the denial of same. Some retailers such as Nike and Ikea actually create *brandscapes* (Sherry, 2005) in which consumers may actively participate with the brand in an almost museum or amusement park type space. Governmental agencies significantly restrict what a brand can mean. They may bring formal legal action when a company produces what is deemed as an inappropriate meaning. Assumptions and estimates of the likelihood of greater regulation, possible class action law suits, and more

FIGURE 7.6

(See color insert.) Repositioning with significant institutional involvement.

restrictive public policy serve to frame the positioning or repositioning of many brands.

The very repositioned Camel cigarette brand of the 1990s is a prime example—from "old outdoor guy" brand to hip and young "Joe Camel" (see Figure 7.6). The "true" goal of the brand's parent, RJR, generated a great deal of speculation. The ad campaign was implicated in bringing about an avalanche of brand advertising regulation ... far beyond tobacco. Some believe it helped freeze cigarette market share, after a big gain by Camel against its number one competitor Marlboro. The ads demonstrate a repositioning that had enormous institutional antecedents and consequences. The presumed action of a major competitor, consumers, collectives of consumers, populations deemed "at risk," numerous state, local, federal, and international governments, NGOs and others all led to the social construction of the new Camel.

The mere presence of regulations and the institutions charged with creating, modifying, and imposing those regulations make a significant impact on what meanings are allowed for a brand and which are not. Likewise, nongovernmental organizations (NGOs) exert a force in the social construction of brands. Brands sanctioned by the Environmental Defense Fund (Federal Express) or the Sierra Club (Clorox) mean something different than those without this blessing.

Processes that act to form brands include the following activities.

Accommodation is a process through which the marketer's intended meaning is given some degree of acceptance by consumers. Consumers typically accommodate some, but not all, of the marketer's desired meaning. The term *accommodation* explicitly acknowledges that some of the marketer's meaning will likely remain (Anderson & Meyer, 1989).

Negotiation refers to a social process in which actors actively "bargain" for something—in this case what the brand means and to whom it belongs. This happens with all brands, but at any given moment in the life of a brand, the meaning of that brand might be closer to the preferred meaning of the marketer or the consumer. Famous instances of brand "hijacks" or "appropriations" by consumers are plentiful in the brand literature (Holt, 2004; Wipperfurth, 2005). However, any one of the other social actors may negotiate as well. Consumer actions took Doc Martins from geriatric gardening shoe to .alt footwear. Did marketers then react and (re)negotiate the meaning with consumers? Sure. In a similar fashion, urban consumers enabled Tommy Hilfiger's metamorphosis from preppy country club attire to hip-hop wear (Gladwell, 1997). Tommy Hilfiger then appeared to softly leverage those associations in marketing to the mainstream. That is accommodation and negotiation at work.

The condom category provides another example. During the early days of the AIDS epidemic, the Reagan administration brought to bear considerable regulatory pressure as to just when, where, where not, and how condoms could be advertised. Here, the government played a role in meaning negotiation by delimiting potential ad space. Certainly these actions made the product taboo at some level. On the other side of the equation, actions by manufacturers further constrained potential ad space and contributed to meaning. Supposedly, some condom brands had a policy not to buy ads in any gay periodicals for fear of becoming the "gay condom." Here, manufacturers were aware of the meaning of particular publications would foster via their association with a brand. Consumers, marketers, and institutions negotiated the social space and meaning of the category, and certain brands.

This trajectory was similar to that of CPG manufacturers who did not use blacks in their ads until the mid-1960s for fear of being the unofficial black detergent or soap (Chambers, 2007; Fox, 1984). Similarly, Coca-Cola and Pepsi have very different brand mythologies where race is concerned in the southern United States (Pendergrast, 2000; Smithsonian Oral History Archives). Even in the cobranding world of social causes, we once heard a Fortune 500 company assert that it could not/would not cobrand with the struggle against breast cancer "because everyone knows that American Express owns that space." The struggle for brand ownership has become even more contested in the contemporary world with consumer-generated content and computer-mediated environments. Who owns the brand is more than a rhetorical question.

COOL CUSTOMERS

More often than not, as O'Guinn and Muniz underscore with their Social Construction Model of Brands, a line from a marketing plan to a brand's meaning in the real world is curved rather than straight. A marketer's intentions may even seem unrecognizable when compared with a product's reputation as it is created through the seven sociological processes the authors identify. In one famous example, the Tommy Hilfiger brand has traveled the road from upper-crust sportswear to favored hip-hop gear through the processes of negotiation and accommodation.

Preppy Hilfiger's move into the upper echelons of the lucrative urban market in the late 1990s was so surprising that even venerable, straight-laced news outlets like *The New York Times* and *PBS* took notice. Writing in *The New Yorker* (March 17, 1997), Malcolm Gladwell cited Hilfiger as he addressed what he called the "cool-hunt"—companies' quest to reach favored status in youth markets. Gladwell pointed out how Hilfiger had successfully taken hold of its unintentionally budding urban market. That popularity, spurred, among other things, by the unsolicited endorsements of rap superstars like Snoop Doggy Dogg, was then turned into a broader selling point for its brand.

Unlike consumer hijacking, wherein a brand's meaning is appropriated by its consumers, the process of negotiation allows for consumers to adopt a brand and for marketers to accommodate and build on those new brand meanings. Hilfiger might have found its name plastered across the stars of MTV unwittingly, but the company quickly spotted the market potential of that development. In a smart move for this iconic brand, Hilfiger sought further celebrity endorsements and reached out to both its new urban adopters and to their core audience of suburban consumers. Still wearing Hilfiger, these seemingly square customers now hoped, instead of country-club cred, to catch some of the rappers' cool.

R.D.M. & L.W.P.

Consider the Sharpie brand of felt tip pens. A series of Sharpie brand communities have formed online, completely independent of managerial action. Members of these collectives assert their ownership by creating elaborate videos of Sharpies in use. Some of these videos resemble advertisements, building on official campaign taglines such as "Write Out Loud." Others offer testimony of their creators' creative prowess by documenting the creation of Sharpie works of art, such as portraits and giant collages. Further asserting their ownership (and illustrating the contested nature of brands), these collectives have largely resisted management entre and involvement.

Brand *communities* often assert negotiating power. Because they are a social structure they can exert the force of many. In their study of brand communities, Muniz and O'Guinn (2001) commented on the *desired marginality* often sought for communal brands. Here, brand community members actively try to keep the community ethos one of marginality. A brand like Apple, with an approximate 7% share of the U.S. computer market, has marginality as part of its core brand meaning. It thrives on being the underdog (Kahney, 2004). Thus, some brand community members actively work against market share growth, or at least the perception of growth. These communities must walk a tricky path between rejecting willing new members and sustaining a large enough market share to keep the brand viable. If the brand gains too much market share or becomes too mainstream then cultural cachet is lost and the brand is no longer as desirable. Here, the boundaries of community and brand are upheld by the collective. By enforcing community standards of *legitimacy*, or who is and who is not a proper owner/user, they ensure marginality. It is also true that if a brand manager violates the essential meaning of the brand, as held by the brand community, the blogosphere can light up in protest within hours.

Cultivation is another process of social construction. O'Guinn and Shrum (1997) demonstrated that goods and services frequently used in television programming are seen by those who watch more television as systematically more plentiful in the social world. That is, consumption life on television helps cultivate a similar world in the minds of those who watch television. This is one reason that branded entertainment is so popular at this time. A significant process in the social construction of brands is those brands' appearance within programming content. They become part of mental representations shared by viewing audiences as representing what other people have and use in their daily lives. Given how much television the average person watches, and the branded plentitude found in contemporary programming content, not to mention the ads between the programs, brand meaning can be significantly constructed through what viewers believe about the social world as delivered to them via television, films, and other mediated content.

Consider Gatorade. The brand is nearly omnipresent on professional sport sidelines. Owing to this saturation, Gatorade is frequently displayed during NFL game broadcasts, even when it is absent in purchased ad time. During the February 2005 broadcast of Superbowl XXXIX, the Gatorade logo was displayed for a total of 6:58 min (Rovell, 2006). Given the worldwide viewership of the event, Nielsen's Sports Sponsorship Scorecard

FIGURE 7.7
The "black power" statement appropriated as "cold power."

estimated that the brand had received more than 590 million impressions (Rovell, 2006).

Polity: Brands and politics were never complete strangers. In the United States, brands have an entanglement with politics that goes to our very founding. The politics of goods and their "branding" was hardly absent in the American Revolution (Axtell, 1999). As several historians have noted, this merging of brand and polity has only accelerated, particularly since the end of World War II (Cohen, 2000). It hit its stride in the cultural revolution of the 1960s, revolution that was very much about the "establishment," material existence, and stuff, including brands. It is here, as Frank (1997) and others have noted, that the revolution paradoxically became about what (brands) you bought, not whether or not you bought. In other words, the nature of making a political statement via consumption choices shifted from not consuming (boycotting) to carefully discriminating among brands and the meaning they evinced. Consider Figure 7.7. In 1968 (a summer of significant racial tension), the then familiar "black power" statement appears oddly appropriated as "cold power." Given that African Americans had only within that decade begun to regularly appear in "mainstream" (white) mass market advertising the headline looks very much like a political appropriation. Today, it is easy to point to a slew of brands that have been overtly politicized (see Crockett & Wallendorf, 2004; Loken & Roedder John, Chapter 11, this volume). Try driving into Santa Cruz, California, in a Hummer and asking where the Wal-Mart is.

Some "revolutionaries" now strike blows against the capitalist empire by buying things (Frank, 1997; Heath & Potter, 2004). As paradoxical as this seems (is), these brands of revolution have been granted community approval. In the new sociopolitical order, revolutionary politics are enacted not through choices of consuming or not consuming, but in identification, group sanctioning, and community championing of brands that are deemed by the collective to be the best vessels of the group's "alternative" politics. Such social processes can be seen in such brands as American Apparel, Apple, Ben & Jerry's, Carhart, Diesel, MAC, REI, The Body Shop, and Tom's of Maine.

Recently, more actively marketer-politicized brands have emerged on the scene. Two examples of this are SweatX clothes and BlackSpot sneakers. SweatX is an anti-sweatshop brand. It is strongly supported by an online brand community. In fact, without the associated collective, it would have far less market meaning and potency. However, the most controversial polit-brand is the so-called "antibrand brand," BlackSpot, by AdBusters, an ostensibly antiadvertising and anticonsumer culture magazine. AdBusters is marketing the BlackSpot to its members (themselves a form of brand community) to challenge a particularly chaotically politicized brand, Nike.

> We're selling real, authentic empowerment. If you wear the BlackSpot sneaker, you're helping to demolish a big, bad corporation [Nike] that has done dirty deeds in the Third World. —Adbuster Publisher Kalle Lasn

By targeting Nike, BlackSpot further complicates the politics of Nike, polarizing both supporter and detractor communities. Very clearly, brands, politics, and national ideology intersect. Politics help give meaning to the contemporary brand.

Rumors play an important role in the social construction of the brand as rumors allow the community to express properties of the brand that might not be true but reflect what the community *wants* to be true. Rumors surrounded the reintroduction of the new VW Beetle in 1997 as community members looked for reasons to be optimistic that the New Beetle would honor its roots (Muniz, O'Guinn, & Fine, 2005). As a result, rumors about the new model, including the use of the original plans and the rehiring of retired designers, were rife in the months leading up to the launch of the New Beetle. Long-time community members wanted to believe that the New Beetle would be true to the ethos of the original, despite fearing otherwise. The belief that the New Beetle had become a "chick" car or a gay car gave additional meaning to the brand. In a similar way, members of the Apple brand community spent considerable time discussing the introduction of the iPhone as community members looked for evidence that the device would revolutionize the smartphone the same way the iPod revolutionized personal MP3 players. We have observed several instances where rumors of an impending line-extension or repositioning have caused sufficient push-back from brand loyalists to get companies to either reconsider or outright abandon their plans. We have seen this in both the consumer electronics and automotive categories.

The brand world is inherently self-reflexive and rumors usually reach the marketer. That is, the social construction of a brand is full of feedback loops and recursive action. Marketers are immersed in feedback from consumers through market research, consumer-generated content, brand blogs, online brand community chatter, etc. They react to one another and perceptions of one another. They "imagine" each other. Consumers perceive the "schemer schema" (Wright, 1986) or the persuasive intent of the brand and beyond. They form ideas as to what the marketer is trying to do with a brand. Sometimes they reject that view altogether, other times they embrace it, but they always have some reaction. They always leave their mark, their fingerprints, on the brand. Consumers are very aware of changes made to their brands and the marketer-preferred meaning, just as they are to the meaning ascribed by social collectives who "appropriate" or "hijack" the brand for their own purposes. In fact, all the institutions and social actors in our model play this role and respond to others in building the meaning of the brand.

Manjoo (2008) provides some excellent examples of how this plays out in the Apple and Windows' brand communities. He relates the experiences of technology reviewers David Pogue (*New York Times*) and Walt Mossberg (*Wall Street Journal*). Both strive for balanced, nonbiased reviews, yet both are routinely taken to task by brand fans for what they perceive to be biased reviews. For example, Pogue once wrote a detailed review of the Windows Vista operating system. Manjoo (2008) notes that the review was generally positive toward both Windows (he found several things to like about it) and Apple (he also noted that several of Vista's innovations had been standard for many years in the Mac OS). Despite such strident attempts at reason and balance, members of both communities saw systematic biases against their OS of choice in the review. "The Mac people saw it as a rave review for Windows Vista," while the Windows folks, focusing on two minor criticisms, "saw it as a vicious slam on Windows" (Pogue, quoted in Manjoo, 2008, p. 160). Mossberg suggests such disproportionate reactions reflect "the Doctrine of Insufficient Adulation" (Mossberg, quoted in Manjoo, 2008, p. 161). It appears that consumer collectives, comprised of a chorus of similarly voiced devotees, creates an understanding of reality that has little room for criticisms from outsiders.

Disruption is a process in which there is a perceptible break in social continuity. This occurs in times of change in a society's circumstance, economics, demography, or along some other social dimension. An early modern historical example is Ivory soap. Ivory along with two or three other major competitors were leaders in turning commodities into the modern CPG industry. When Ivory staked out the "purity space" it was leveraging a major social disruption. Urban modernity had brought enormous disruption to American society—a period of massive in-migration, movement to cities, and widespread changes in social character and norms of behavior, not to mention personal hygiene and daily practices of living.

The average life expectancy in the United States in 1900 was 49.2 years (Sullivan, 1926). Infant mortality was twice what it would be just 25 years later (Sullivan, 1926). A concerned public pushed Congress to pass the

FIGURE 7.1
This Swatch in-store display invokes brand community.

FIGURE 7.3
Tupperware cofounder Brownie Wise was the force behind one of the first popular brand communities.

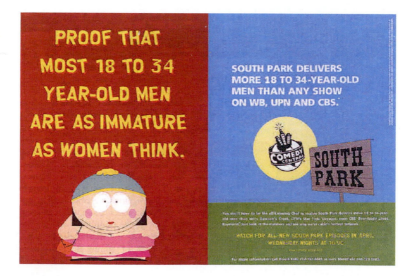

FIGURE 7.5
Here, the producers of *South Park* appeal in the trade press to media buyers with the promise that their show can effectively deliver a valuable demographic.

FIGURE 7.6
Repositioning with significant institutional involvement.

FIGURE 7.8
Virginia Slims came to much of its meaning by its resonance with the second wave of American feminism.

Open House...Have a Coke

...there's nothing like the friendly pause

After school is the happy time when young folks like to get together to discuss "what's new" and pass the time of day. And to add to the fun, of course, there's nothing like frosty bottles of sparkling Coca-Cola. Yes, when Sue or Sal says "Come over and *Have a Coke*" —that's the high-sign for *the pause that refreshes*. It's the simplest, friendliest way in all the world to say, *You're welcome, folks*, to one and all.

Coke = Coca-Cola

"Coca-Cola" and its abbreviation "Coke" are the registered trade-marks which distinguish the product of Coca-Cola Ltd.

Serve
Coca-Cola
at home

FIGURE 7.10
Coke insinuates itself into social gatherings.

Pure Food and Drug Act in 1906. Purity was more than a word; it was, at that time, one of the few things the public believed might prevent them or their children from dying young. So, Ivory floats. Its purity was demonstrated by a market logic. No one really had to understand the physical mechanism relating purity to floating; it became a marketplace myth. Social context gave meaning to Ivory's branding, its advertising claim, its marketplace logic, and the meaning of a bar of soap that floated. Ivory *meant* something. It was pure, "ninety-nine and forty-four one hundredths percent pure." Ivory was no longer a commodity; its set of acceptable substitutes shriveled. The same was true of countless other branded goods and services.

Likewise, many other brands leveraged social disruption and took meaning from them (also see Torelli & Keh, Chapter 6, this volume). Virginia Slims came to much of its meaning by the marketers and all the other interested parties' resonance with the second wave of American feminism (see Figure 7.8). The brand's social construction was part Philip Morris's and part cultural resonance. Similarly, Gatorade's "Be Like Mike" campaign (centered on NBA icon Michael Jordan) is widely regarded as one of the most successful uses of a sports celebrity endorser (Rovell, 2006). Here, the brand's social construction was part Gatorade (a brand with an already powerful history), part Michael Jordan (the world's greatest athlete was making more in endorsements than he was as a basketball player), and part of the cultural resonance of the two.

Other times, a brand came to its meaning through a largely consumer-oriented response or resonance, which in turn, was then appropriated from the consumer collective. Holt (2004) provides other examples, such as Mountain Dew going from a Hillbilly NASCAR Belt brand to the official brand of Gen-X skateboard dudes. What consumers create is then often called "insight" by

FIGURE 7.8
(See color insert.) Virginia Slims came to much of its meaning by its resonance with the second wave of American feminism.

brand managers and then the brand is officially repositioned. Brand managers may react to culturally resonant consumer appropriations of brands and then call them their own. Rather than purely random, these consumer appropriations and marketer reappropriations work because they can function as channel markers in the shifting social currents.

Suggestions on Method

In the model just outlined above we call for a new approach, or at least a different one, to the study and theorizing of brands. We fully admit that our model is bare bones and a first attempt. We believe we have put the essentials in place.

In terms of method we make a few suggestions. First, we believe brands could and should be studied in a near-endless number of ways. We are big believers in multimethod approaches. We make a plea for history because we honestly don't know how you ever understand a brand apart from its history. We hope that those trained and experienced in historical method will apply themselves to the study of brands. At a minimum, we hope that a historical consciousness informs brand research going forward. We also firmly believe that ethnographic work is critical. Absent social meaning, we don't think there is a brand. We also believe that social network and community research on and off the Internet remains vital. We believe that textual, rhetorical, and visual-based work on brands is vital. We encourage those who work in reader response, textual analysis, and semiotics to work in the branding area. Finally, we encourage demographers and other quantitative sociologists to bring their tools to bear on the social construction of brands.

Conclusion

In the late 19th century, brands replaced many unmarked commodities. While it is true that there were some branded products prior to this period, it is during the last two decades of the nineteenth century that the ubiquitous branding we know today began. Between 1875 and 1900, thousands of branded products replaced unbranded commodities. The phenomenal growth first took place in package goods. Soap, previously sold by weight from a generally unbranded cake, becomes Ivory (1882) and Sapolio (circa 1875). Beer, previously drawn from an unnamed keg, becomes Budweiser (1891) and Pabst (1873). All across the spectrum of goods and services, existing commodities became brands, as did the flood of new things designed for the modern marketplace of 1900.

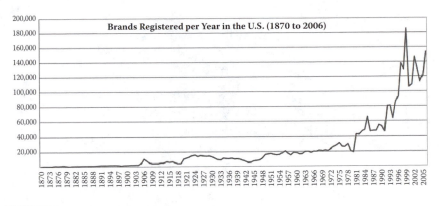

FIGURE 7.9
Brand registrations increased dramatically in the last part of the 20th century.

To most scholars, it is absolutely axiomatic that there is no such thing as just a thing. To sociologists, anthropologists, and many more, all material objects carry with them meaning—even the ones grossly mislabeled as "utilitarian." This point has been made too many times by too many celebrated scholars (Goody, 1993; Sahlins, 1972; Schudson, 1984) to belabor it here, although it does apparently need saying in contemporary consumer behavior. The entire human record consists of no place where materiality, social construction, and meaning are strangers. Goods have always had social meaning. The same holds true for *branded* goods. How could they not?

During the last years of the nineteenth and the first two decades of the twentieth century, branding exploded (see Figure 7.9). Advertising and branding pushed marketplace modernity along; they were its engines, its mode. Over the next eight or so decades, the branding tide rose to cover just about everything.

By the end of the twentieth century, religious sects publically discussed branding (Jones, 2003), as did universities, cities, and national parks (Twitchell, 2004). Even dirt and water are now branded. Brands came to be important in the lives of citizens. Citizens became consumers.

It is time to see brands as more than summed attributes floating in preference factor space. They may be that,

$$\text{Coke attitude} = \Sigma a_i b_i$$

where:

$$a_1 = \text{sweet } a_2 = \text{fizzy etc.}$$

but they are a whole lot more (see Figure 7.10).

We need to see them as vessels of meaning. Brands have co-mingled with or substantially emulated the form and function of traditional social institutions. In this chapter we argue that we must significantly rethink

Open House...Have a Coke

. . . *there's nothing like the friendly pause*

FIGURE 7.10
(See color insert.) Coke insinuates itself into social gatherings.

our views of brands and the singular obsession with the individual consumer and his or her thoughts. Contemporary society floats on a true
sea-change in mediated human communication that makes it easier for
consumers to exchange information and organize. Brands are social creations, and this reality has never been more important. Brands are not
just names of things, but increasingly an important part of the social fabric and centers of social organization. Our models, our thinking, and our
practice need to catch up with this reality.

References

Anderson, B. (1983). *Imagined community*, London: Verso.

Anderson, C. (2006). *The long tail: Why the future of business is selling less of more.*
New York: Hyperion.

Anderson, J.A., & Meyer T.P. (1989). *Mediated communication: A social interaction
perspective*. Newbury Park, CA: Sage.

Axtell, J. (1999). The first consumer revolution. In L.B. Glickman (Ed.), *Consumer
society in American history: A reader*. Ithaca, NY: Cornell University Press.

Bagozzi, R.P., & Dholakia, U.M. (2006). Antecedents and purchase consequences
of customer participation in small group brand communities. *International
Journal of Research in Marketing, 23* (March), 45–61.

Boorstin, D.J. (1961). *The image: A guide to pseudo-events in America*. New York: Antheum.

Chambers, J. (2007). *Madison Avenue and the color line: African Americans in the advertising industry*. Philadelphia: University of Pennsylvania Press.

Cohen, L. (2000). From town center to shopping center: The reconfiguration of community marketplaces in postwar America. In J. Scanlon (Ed.), *The gender and consumer culture reader*. New York: New York University Press, 243–266.

Cooper, E. & Jahoda, M. (1947). The evasion of propaganda: How prejudiced people respond to anti-prejudice propaganda. *Journal of Psychology* , 23, 15–25.

Cova, B. & Cova, V. (2002). Tribal marketing: The tribalisation of society and its impact on the conduct of marketing. *European Journal of Marketing, 36 (5)*, 595–520.

Cova, B. & Pace, S. (2006). Brand community of convenience products: New forms of customer empowerment—the case of my Nutella The Community. *European Journal of Marketing, 40 (9–10)*, 1087–1105.

Cova, B., Pace, S., & Park, J.D. (2007). Global brand communities across borders: The Warhammer case. *International Marketing Review. 24 (3)*, 313–329.

Crockett, D. & Wallendorf, M. (2004). The role of normative political ideology in consumer behavior. *Journal of Consumer Research. 31 (3)*, 511–528.

Elliott, S. (2007, May 21). In a time of high anxiety, a sedative of the occult. *The New York Times*, p. C5.

Etgar, M. (2008). A descriptive model of the consumer co-production process. *Journal of the Academy of Marketing Science, 36* (March), 97–108.

Fischer, E., Bristor, J., & Gainer, B. (1996). Creating or escaping community? An exploratory study of internet consumers' behaviors. In *Advances in consumer research* (Vol. 23). Provo, UT: Association for Consumer Research, 178–182.

Fishbein, M. (1963). An investigation of the relationships between beliefs about an object and the attitude toward that object. *Human Relations, 16 (3)*, 233–239.

Fishbein, M., & Ajzen, I. (1975). *Belief, attitude, intention, and behavior: An introduction to theory and research*. Reading, MA: Addison-Wesley.

Fox, S. (1984). *The mirror makers: A history of American advertising and its creators*. New York: Vintage.

Frank, T. (1997). *The conquest of cool: Business culture, counterculture, and the rise of hip consumerism*. Chicago: University of Chicago Press.

Gladwell, M. (1997, March 17). The coolhunt. *The New Yorker,* pp. 78–88.

Halberstam, D. (1993). *The fifties*, New York: Fawcett.

Hays, C.L. (2004). *The real thing: Truth and power at the Coca-Cola Company*. New York: Random House.

Heath, J., & Potter, A. (2004). *Nation of rebels: Why counterculture became consumer culture*. New York: Harper Collins.

Holt, D.B. (2004). *How brands become icons: The principles of cultural branding*. Cambridge, MA: Harvard Business School Publishing.

Jones, M.C. (2003). Case study—Religion: A is for Alpha, C is for Christ. *Brand Strategy, 176* (October), 23.

Kahney, L. (2004). *The cult of Mac*. San Francisco: No Starch.

Kates, S.M. (2004). The dynamics of brand legitimacy: An interpretive study in the gay men's community. *Journal of Consumer Research, 31 (2)*, 455–464.

Maffesoli, M. (1996). *The time of the tribes: The decline of individualism in mass society.* Thousand Oaks, CA: Sage.

Martineau, P. (1957). *Motivation in advertising.* New York: McGraw Hill.

McCloskey, D.N. (2006). *The bourgeois virtues: Ethics for an age of commerce.* Chicago: University of Chicago Press.

Muniz, A.M., Jr., & O'Guinn, T.C. (1995). Brand community and the sociology of brands. Paper presented at Association for Consumer Research Annual Conference. Minneapolis, MN.

Muniz, A.M., Jr., & O'Guinn, T.C. (2001). Brand community. *Journal of Consumer Research, 27(4)* (March), 412–431.

Muniz, A.M., Jr., O'Guinn, T.C., & Fine, G.A. (2005). Rumor in brand community. In *Advances in theory & methodology in social & organizational psychology: A tribute to Ralph Rosnow.* Mahwah, NJ: Lawrence Erlbaum Associates.

Muniz, A.M., Jr., & Schau, H.J. (2005). Religiosity in the abandoned Apple Newton brand community. *Journal of Consumer Research, 31:4,* 737–747.

Muniz, A.M. Jr., & Schau, H.J. (2007). Vigilante marketing and consumer created communications. *Journal of Advertising, 36(3),* 35-50

O'Guinn, T.C., & Muniz, A.M., Jr. (2004). The polit-brand and blows against the empire. Paper presented at Association for Consumer Research Annual Conference. Toronto, ON.

O'Guinn, T.C., & Shrum, L.J. (1997). The role of television in the construction of consumer reality. *Journal of Consumer Research* (March), 278–294.

Pendergrast, M. (1993). *For God, country, and Coca-Cola: The unauthorized history of the great American soft drink and the company that makes it.* New York: Scribner.

Putnam, R.D. (2000). *Bowling alone: The collapse and revival of American community.* New York: Simon & Schuster.

Rockwood, T.H, Sangster, R.L., & Dillman, D.A. (1997). The effect of response categories on questionnaire answers: Context and mode effects. *Sociological Methods of Research, 26 (1),* 188–140.

Rothenberg, R. (1994). *Where the suckers moon: An advertising story.* New York: Alfred A. Knopf.

Rovell, D. (2006). *First in thirst: How Gatorade turned the science of sweat into a cultural phenomenon.* New York: AMACOM.

Sahlins, M. (1972). The first affluent society. In Marshall Sahlins (Ed.), *Stone Age economics.* Chicago: Aldine.

Schouten, J.W., & McAlexander, J. (1995). Subcultures of consumption: An ethnography of the new bikers. *Journal of Consumer Research, 22* (June), 43–61.

Schramm, W., & Roberts, D.F. (1971). *The process and effects of mass communication.* Urbana, IL: University of Illinois Press.

Schudson, M. (1984). *Advertising, The uneasy persuasion.* New York: Basic Books, 129–146.

Sherry, J.F., Jr. (2005). Brand meaning. In A.M. Tybout & T. Calkins (Eds.), *Kellogg on branding: The Marketing Faculty of the Kellogg School of Management.* New York: Wiley, 40–69.

Shirky, C. (2008), *Here comes everybody: The power of organizing without organizations.* New York: Penguin Press.

Simmel, G. (1981) [1904]. Fashion. In G.B. Proles (Ed.), *Perspective on fashion.* Minneapolis, MN: Burgess, 130–155.

Sullivan, M. (1926). Immense Decrease in the Death Rate. In R. Rhodes (Ed.), *Visions of technology: A century of debate about machines, systems and the human world*. New York: Touchstone, 88–89.

Sunderland, P.L., & Denny, R.M. (2007). *Doing anthropology in consumer research*. New York: Left Coast Press.

Thompson, C.J., & Coskuner-Balli, G. (2007). Countervailing market responses to corporate co-optation and the ideological recruitment of consumption communities. *Journal of Consumer Research, 34 (2)*, 135.

Twitchell, J.B. (2004). *Branded nation: The marketing of Megachurch, College Inc., and Museumworld*. New York: Simon & Schuster.

Von Hippel, E. (1986). Lead users: A source of novel product concepts. *Management Science, 32* (July), 791–805.

Wipperfurth, A. (2005). Brand hijack. New York: Portfolio.

Wright, P. (1986). Schemer schema: Consumers' intuitive theories about marketers influence tactics. *Advances in Consumer Research, 13*, 1–3.

Section IV

New Directions in Measurement of Brand Equity

8

Measuring Brand Equity: The Marketing Surplus and Efficiency (MARKSURE)-Based Brand Equity*

C. Whan Park
University of Southern California

Deborah J. MacInnis
University of Southern California

Xavier Drèze
University of Pennsylvania

Jonathan Lee
California State University

Introduction

The equity associated with brands has been identified as one of the most powerful intangible assets driving corporate value (others include investments in R & D, patents, databases, human capital, software development ([Lev, 2001]). Some suggest that brands represent large assets with approximately 40% of the market value of firms (Barth, Clement, Foster, & Kasznik, 1998). In fact, the brand may be regarded as the fifth major business resource following human resources, goods, money, and information. The concept of brand equity has thus been of interest to marketing academics and practitioners alike (Aaker, 1991; Farquhar, 1989; Keller, 1993; MSI, 1999; Park, Jaworski, & MacInnis, 1987). An issue of considerable relevance concerns how brand equity should be defined and measured. This issue is critical in two ways.

First, a valid measure of brand equity would enable an *assessment of a firm's brand on its balance sheet*, particularly if it were theoretically based and consistent with accounting standards. In accounting, the development of

* The authors gratefully acknowledge valuable comments offered by Professor K.R. Subramanyam at Marshall School of Business, University of Southern California.

a measure suitable for disclosure on a balance sheet is stymied by what accounting academics regard as problematic treatment of intangible assets like brands in accounting practice (Barth et al., 1998). Unlike the practice of some countries (e.g., Canada, Japan, Australia, France, and the United Kingdom), the U.S. Financial Accounting Standards Board (FASB) has historically viewed the estimation of intangible assets like brands as unreliable (Barth et al., 1998). As such, generally accepted accounting principles (or GAAP), dictate that only externally acquired (versus internally developed) brands are recognized as assets and amortized against net income over the brand's estimated useful life (which cannot exceed 40 years). The failure to include the value of internally developed brands in standard financial statements renders accounting information in financial reports misleading, and results in a severe underestimation in the asset valuation of firms and excessive cost of capital, hindering business investment and growth (Lev, 2001).

Second, measuring brand equity is critical for purposes of assessing the performance of the brand's marketing activities. Measuring brand equity can provide useful information regarding the effectiveness of marketing decisions. Brand equity measures can also be used to track the brand's health compared to that of competitors and over time. Indeed, a marketing-relevant brand equity measure that is not confounded with nonmarketing factors would be highly useful for monitoring the brand's health and the effectiveness of the marketing strategy that drives it. Understanding the factors that drive brand equity could also provide insight into decisions that must be altered or monitored so as to enhance equity.

The concept of "brand equity" has been defined and measured in a number of ways. As such, it is helpful to explore several conceptual issues concerning the construct before addressing its measurement. These issues are described below. We then develop an alternative perspective on the construct and its measurement. This alternate perspective, termed marketing surplus and efficiency (or MARKSURE) metric, takes a specific stance on each of these issues. We discuss several operational issues regarding this alternative view. Finally, we describe the limitations and the boundary conditions for this alternative perspective on brand equity assessment.

Perspectives on Brand Equity

Table 8.1 reviews a set of different perspectives on the meaning and measurement of brand equity. The diversity of meaning and measurement

TABLE 8.1

Review of Existing Measures of Brand Equity (BE)

Perspectives	Customer Based		Performance Outcome Based			Financial Marketplace Based	A Brand Holder's Perspective
Authors	Park & Srinivasan (1994)	Kamakura & Russell (1993)	Swait et al. (1993)	Ailawadi et al. (2003)	Interbrand	Simon & Sullivan (1993)	MARKSURE model
View of BE	Added value endowed by a brand as perceived by a consumer	Component of the brand's value that cannot be directly attributed to its physical features	Equalization price (EP), which equates the utility of a brand with the utility of a brand in a market with no brand differentiation	Revenue premium of the brand compared to a private label brand	Excess of the brand's estimated after-tax profits over the generic after-tax profits multiplied by brand strength	Intangible asset that is the fraction of firm's replacement value	Value of a brand is determined by considering both customers' input (i.e., sales revenue) and the firm's input (i.e., marketing costs)
Sources of data used to compute the BE measure	Every survey and consumer survey	Single-source scanner panel	Discrete choice experiment	Store-level scanner data	Financial statement and brand strength multiplier	Stock price and compustat financial statement	A firm's internal accounting data

TABLE 8.1 (continued)

Review of Existing Measures of Brand Equity (BE)

Perspectives	Customer Based		Performance Outcome Based			Financial Marketplace Based	A Brand Holder's Perspective
Determinants of BE	Difference between consumer's overall preference and objective multi-attribute preference	Brand intangible value created by brand name associations and perceptual distortions	Brand name, product attributes, brand image, consumer heterogeneity, and usage	Own marketing mix/price; competitor mix/price; category characteristics; firm strength (e.g., image, R & D capabilities)	Net brand-related profits and brand strength	Current and past advertising; advertising share; brand age; order of entry	Marketing surplus (TRt. TMCt) and marketing efficiency (1-(TMCt / TRt))
Nature of input data	Non-attribute-based and attribute-based	Remainder of brand value after accounting for price and advertising	Price of a brand, total utility of a brand, and price coefficient	Volume of brand; price of brand; volume of private label; price of private label	Operating income of a brand and a generic brand, a brand strength multiplier	Demand enhancing components; cost-reducing components	Price and the quantity sold at the intermediary level (wholesale or retail) and all the itemized marketing costs

Referent	Mean equity scaled to zero	Mean equity scaled to zero	Brand in a market with no product differentiation	Private label brand	Generic brand	Unbranded product	No referent
BE Estimation	BE = non-attribute-based + attribute-based component	Brand value = intangible value (BE) + tangible value	EP = price – (total brand utility of consumer + price coefficient)	BE = revenue (brand) – revenue (private label)	BE = (brand profit – generic profit) x brand strength	BE = adv(t) +adv (t–1) + age + brand-based share	$BE = (TR_t \cdot TMC_t) \times (1 - (TMC_t / TR_t))$

perspectives itself illustrates why the brand equity construct has been so nettlesome. Until there is agreement on the construct and its properties, clarity on how the construct should be measured will be difficult.

As Table 8.1 shows, several metrics examine brand equity from the standpoint of the customer, focusing on the added value or utility that *customers perceive* from the brand (Park & Srinivasan, 1994)—value that cannot be explained by physical product features (Kamakura & Russell, 1993; Swait, Erdem, Louviere, & Dubelaar, 1993). Consistent with this customer focus, these metrics utilize consumer data from surveys, scanner panels, or discrete choices as inputs. Brand equity is typically conceptualized as deriving from associations linked to the brand and its attributes.

Other metrics reflect a *performance outcome-based perspective.* Ailawadi, Lehmann, and Neslin's (2003) conceptualization of brand equity as the revenue premium that accrues to a brand compared to a private label counterpart is illustrative of this perspective. *Financial World's* Interbrand model adopts a similar perspective, operationalizing brand equity as the relative after-tax profit of the brand in comparison with a generic brand multiplied by an index of brand strength (based on the seven subjective factors).

Simon and Sullivan (1993) adopt a *marketplace metric* of brand equity, designed to assess the value of the brand as determined by the financial marketplace. Consistent with this perspective, brand equity is based on stock prices and financial statement data, specifically "the incremental cash flows which accrue to branded products over and above the cash flows which would result from the sale of unbranded products" (p. 29).

Interestingly, one perspective on brand equity has not been elucidated— the value of the brand from the *brand holder's perspective.* This perspective on brand equity is relevant as it links the three perspectives described above. It does so by considering the brand's relationship with its customers, the firm's effort at developing this relationship, and hence the potential value of the brand to the financial marketplace. Existing measures of brand equity are incomplete in representing this brand holder's perspective. No matter how great a brand's relationship is with customers (e.g., reputation and goodwill), it is not valuable to a firm (or investors and prospective corporate buyers) if it requires excessive firm efforts (e.g., marketing costs) to develop and maintain this relationship. The marketplace metric of brand equity (e.g., stock price) measures the equity of a brand at a corporate level, not at an individual product level. Hence, it provides little guidance to the brand holder on equity-building possibilities for individual products produced by the firm.

More specifically, there are several uniquely differentiating characteristics of the brand equity measure that represents the *brand holder's* perspective. They are discussed next.

Costs to the Firm to Secure Customer Relationships (Firm Effort)

To serve as a useful construct that describes a brand's value to the brand holder, brand equity must be distinguished from other key performance indicators such as brand revenue or profit. Building and maintaining relationships with customers clearly involves real dollar costs to the firm. However, Ailawadi et al.'s (2003) revenue premium model does not incorporate costs (though their alternative theoretical model includes total variable costs). At issue here is not only whether costs should be included in the measure of brand equity, but also which costs are informative.

We argue that a measure of brand equity from the brand holder's perspective should include those *costs incurred in developing and maintaining a relationship between customers and the brand.* Unlike Ailawadi et al.'s alternative model, we do not believe that all variable costs should be considered in such a metric. Costs such as manufacturing or administrative costs are internal and hence hidden from customers' relationship with a brand. While they constitute costs borne by the firm, they do not directly impinge on customers' perceptions of the brand's benefits or their desires to stay in a long-term brand relationship. On the other hand, the *marketing costs* that the firm invests in a brand are primarily designed to develop customer relationships (e.g., creating, communicating, and delivering brand benefits for customers). They are the primary source of information from which customers infer brand benefits and develop a transactional brand relationship. Thus, marketing costs, not total costs invested in a brand, should constitute the relevant costs to be incorporated in the brand equity measure (see the forthcoming discussion about what constitutes marketing costs).

The separation of marketing from nonmarketing costs is an important departure from previous approaches. As we demonstrate later, a measure of brand equity based on marketing (versus total costs) need not correlate with a brand's profit as marketing and nonmarketing costs may differ in their operational efficiency (e.g., very inefficient manufacturing and very efficient marketing costs). Thus, a brand equity measure that considers only marketing costs serves as a unique performance measure that is different from profit, sales, market share, brand reputation, or goodwill. The two measures are, however, complementary. Hence, it is highly informative for a firm to examine performance measures (e.g., profit, sales, market share, etc.) that assess brand operations and to examine brand equity as an indicator of brand health.

The "Referent Brand"

Common to a number of brand equity definitions (see Table 8.1) is the inclusion of a *comparative entity or referent.* Typically, the referent is an "unnamed," "generic," or "private label brand." For example, Ailawadi et al. (2003) defined brand equity as "The marketing effects or outcomes that accrue to the product with its brand name as compared to the outcomes that would accrue if the same product did not have the brand name." Other definitions (Aaker, 1991; Farquar, 1989; Keller, 1993) benchmark the equity of a brand relative to a fictitious (generic or private) brand.

Although consideration of such a referent may be useful in the assessment of brand equity, use of an unnamed, fictitious, or generic brand has some significant shortcomings. To illustrate, consider the celebrity brand "Angelina Jolie". This brand name would be valued highly even if the famed actress had a fictitious name; part of the value of her name lies with her physically attractive features. Therefore, the difference between the real and an unknown or fictitious Angelina Jolie would not reflect the true value of Angelina Jolie. Consider another example—the iPod. The iPod's distinctive design is a fundamental contributor to the value consumers place on the brand and is essential to the brand's value (it must have contributed to the development of its brand equity in the first place.). Since this brand characteristic is salient and forms a basis for initial and continuing brand relationships, an unnamed brand that also has these attributes would still be valued—at least to some extent. Consequently the difference between the brand and an unnamed counterpart would be smaller than the real value of iPod. Hence, the true value of a brand should include not just the value of its name but also other product characteristics associated with that name.

The present chapter proposes that brand equity must be understood in terms of the value of a *brand*, not the value of its name (if this were the case, we would also have package design equity, product design equity, etc.). Hence, we recommend avoiding use of an unnamed, generic, or private label brand as referents. Avoiding the use of a referent brand also resolves some *operational* problems that make reliable assessment of brand equity difficult. In some industries, a private label or generic counterpart does not exist. Moreover, if multiple private label and/or generic brands are available it is not clear on the basis of which private label or generic brand equity should be assessed. Comparisons to one may yield quite different values than comparisons to another. Finally, it is difficult to measure brand equity relative to an unnamed (generic or private label) brand when the brand lacks physical, substantive, or explicit transaction properties. For example, brands representing services, places, countries, organizations, or sports teams (e.g., AT&T, New York, Japan, Stanford University, or the L.A. Dodgers) do not have specific referents that can be separated from their names. It is unclear how the equity of New York, Stanford University, or the L.A. Dodgers can be measured against an unnamed or private label New York, Stanford, or L.A. Dodgers.

Rather than specifying how valuable a brand is relative to an unnamed, generic, or private label referent brand, perhaps brand equity assessment is better assessed in terms of its absolute value to the firm (the brand holder). Brand equity measured in an absolute sense allows firms to compare the equity of one brand to a private label or generic referent brand, other brands within the same company, or with other brands in the same or a different industry. Hence comparison with any referent is possible. Such comparisons are more difficult when brand equity is conceptualized and measured based on a comparison between a target and a fictitious (generic or private) brand. Importantly, the proposed conceptualization and measurement perspective allows for the comparison of the value of a brand to any referent (not just an unnamed, generic, or private label brand). However, the referent brand is compared after an assessment of brand equity has been made. The referent is *not* part of the assessment of the brand's equity.

Measuring brand equity in terms of current value raises another related issue. It involves the distinction between the flow and stock concept of brand equity. The current-value-based brand equity is more a flow (e.g., income) concept than a stock (e.g., wealth) concept. The two have different meanings. One can have low income and still be wealthy, or have high income but not yet be wealthy. In accounting, equity like an asset is a stock concept, not a flow concept. Thus, the current-value-based equity measure appears to be the per-period measure of brand equity, not the total value of a brand at a point in time. It is in this sense that the current-value-based brand equity may be appropriate for the income statement but not part of the balance sheet. In order for this measure to be included in a firm's balance sheet, it may have to be converted to the measure that satisfies the stock concept of brand equity. Addressing this issue, albeit critically important, is beyond the scope of this chapter.

Temporal Issues Involving Brand Equity

Another thorny issue when measuring brand equity concerns the temporal perspective that should be adopted in conceptualizing and measuring brand equity. Current perspectives disagree on whether brand equity should be based on the brand's current value, or its current value and future expected value. For example, the Interbrand model incorporates a brand's future growth potential while others (Ailawadi et al., 2003) focus on the current value of a brand.

Conceptually, a brand's future growth potential is an important consideration for certain decision making situations (e.g., mergers and acquisitions). It does not, however, justify why a future growth potential should be intrinsic to the conceptualization and measurement of brand equity itself. As Ailawadi et al. (2003) note, including future growth potential brings a high degree of uncertainty and judgment into the measure, making the measure subjective and speculative. We believe that brand equity is best conceptualized and measured in terms of current value. While assessments of future value may be added subsequently, developing an accurate and non-subjective estimate of current value would produce a more reliable estimate. Notably, the calculation of current value enables a comparison of the brand's current value relative to the value attained in the past. Such comparisons may be extremely informative to internal brand strategy decisions.

Marketing Surplus and Efficiency (MARKSURE)-Based Brand Equity

With these considerations in mind, we develop a new perspective on brand equity and its measurement called the marketing surplus and efficiency (MARKSURE) measure. The metric bears some similarities to that of Ailawadi et al. (2003). Their metric is based on brand unit sales and price in comparison with a private label counterpart. Unit sales and price are derived from purchase behavior, and assessed from scanner data. Their revenue premium measure is as follows: $(\text{Volume}_b) \times (\text{Price}_b) - (\text{Volume}_{pl}) \times (\text{Price}_{pl})$ where subscripts b and pl refer to the focal national brand and the equivalent private label, respectively. Their model is interesting and useful as a reference to proposed MARKSURE because it deals with two of the three key variables that our newly proposed model relies on (unit price and the quantity sold).

However, our MARKSURE model differs *conceptually* and *operationally* from that of Ailawadi et al. (2003). We redefine brand equity by incorporating both inputs of a firm and its customers. We also extend Ailawadi et al.'s model *operationally* by specifying different procedures for brand equity assessment. The latter is achieved by (1) including marketing costs as a relevant input for measuring brand equity, (2) removing the private label referent brand (or unidentified brand name) as part of the measure, and (3) including the efficiency ratio of a firm's marketing costs. We believe that these extensions are fundamental and significant to a more useful metric. Specifically, the proposed measure entails several desirable features that address some of the issues described earlier. It also allows the firm to (1) assign a financial value to the brand in financial transactions and (2) to track brand health vis-à-vis competitors and over time. The next section discusses how the proposed measure performs these two different functions.

Revised Definition of Brand Equity

In light of the issues described earlier, we propose a new definition of brand equity, defining it as the current financial value of the brand to its holder (the firm) at a specific point in time. Conceptually, this value assessment is based on *the difference between customers' willingness to bear the costs to obtain the brand's benefits and the firm's costs expended to create these benefits in the minds of customers.* In other words, brand equity is *the difference between customers' endowment to a brand and the investment the brand holder has had to bear to secure this endowment from customers.* This conceptual perspective is operationalized by considering how the following three key variables drive brand value: (1) unit price (P), (2) unit marketing cost (MC), and (3) the quantity sold (Q).

Unit Price

Abundant empirical evidence supports the strong positive relationship between the strength of customers' relationship with a brand and the unit price level they are willing to bear (Aaker, 1996; Doyle, 2001; Erdem, Swait, & Louviere, 2002; Firth, 1993; Keller, 1993; Lassar, Mittal, & Sharma, 1995; Park & Srinivasan, 1994; Randall, Ulrich, & Reibstein, 1998; Swait et al., 1993; Yoo, Donthu, & Lee, 2000). Accordingly, evidence for an increase in brand equity would be revealed when a firm increases its unit price (P) from time t-1 to t but does so with no negative impact on demand (Q) and no additional marketing costs (MC) during the same time period (i.e., $Q_{t-1} = Q_t$; $MC_{t-1} = MC_t$).

Quantity Sold

Research similarly supports the relationship between the value customers place on their relationship with a brand and quantity sold (Aaker, 1992, 1996; Cobb-Walgren, Erdem & Swait, 2004; Keller, 1993; Park & Srinivasan, 1994; Ruble, & Donthu, 1995; Smith & Park, 1992). Customers who value their relationship with a brand are more willing to forgive brand mishaps and to be loyal to it (Ahluwalia, Burnkrant, & Unnava, 2000). Accordingly, brand equity should be revealed when demand for a brand increases from *t*-1 to *t* without (1) an associated unit price reduction (P), or (2) an increase in unit marketing cost (MC) during the same time period.

Marketing Costs

Finally, research supports the relationship between the value consumers place on their relationship with the brand and marketing costs (Aaker, 1992; Keller, 1993; Smith & Park, 1992). A brand with strong equity influences customers' trust in the brand, their willingness to promote positive word-of-mouth, and their relative insensitivity to reciprocity in communications by the firm (e.g., neither expecting nor requiring extensive marketing effort to remain loyal). Accordingly, brand equity should increase when a firm can (1) reduce marketing costs (MC) at time *t* from *t*-1 without an associated reduction in revenue, or (2) realize a revenue increase without an associated increase in marketing costs (MC).

Two Key Components of the MARKSURE Metric

The above three variables provide the basis for measuring two key components of the proposed brand equity metric—the *magnitude* of value generated by the brand (or marketing surplus) and the *efficiency* at which such value is achieved. These two components are examined below.

$$\text{Marketing Surplus: } (p_{jt} - mc_{jt})q_{jt}$$

$$\text{Marketing Efficiency: } 1 - \frac{mc_{jt}q_{jt}}{p_{jt}q_{jt}}$$

where:

p_{jt}: Price of the brand *j* at time *t*
mc_{jt}: Marketing cost of the brand *j* at time *t*
q_{jt}: Quantity sold for the brand *j* at time *t*
$mc_{jt}q_{jt}$: Total marketing cost
$p_{jt}q_{jt}$: Total revenue

$$\text{Total Marketing Surplus: } (P_t - MC_t) * Q_t$$

$(P_t - MC_t)$ represents the difference between the customer's costs at time t and the brand holder's costs at time t (hereafter, we drop the brand subscript j). The difference between customers' willingness to pay a certain cost (unit price, P_t) to obtain the benefits of a brand and the firm's unit marketing cost to create, communicate, and deliver such benefits is called "unit marketing surplus." Multiplying unit marketing surplus by the number of units sold (Q_t) yields total marketing surplus. Since willingness to pay represents the customer's side and the unit marketing costs represent the firm's side, both customer and firm perspectives are reflected in *marketing surplus*. To the extent that a firm can create, communicate, and deliver brand benefits at a lower cost than the price customers are willing to pay, the brand enjoys a *marketing surplus*. The greater the total marketing surplus is, the greater the brand's value becomes. Thus, total marketing surplus reflects the *magnitude* of brand value.

Unit price in the above formula reflects the wholesale price. Wholesale price is determined by total revenue divided by the number of units sold at the wholesale level. Total marketing costs (aimed at both middlemen and end users) represent the expenditures the firm has borne to generate this revenue during time t. While a time lag is sometimes observed between marketing costs and resultant revenue, we do not formally include time lag effects in the model given the myriad issues associated with estimating lag length and magnitude (discussed later). Failure to incorporate lag effects may also be less problematic if the brand equity measure allows a sufficient time period to make the inclusion of a lag unnecessary.

$$\text{Marketing Efficiency: } (1 - [TMC_t / (P_t * Q_t)])$$

The ratio of total marketing costs to total revenue reflects the proportion of revenues that are allocated to creating customer value. One minus this ratio represents *marketing efficiency*. The lower the marking costs in relationship to the revenues, the greater the firm's marketing efficiency. Brand equity increases as marketing efficiency increases. Thus, the less a firm spends on brand marketing to generate a specific revenue level, the greater is the brand's equity. Unlike Ailawadi et al.'s model, this metric explicitly considers the brand's return on marketing investments. *Marketing efficiency* therefore reflects the efficiency with which the brand achieves its marketing surplus. This variable assumes that the brand's revenue is greater than 0. As with *total marketing surplus, marketing efficiency* involves both customers' input (customers' responses in the form of total revenue) and a firm's input (total marketing costs).

Importantly, *marketing efficiency* and *marketing surplus* are independent entities; each serves as an independent dimension according to which the levers of brand value can be judged. Combined, these variables also offer an overall assessment of brand equity. In this case, *marketing efficiency* serves as a weight for *marketing surplus*. It adjusts *total marketing surplus* because the same amount of marketing surplus can be obtained at different levels of efficiency. Specifically, even if two brands have the same total marketing surplus $((P_t - MC_t) * Q_t)$, they may not reflect the same brand value when they differ in the ratio of marketing investments over total revenue.

To illustrate, consider the two brands shown in Table 8.2. Brand A has $100 in total revenue ($10 in unit price and 10 units sold) and $10 in marketing investment ($1 in unit marketing investment). Brand B has $200 in total revenue ($20 in unit price and 10 units sold) and $110 in total marketing investment ($11 in unit marketing investment). Both brands have the same total marketing surplus ($90). However, they differ greatly in their marketing efficiency. The former should be higher in value since the latter spent more to achieve the same marketing surplus. Assuming that all other costs for the two brands are equivalent, the difference between the two brands suggests that Brand B spent eleven times more in marketing dollars to generate the same unit profit (P – MC – all other costs). This adjustment yields value of $81 for brand A and value of $40.5 for brand B. This adjustment (1– (total marketing costs/total revenue)) is based on the logic that the brand's value is positively related to the proportion of marketing spending given its total revenue. Simply stated, a brand enjoys the highest (lowest) value when it generates substantial (limited) revenue with no (extensive) marketing costs.

Brand Equity Measure

Marketing surplus and marketing efficiency combined reflect the proposed brand equity metric. The composite MARKSURE measure is thus operationally defined as:

TABLE 8.2

An Example for Adjusting Marketing Surplus with Marketing Efficiency

Factors	Brand A	Brand B
Price	$10.00	$20.00
Q	10	10
Marketing costs	$1.00	$11.00
Marketing surplus	$90.00	$90.00
Marketing efficiency	0.9	0.45
Brand equity	$81.00	$40.50

Note: Where Marketing Surplus $((P_t - MC_t) * Q_t)$ is $9 x 10 = $90 for Brand A and $9 x 10 = $90 for Brand B, respectively, and Marketing Efficiency (1– [TMC_t/P_t*Q_t]) is 1 – 01= 0.9 for Brand A and 1 – 0.55 = 0.45 for Brand B, respectively.

$$BE_t = (p_t - mc_t)q_t \left| 1 - \frac{mc_t q_t}{p_t q_t} \right|$$

That is, brand equity reflects the difference between the brand's unit price at time t and its unit marketing cost at time t, multiplied by the total number of units sold at time t, adjusted by the ratio of total marketing investments over total revenue (the lower this ratio is, the less the adjustment becomes). Note that when a brand spends more money for marketing than its total revenue ($mc > p$), brand equity becomes negative.* Illustrative examples of brand equity measure are found in the Appendix. They clearly show the value of the MARKSURE measure.

According to the MARKSURE measure, brand equity at any given point in time cannot exceed total revenue. This assumption is reasonable because brand revenue at a particular point in time represents the total possible value of that brand judged by customers at that time. Note also that the composite MARKSURE measure is a joint product of (1) the magnitude of a brand's value (total marketing surplus) and (2) the efficiency at which such magnitude was obtained. Extending from an individual product level to a corporate level, we propose that corporate brand equity is assessed based on the same marketing surplus and efficiency components. In this case brand level revenue and marketing costs are replaced by corporate revenue and marketing costs (for more about this issue, see the Discussion section).

Operational Characteristics of the Marketing Surplus and Marketing Efficiency-Based Brand Equity Measure

Several additional factors, described below, distinguish the operational characteristics of the MARKSURE measure.

Operational Definition of Marketing Costs

From an operational standpoint, we focus on costs incurred to create, communicate, and deliver brand value to customers over time. Any costs

---

* Brand equity would be negative when mc is greater than p. Current accounting practice does not recognize negative brand equity. Thus, the measure may not be used for purposes of disclosure on balance sheets when brand equity is negative. However, observing and tracking equity when it is negative (or positive) likely has an important role for internal management control purposes.

associated with *value-creating and communicating* activities (e.g., 4P-related activities such as advertising, trade show, publicity, package design, product design, etc.) and other activities (e.g., marketing research expenses) engaged in to improve their effectiveness belong to marketing costs. Costs associated with 4P-related activities designed to *remove transaction barriers* should also be a part of marketing costs. Thus, costs associated with activities that remove time (a brand must be available at the right time), place (a brand must be available in the right place), ownership (a brand must be designed and priced to facilitate its ownership), and intimacy barriers (aesthetic aspects of a brand and services associated with buying, using, and disposing of a brand) should be considered as part of marketing costs. Costs associated with various activities that remove these transaction barriers such as logistics, personal selling, sales promotion, and warehousing, belong to marketing costs. In general, variable costs incurred to facilitate the transaction between the customer and the brand (variable costs associated with activities at the before-purchase, during-purchase, during-use, and/or the disposal stages) should be included in unit marketing costs.*

Since 4P-related activities are designed to address the needs of customers and directly affect customers' perceptions of a brand value and their purchase and repeat purchase decisions, their costs and the marketing costs defined above are consistent with each other. However, identifying marketing costs in accordance with this perspective is not as straightforward as it initially appears. This difficulty arises from the fact that various activities for brand management and their associated costs need to be reclassified because many costs related to these activities have traditionally been assigned to other cost categories, but not to the marketing cost category. In addition, there is conceptual confusion about the definition of the term product as one of the 4Ps. These two issues are discussed below.

To illustrate the need to reclassify existing costs, consider for example the following costs: order handling and processing costs (relevant at the during-purchase stage), call center operating costs (relevant at the before-purchase stage), and customer service center operating costs (relevant at the post-purchase stage). These costs are not traditionally considered to belong to marketing costs. To illustrate another cost that is not traditionally assigned to marketing costs, consider a patients : nurses ratio in the hospital brand. This ratio may matter a great deal to patients because it affects the quality of the service (relevant to the during-use stage). Notably, current accounting practices do not assign such costs to marketing.

---

* When a firm has multiple product lines or share the same production or distribution resources together, activity-based cost accounting is needed to accurately reflect each brand's marketing costs.

The reclassification of marketing costs that are recommended in this paper is based on the theoretical notion that marketing activities occur across four transaction stages: before-purchase, during-purchase, during-use, and disposal. Therefore, any costs that incur at any one of these four transaction stages should be considered to be marketing costs. While this approach to marketing costs maps well to the traditional classification of the 4Ps, there is one thorny issue that needs to be resolved. It pertains to the definition of product as one of the 4Ps. While activities related to price, promotion, and place are relatively clear, the same may not be argued for product. It is important to define the term product and activities associated with it in order to specify marketing costs relevant to product.

In this chapter we propose that the term product as one of the 4Ps should be understood in terms of its raw materials, functions, and its form design and specification. According to this view, raw materials costs, costs incurred to develop product functions (a portion of R&D costs), and product design development costs (a portion of R&D) should be reflected in marketing costs. Activities associated with these product-related costs are highly relevant to customers' decisions to choose a brand. For example, raw materials (steel versus plastic, organic versus nonorganic, silk versus synthetic fiber, etc.) matter a great deal to customers. According to this view, any other part of R&D costs, production costs, labor costs, administrative costs, and financial costs (depreciation, interest charges, etc.) should not be included in marketing costs. These costs are internal to a firm and do not bear any relevance to customers' brand preference and loyalty.

One may argue that there may be other internal costs that should be considered to be marketing costs when following the above classification logic. For example, there may be value-added production costs (e.g., hand-made versus machine-made) that are internal to the firm, yet relevant to the customers' brand preference and loyalty. They are not, however, included in marketing costs since it is difficult to judge a priori what constitutes value-added production activities. While acknowledging the possibility that the marketing costs classification proposed in this chapter may not fully represent *true* marketing costs defined in this chapter, we nevertheless follow the common denominator approach.

Note that the definition and specification of marketing costs proposed in this chapter are an improvement over traditional perspectives that include total costs when measuring brand value. Moreover, the incorporation of the marketing costs identified here provides a more comprehensive view of marketing's contribution to the brand value creation and fortification. Incorporating communication costs and those that remove transaction barriers better reflect marketing's role in creating and sustaining brand value.

Using MARKSURE to Assess Marketing Activities

The value of the brand, derived from customers' response (i.e., revenue) to the firm's marketing effort (i.e., marketing costs), not only represents the value of a brand to the firm. It also serves as an accountability metric for marketing expenditures. Specifically, the metric can also be used to track the brand's health vis-à-vis competitors and over time. Information about marketing surplus and marketing efficiency offers diagnostic benefits to a firm. This information may be examined in two ways: one is based on the absolute level, and the other one is based on the relative changes over time. We suggest that the effective way to examine the contribution of marketing and the brand's health over time is to examine changes in brand equity from one point in time to the next. These changes would reflect marketing accountability, which may be used in turn to diagnose brand health, and evaluate and reward employees responsible for brand management.

The relative changes of marketing surplus and efficiency, as opposed to their absolute level, would resolve the thorny issue involved in assessing customers' response to a firm's marketing effort for its brand. One may argue that the way marketing costs are measured does not fully include the contributions made by other departments of a firm for the brand's market performance. For example, a reliable production process with few defects, motivated employees, and their market sensing and responding capabilities may also directly or indirectly influence the effect of marketing costs on the market performance of a brand. We recognize this potential, and suggest that relative change is a way to resolve this problem. Since these other contributions are relatively stable over time, relative changes in marketing surplus and efficiency would reflect the contribution by marketing more accurately than the absolute level measure. The positive, negative, or no change would be useful information for the brand management control.

Including Lag Effects

The MARKSURE measure does not incorporate a time lag between some marketing investments (costs) and their revenue return. While considerable research (Dekimpe & Hanssens, 1995; Mela, Gupta, & Lehmann, 1997 Pauwels, Hanssens, & Siddarth, 2002) suggests that outputs of marketing efforts are observed only after a time lag, we exclude a lag for several reasons. First, the time lag varies, depending on the types of investment (e.g., advertising, package design, sales promotions, etc.). Since different types of marketing investments have different return horizons, a different time lag must be specified for each type of marketing investment. Estimating the magnitude of the lag effect over time is equally challenging as it is not only affected by the nature of marketing investments (the goodwill or demand-stimulating advertising) but also by the effectiveness of the marketing investment (e.g., how good the advertising campaign is). Lag effects may also be highly dependent on market and competitive factors, which may change over time. We avoid use of multiple time lags for different investments by suggesting that brand equity be measured on a one-year time horizon. This horizon is sufficiently long to incorporate short- and moderate-term time horizons. By measuring brand equity over a relatively longer time interval (longer than one year), lag effects should also be minimized to the extent that the longer time horizon should reflect short-, medium-, and long-term lag effects.

Practitioner Appeal

The Marketing Science Institute (MSI, 1999) identified operational issues relevant to practitioners in the assessment of brand equity. Such metrics would have more widespread appeal to the extent that they provide (1) ease of measure, (2) ease of use, (3) diagnostic value, and (4) intuitive appeal. Existing brand equity metrics vary considerably on these operational criteria. The MARKSURE has distinctive advantages over other metrics on these criteria.

With respect to ease of measurement and use, the MARKSURE metric does not require new data. The three variables that it includes are based on available brand information. Moreover, the variables are objectively identifiable, reliable, and tractable. The metric also involves ease of use by virtue of its computational simplicity. The measure provides diagnostic value as the marketing surplus and efficiency components provide independent information regarding the brand's health. Finally, the measure's intuitive appeal has hopefully been elucidated in the discussion of the marketing surplus and marketing efficiency components.

The MARKSURE metric is also easy to operationalize and use as it does not require data from a referent brand. Conceptually, brand equity is driven by the brand's ability to create strong *marketing surplus* and *efficiency*, not by its ability to outperform specific competitors. Operationally, the omission of information about competing brands makes the input required to compute the brand equity metric less onerous, facilitating its use for internal and accounting-based purposes. While comparisons can be made between brands in terms of their relative equity, these comparisons are not endemic to the measure of brand equity itself and are made for diagnostic (not value assessment) purposes.

Notably, the proposed metric can be used to diagnose brand health independent of a referent brand. The magnitude of marketing surplus and the level of marketing efficiency individually offer critical information about the relationship among the price level, demand, and marketing costs ($(P_t - MC_t) * Q_t$). Each entity carries critical information about the status of a brand's value. By plotting a brand's value on two axes (one axis

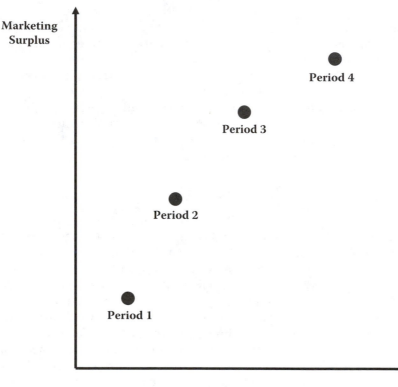

FIGURE 8.1
Illustration of the use of two dimensions of brand equity.

representing marketing surplus and the other axis representing market-ing efficiency) one can locate the status of a brand's value (see Figure 8.1). This assessment may then be compared with value attained at a previous period or with the values of the competing brands. The former suggests the information about how the marketing investment in a brand performs over time. The latter offers information about the relative competitive advantages in the brand's marketing effort.

The MARKSURE metric may also be used with other performance indica-tors to augment a firm's diagnosis of improvement potential. Specifically, the metric may be compared with brand profit so as to examine changes from the previous period (see Figure 8.2). This comparison would offer information about the source of potential discrepancies between brand value and profit. For example, if brand value improves from the baseline period while profit decreases, one can conclude that the decrease in profit from the baseline

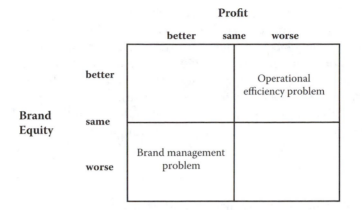

FIGURE 8.2
Brand equity as an independent key performance indicator.

period is due to problems in internal operations such as inefficiency with the manufacturing and/or other administrative costs. On the other hand, if the reverse occurs, the problem exists with the brand's marketing effectiveness.

The proposed metric also enables the additional diagnostic assessments. Specifically, information on the speed at which the marketing investment is reflected in the brand's revenue offers important information about the marketing effectiveness. Highly effective marketing will realize returns on marketing investments sooner as opposed to later. Moreover, such information may aid a firm in its decision to increase its marketing investments for further revenue growth.

Discussion

While the proposed measure is a move toward an accounting- and marketing-relevant metric, it should be evaluated in the context of the boundary conditions described below that may limit its usefulness.

The Boundary of Marketing Functions

As noted earlier, marketing costs in the proposed measure are defined and measured in a manner that differs from traditional conceptualizations. Marketing functions are described as those activities (performed by various departments) designed to facilitate customer acquisition and retention. They include costs associated with deriving and communicating brand value and removing transaction barriers between the firm and its customers. This expanded view of marketing (and hence marketing costs) is justified by the fact that when customers assess the value of a brand for purchase or repurchase, they do not consider the performance of different departments of the organization. They simply consider the brand's performance, symbolic, aesthetic, and acquisition benefits and costs of the brand relative to competing brands. Their endowment to a brand is heavily influenced by all the activities required for customer acquisition and retention. Marketing functions and costs should thus be understood and measured accordingly.

Potential Inflation of Measured Brand Equity

No measure, including the MARKSURE metric, is immune to the misuse or the undesirable manipulation of the measure by brand holders. With the MARKSURE metric, for example, brand holders may be tempted to reduce marketing costs so as to increase brand equity. Brand holders may engage in aggressive short-term sales promotions, creating short-term revenue spikes. Notably though, these tactics come at the expense of long-term brand equity. These temptations and effects may also be minimized if brand equity is assessed on a yearly basis—when short-term effects may have settled out. Comparisons across years should also minimize temptations to game the measure so as to look optimally strong in the long run. To discourage a short-term orientation, one might also recommend a relatively long-term basis (e.g., 3 years) on which a brand manager's performance can be judged.

Incorporating Expected Future Earning

Unlike other measures (e.g., Interbrand), MARKSURE does not incorporate expected future earnings as part of the brand equity metric. Their inclusion would violate criteria of objectivity and reliability that are critical to an accounting-based metric. Estimates of future earnings potential involve both subjective judgment and uncertainty (Ailawadi et al., 2003), which negatively impact agreement on assessment. Nevertheless, those who are interested in the future earnings potential of a brand (e.g., financial analysts) could incorporate future values *after* the MARKSURE metric has been derived. As is true with the use of an unnamed or referent brand, future earnings potential may be considered as an operational adjustment to the proposed brand equity measure, not endemic to its conceptualization or operationalization.

Brand Equity of Not-For-Profit Brands

The proposed MARKSURE measure considers only the equity of profit-oriented firms. Clearly, however, there are numerous respected and trusted brands in the nonprofit sector, including Amnesty International, World Wildlife Fund, Greenpeace, International Red Cross, Human Rights Watch, Oxfam, and CARE (Quelch & Laidler-Kylander, 2005). Development of a brand equity measure for not-for-profit brands is clearly warranted.

The Unit of Analysis for Brand Equity

The unit of analysis for the proposed measure is a branded product. We recommend that variations (e.g., line extensions) of the initial brand should be treated as part of the initial brand. However, a new product (e.g., brand extensions) that extends from this existing brand would therefore have its own equity. Hence, we distinguish the equity of the original brand from that of its extension. Thus, for example, the equity of Heinz pickles and the equity of Heinz ketchup are estimated separately. Assessing equities separately is justified since they differ in ways that affect brand equity (differences in markets and the firm's relative emphasis on resource investment, etc.).

It is also possible to measure brand equity at the higher level of aggregation. Specifically, brand equity may also be measured at the product line level, SBU level, or the corporate level. Specifically, there are two different ways in which one can estimate brand equity at the higher level of aggregation. One way is to measure the equity of the corporate brand, for example, Gap, based on total sales revenue and total marketing costs using the MARKSURE formula. Here, brand equity is not the sum of the equity of its individual product brands but rather the equity of the overall company. This is because while the marketing surplus component of the MARKSURE-based brand equity measure can be aggregated up from a single brand to a complete line of products (i.e., the marketing surplus of a product line is the sum of the marketing surpluses of each product), the marketing efficiency multiplier cannot be aggregated so readily. Another way is to multiply the sum of the marketing surplus of each product brand of a corporation by a weighted average of the marketing efficiency of each product. The marketing efficiency of a corporate brand (or a whole product line) is a weighted average of all the individual product-level marketing efficiencies where the weight associated with each product is its dollar share of the whole corporation (or a whole product line).

To illustrate, let us compare the marketing efficiency of a whole product line to the marketing efficiency of each of its individual products. The marketing efficiency of a product line is

$$ME_{Line} = 1 - \frac{\text{Total Marketing Costs}}{\text{Total Revenues}} = 1 - \frac{\sum_{i=1}^{N} mc_i q_i}{\sum_{i=1}^{N} p_i q_i}.$$

The marketing efficiency of product *i* in the product line is

$$ME_i = 1 - \frac{mc_i q_i}{p_i q_i}$$

We can thus express the marketing efficiency of the product line as a weighted average of the efficiency of each of its products, as follows:

$$ME_{Line} = \sum_{i=1}^{N} w_i ME_i = \sum_{i=1}^{N} w_i \left(1 - \frac{mc_i q_i}{p_i q_i}\right) = \sum_{i=1}^{N} w_i - \sum_{i=1}^{N} w_i \frac{mc_i q_i}{p_i q_i} = 1 - \frac{\sum_{i=1}^{N} mc_i q_i}{\sum_{i=1}^{N} p_i q_i}$$

The last equality is true only if we set the weights to be equal to the share of each product in the product line:

$$\text{i.e., } w_i = \frac{p_i q_i}{\sum_{i=1}^{N} p_i q_i}$$

In short, the marketing efficiency of a product line is equal to the sales weighted average of the marketing efficiency of each of its products.

Finally, measuring brand equity at the individual firm level may offer important implications for assessing royalty fees to be charged by a conglomerate to its subsidiaries for use of its brand name. For example, many conglomerates such as GE, Sony, Samsung, Nestle, Hitachi, etc., have their own subsidiary firms that use their names. Since each subsidiary firm's equity directly and indirectly influences the conglomerate's brand equity, it is important for the conglomerate to ensure that each subsidiary strives for improving its own brand equity. Therefore, conglomerates may have to envision compensation systems (e.g., royalty fee assessment) that reward CEOs of individual subsidiary firms based on their performance on their brand equity. For example, those who performed well in the previous year may be charged less royalty fee than those who did not.

Appendix

Two illustrative examples using the MARKSURE metric are shown below. The information in Table 8.3 (A and B) shows the internal financial data for an individual brand (readily available to a firm). In these examples brand-equity-related metrics are used to assess the total value of a brand, as well as how a firm performs its marketing operations (Table 8.3C).

Referring to Table 8.3A, consider the internal financial data about the brand Cruise. From this information, it is quite difficult to readily identify whether or not there is a problem (opportunity) with respect to the brand's operations and value. Several key statistics draw our attention. First, the continuous revenue increase over the 5 years is a good sign. So is the continuous increase in margin before marketing during the same period. The brand's profit, ROI, and marketing/sales have been steady over the 5-year period. On the other hand, the continuous decrease in ROS (return on sales) is somewhat troublesome. One may certainly identify the decreasing

TABLE 8.3A

Illustrative Examples for Assessing Brand Equity and Marketing Performance

Assessment (in $1,000)	Cruise				
	Year 1	Year 2	Year 3	Year 4	Year 5
Revenue	$1,320	$1,385	$1,463	$1,557	$1,670
Margin before marketing	$198	$208	$219	$234	$251
Marketing	$173	$183	$194	$209	$226
Profit	$25	$25	$25	$25	$25
Margin (%)	15%	15%	15%	15%	15%
ROS	1.9%	1.8%	1.7%	1.6%	1.5%
Year-on-year revenue growth	—	5%	6%	6%	7%
Invested capital	$500	$501	$503	$505	$507
ROI	5.0%	5.0%	5.0%	5.0%	4.9%

Note: Farris, Bendle, Pfeifer, Reibstein (2006). Philadelphia: Wharton School Publishing.

TABLE 8.3B

Illustrative Examples for Assessing Brand Equity and Marketing Performance

Assessment (in $1,000)	Boom				
	Year 1	Year 2	Year 3	Year 4	Year 5
Revenue	$183	$1,167	$1,700	$2,553	$3,919
Margin before marketing	$125	$175	$255	$383	$588
Marketing	$100	$150	$230	$358	$563
Profit	$25	$25	$25	$25	$25
Margin (%)	15%	15%	15%	15%	15%
ROS	3.0%	2.1%	1.5%	1.0%	0.6%
Year-on-year revenue growth	—	40%	46%	50%	53%
Invested capital	$500	$520	$552	$603	$685
ROI	5.0%	4.8%	4.8%	4.1%	3.6%

Note: Farris, Bendle, Pfeifer, Reibstein (2006). Philadelphia: Wharton School Publishing.

ROS figures as a possible cause for concern. But how should one interpret these figures in terms of the marketing performance of a brand and its value? Do these decreasing figures necessarily mean the decreasing marketing performance and its value?

The analyses become even more complicated when Cruise is compared with another brand, Boom. Boom's financial statements are shown in Table 8.3B. Boom's revenue growth is quite substantial while profit remains both steady and identical to that of Cruise. However, its ROS and ROI have declined over time. Given this information, it is difficult to assess which brand is better in their equity management and marketing performance. By applying marketing surplus and efficiency indicators, one may be readily able to make such assessments.

Table 8.3C contains information about marketing surplus, marketing efficiency, and brand equity (value) for Cruise and Boom. Considering the conflicting information between the two brands, the verdict is quite clear when one compares the two in terms of marketing surplus, marketing efficiency, and the brand equity. While the two are rather similar in marketing efficiency, Boom is much stronger in marketing surplus and thus brand equity (more than twice in brand equity at the end of year 5). Moreover, the Boom brand manager is doing a much better job than his counterpart at Cruise as revealed by changes in brand equity over time. The magnitude of increase in brand equity over the 5-year period clearly shows far greater potential for Boom than for Cruise.

TABLE 8.3C

Illustrative Examples for Assessing Brand Equity and Marketing Performance

Assessments	Cruise					Boom				
	Year 1	Year 2	Year 3	Year 4	Year 5	Year 1	Year 2	Year 3	Year 4	Year 5
Total revenue	1,320	1,385	1,463	1,557	1,670	183	1,167	1,700	2,553	3,919
Total marketing cost	173	183	194	209	226	100	150	230	358	563
Marketing surplus	1,147	1,202	1,269	1,348	1,444	83	1,017	1,470	2,195	3,356
Marketing efficiency	86.9%	86.8 %	86.7 %	86.6%	86.5%	46.0%	87.1 %	86.5 %	86.0 %	
Brand equity	997	1,043	1,101	1,167	1,249	38.18	886	1,271	1,887	2,874

References

Aaker, D.A. (1991). *Managing brand equity*. New York: The Free Press.

Aaker, D.A. (1992). The value of brand equity. *Journal of Business Strategy, 13* (July/August), 27–32.

Aaker, D.A. (1996). Measuring brand equity across products and markets. *California Management Review, 38* (Spring), 102–120.

Ailawadi, K.L., Lehmann, D.R., & Neslin, S.A. (2003). Revenue premium as an outcome measure of brand equity. *Journal of Marketing, 67* (October), 1–17.

Ahlwalia, R., Burnkrant, R.E., & Unnava, H.R. (2000). Consumer response to negative publicity: The moderating role of commitment. *Journal of Marketing Research, 37* (May), 203–214.

Barth, M.E., Clement, M.B., Foster, G., & Kasznik, R. (1998). Brand values and capital market valuation. *Review of Accounting Studies, 3*, 49–68.

Cobb-Walgren, C.J., Ruble, C.A., & Donthu, N. (1995). Brand equity, brand preference, and purchase intent. *Journal of Advertising, 24* (Fall), 25–40.

Dekimpe, M.G., & Hanssens, D.M. (1995). The persistence of marketing effects on sales. *Marketing Science, 14* (3), 1–21.

Doyle, P. (2001). Building value-based branding strategies. *Journal of Strategic Marketing, 9* (4), 255–68.

Erdem, T., & Swait, J. (2004). Brand credibility, brand consideration, and choice. *Journal of Consumer Research, 31* (June), 191–198.

Erdem, T., Swait, J., & Louviere, J. (2002). The impact of brand credibility on consumer price sensibility. *International Journal of Research in Marketing, 19* (March), 1–19.

Farquhar, P. (1989). Managing brand equity. *Marketing Research, 1* (September), 24–33.

Farquhar, P. (1990). Managing brand equity. *Journal of Advertising Research, 30* (August–September), RC7–RC12.

Farris, P., Bendle, N., Pfeifer, P., & Reibstein, D.J. (2006). *Marketing metrics: Fifty + metrics every marketer should know.* Philadelphia: Wharton School Publishing.

Firth, M. (1993). Price setting and the value of a strong brand name. *International Journal of Research in Marketing. 10* (December), 381–386.

Kamakura, W., & Russell, G.J. (1993). Measuring brand value with scanner data. *International Journal of Research in Marketing: Special Issue on Brand Equity, 10* (March), 9–22.

Keller, K.L. (1993). Conceptualizing, measuring, and managing customer-based brand equity. *Journal of Marketing, 57* (January), 1–22.

Lassar, W., Mittal, B., & Sharma, A. (1995). Measuring customer-based brand equity. *Journal of Consumer Marketing, 12* (4), 11–19.

Lev, B. (2005). *Intangibles: Management, measurement, and reporting.* Washington, D.C. The Brookings Instition.

Mela, C.F., Gupta, S., & Lehmann, D.R. (1997). The long-term impact of promotions and advertising on consumer brand choice. *Journal of Marketing Research, 34* (May), 248–261.

MSI (1999). Value of the brand. Workshop at Marketing Science Institute Conference on Marketing Metrics, Washington, DC (October 6–8).

Randall, T., Ulrich, K., & Reibstein, D. (1998). Brand equity and vertical product line extent. *Marketing Science, 17* (4), 356–379.

Park, C.W., Jaworski, B.J., & MacInnis, D.J. (1986). Strategic brand concept-image management. *Journal of Marketing, 50* (October), 135–146.

Park, C.S., & Srinivasan, V. (1994). A survey-based method for measuring and understanding brand equity and its extendibility. *Journal of Marketing Research, 31* (May), 271–288.

Pauwels, K., Hanssens, D.M., & Siddarth, S. (2002). The long-term effects of price promotions on category incidence, brand choice, and purchase quantity. *Journal of Marketing Research, 34* (November), 421–439.

Quelch, J.A., & Laidler-Kylander, N. (2005). *The new global brands: Managing non-governmental organizations in the 21st century.* Belmont, CA: Thomson South-Western.

Simon, C.J., & Sullivan, M.W. (1993). The measurement and determinants of brand equity: A financial approach. *Marketing Science, 12* (Winter), 28–52.

Smith, D.C., & Park, C.W. (1992). The effects of brand extensions on market share and advertising efficiency. *Journal of Marketing Research* (August), 296–313.

Swait, J., Erdem, T., Louviere, J., & Dubelar, C. (1993). The equalization price: A measure of consumer perceived brand equity. *International Journal of Research in Marketing, 10,* 23–45.

Yoo, B., Donthu, N., & Lee, S. (2000). An examination of selected marketing mix elements and brand equity. *Journal of the Academy of Marketing Science, 28* (2), 195–211.

9

Revisiting the Customer Value Proposition: The Power of Brand Emotion

Baba Shiv
Stanford University

Antoine Bechara
University of Southern California

Arguably, at its core, the fundamental goal of marketing is to create, sustain, and monetize a competitive advantage through a superior customer value proposition (CVP). How has our thinking about the CVP been shaped over the years? What are some of the emerging trends related to the CVP, particularly regarding the role of emotion in the "branding route" to the CVP? What are the implications of these emerging trends for marketing strategy and tactics? The thrust of this chapter is to answer such questions and, thereby, enrich our understanding of the CVP.

The journey that the reader is about to take is organized as follows. The next section will highlight the evolution of the CVP across the years. The subsequent sections will highlight the emergent "third-wave" viewpoint of the CVP, at the core of which is brand emotion and its power in shaping a sustainable CVP. The journey will finally end with an eye on the future, the promise that the future holds for the practice and science of marketing.

Customer Value Proposition— Tracing the Historical Viewpoints

The traditional view that prevailed until the 1980s and even into the 1990s was that marketers could shape the value proposition by focusing on one or both of two routes. One route is the "branding route," where the marketer shapes the CVP through a product differentiation strategy by offering a superior value in terms of the benefits (Vb), both tangible and intangible (e.g., Keller, 1993; Park, Jaworski, & MacInnis, 1986). A second route to shaping the value proposition is the "pricing route," where the marketer shapes the CVP by offering superior value in terms of lower prices (Vp), either momentarily through discounts, rebates, etc., or by adopting a price-leadership strategy (e.g., by eliminating inefficiencies in the supply chain and passing on the reduced costs to customers). Stated differently, as per the traditional viewpoint, the CVP could be captured by the following simple equation, CVP = Vb + Vp. The marketer could thus increase the attractiveness of the CVP and thereby enhance its competitive advantage by focusing its efforts on Vb through product improvements, more convenient packaging, etc. and/or focusing its efforts on Vp.

By the end of the 1990s, one additional component began to be pictured in the CVP, giving rise to the "second-wave" view of the CVP—the explicit appearance of brand emotion (E) in the CVP.* Two developments during this period shaped this revision of the CVP, wherein CVP = E + Vb + Vp.† The first was a recognition that emotions are key component of a brand's inventory (see, Keller, 2001; Keller, 2002). The second critical development was that brand emotion could be shaped by the marketer through aspects that are completely unrelated to Vb, particularly through the use of emotional advertising (e.g., Batra & Ray 1986; Mitchell & Olson 1981). More important was the recognition that such brand emotion, shaped independent of Vb, are often nonconscious (Gorn, 1982; Zajonc, 1980; Zajonc & Markus, 1982) and can have a direct impact on customer choices (Gorn, 1982; Miniard, Sirdeshmukh, & Innis, 1992).

At this point, the reader might wonder why including E as a separate component in the CVP was an important development over the traditional perspective involving only the Vb and Vp components.

Consider the following situation in the marketplace (Table 9.1): a marketer and a competitor in dead-heat in terms of the CVP, resulting in an equal likelihood of the customer choosing the marketer's and the competitor's brand. According to the traditional perspective, the marketer had only two options to break the tie—go in for a product differentiation strategy by offering more benefits to the customer through product improvements, adding new attributes, etc., or go in for a pricing strategy by reducing prices either momentarily or for the long haul. The modified CVP with E in the picture allowed the marketer to break the tie and

---

* In all fairness to the traditional perspective, emotion was implicitly considered part of the CVP, albeit as arising from Vb elements (e.g., design, packaging, etc.).

† The components of this equation can also be construed in terms of constructs in the attitude literature. For instance, E shares kinship with affective attitudes, Vb shares kinship with multiattribute cognitive attitudes (attributes with the exception of price-related attributes), and Vp can be construed as cognitive attitudes related to price, momentary incentives such as rebates, etc.

TABLE 9.1

Two Routes for Marketers/Competitors to Shape Value Perception

Product Strategists	Branding Route Vb	+	Pricing Route Vb	= CVP
Marketer	4		4	= 8
Competitor	4		4	= 8

create a competitive advantage by efforts aimed at building brand emotion through emotional advertising, product placements, event sponsorship, etc., without the need to engage in expensive product improvements (Vb) or in reducing prices (Vp).

While the emergence of E in the CVP was an important development, note that in the revised formulation, E is treated as an add-on to the value proposition. An important implication of this feature in the revised second-wave view of the CVP is that the marketer has the luxury of focusing either on E or on Vb under the branding route. Stated differently, as per the second-wave view, the marketer can completely ignore E and yet expect to enjoy a sustainable competitive advantage as long as Vb + Vp is more favorable for the marketer's brand than the competitors' brands. In the next section, we will delve into the demerits of this rather simplistic viewpoint and argue that brand emotion might actually be essential for and fundamental to creating a sustainable competitive advantage through a superior E-based CVP.

The "Third-Wave" View—The Power of Brand Emotion

To frame the discussion in this section, let us revisit a fundamental question that has been debated for centuries from the time of the Greek philosopher Plato through the time of medieval Christian philosophers such as Leibniz and Descartes to modern philosophers such as Hare and Rawls. The question is, are emotions *by and large* beneficial for human decision making or are they detrimental? The consensus view to this fundamental question that prevailed over the centuries was that emotions are by and large detrimental to human decision making. In other words, if the philosophers of yesteryears had been familiar with the Vulcan Mr. Spock in *Star Trek*, they would have argued that the emotionless Mr. Spock will end up making better decisions.

While this consensus view of the role of emotion in decision making was questioned from time to time across the centuries (e.g., Hume in the

1700s), it was not until the 1970s that a diametrically opposite viewpoint (that emotions by and large are beneficial to decision making) began to gain traction. Notable among the proponents of this diametrically opposite viewpoint were social psychologists such as Robert Zajonc (1980), moral psychologists such as Lawrence Kohlberg (1971), and evolutionary psychologists such as Leda Cosmides and John Tooby (e.g., Cosmides & Tooby, 2000), who made compelling arguments in favor of the evolutionarily adaptive function of emotion in decision making. While psychologists were building a strong case for the diametrically opposite view, by the 1990s neuroscientists were also beginning to address this issue, notable among the proponents being Antonio R. Damasio and his colleagues (Hanna Damasio and Antoine Bechara, to name a few). Particularly notable was that the neuroscientists began to present compelling clinical as well as empirical evidence in support of this diametrically opposite viewpoint (Bechara & Damasio, 2005; Damasio, Everitt, & Bishop 1996). Probably the earliest recorded clinical evidence derives from the unfortunate story of Phineas Gage.

The Story of Phineas Gage

The story of Phineas Gage is set in the mid-1800s. Gage was a construction foreman for the Rutland and Burlington Railroad Company in New England and was noted for being very responsible as a manager of people, respectful of authority, doing reasonably well financially and very well socially. On a fateful day in September 1848, Gage fell victim to an accident, wherein an explosion hurled a tamping iron about an inch in diameter through his left cheek, skull, and finally out of the front of his head. To everyone's surprise, Gage recovered from the accident and was soon able to walk, talk, and even engage in his normal activities. Or was this the case?

Following the accident, Gage's acquaintances began to notice a marked change in his personality. Capturing these marked changes are the following excerpts from the report by Gage's doctor:

> Previous to his injury, although untrained in the schools, he possessed a well-balanced mind, and was looked upon by those who knew him as a shrewd, smart businessman, very energetic and persistent in executing all his plans of operation.
>
> [After the injury] Gage was fitful, irreverent, indulging at times in the grossest profanity (which was not previously his custom), manifesting but little deference for his fellows, impatient of restraint or advice when it conflicts with his desires, at times pertinaciously obstinate, yet capricious and vacillating, devising many plans of future operations, which are no sooner arranged than they are abandoned in turn for others appearing more feasible.

For the purposes of the exposition regarding the power of emotion (E) in the customer value proposition (CVP), the focus will be on one part of the doctor's report—the observation that following the accident, Gage became capricious and indecisive, akin to the proverbial Buridan's ass. (For the reader who is not familiar with the story of Buridan's ass, it goes as follows. A completely rational ass was placed between two stacks of hay of equal size and quality. The rational ass starved to death, not being able to decide which stack to start eating from.) But, before focusing on that aspect of the report, let's continue with the unfortunate story of Phineas Gage.

Following his tragic accident, Gage went on to live for another 12 years! During this time, he wandered from one job to another, made bad financial and social decisions, and literally died a pauper financially as well as socially. What might have caused this drastic change in Gage's behavior? Why did Gage end up making bad decisions following his accident? Preliminary answers to these questions emerged from a study conducted by Hanna Damasio and her colleagues (Damasio, Grabowski, Frank, Galaburda, & Damasio, 1994). In this study, Gage's skull, which is still preserved in the Warren Anatomical Medical Museum at Harvard University, was subject to a forensic neuroscience examination. A series of analyses revealed that the accident had damaged a very critical component of the brain's emotional circuitry, namely the ventro-medial prefrontal cortex (VMPC).

Recall the original question, are emotions beneficial or detrimental to human decision making? The story of Phineas Gage and the forensic examination of his skull provide a possible answer to this question; emotions might actually be beneficial to human decision making. Phineas Gage loses a critical component of his brain's emotional circuitry and ends up making bad decisions for the rest of his life! But, can one come to this conclusion with just a single data point?

More Evidence From Neurological Patients

Phineas Gage is not alone in terms of displaying marked changes in behavior following damage to components of the brain's emotional circuitry. Similar "before–after" alternations in behavior have since been observed in several neurological patients with damage to various areas of the brain's emotional circuitry (see Figure 9.1): amygdala, insula, somatosensory cortex, and the ventromedial prefrontal cortex.

As with Phineas Gage and his doctor's observations, typical changes that are observed in such patients are unrestrained (impulsive) behaviors, inability to learn from previous "slaps on the wrist," and most pertinent for this chapter, the inability to make good decisions (Bechara & Damasio, 2005; Naqvi, Shiv, & Bechara, 2006).

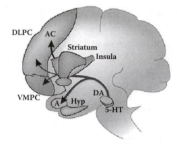

FIGURE 9.1
Areas of the brain's emotional circuitry. A = Amygdala; SS = somatosensory cortex; VMPC = ventromedial prefrontal cortex; DLPC = dorsolateral prefrontal cortex ("working memory").

By now, the perceptive reader would have noted the use of terms such as "bad decisions" and "good decisions" and begun to wonder, "How does one characterize a decision as being good or bad?" And, "Why would damage to the emotional circuitry result in an inability to make good decisions?" These questions will be addressed in the next section, which will be followed by a discussion of the theoretical as well as the managerial implications of this discourse for the customer value proposition.

Decision Quality, Emotions, and the Brain

In this section, we will first present our perspective on what makes a decision good or bad. We will then revisit observations of individuals with damage to the emotional circuitry and subsequently posit reasons why such individuals end up unable to make good decisions.

When Is a Decision Good or Bad?

One way of answering this question is to rely on two basic rational axioms of rational preference relations in economics—*dominance* and *transitivity* (Mas-Colell, Whinston, & Green, 1995). Dominance implies that for a set of options a and b, if $a > b$ then a decision is bad when the individual chooses the dominated option b. Stated in simple words, if an individual prefers a Toyota Prius over a BMW but chooses the BMW, then his/her decision should be characterized as being bad. Transitivity implies that a consumer should have a well-defined preference structure, such that for any set of bundles: a, b, and c, if $a \geq b$ and $b \geq c$, it must also be the case that $a \geq c$ (where $\geq$ denotes relative preference). In other words, when an individual is presented with a Toyota Prius and a BMW s/he indicates a preference for the former over the latter. When presented with a BMW and a Cadillac, s/he indicates a preference again for the former over the latter.

But, when presented with a Toyota Prius and a Cadillac, if s/he prefers the latter then one would characterize the decision as being bad (normatively, s/he should prefer the Prius over the Cadillac).

Normative benchmarks exist in other forms as well. For instance, consider the following task.

> You will engage in several rounds of investment decisions. Before you begin to make your decisions, I will endow you with $20 in $1 bills. On each round, you can decide not to invest, in which case I will proceed to the next round. Alternatively, you can invest a dollar, in which case I will toss a fair coin. If the outcome is "heads" you will lose your investment. If the outcome is "tails" I will add $1.50 to your investment of a dollar. In other words, I will give you $2.50.

If you, the reader, were faced with this task, what would you do? We are quite sure that the answer would be, "Keep investing in every single round—the expected value from investing ($1.25) is greater than the expected value from not investing ($1)." Yet, as demonstrated by Uri Gneezy (Gneezy & Potters, 1997) and Baba Shiv (Shiv, Loewenstein, Bechara, Damasio, & Damasio, 2005), individuals often invest in fewer rounds (especially as the task progresses) than that suggested by normative principles.*

Decision Making in the Absence of Normative Benchmarks

While we as decision makers do frequently face decisions that offer normative benchmarks, arguably such situations are far less frequent than those that offer no such benchmarks and yet present us with trade-off conflicts (i.e., the choice options *a* and *b* are equally preferred such that *a* = *b*). The question is how does one go about making good decisions under these circumstances? One perspective on resolving such decision conflicts is to adopt the completeness principle, a notion that is grounded in economics (e.g., Sugden, 1991) and shared by decision-making researchers (e.g., Payne, Bettman, & Johnson, 1993). According to this perspective, the way to resolve the conflict is to collect as much information on the options as feasible (with some cut-off rule, if needed). If a dominance structure emerges from this exercise, then choose the dominating option; if the trade-off conflict remains, then decide by simply tossing a coin. Note that this perspective focuses on the "input side" to the decision.

---

* We view normative principles as not only rooted in rational economic theory but also rooted in internalized sociocultural norms. For instance, the decision by a substance abuser to abuse rather than abstain would be considered by most of us as violating a normative benchmark, this time as defined by internalized social norms.

An alternate perspective, which we adopt for the rest of our exposition focuses on the "output side" to the decision. According to this perspective, a good decision is one where the decision maker is satisfied with, confident about, and thus committed to the chosen option.* In a sense, this perspective is consistent with how firms would characterize (their) customers' decisions as being good—after all, a satisfied and committed customer is likely to exhibit greater loyalty, and result in fewer cases of product returns (i.e., switching behaviors) and greater word of mouth. Interestingly, this perspective is in line with the Latin root of the word decision—*decidere*, which in turn is derived from *caedere*, which means *to cut* (words such as *excise* and *circumcise* share the same Latin root). This Latin root implies that when one is faced with a trade-off conflict, one has made a decision if one "cuts oneself from off from the past, from reexamining the decision," and thus is no longer in a state of indecision. "State of indecision" … does this remind the reader of the proverbial Buridan's ass that was featured earlier in this chapter? Well, let us get back to this proverbial ass and to the story of Phineas Gage.

Compromised Emotional Circuitry and the Inability to Make Good Decisions

Recall the following observation made by Gage's doctor: "*[After the injury, Gage became] capricious and vacillating, devising many plans of future operations, which are no sooner arranged than they are abandoned in turn for others appearing more feasible.*" Similar observations have been made by Damasio and his colleagues on patients with damage to the emotional circuitry (Damasio, 1994). When faced with trade-off conflicts,† such patients have been observed to exhibit a lack of commitment to the chosen option following a decision, resulting in considerable vacillation, frequent changes of mind, and thus the inability to make good decisions (as viewed from the output side and particularly as viewed from the Latin root of the word "decision").

---

* This output perspective is bound to raise criticism from readers. For example, if an addict chooses to abuse himself rather than abstain, and is happy about the decision, the output perspective would view his decision as being good; yet most of us would agree that his decision was bad. Rather than entering into debate on this issue, we qualify this perspective as being applicable to decisions where a normative benchmark, as broadly defined by axioms of rational choice, by the society (e.g., substance abuse is not normatively advantageous), etc., does not exist; yet the decision maker is confronted with a trade-off conflict.

† It should be noted that when such patients face choice options with a clear dominance structure, they have little problem in making good (i.e., committed) decisions. It is when they face trade-off conflicts, wherein the choice options are equally preferred (i.e., there is no dominance structure), that their ability to make good decisions breaks down.

Evidence from "Normal" Individuals

It is not just patients who exhibit the inability to make good decisions. In a study that we conducted with normal individuals, we examined if those with a more "muted" emotional circuitry (we term such individuals "vulcans" in our research) will exhibit greater inability to make good (i.e., committed) decisions compared to those (i.e., the "emotional") with a more sensitive emotional circuitry. In order to categorize individuals as either vulcans or emotionals, we first administered the affect intensity measure (AIM) scale (Larsen, Diener, & Emmons, 1986) as part of a purportedly unrelated series of studies. After a short filler task, participants moved on to the next task, which was an adaptation of Wilson et al.'s change-of-mind experimental paradigm (Wilson, Lisle, Schooler, Hodges, Klaaren, & LaFleur, 1993). In this task, participants first chose among eight Stanford memorabilia (as a token of our appreciation for their participation in this study). After a brief filler task and prior to being thanked and debriefed, participants were told that we were about to place the order for the item they had previously selected. Participants were asked if they would like to revisit the options before making up their minds. The proportion of participants who decided to revisit the options and the proportion of participants who changed their minds (i.e., ended up selecting an option that was different from the one previously selected) served as the key dependent variables. The results from this study are presented in Table 9.2.

Consistent with observations about Phineas Gage and patients with damage to the emotional circuitry, the results from this study suggest that vulcans have a greater propensity to vacillate and change their minds, and thus a greater propensity to make bad (i.e., less committed) decisions compared to emotionals. The question is, why? What do emotions have to do with the ability to make good (i.e., committed) decisions?

Emotions and the Ability to Make Good Decisions

The *somatic marker hypothesis* posited by Damasio and his colleagues (Bechara & Damasio, 2005; Damasio et al., 1996) provides potential answers to why emotions are crucial for and fundamental to making good (i.e.,

TABLE 9.2

Results from Decision Change-of-Mind Study Comparing Vulcans versus Emotionals

	Vulcans	Emotionals
% Revisiting	40.4	17.5
% Changing minds	21.4	5.0

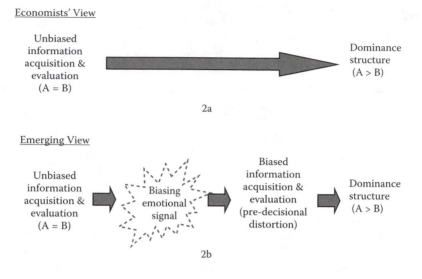

FIGURE 9.2
Emerging view of the decision-making process contrasted with the traditional (economists') view.

committed) decisions. According to the somatic marker hypothesis, the way the brain goes about resolving trade-off conflicts is *not* as shown in Figure 9.2a. That is, the brain does not follow the economist's perspective of what makes good decisions—following the completeness principle by engaging in an unbiased acquisition and evaluation of information until hopefully a dominance structure emerges. Instead, the brain seems to resolve trade-off conflicts in an arguably more efficient manner.

As shown in Figure 9.2b, the brain might begin the decision making through an unbiased information acquisition and evaluation process ("might," because this step can be skipped if one of the options is already enriched with positive emotions); however, as the process begins to unfold, a positive emotional signal (somatic marker) gets generated in favor of one of the options. The source of this emotional signal is a prior positive or negative experience that becomes associated with a particular thought or scenario conjured up during the pondering of a decision. Thereafter, often unbeknownst to the decision maker, the process that ensues becomes biased toward the emotionally enriched option. In other words, the brain engages in what Jay Russo and his colleagues have termed as predecisional distortion (Russo, Meloy, & Medvec, 1998; Russo, Meloy, & Wilks, 2000), wherein the brain shifts the evaluation of attribute information and the importance weights associated with such information in favor of the emotionally enriched option and against the emotionally impoverished option. The biased processing that is rooted in an emotion now enables the brain to create a clear dominance structure (i.e., $a > b$) and, thus, make good (i.e., committed) decisions.

The propositions stated above can account for why individuals with a muted emotional circuitry exhibit indecisiveness in the form of vacillation, which can manifest in the form of trade-off aversion (see Luce, 1998), changes of mind, and a lack of commitment to the option that is chosen following the decision. With no biasing emotional signals to trigger the biased processing and, in turn, to create the dominance structure, such individuals are left to the mercy of the "rational" brain— unless the information being acquired clearly favors one of the options, such individuals are stuck with where they started, namely $a = b$. Thus, the vacillation, trade-off aversion, the changes of mind, and the inability to make good (i.e., committed) decisions.

Preliminary evidence from a study that we conducted using the predecisional distortion paradigm seems to support the above propositions. Participants in this study were first categorized as being either vulcans or emotionals (as described earlier). The participants were then taken through a task adapted from the work by Russo and his colleagues (e.g., Russo et al., 1998). Specifically, one group (treatment condition) was asked to imagine the task as being a horse race and told that after each piece of information on two smart phones, A and B, they would rate them by how much one option was ahead of the other in the race (on an 11-point scale). Another group (control condition) rated a set of binary smart phone options (again on an 11-point scale), which were labeled differently across the pieces of attribute information (e.g., A and B, followed by T and U).

The level of distortion in the treatment condition (across the various attributes) was computed by comparing the ratings given by each participant on each attribute in the treatment condition with the mean ratings for the same attribute across all participants in the control condition. A comparison of the results on the cumulative distortion across the sequence of attributes that were presented in the treatment conditions revealed a clear distortion among emotionals; vulcans on the other hand barely distorted the information—their ratings were no different than those in the control condition. More importantly, participants in the treatment condition were asked to choose between the smart phones and then asked to rate how satisfied they were with their selection. Not surprisingly, vulcans were less satisfied with their chosen option compared to emotionals. Evidence from this preliminary study suggests the following. Vulcans, with relatively more muted emotional signals to trigger the biased processing and, in turn, to create the dominance structure, were stuck at where they started, namely an indifference between the two smart phones. Thus, we see the dissatisfaction among vulcans with their choices.

Back to the Customer Value Proposition

It is time to get back to where we started our journey: the role of emotion (E) in the customer value proposition (CVP). Recall an important development in the 1980s related to the CVP, namely the emergence of E as an explicit component in the second-wave view of the value proposition. Also recall E being treated as an add-on to the value proposition, implying that the marketer can completely ignore E as part the branding route and yet expect to enjoy a sustainable competitive advantage as long as $Vb + Vp$ is more favorable for the marketer's brand than the competitors' brands. Now juxtapose this second-wave view with the exposition in the previous section; it would become readily apparent to reader why the second-wave view, while a significant development over the traditional first-wave view, by advocating the notion that E is merely an add-on to the CVP is quite simplistic. Rather than being an add-on, the growing evidence seems to point to the notion that E is interactive, shaping Vb and Vp through predecisional distortion processes. In sum, E might actually be essential for and fundamental to creating a satisfied and committed customer, resulting in a *sustainable* competitive advantage through greater brand loyalty, favorable word of mouth, and fewer product returns.

The exposition thus far has attempted to convince the reader about the power of emotional branding in the third-wave view of the CVP— its power to shape the CVP by setting into motion mental processes that yield a satisfied and committed customer. In our opinion, this journey into the third-wave of branding has only begun. The future of the third-wave view is full of promising opportunities, both in terms of academic research and managerial applications, which we discuss next.

Journey Into the Future

In this section, we will highlight some promising opportunities related to the third-wave view, wherein E plays a more central and powerful role than previously envisaged in shaping the CVP. These include (1) developing appropriate measures for the E component, (2) examining the array of tactical means of shaping E, and (3) gaining richer insights into the CVP by adding β-weights to the various components (i.e., E, Vb, and Vp) and examining the nature of these weights for different product categories, including those in the B-to-B space.

EMOTIONAL DIFFERENTIATION TAKES FLIGHT

In 2004, American Airlines' marketing team launched an ad campaign based on the simple tagline, "We know why you fly." Former advertising director Rob Britton explains, "Looking at our relationship with our customers, we saw that, while we, as an airline, flew to JFK International, our passengers were flying to see a play on Broadway, to see their grandma in the Bronx, or to go to a meeting on Wall Street."

Britton notes that the airline business is only getting tougher. "This decade hasn't been kind to our industry, and by about 2002, American knew that we had to try to create meaningful and sustainable differentiation in a new way. We'd already tried the functional routes on-time performance, leg room, and that sort of thing." says Britton. "That's when we really took notice that many companies outside our industry, like soft drink makers and cosmetics firms, were creating great business by using *emotional* differentiation. L'Oreal, for instance, has built long-term brand preference, price premiums, and market share using emotional differentiators."

By adding emotion into their calculation of customer value, American was able to approach the marketplace differently from its competitors. American sought to communicate that "nobody understands airline travelers like we do" through a coordinated and long-term marketing campaign, now in its fifth year. "That word *understands* is key," Britton points out. "The idea is that we get it. American knows that we have the duty to get you there safely, reliably, and comfortably, but that our customers are going someplace other than the airport. We use that emotional appeal to set us apart."

Although many challenges remain, American's emotional capital continues to serve it well. "Looking at our customer value proposition as a three-part plan showed us that, without a doubt, emotion is a significant and durable differentiator," Britton concludes.

R.D.M. & L.W.P.

Developing Appropriate Measures for the E Component

Given how central E is to the third-wave view of the CVP, developing appropriate measures related to this component is likely to become more important than ever in the near future. The primary challenge is that with arguably most of the brain's emotional processes being inaccessible to our conscious awareness (e.g., Kihlstrom, Mulvaney, Tobias, & Tobis, 2000), traditionally used self-reported measures might be tapping into merely the tip of the emotional iceberg. The question is, how can we gain access to nonconscious emotional processes? Advances in neuroimaging (e.g., functional magnetic resonance imaging) might provide an answer to the question, but the costs involved in using this relatively modern technology and the complexity involved in executing the studies as well as interpreting the data are formidable enough that we are unlikely to see widespread use of this approach in the near future.

A promising direction might come from making traditional measures of the physiological correlates of E more accessible and user-friendly to marketing researchers. These measures include face tracking, cardio activity, and skin conductance, etc., apart from scalp-recorded brain electrical activity, which have been shown to be sensitive to measuring both the valence as well as the arousal dimensions of emotions (e.g., Cacioppo et al., 2000). The rationale behind these physiological measures is that emotional processes that occur in the brain and the viscera manifest themselves in the form of changes to the facial musculature, heart rate, skin conductance, etc.

One promising approach to making such traditional physiological measures more accessible and user-friendly has been developed by a team of researchers at Stanford University (Bailenson et al., 2008). A schematic of this approach presented in Figure 9.3 combines face-tracking with other physiological measures, all of which are automatically fed into an algorithm that yields two dimensions of the emotions being

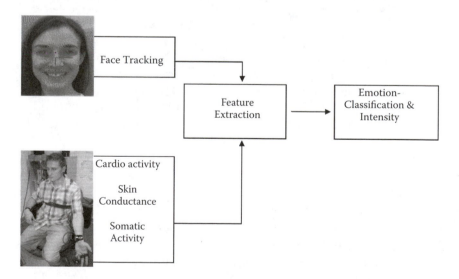

FIGURE 9.3
A promising approach to measuring (non-conscious) emotions (Bailenson et al. 2008).

experienced in real time by the individual—valence and intensity of the experienced emotions.

Exploring Tactical Approaches to Shaping E in the Age of the Internet

Since E emerged as a separate component of the CVP in the 1980s, considerable research has been conducted on the effectiveness of various means of shaping this component. The notion behind the use of these tactics is as follows. Emotions that are triggered by a stimulus (e.g., an attractive celebrity, music, humor, etc.) in the presence of the featured brand have the potential to get associated with the brand (for a recent exposition on this notion, see Niedenthal, 2007). In this regard, the general consensus has been that the most effective media vehicle to shape E is audio-visual advertising, given the range of executions it offers. While this consensus view has been prevalent now for more than two decades, more research is needed on media and execution-related factors that are likely to engender the most favorable and the most intense brand emotion in the quickest and most cost-effective fashion. Identifying such factors is likely to gain in urgency given the shift in media-consumption behavior—emergence of the notion of "wee-wee-wee," with technological advances giving customers the option of consuming what they want, where they want, and when they want.

Apart from audio-visual advertising, other tactics that can shape E, and thus the CVP, merit consideration in future research. First is the use of outdoor and in-store signage, event sponsorship, etc., that are known to enhance brand salience (i.e., the top-of-mind awareness of the brand name, logos, etc.). While brand salience is believed to be critical in the formation of the consideration set (see Keller, 2003), it may also shape E through the mere-exposure effect (Zajonc, 1980), which was built on Titchener's (1910) thesis on familiarity. Titchener argued that we, as decision makers, have an inherent preference for familiar options because such options give us a "glow of warmth, a sense of ownership, a feeling of intimacy" (p. 411). Titchener's thesis needs further testing, especially given the advances in the measurement of emotions.

A second approach that offers rich opportunities for future research is the use of tactics that enhance a feeling of ownership, often termed *endowment effect* in the literature (Kahneman, Knetsch, & Thaler, 1991). These tactics could include putting in effort by consumers for an option through contests, opportunities to customize options, etc. A recent piece of work on the "IKEA effect" (Norton, Mochon, & Ariely, forthcoming) provides evidence in support of the notion that effort increases the value of the option the effort was directed toward. In one study, participants were asked to create an origami frog or crane, and then asked them to buy their creations with their own money. Participants, in general, bid higher amounts than a different set of participants who did not put in effort to create the objects. Future research needs to delve deeper into the underlying mechanism giving rise to the IKEA effect. Our thesis is that effort put into an option enhances predecisional distortion toward the option, resulting in greater willingness to pay and greater commitment to the chosen option.

Promising opportunities are also likely to emerge by focusing not merely on the encoding (of advertising, creation of options, etc.) stage but also on the retrieval stage—identifying factors that will be most effective at retrieving E during the decision making process so as to increase chances that biased predecisional distortion processes will ensue (see Keller, 1987).

Adding Beta-Weights to the Components of the CVP

In the formulation at the beginning of the chapter, the CVP was expressed as $E + Vb + Vp$. This was later modified to the interactive effect of E on Vb and Vp, yielding a formula such as $E + Vb + Vp + E^*(Vb) + E^*(Vp)$. The more interesting questions that are likely to arise are when β-weights are added to the various components. One can begin to explore the following: Which product categories are likely to have bigger betas, both in terms of the main effects and in terms of the interactions, and why? How will these betas manifest for products in the B-to-B space? Are these betas likely to be small, or counter-intuitively, are these betas likely to be large? What are the situational and individual-difference factors that are likely to moderate these β-weights? For example, can tactics focusing on Vp (e.g., rebates, coupons, discounts, etc.) enhance not only price sensitivity in the form of greater β-weight on this component but also enhance vulcanism, leading to reduced β-weights on the interaction of E with Vb, increased indecisiveness, and reduced commitment to the chosen options? Addressing these questions can yield significant insights not merely into the strategic and tactical aspects of the CVP but also into the underlying processes giving rise to good decisions.

Some Final Words

The broad objective of this chapter was to take the reader on a journey involving the customer value proposition. A journey that was aimed at unraveling the importance of emotion in the value proposition—not merely as an add-on as previously envisaged in the "second-wave" view, but as a component that can actively shape Vb and Vp. We also presented empirical evidence in support of the third-wave view of the CVP, and highlighted some promising opportunities for the future. Most importantly, we hope that this journey has left the reader with a desire to learn more about the third-wave view of the CVP and its ramifications for research on decision making as well as for the practice of marketing.

References

Bailenson, J.N., Pontikakis, E.D., Mauss, I.B., Gross, J.J., Jabon, M.E., Hutcherson, C.A.C., Nass, C., & John, O. (2008). Real-time classification of evoked emotions using facial feature tracking and physiological responses. *International Journal of Human-Computer Studies, 66,* 303–317.

Batra, R., & Ray, M.L. (1986). Affective responses mediating acceptance of advertising. *The Journal of Consumer Research, 13 (2),* 234–249.

Bechara, A., & Damasio, A.R. (2005). The somatic marker hypothesis: A neural theory of economic decision. *Games and Economic Behavior, 52 (2),* 336–372.

Cosmides, L., & Tooby, J. (2000). Evolutionary psychology and the emotions. In M. Lewis & J.M. Haviland-Jones (Eds.), *Handbook of emotions, 2.* New York: Guilford.

Damasio, A.R. (1994). *Descartes' error: Emotion, reason, and the human brain.* New York: Grosset/Putnam.

Damasio, A.R., Everitt, B.J., & Bishop, D. (1996). The somatic marker hypothesis and the possible functions of the prefrontal cortex (and discussion). *Philosophical Transactions: Biological Sciences, 351 (1346),* 1413–1420.

Damasio, H., Grabowski, T., Frank, R., Galaburda, A.M. & Damasio, A.R. (1994). The return of Phineas Gage: Clues about the brain from the skull of a famous patient. *Science, 264 (5162),* 1102–1105.

Gneezy, U., & Potters, J. (1997). An experiment on risk taking and evaluation periods. *Quarterly Journal of Economics, 112 (2),* 631–645.

Gorn, G.J. (1982). The effects of music in advertising on choice behavior: A classical conditioning approach. *Journal of Marketing, 46 (1),* 94–101.

Kahneman, D., Knetsch, J.L., & Thaler, R.H. (1991). The endowment effect, loss aversion, and status quo bias. *Journal of Economic Perspectives, 5 (1),* 193–206.

Keller, K.L. (1987). Memory factors in advertising: The effect of advertising retrieval cues on brand evaluations. *Journal of Consumer Research, 14 (3),* 316.

Keller, K.L. (1993). Conceptualizing, measuring, managing customer-based brand equity. *Journal of Marketing, 57 (1),* 1–22.

Keller, K.L. (2001). Building customer-based brand equity. *Marketing Management, 10 (2),* 14–19.

Keller, K.L. (2002). Branding and brand equity. In B.A. Weitz & R. Wensley (Eds.), *Handbook of marketing*. London: Sage Publications, 151–178.

Keller, K.L. (2003). *Strategic brand management: Building, measuring, and managing brand equity*. Upper Saddle River, NJ: Prentice Hall.

Kihlstrom, J.F., Mulvaney, S., Tobias, B.A., & Tobis, I.P. (2000). The emotional unconscious. In E. Eich & J.F. Kihlstrom (Eds.), *Cognition and Emotion*, p. 30–86.

Kohlberg, L. (1971). From is to ought: How to commit the naturalistic fallacy and get away with it in the study of moral development. *Cognitive Development and Epistemology*, 151–235.

Larsen, R.J., Diener, E., & Emmons, R.A. (1986). Affect intensity and reactions to daily life events. *Journal of Personality and Social Psychology, 51 (4)*, 803–814.

Luce, M.F. (1998). Choosing to avoid: Coping with negatively emotion-laden consumer decisions. *Journal of Consumer Research, 24 (4)*, 409–433.

Mas-Colell, A., Whinston, M.D., & Green, J.R. (1995). *Microeconomic theory*. New York: Oxford University Press.

Miniard, P.W., Sirdeshmukh, D., & Innis, D.E. (1992). Peripheral persuasion and brand choice. *The Journal of Consumer Research, 19 (2)*, 226–239.

Mitchell, A.A., & Olson, J.C. (1981). Are product attribute beliefs the only mediator of advertising effects on brand attitude? *Journal of Marketing Research, 18 (3)*, 318–332.

Naqvi, N., Shiv, B., & Bechara, A. (2006). The role of emotion in decision making: A cognitive neuroscience perspective. *Current Directions in Psychological Science, 15 (5)*, 260–264.

Niedenthal, P.M. (2007). Embodying emotion. *Science, 316 (5827)*, 1002–1005.

Norton, M.I., Mochon, D., & Ariely, D. (forthcoming). The IKEA effect: When labor leads to love. *Journal of Consumer Research*.

Park, C.W., Jaworski, B.J., & MacInnis D.J. (1986). Strategic brand concept-image management. *Journal of Marketing, 50 (4)*, 135–45.

Payne, J.W., Bettman, J.R., & Johnson, E.J. (1993). *The adaptive decision maker*. Cambridge: Cambridge University Press.

Russo, J.E., Meloy, M.G., & Medvec, V.H. (1998). Predecisional distortion of product information. *Journal of Marketing Research, 35 (4)*, 438–452.

Russo, J.E., Meloy, M.G., & Wilks, T.J. (2000). Predecisional distortion of information by auditors and salespersons. *Management Science, 46 (1)*, 13–27.

Shiv, B., Loewenstein, G., Bechara, A., Damasio, H., & Damasio, A. (2005). Investment behavior and the negative side of emotion. *Psychological Science, 16 (June)*, 435–439.

Sugden, R. (1991). Rational choice: A survey of contributions from economics and philosophy. *The Economic Journal, 101 (407)*, 751–785.

Titchener, E.B. (1910). *A textbook of psychology*. New York: Macmillan.

Wilson, T.D., Lisle, D.J., Schooler, J.W., Hodges, S.D., Klaaren, K.J., & LaFleur, S.J. (1993). Introspecting about reasons can reduce post-choice satisfaction. *Personality and Social Psychology Bulletin, 19 (3)*, 331–339.

Zajonc, R.B. (1980). Feeling and thinking: Preferences need no inferences. *American Psychologist, 35 (2)*, 151–175.

Zajonc, R.B., & Markus, H. (1982). Affective and cognitive factors in preferences. *The Journal of Consumer Research, 9 (2)*, 123–131.

10

Utility-Based Models of Brand Equity

Tülin Erdem
New York University

Joffre Swait
University of Alberta

Introduction

Brand equity has been a key evolving concept in marketing for the last two decades. Brand equity is often referred to as the added value to the firm, the trade, or the consumer with which a brand endows a product (Farquhar, 1989) or, similarly, as the difference between the value of the branded product to the consumer and the value of the product without that branding (McQueen, 1991).

There exist many definitions and conceptual frameworks of brand equity. Aaker (1991) defined brand equity as a collection of brand assets and liabilities linked to a brand, its name, and symbol, which add to or subtract from the value provided by a product or service to a firm and/or to the firm's customers. In Aaker's framework, brand awareness, perceived quality, brand associations, and brand loyalty are the main components of brand equity. Keller (1993) offered a cognitive psychology perspective, defining customer-based brand equity as the differential effect that brand knowledge has on consumer response to the marketing of that brand. In Keller's framework, brand knowledge has two components: brand image (based on brand associations) and brand awareness. Keller emphasizes the importance of uniqueness, favorability, and strength of brand associations. Young and Rubicam's Brand Asset Valuator posits brand equity to have four dimensions, namely, knowledge, esteem, differentiation, and relevance. Adopting an information economics view, Erdem and Swait (1998) argue that consumer-based brand equity is the value of a brand as a credible signal of a product's positioning. In their framework, the content, clarity, and credibility of the brand signal creates intangible benefits, enhances perceived quality, and decreases consumer perceived risk and information costs, and hence increases consumer utility, which underlies the added value associated with a brand.

These definitions and frameworks share the view that the value of a brand to a firm is created through the brand's effect on consumers. Thus, most customer-based brand equity conceptualizations emphasize consumer-based concepts such as brand associations (Aaker, 1991), brand knowledge (Keller, 1993), perceived clarity, and credibility of the brand information under imperfect and asymmetric information (Erdem & Swait, 1998). The common thread in these conceptualizations is that, implicitly or explicitly, brands provide utility or value to consumers, and, hence, affect different stages of the decision and choice process, ranging from preference and perception formation, information search, consideration and choice set formation, and choice itself.

Consistent with the variety of conceptualizations of brand equity, there have also been proposed different measurement approaches and models of brand equity. In this chapter, we focus on consumer-based brand equity models that utilize the utility maximization and random utility framework. However, for completeness, we would like to note that to date brand equity measurement schemes can be categorized as component-based versus holistic and source-oriented (brand equity to customers) versus outcome-oriented (brand equity to firms, retailers, etc.). Table 10.1 lists examples of each type of approach.

Source-oriented approaches aim to measure brand equity to the customer, that is, customer-based brand equity. Outcome-oriented approaches, on the other hand, focus on the brand equity to the firm or the trade as a result of customer-based brand equity (i.e. brand-related marketplace behaviors that create value to the firm and affect a brand's market performance). Brand equity measurement approaches can also be differentiated by whether they are component-based or holistic. Component-based systems first define and then calibrate the individual elements of consumer brand equity (such as brand awareness) separately, while holistic systems have as their objective an overall evaluation of the brand (even if most of the holistic approaches measure at least some of the individual components of brand equity, such as perceived quality). Thus, component-based and holistic approaches to customer-based brand equity measurement can be easily linked since the total value of the brand may be modeled in terms of its components.

Furthermore, in the case of customer-based brand equity, holistic approaches aim to provide an overall measure of customer-based brand equity (source-oriented), either in terms of utilities or willingness to pay (based on survey, experimental or transactional data such as scanner

TABLE 10.1

Extant Approaches to Brand Equity Measurement

	Source-oriented: customer- based	Outcome-oriented: firm-based (or trade-based)
Component-based	Aaker (1991, 1996), Keller (1993, 1998)	Keller (1993, 1998)
Holistic	*Utility-based (cross-sectional): Swait et al. (1993), Park & Srinivasan (1994)*	
	Utility-based (panel data): Static: Kamakura & Russell (1993) Dynamic: Erdem (1998)	*Utility-based (time series): Kartuno and Rao (2007), Goldfarb, Lu, Moorthy (2007)*
		Financial value (inter-firm analysis): Simon & Sullivan (1993)
		Financial value (intra-firm analysis): Farquhar et al. (1991)
		Profits–revenue (Ailawadi et al. 2003)

panel data). Holistic approaches to brand equity to the firm (outcome-oriented approaches) do so in terms of additional profits, revenues or stock returns due to brand (calculated from observed market data), compared to a non-branded product.

Finally, customer-based brand equity can be linked to firm-based brand equity, that is, a brand's impact on market performance. For example, Aaker and Jacobsan (1994) link perceived quality to firms' stock prices; Kim, H., Kim, W.G., and An (2003) study the correlations among individual customer-based brand equity components such as awareness, image, loyalty, and the firm's revenue. Srinivasan, Park, and Chang (2005) link the effect of consumers' incremental choice probabilities to brands' contribution margins. In this chapter, we will only focus on approaches based on utility and profit maximization that attempt to link customer-based brand equity to brand equity to the firm and/or market performance.

The first objective of this chapter is to summarize customer-based holistic brand equity models based on utility maximization, including very recent work that models both customer-based brand equity and brand equity to the firm, using utility and profit maximization frameworks in an equilibrium setting. The areas we focus on are highlighted in bold italics in Table 10.1. The second objective of the chapter is to provide an integrative framework based on utility maximization and discrete choice modeling, within which psychological (e.g., Keller, 1993) and information economics theoretic (e.g., Erdem & Swait, 1998) perspectives of brand equity can be explained and measured, while also allowing for a holistic measurement of overall customer-based brand equity. A third objective is to suggest avenues for future research in utility-based brand equity modeling, as well as propose further integration of different approaches, such as relating utility-based measures to financial measures of brand equity.

A variety of customer-based brand equity conceptualizations can be unified in the context of a dynamic brand choice model with a behaviorally motivated and process-oriented utility specification. Building upon Erdem et al. (1999), we provide such a modeling framework below. We will use this modeling framework to discuss various utility-based modeling efforts in the following sections.

The second section introduces the utility-based modeling framework to customer-based brand equity, The third section outlines different streams of literature that adopt the utility maximization framework to measure brand equity. The fourth section discusses the recent approaches to link the utility-based approaches to market performance of a brand (firm-based brand equity). Finally, the fifth section discusses directions for future research.

A Utility-Based Modeling Framework for Customer-Based Brand Equity

A variety of customer-based brand equity conceptualizations can be unified in the context of a dynamic brand choice model with a behaviorally motivated and process-oriented utility specification. Building upon Erdem et al. (1999), we provide such a modeling framework below. We will use this modeling framework to discuss various utility-based modeling efforts in the following sections.

Multiattribute utility theory implies that the main building blocks of the consumer choice process are consumer attribute perceptions or beliefs (X^*), which involve encodings of actual product attributes (X), and consumer taste or utility weights (β). This basic proposition may be extended by incorporating consumer uncertainty about product attributes, so that beliefs about attribute levels are characterized as distributions with mean (μ) and variance (σ^2). The mean represents the perception of the expected value of an attribute level, whereas the variance reflects the consumer's uncertainty about that level, thus capturing perceived risk associated with the attribute. Consumers may also be uncertain about the attribute weights to use in evaluating attribute partworths or how to combine the partworths to evaluate utility. Finally, in the presence of consumer uncertainty, consumer utility will also depend on information costs associated with attribute perceptions and the taste weights. This individual utility or assessment of the product/service attractiveness is additively decomposable into two parts, systematic (V_i) and stochastic (ε_i) utility. According to a combination rule, consumer-perceived attribute levels (X^*) and tastes (β) are combined to form the systematic utility, V_i. A similar process for other products (or brands, i) defines the choice set C of objects that subjects actively evaluate during the decision process.

Since total utility has a stochastic component, choice is modeled probabilistically rather than in a deterministic framework. We view the choice stage from the perspective of random utility choice theory (McFadden, 1981, 1986). The stochastic utility component, which gives the framework its name, is usually thought of as capturing analyst-based observation errors (e.g., random taste shocks, unobserved product characteristics). In this framework, choice is assumed to be exercised from among the choice set C of objects, which can itself be latent (see Manski, 1977). As depicted in Figure 10.1, at any point in time certain brands may be in the choice set C_t (brands i, j and k are included in the example) and others excluded (brand l is excluded), partly as a function of brand-related activities.

Figure 10.1 suggests that the various elements of the choice process are individual- (p), brand- (i) and time- (t) specific. Not only may consumers have different tastes and perceptions, but a particular consumer's perceptions and tastes may also evolve over time. Although the cognitive psychological and information economics views of brand equity focus on different aspects of the choice process, Figure 10.1 accommodates a broad set of phenomena associated with brand equity. For example, Keller (1993) suggests that brand equity arises from two major elements: awareness and associations. Awareness, whether assessed in terms of recall or recognition, rests essentially on the brand's salience (i.e., the consumer's ability to retrieve the target brand with or without associated cues). Awareness is also one of the four components of brand equity in Aaker's (1991) framework. It can best be captured by a more detailed formulation of the choice set formation process in Figure 10.1. Consideration may be modeled as contingent on awareness, which in turn is a function of exposure to, and the credibility of, information, as well as the importance of communicated attributes. Since such processes occur as information is encountered initially, and also from choice-event feedback, the picture of consumer learning invoked here is consistent with a dynamic, information-theoretic framework.

The other major source of brand equity in Keller's framework, and a major component of brand equity in Aaker's framework, is the set of associations that the consumer holds about the brand. Keller suggests that valuable brand associations are strong, favorable, and unique. Strength and favorableness have received considerable attention in multi-attribute utility modeling. Belief strength may be loosely related to the consumer's

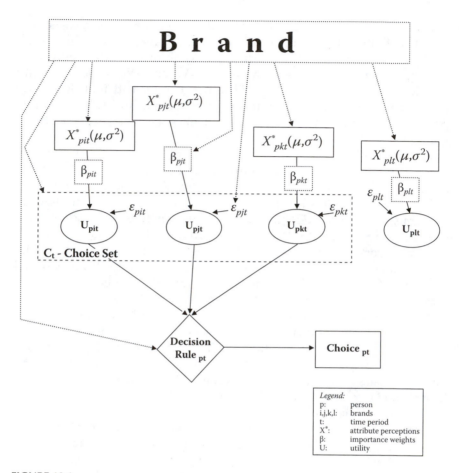

FIGURE 10.1

Brand equity—generalized impact of the brand on choice. From Erdem et al. (1999). Used with permission.

perception of the products' attribute levels (X^*_{jm} in a standard multi-attribute model, where m is an attribute and j denotes the brand) and favorableness is represented in the sign and size of the importance weight in a multi-attribute utility model (β_m). In this representation, the overall utility of a brand would be represented as $V_j = \Sigma_m \beta_m X^*_{jm}$. The new element introduced by Keller is uniqueness, which is not directly captured by most multi-attribute utility models. This is an important aspect to branding, with brand strength stemming from points of parity and competitive advantages being generated by points of difference. Krishnan (1996) provides theoretical and empirical evidence of the importance of uniqueness in brand evaluation. In the present framework, one might accommodate uniqueness notions through an increase in the weights attached to the attributes that are perceived to be unique, or by adopting a factor-analytic approach to multi-attribute utility theory. For example, Elrod and Keane (1995) estimate a factor-analytic probit model that includes between-brand common factors (attributes), whose levels differ among brands but are shared by all brands, and a unique brand factor (attribute).

Figure 10.1 therefore includes many of the key constructs used in cognitive psychology views of brand equity. At the same time, the framework also incorporates the basic information economics constructs such as consumer uncertainty about preferences and tastes, and the associated perceived risk and information costs. Erdem and Swait (1998) suggest that (a) brand investments and (b) consistency of marketing actions over time and across marketing mix elements increase the credibility of a brand as a signal of a product's position. This leads to increases in perceived quality and to decreases in perceived risk and information costs. Similarly, consistency may also affect the clarity of the brand signal. In addition, constructs such as credibility may affect consumer utility weights, e.g., by reducing price sensitivity (Erdem, Swait, & Louviere, 2002). It has also been shown that brand credibility has a role in the composition of the consideration set (Erdem & Swait, 2004) and the choice set (Swait & Erdem, 2007), thus emphasizing the non-utility brand impacts that are depicted in Figure 10.1. The brand investments and consistency constructs (Erdem & Swait, 1998) also fit into Figure 10.1 as exogenous variables that affect consumer perceptions (both mean and variance), as well as utility weights and information costs. As Morrison and Roberts (1998) show, consistency between the distribution elements of a financial service and its features is more important than either mix element in isolation.

The complementary nature of the cognitive psychological and information economics views of brand equity is also illustrated in Figure 10.1. In the cognitive psychology view, brand equity stems from awareness of brand features and associations that drive attribute perceptions, whereas the information economics view emphasizes consumer uncertainty and its impact on consumer choice via perceived risk and information costs. The two perspectives also share similar ideas regarding the market consequences of brand equity (Erdem & Swait, 1998), or what Keller terms the "outcomes" of brand equity (Keller, 1993). In the information economics framework, a brand's added market performance (greater consumer loyalty, more aggressive pricing, enhanced capability for extensions, etc.) are the results of increased perceived quality and reduced risk and information costs. In the cognitive psychology perspective, these marketplace outcomes are attributed to the existence of strong, favorable and unique associations in the minds of consumers.

To recapitulate, the main point of Figure 10.1 is that the brand can affect several components of the choice process. For example, suppose a brand undertakes an advertising campaign that raises doubts about a competitor's ability to deliver on product claims. Such advertising may not affect consumer tastes, attribute evaluation and combination rules, or decision rules, but could influence how consumers encode the attributes and form choice sets. In contrast, if a brand is the first to introduce a new attribute into a product category, the brand's advertising and consumer experience with the pioneering product should influence consumer tastes, perhaps to the advantage of the pioneering brand (Carpenter & Nakamoto, 1989).

Furthermore, one of the more intriguing possibilities created by this framework is the incorporation of choice consistency over time and within segments. A recent research stream suggests that the stochastic utility component of choice models can capture a number of effects that are related to utility variance rather than utility mean (see, e.g., Swait & Adamowicz, 2001; Hensher, Louviere, & Swait, 1999; Swait & Erdem, 2007). In other words, the credibility of a brand's positioning information can promote more consistent choice behavior within and across consumers by reducing perceived risk and information search costs (Erdem & Swait, 1998). The random utility framework can represent such effects by specifying the scale of the error term as a function of appropriate individual characteristics, context variables, and experimental manipulations (Swait & Erdem, 2007; Swait & Louviere, 1993).

Finally, the basic structure used in Figure 10.1 could be the guiding framework for exploring dynamic brand equity formation, a topic we will discuss in more detail later.

Consumer Choice Processes and Brand Equity Measurement

Cross-Sectional Models

The models reviewed in this section are based on cross-sectional data, usually elicited as some form of revealed or stated preference. The salient difference, then, with the models of the following section, is in respect to the absence of dynamic factors underlying the utility measure. When stated preferences are used, these are usually obtained through some variant of conjoint, particularly discrete choice experiments.

In regard to holistic approaches involving cross-sectional models, Swait, Erdem, Louviere, and Dubelar (1993) used random utility theory to calibrate the reservation price of consumers as an indicant of how much the brand name is worth. Central to their concept of brand equity is the idea of an equalization price, defined thusly for brand j:

$$EP_j = p_j - V_j / \beta_p, \tag{1}$$

CONSISTENCY OF MARKETING ACTIVITIES PREDICTS BRAND EQUITY

The insights that can be gained by employing utility-based models of brand equity are illustrated by an analysis of the fabric softener product category. How do people choose a fabric softener brand? A 2002 study by this chapter's authors, Swait and Erdem, used the information economics framework the researchers had developed to look at this category and its brands' equity.

Employing a utility-based model of brand equity, using the general schematic shown in Figure 10.1, the authors demonstrated that customers' preferences for specific fabric softeners were not only based on the product's delivery of direct benefits such as smell, static reduction, or a wrinkle-free appearance. Their choice was also based on the consistency of that brand's marketing activities, including consistency over time in pricing, the availability of the product on the store shelf, and promotional activities such as weekly newspaper inserts or in-store displays, all of which help support a brand. The authors found, for example, that the simple act of making sure your fabric softener brand is consistently present on a store's shelves can increase your brand's attractiveness.

"From the information economics perspective, brands are important to consumers because they offer a convenient short-cut to making reliable decisions." For the customers trying to choose a fabric softener, the authors said, "A strong brand with high equity, like Downy, provided credible information, compensating for the consumers' lack of knowledge about the product. Further, the consistency of availability of a strong brand—knowing that it would very likely be on the shelf the next time you went to buy fabric softener—affected choice." They explain, "When a brand fails to be present on the shelf, this reduces its usefulness to the consumer and increases consideration of competing brands, leading not only to the obvious loss of the immediate sale, but ultimately, to long-term erosion of the brand's equity. Why pick a brand if you're not sure it will be available consistently in the future?"

Price also plays an important role in the utility-based model of brand equity. In the short-term, price promotions and discounts add utility to a given product, boosting its sales. But, if consumers notice a discounting trend over time, they may become wary of the product, doubting the consistency of the brand's pricing strategy and the quality of its products.

Erdem and Swait's research shows that brand managers need to not only look at short-term goals like increasing current sales, but also take into consideration the overall management of their brand's equity in the long term.

R.D.M. & L.W.P.

where p_j is the market price, V_j is the utility of its constituent attributes, and β_p is the consumer's price sensitivity (here, assumed generic, not brand-specific). Essentially, EP is the consumers' willingness-to-pay (WTP) for objective and symbolic attributes, anchored on the brand's market price; thus, it represents an individual-specific price equivalent for the brand. It may be smaller or larger than the market price, depending upon the sign of V (since the sign of β_p is expected to be negative). From its derivation (see Swait et al., 1993), equalization price is seen to be a normalized measure of the net value of a brand relative to the value of all brands in the consumer's choice set. Swait et al. show that EP can be divided into three components: (1) an intangible brand effect, (2) the utility due to objective attributes, and (3) the utility due to perceptions of brand positions (or the utility of symbolic attributes). Thus, while they study the overall value of a brand on a holistic basis, it is also broken down into component parts. This approach, which permits mapping of brand perceptions, brand by price interactions, and attribute by price interactions, provides managerial diagnostics not only about the strength of the brand, but also the sources of that strength (see also Rangaswamy, Burke, & Oliva, 1993, concerning attribute brand interactions in the context of brand extensions). Swait et al. (1993) also demonstrate that EP has a functional relationship to the brand equity intangible valuation measure by Kamakura and Russell (1993), based on scanner panel data.

While Rangaswamy et al.'s (1993) interest was primarily on the extendibility of brands, and therefore defined brand equity "... as a residual value in the form of favorable impressions, attitudinal dispositions, and behavioral predilections among all those who are exposed to the marketing activities related to the brand" (Rangaswamy et al., 1993), they added to the discussion about brand equity measure the idea that this residual value could be captured through the introduction of brand by attribute interactions. From the perspective of choice model specification, this is equivalent to arguing that utility-based models should have brand-specific coefficients. Referring back to our discussion concerning Figure 10.1, they essentially allow encodings of product attributes to be brand-specific. They also decompose the utility measure into (1) a brand component, (2) an attribute-based component, and (3) a brand by attribute component.

A strong brand by attribute utility component in a core product class is indicative, according to Rangaswamy et al. (1993), to greater difficulty in brand extendibility to a more dissimilar product class. Due to their focus, no specific measure of brand equity is proposed by Rangaswamy et al.

Park and Srinivasan (1994) took a similar approach to Swait et al. (1993) for measuring the total equity of a brand. Brand equity for brand j is defined by them as

$$BE_j = (V_{pj} - V_{oj}) = \beta' \times (X_{pj} - X_{oj}),\tag{2}$$

where β is a column vector of taste/partworth coefficients, V_{pj} is the total utility of the product under brand j, based on user perceptions of its attributes (vector X_{pj}), while V_{oj} is the total utility of the product under brand j, based on objective attributes (vector X_{oj}). (The second expression in (2) follows assuming a linear-in-the-parameters utility function.) Dividing (2) by the price coefficient will transform the units of this brand equity measure from utiles to a monetary metric. So, the essential basis for Park and Srinivasan's brand equity measure is the gap existing between brand-driven attribute perceptions and their objective counterparts. It is expected that strong brands will create larger, favorable attribute gaps, hence leading to higher brand equity values. They partitioned brand effects on utility into attribute-based and nonattribute-based components. The reader is urged to consult Park and Srinivasan (1994) for details on the measurement technique used to support this definition of brand equity. Since the method requires knowledge of the perceptual/objective gap at the attribute level, a number of different stages are necessary during measurement. Like Swait et al. (1993), this approach also provides specific managerial guidance about areas in which a brand is weak or strong.

It was noted before that one of the streams of brand equity research has based itself on concepts from information economics (see Erdem & Swait, 1998). This stream views the brand as a signaling mechanism for its position in attribute space, and has associated with this mechanism the critical property of credibility (or believability, based on trustworthiness and expertise). The brand is seen to have value to consumers because it reduces both decision-making costs and risk perceptions. Based on this framework, Erdem, Swait, and Louviere (2002) focus on testing the basis for the existence of price premia for strong (i.e., credible) brands. They show that strong brands have lower price sensitivities due to high credibility levels, specifically by demonstrating that a significant price by credibility interaction (with positive sign, thus decreasing overall price sensitivity) can be identified. In addition, they suggest the use of a value of credibility (VOC) measure to describe brand strength, defined as follows:

$$VOC_j = \frac{\partial p}{\partial C_j} = \frac{\partial V_j}{\partial C_j} \left[\frac{\partial V_j}{\partial p} \right]^{-1} \tag{3}$$

where C_j is the credibility of brand j, V_i is systematic utility, and p is price. (This measure is akin to the value of time measures used in cost/benefit analyses for engineering projects.) VOC expresses the monetary equivalent of a unit of brand credibility. While not a brand equity measure per se, in the sense that it does not express a valuation of the entire brand's impact, it can be seen as a direct measure of the brand's strength on consumer preference.

Up to this point, the approaches and models reviewed have taken the position that brand equity is inferred from all or part of the utility function. However, the frameworks of Aaker (1991) and Keller (1993), as well as the considerations detailed above, suggest that brands play manifold roles in consumers' decision processes. For example, as noted above, the results of Erdem, Swait, and Louviere (2002) suggest that the brand's strength (as expressed via credibility) affects consumers' sensitivity to price changes. Similarly, Erdem and Swait (2004) show that brand credibility is a strong explanator of brand consideration over a wide range of product classes. Thus, upon further thought, it would seem that brand equity measures based solely on systematic consumer utility tell only a partial story.

Srinivasan et al. (2005) take a significant step in measuring brand equity under more general conditions, presenting an extension to the prior approach of Park and Srinivasan (1994). Srinivasan et al. define brand equity for a given consumer and brand j as

$$BE_j = q(\Delta P_j)g_j, \tag{4}$$

where q is the category purchase for the individual during a given time period (e.g., a year), g is the unit contribution margin (= unit price – unit variable cost) for the brand, and ΔP_j is the difference in choice probability between brand j and a nonbranded product. Note how this measure differs from (2), since it expresses a clearer dependence on outcomes rather than just preferences. In addition, through the empirically determined measure q, expression (4) also captures indirectly impacts of choice set formation (via, e.g., reflecting the availability of the brand for it to be chosen).

Working within the random utility paradigm, and using the information economics paradigm as the basis for explaining brand effects, Swait and Erdem (2007) extend the basic measurement method covered in this section to explain the role of brand in (1) choice set formation, (2) systematic utility, and (3) stochastic utility. They find significant brand credibility impacts in all three components, in two product classes (PCs and orange juice). Their results suggest that (a) the brand plays a role in the simplification of decision making by eliminating low credibility brands from further study, (b) confirms that higher credibility brands have higher systematic utility, ceteris paribus, and (c) that as credibility increases, the contribution of stochastic utility (i.e., utility arising from unmeasured/unspecified sources) decreases, implying that uncertainty is reduced and evaluation of attribute-based systematic utility approaches total utility. Given these multiple roles for the brand, it seems something of a challenge to propose straightforward measures of brand equity of the type suggested by Swait et al. (1993), Park and Srinivasan (1994), or even that of Erdem, Swait, and Louviere (2002).

However, building on the idea of Srinivasan et al. (2005), consider a market with branded products contained in the set M. Let p_j be the price of brand j, and A_j be the probability that j is included in a consumer's choice set. Then it is possible to generalize the equalization price measure (Expression 1) as follows to account for the multiple effects identified by Swait and Erdem (2007):

$$GEP_j = \sum_{B \subseteq M} Q(B)\left(EP_j\right), \qquad (5)$$

where GEP is the generalized equalization price measure; EP_j is the brand-specific, utility-based equalization price given by Expression (1), based on the conditional choice model; and Q(B) is the probability that $B \subseteq M$ is the true choice set of the individual. Thus, GEP takes into account the structure of the market (like EP does), but generalizes that structure by accounting for the brand's role during choice set formation through probability Q(B). As with EP, the unit of GEP is monetary. If we don't have direct measures of Q(B), we can approximate it by assuming brand availability is independent across brands, leading to this expression:

$$Q(B) = \frac{\prod_{k \in B} A_k \; \prod_{l \in M-B}\left(1 - A_l\right)}{1 - \prod_{m \in M}\left(1 - A_m\right)}, \quad B \subseteq M. \qquad (6)$$

This probability is conditional on the choice set being nonempty.

Agrawal and Rao (1996) present a comparison of a number of survey- and conjoint-based measures of brand equity, measured at the individual consumer level. Their interest lay particularly in the convergent validity of a set of eleven measures, varying from unaided brand awareness to preference and dollar-metric measures similar to those discussed above. They found strong evidence of convergent validity among the measures, with the exception of unaided brand awareness. They point out that the preference measures have greater face validity than some of the other measures because of their ability to predict market share well; on the other hand, obtaining such measures does involve a greater cognitive burden for respondents.

Panel Data Models

Static Models

In contrast to the above measurement approaches using cross-sectional data, brand equity for different brands may be inferred from studying brand choices of individual consumers over time. Most such models utilize transactional data like that arising from scanner panels. In a seminal paper, Kamakura and Russell (1993) estimated a latent-class choice model to infer brand values. They used the segment-specific brand constant as a measure of segment-level brand equity, after controlling for valuation of tangible product attributes (labeled as tangible brand value), price, and advertising. These brand specific constants can be thought of as a linear combination

$$\alpha_{pj} = \sum_{n=1}^{N} \beta_{pnj} X_{pnj}^{*} , \qquad (7)$$

where X^{*} stands for intangible product attribute perceptions or any other attribute perceptions that are not controlled for, and β stands for utility weight as per Figure 10.1. The index p stands for person or segment, N is the total number of such attributes where n stands for a specific attribute perception. In the static models, there are no time subscripts (t).

Kamakura and Russell (1993) postulated overall brand equity to be the summation of segment level brand equities. This paper was one of the first to model heterogeneity in consumer preferences and perceptions and hence, the resulting heterogeneity in brand values across consumer segments. A managerially useful concept in the study is a brand's dominance value, defined as the ratio of the brand's vulnerability (to attack by other brands) to its clout (its power to attack other brands).

Dynamic Models

Brand equity formation is inherently a dynamic phenomenon. Yet most of the modeling literature that directly addresses issues of brand equity measurement has taken a static view, mainly because of data limitations. One of the few exceptions is work by Sriram, Balachnader, and Kalwani (2007) that estimates quarterly brand-specific constants as measures of brand equity, then regresses these on lagged brand-specific constants (to capture state dependence such as inertia in brand equity formation), marketing mix variables such as price, advertising, promotions, etc., as well as variables such as new product introductions. The researchers find that there is high and positive state dependence in brand equity (pointing at brand equity dynamics).

Thus, it is not surprising that the vast literature on dynamic choice would have implications for customer- or consumer-based brand equity. Particularly, the structural dynamic choice literature has implications for brand equity measurement, even if this stream of work has not been necessarily positioned as work on "brand equity measurement" per se.

Before we establish the link between the dynamic structural choice literature and brand equity measurement, we need to make some definitions. We use the term *structural modeling* here in the context of models that are based on objective function maximization (utility for consumers and profits for firms), and the model in question is based on the primitives of these functions such as consumer preferences, perceptions, and expectations. Structural dynamic choice models specify the exact behavioral source of choice dynamics. For example, positive state dependence, that is, choice probabilities conditional on prior purchase being higher than unconditional ones, could be due to a variety of reasons such as inertia, habit persistence or learning, and associated risk aversion and familiarity, etc. A dynamic structural model specifies the process of this dynamics, rather than capturing the dynamics in a reduced-form way through some formulation of past purchases (e.g., the brand loyalty or purchase feedback variable of Guadagni and Little, 1983).

One advantage of structural models is that the estimated parameters are policy invariant (Lucas, 1976). For example, assume that consumers have forward-looking price and promotion expectations. If a firm promotes frequently, consumers will eventually learn that the brand will be on deal at some subsequent and predictable point of time. This may influence consumers' purchase timing, brand and quantity decisions, and increase consumer price sensitivity (see, e.g., Swait & Erdem, 2002). Under such a scenario, if one estimates a reduced-form model without modeling how consumers form forward-looking price expectations, the parameter estimate for price cannot be used to evaluate possible changes in brand choice probabilities under alternative pricing strategies. This is because every change in pricing strategy will also alter price sensitivity (i.e., price sensitivity is not policy-invariant). However, in a structural model that explicitly incorporates the impact of price expectations on consumer behavior, the price sensitivity parameter will (arguably) have captured the underlying mechanism. Hence, the estimated parameter can be used to evaluate alternative pricing strategies.

Learning plays a key role in dynamic brand equity formation. Brands may affect consumer preferences and perceptions over time. Thus, a structural modeling approach that explicitly models the process by which consumers learn about brands and their preferences through brand activities and other sources would provide a more complete representation of how brand equity develops over time in a dynamic consumer choice process.

One of the early examples of a structural learning model with myopic consumers (consumers who maximize immediate utility rather than being forward-looking and maximizing long-run expected utility) is the model proposed by Roberts and Urban (1988), who modeled learning about product attributes through word-of-mouth and test-driving in car markets (note that theirs was not a structural model). Erdem and Keane (1996) estimate a structural model with forward-looking customers who learn about quality levels of brands through sampling and use experience, as well as advertising (where the content of the advertising message provides direct quality information) in frequently purchased product categories. The dynamic structural learning model they estimate shows how advertising messages and positive use experience can increase perceived quality, as well as how advertising messages and use experiences may decrease perceived risk, both of which increase brand utility. In this context, the increase in mean quality perceptions and decrease in the variance of these perceptions (perceived risk) constitutes a measure of consumer-based brand equity. Following Erdem and Keane (1996), there have been a number of papers that modeled consumer learning through use experience (Crawford & Shum, 2005), advertising content (Byzalov & Schachar, 2004), advertising frequency (advertising signaling quality; see Ackerberg, 2003), price (price signaling quality Erdem, Keane, & Sun, 2008); and the like. Finally, Erdem (1998) estimates a learning model with myopic consumers allowing use experience in one category to affect consumer perceptions of the same brand in another category for umbrella brands. The main premise of all these models is that consumers have priors about mean brand "quality" (which may involve both tangible and intangible dimensions), and their quality beliefs are distributed with some variance; through use experience and marketing mix activities they update both mean expectations and variance of their beliefs. In such a setting, high equity brands are associated with high means and low variances (i.e., reduced uncertainty).

There are four noteworthy aspects of these learning models. First, these models incorporated one consumer attribute perception, labeled as perceived quality. Perceived quality, in these models, is thought of as being a "summary statistic" of multiple subdimensions. Thus, referring back to Figure 10.1, the analyst is interested in modeling the evolution of the mean and variance of consumer quality perceptions $X_{pjt}^*(\ , \sigma^2)$. Second, in these models the "noisiness" of each information source is estimated, and according to Bayesian theory, the noisier the information, the less that information source will be used to update quality expectations. Thus, for example, the noisiness of advertising as an information source will be lower the more consistent the advertising messages. Consequently, these learning models also measure some of the concepts mentioned in the brand equity literature (such as consistency of brand communications).

Third, most work on brand equity discusses the link between marketing activities and brand equity (advertising, for example, builds brand equity). Yet, most measurement approaches measure brand equity after controlling for advertising, although in fact advertising expenditures are part of brand investments (Erdem & Swait, 1998). The dynamic learning models directly incorporate the effects of marketing mix activities such as advertising by modeling their impact on consumer expectations and uncertainty, and consequently, on brand equity. Indeed, advertising may play multiple roles in brand equity formation, and these different roles can be modeled and differentiated within the dynamic structural modeling framework (Nitin et al., 2007).

Fourth, for mathematical tractability reasons, such models have typically used a Bayesian updating mechanism to represent how consumers learn (e.g., about product quality). However, such mechanisms cannot directly handle the reality of consumer learning, in which attribute perceptions and tastes may be learned implicitly, biased initially and, furthermore, updated via a mechanism susceptible to confirmatory biases. We will discuss the future research implications of this below.

Linking Customer-Based Brand Equity to Market Performance

Kartuno and Rao (2007) and Goldfarb, Lu, and Moorthy (2007) develop and estimate a full equilibrium model (modeling both the demand and supply) to capture the structural link between consumer-based brand equity derived from a utility maximization framework and the brand's market performance. Kartuno and Rao model consumer-based brand equity using a logit model that accounts for the product's physical characteristics, marketing mix variables, as well as perceived quality and satisfaction with the brand. Their consumer-based brand equity measure has a time-constant and a time-varying component, the time varying-component consisting of variables such as satisfaction and perceived quality. Tangible attributes of the brand are assumed not to be a part of the brand equity measure. They also account for firm competition in pricing and advertising. They model the brand's market performance using financial measures of the brand's profit, profit premium and revenue, and revenue premium. Their application is in the U.S. car industry.

Goldfarb et al. (2007) define brand value as the difference in equilibrium profit between the brand in question and its counterfactual unbranded equivalent on search attributes. They adopt an oligopoly with a common retailer framework to model the supply side, but do not make advertising endogenous (i.e., they do not model firms' advertising decisions). Consumer-based brand equity in their framework is measured as the brand constants, after controlling for search attributes.

In short, both approaches use discrete choice modeling based on random utility theory to measure brand equity, while also modeling firms' pricing and/or advertising decisions.

Future Research

Our emphasis in this chapter has been on the measurement and modeling of brand equity at the individual level using utility-theoretic methods, whether cross-sectional or dynamic in specification. This stream of research has given rise to a number of measures of brand equity and strength based on consumer preferences, some of which have been discussed above. The literature, however, has not generally and formally addressed issues of aggregation from the individual consumer level to the brand, firm, and market levels (though see Srinivasan et al., 2005). In addition, it is necessary to construct explicit links between these levels of aggregation of brand equity measures and more commonly understood financial and accounting measures (e.g., elements of balance sheets, stock prices). There is also a need to test the capability of measurement frameworks to reflect the brand equity impacts of specific actions of firms (e.g., product repositionings, brand extensions, price policy alterations), environmental factors (e.g., stock market conditions, entry or failure of competitors, introduction of new substitutes), random shocks (e.g., product recalls, service failures, financial scandals), and so forth. Such research might form part of the basis for contingency planning on the part of firms to mitigate adverse impacts to brands, both in preventive and corrective modes of action.

One main area of future research is linking both consumer-based and firm-based brand equity to financial metrics, such as stock prices. There is a strong tradition in both marketing and accounting of studying the value of the brand in the market place on a holistic basis. Simon and Sullivan (1993) regard the value of the firm to be the value of its tangibles and intangibles. They break up the value of the intangibles into brand intangibles (demand-enhancing and efficiency-producing intangibles), nonbrand firm-specific intangibles, and industry intangibles. The demand-enhancing brand intangibles accrue as a result of marketing activity (e.g., order-of-entry advantages and advertising share), and thus represent brand equity on the balance sheet. Simon and Sullivan do a cross-sectional analysis with different companies, decomposing brand equity into share advantage, age, and advertising. This enables an examination of the relative value of brand intangibles, which they then monitor over time. Farquhar, Han, and Ijiri (1991) adopt a similar approach but look within the firm to identify the financial implications of brand equity. They introduce the term "momentum accounting" to study the enduring value of the brand over time, after smoothing out the short-term fluctuations due to company and environmental factors. This momentum is the cumulative value of marketing impulses to the brand by advertising, promotion, and other marketing activity. The concept provides a useful link between the accounting view of brand valuation through the balance sheet and marketing methodology for calibrating the value of brand activity (e.g. knowledge of decay rates of advertising effects on consumer behavior; see Kapferer [1997, Chapter 13] for a discussion of the link between brand marketing activity and accounting practices). A good review of recent work on linking brand equity to financial metrics can be found in Srinivasan and Hanssens (2007).

Another area of future research is linking consumer-based brand equity to firm brand equity. We discussed some very recent work that used utility and profit maximization frameworks. However, modeling both utility maximization of consumers and profit maximization of firms is challenging. For example, to date, research efforts have adopted simple demand specifications. One future challenge will be to estimate full equilibrium models that may render brand equity estimates while incorporating a rich demand specification, as in the case of dynamic structural demand approaches.

Furthermore, as discussed in previous sections, the dynamic nature of brand equity, and of the behavioral processes that underlie the formation and evolution of brand equity, suggest that it is important for brand equity measurement models to capture dynamics. This is true for both individual-level choice-theoretic models of brand equity (e.g., Park & Srinivasan, 1994, Swait et al., 1993), as well as aggregate models of brand equity (e.g., Simon & Sullivan, 1993). In the context of choice-theoretic approaches, one useful future avenue for research is to develop and estimate richer dynamic structural models of consumer brand choices to measure consumer-based brand equity.

Our emphasis on dynamic models is not meant to imply that cross-sectional efforts are either not of interest or incapable of producing results of great use. Cross-sectional efforts can lead to accurate "snapshot" representations of brand equity; furthermore, cross-sectional approaches are quite useful for testing certain basic premises and components of more general time-varying models, especially given that cross-sectional data are generally more easily and cheaply collected than their dynamic counterpart.

To capture the richness of the processes that underlie the evolution of brand equity, researchers should seriously consider the possibility of using both experimental cross-sectional discrete choice data as well as transactional panel data (e.g., Swait & Andrews, 2003) in future work. This union of different data sources may enable better discrimination of brand equity effects through improved control over the exogeneity, ranges, and other statistical characteristics of variables central to the questions of interest, while also enhancing our understanding of brand equity dynamics.

In order to develop and estimate models of the type represented in Figure 10.1, we need to better understand consumers' learning processes. This involves understanding the mechanisms involved in attribute encoding as well as the manner in which attribute perceptions and tasks are updated. To be useful, this new knowledge must be specific enough to support mathematical and statistical specification of alternative encoding and updating mechanisms.

As an example, implicit learning phenomena and biased attribute encoding may be represented in our structural models by estimating psychophysical transformations of objective levels, if such data are available, into subjective perceptions. Moreover, the possibility of confirmatory biases can be incorporated into our current models by allowing Kalman gain coefficients (weights attached to new pieces of information) to be asymmetrically affected by confirmatory versus disconfirmatory information. Leveraging on research in psychology and behavioral marketing on learning (e.g., Klayman & Ha, 1987, Snyder & Swann, 1978), one may explicitly model alternative learning and belief updating mechanisms, such as an anchoring and adjustment process, which involves more conservative updating of priors than in a Bayesian updating mechanism.

Comparing such enriched structural models to those incorporating traditional assumptions (e.g., Bayesian updating) in terms of their ability to explain data allows us to gauge the extent to which the proposed cognitive phenomena influence choice. The results may then guide future experimental research.

References

Aaker, D.A. (1991). Managing brand equity. New York: The Free Press.

Aaker, D.A. (1996). *Building strong brands.* New York: The Free Press.

Aaker, D.A., & Jacobsan, R. (1994). The financial information content of brand equity. *Journal of Marketing Research*, 31 (May), 191–201.

Ackerberg, D. (2003). Advertising, learning, and consumer choice in experience good markets: A structural empirical examination. *International Economic Review, 44* (3), 1007–1040.

Agrawal, M., & Rao, V. (1996). An empirical comparison of consumer-based measures of brand equity. *Marketing Letters*, 7 (3), 237–247.

Byzalov, D., & Shachar, R. (2004). The risk reduction role of advertising. *Quantitative Marketing and Economics*, 2 (4), 283–320.

Carpenter, G.S., & Nakamoto, K. (1989). Consumer preference formation and pioneering advantage. *Journal of Marketing Research*, 26 (3), 285–298.

Crawford, G.S., & Shum, M. (2005). Uncertainty and learning in pharmaceutical demand: Anti-ulcer drugs. *Econometrica*, 73 (July), 1137–1174.

Elrod, T., & Keane, M.P. (1995). A factor-analytic model for representing the market structure in panel data. *Journal of Marketing Research*, 32 (February), 1–16.

Erdem, T. (1998). An empirical analysis of umbrella branding. *Journal of Marketing Research, 35* (3), 339–351.

Erdem, T., & Keane, M. (1996). Decision making under uncertainty: Capturing dynamic brand choice processes in turbulent consumer goods markets. *Marketing Science,* 15, 1–21.

Erdem, T., Keane, M., & Sun, B. (2008). A dynamic model of brand choice when price and advertising signal product quality. Forthcoming in Marketing Science.

Erdem, T., & Swait, J. (1998). Brand equity as a signaling phenomenon. *Journal of Consumer Psychology,* 7 (2), 131–157.

Erdem, T., & Swait, J. (2004). Brand credibility, brand consideration, and choice. *Journal of Consumer Research,* 31 (June), 191–198.

Erdem, T., Swait, J., Broniarczyk, S., Chakravarti, D., Kapferer, J., Keane, M., Roberts, J., Steenkamp, J., & Zettelmeyer, F. (1999). Brand equity, consumer learning and choice. *Marketing Letters,* 10 (3), 301–318.

Erdem, T., Swait, J., & Louviere, J. (2002). The impact of brand credibility on consumer price sensitivity. *International Journal of Research in Marketing,* 19 (2002), 1–19.

Farquhar, P.H. (1989). Managing brand equity. *Marketing Research,* 24–33.

Farquhar, P.H., Han, J.Y., & Ijiri, Y. (1991). Recognizing and measuring brand assets. *Marketing Science Report,* 91–119 (July). *Cambridge: Marketing Science Institute.*

Goldfarb, A., Lu, Q., & Moorthy, S. (2007). Measuring brand value in an equilibrium framework. Working Paper.

Guadagni, P.M., & Little, J.D.C. (1983). A logit model of brand choice calibrated on scanner data. *Marketing Science,* 2 (Summer), 203–238.

Hensher, D., Louviere, J., & Swait, J. (1999). Combining sources of preference data. *Journal of Econometrics,* 87 (1–2), 197–221.

Kamakura, W.A., & Russell, G.J. (1993). Measuring brand value with scanner data. *International Journal of Research in Marketing,* 10 (1), 9–22.

Kapferer, J. (1997). *Strategic brand management: Creating and sustaining brand equity long term,* 2. London: Kogan Page.

Kartuno, B., & Rao, V.R. (2005). Linking consumer-based brand equity to market performance: An integrated approach to brand equity management. Working Paper.

Keller, K.L. (1993). Conceptualizing, measuring, and managing consumer-based brand equity. *Journal of Marketing,* 57, 1–22.

Kim, H., Kim, W.G., & An, J.A. (2003). The effect of consumer-based brand equity on firms' financial performance. *Journal of Consumer Marketing,* 20 (4), 335–351.

Klayman, J., & Ha, Y. (1987). Confirmation, disconfirmation, and information in hypothesis testing. *Psychological Review,* 94 (April), 317–330.

Krishnan, H.S. (1996). Characteristics of memory associations: A consumer-based brand equity perspective. *International Journal of Research in Marketing,* 13, 389–405.

Lucas, Jr., R.E. (1976). Econometric policy evaluation: A critique. In K. Meltzer, & A.H. Meltzer (Eds.), The Philips curve and labor markets, supplement to the *Journal of Monetary Economics.*

Manski, C. (1977). The structure of random utility models. *Theory and Decision,* 8, 229–254.

McFadden, D. (1981). Econometric models of probabilistic choice. In C.F. Manski, & D. McFadden (Eds.), *Structural analysis of discrete data with econometric applications.* Cambridge, MA: MIT Press, 198–272.

McFadden, D. (1986). The choice theory approach to market research. *Marketing Science,* 5 (4), 275–297.

McQueen, J. (1991). Leveraging the power of emotion in building brand equity. ARF Third Annual Advertising and Promotion Workshop, February 5–6.

Morrison, P.D., & Roberts, J.H. (1998). Matching electronic distribution channels to product characteristics: The role of congruence in consideration set formation. *Journal of Business Research,* 41 (March), 223–229.

Mehta, N., Chen, X., & Narisimhan, O. (2008). Informing, transforming and persuading: Disentangling the multiple effects of advertising on brand choice decisions. Forthcoming in Marketing Science.

Park, C.S., & Srinivasan, V.S. (1994). A survey-based method for measuring and understanding brand equity and extendibility. *Journal of Marketing Research,* 21, 271–288.

Rangaswamy, A., Burke, R.R., & Oliva, T.A. (1993). Brand equity and the extendibility of brand names. *International Journal of Research in Marketing,* 10 (1), 61–75.

Roberts, J.H., & Urban, G.L. (1988). Modeling multiattribute utility, risk and belief dynamics for new consumer durable brand choice. *Management Science*, 34 (February), 167–185.

Simon, C.J., & Sullivan, M.W. (1993). The measurement and determinants of brand equity: A financial approach. *Marketing Science*, 12 (1), 28–52.

Snyder, M., & Swann, W.B. (1978). Hypothesis testing in social interaction. *Journal of Personality and Social Psychology*, 36 (11), 1202–1212.

Srinivasan, S., & Hanssens, D.M. (2007). Marketing and firm value: Metrics, methods, findings and future directions. Forthcoming in Journal of Marketing Research.

Srinivasan, V., Park, C.S., & Chang, D.R. (2005). An approach to the measurement, analysis, and prediction of brand equity and its sources. *Management Science*, 51 (9), 1433–1448.

Sriram, S., Balachnader, S., & Kalwani, M.U. (2007). Monitoring the dynamics pf brand equity using store-level data. *Journal of Marketing*, 71 (April), 61–78.

Swait, J., & Adamowicz, W. (2001). Incorporating the effect of choice environment and complexity into random utility models. *Organizational Behavior and Human Decision Processes*, 86 (2), 141–167.

Swait, J., & Andrews, R. (2003). Enhancing scanner panel models with choice experiments. *Marketing Science*, 22 (4) (Fall), 442–460.

Swait, J., & Erdem, T. (2002). Temporal consistency of sales promotions and consumer preferences. *Journal of Marketing Research*, 39 (August), 304–320.

Swait, J., & Erdem, T. (2007). Brand effects on choice and choice set formation under uncertainty. *Marketing Science,* 26 (5), 679–697.

Swait, J., Erdem, T., Louviere, J., & Dubelar, C. (1993). The equalization price: A measure of consumer perceived brand equity. *International Journal of Research in Marketing*, 10, 23–45.

Swait, J., & Louviere, J. (1993). The role of the scale parameter in the estimation and comparison of multinomial logit models. *Journal of Marketing Research*, 30, 305–314.

Section V

Protecting Brands

11

When Do Bad Things Happen to Good Brands? Understanding Internal and External Sources of Brand Dilution*

Barbara Loken
University of Minnesota

Deborah Roedder John
University of Minnesota

Firms build strong brands by communicating positive and unique brand identities to consumers. By doing so, brands develop special meanings and associations for consumers, sometimes to the point of achieving iconic status. Disney is associated with childhood, fantasy, and family entertainment. McDonald's is associated with hamburgers and fries, the Golden Arches, and Ronald McDonald House. BMW is associated with driving excitement, German engineering, sophistication, and prestige. As these examples suggest, brands can be thought of as a network of associations that carry meaning—including attributes, emotional and self-expressive benefits, personality traits, country of origin, visual symbols and logos, and charitable causes.

However, brands are not immune to situations that can weaken or diminish these important brand associations. For example, negative media publicity or poor quality products can weaken the extent to which consumers associate a brand with making high quality products, being environmentally conscious, or ethical. We refer to this phenomenon as brand dilution and define it as the weakening of positive brand associations or strengthening/addition of negative brand associations. In the marketplace,

* The authors wish to thank Sonia Basu Monga, Chris Joiner, Mimi Morrin, and C.W. Park for their thoughtful comments and suggestions.

dilution may be detected in a variety of ways, including (1) a negative change in consumer brand perceptions and associations, (2) a decrease in overall brand attitude or preference, and (3) a decrease in brand sales, market share, or stock valuation. For example, consider the media publicity over a recent product recall of Medtronic's Sprint Fidelis defibrillator lead, which is used to connect a cardiac defibrillator (an implantable device for shocking irregular heartbeats back into a normal rhythm) to a patient's heart. Preference for the Sprint Fidelis lead dropped among cardiologists, usage of alternative brands of defibrillator leads increased, and the negative impact on Medtronic's defibrillator business for the quarter was estimated to be in the neighborhood of $115 million (*Wall Street Journal*, November 20, 2007). Thus, brand dilution can affect the brand at a cognitive level (brand perceptions), affective level (brand attitudes and preferences), and/or behavioral level (sales, market share, stock valuation).

Our definition of brand dilution incorporates several important themes. First, we define dilution in terms of its proximate cause (changes in brand associations) and subsequent consequences (reduction in brand attitude, preference, sales). In the marketplace, brand dilution may be observed by any or all of these consequences; in addition, empirical research on brand dilution spans a wide range of consequences included in our definition. Second, we define dilution as a negative and harmful change in the way consumers relate to a brand on a cognitive, affective, or behavioral basis. This excludes situations in which firms deliberately weaken certain brand associations to a specific product category (e.g., Campbell's and soup) or user group (e.g., BMW and yuppies) in order to broaden the appeal of the brand. Finally, we do not require the negative change to be of a particular magnitude or duration. Our definition includes brand dilution that occurs for one brand offering or multiple offerings across the entire brand portfolio, as well as dilution that is momentary in duration or long term.

Understanding when brand dilution occurs is the purpose of this chapter. We discuss two major sources of brand dilution—external and internal sources of dilution (see Figure 11.1). External sources of dilution are defined as activities undertaken by parties outside the firm that are capable of diluting the brand. Included in this discussion are negative media publicity, unauthorized uses of trademarks, distribution channel problems, consumer boycotts, and negative word-of-mouth communications. Internal sources of dilution are defined as activities undertaken by parties inside the firm that are capable of diluting the brand. Included in our discussion are inappropriate marketing mix decisions and ill-advised brand leveraging strategies (brand extensions, brand alliances). We note that some sources of dilution, such as negative media publicity surrounding a product crisis, could be categorized as either internal (company decisions resulted in product problems) or external (media raised awareness

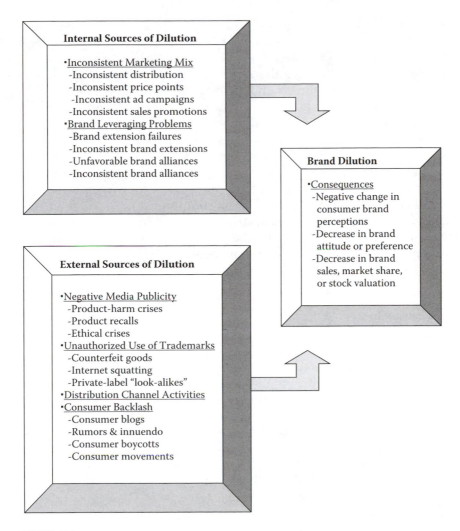

FIGURE 11.1
Sources of brand dilution.

of product problems) in nature. As such, our categories of internal and external sources of dilution should be viewed as a pedagogical device, not a statement of process.

We take a broad view of sources of brand dilution, unlike prior research that has focused solely on brand dilution related to brand leveraging strategies, such as brand extension activity. Although brand extension activity has dominated research published under the "brand dilution" rubric, it is also the case that many areas of consumer research address activities that bring harm to companies and their brands. For the first time, we bring together these disparate streams of research into an overarching framework that identifies many sources of brand dilution and their effects. We review the scholarly literature on each topic, selecting representative articles from the marketing literature published in the past 25 years, to describe brand dilution risks and identify the moderators of these risks. On occasion, we include research that predates our 25-year mark and research outside the marketing discipline to round out our discussion.

We proceed as follows. First, we discuss external sources of dilution, identifying major activities outside the firm that carry the risk of diluting brands. Second, we discuss internal sources of dilution, pointing out internal company decisions that have the capacity to harm brands. Next, we identify several strategies for protecting brands from dilution, suggested by our review of the scholarly literature. Finally, we put forward ideas for future research in brand dilution, suggesting topics that have received limited attention and warrant additional study.

External Sources of Dilution

When we think about situations that are likely to cause harm to a brand, external sources of dilution come to mind quite easily. For example, negative media publicity and consumer boycotts are very visible situations that are readily viewed as representing a risk to the companies and brands that are under attack. In this section, we identify and summarize scholarly research on a variety of external sources of dilution.

Negative Media Publicity

Product-Harm Crises

Media coverage of defective and dangerous products presents negative information that can result in brand dilution. Media stories often feature extremely negative and vivid events, such as reports of severe injuries and deaths. Because these incidents are so negative and so vivid, they are likely to be weighted heavily in consumer perceptions and attitudes about a brand. Although product-harm crises are usually discrete one-time occurrences, they can undo years of branding investments overnight.

Much of the academic literature in this area consists of case studies of real product-harm crises, attempting to draw conclusions for what managers should do when facing a crisis. There are, however, a number of empirical studies that document the consequences of product-harm crises in terms of diluting brand beliefs and attitudes (Coombs

& Holladay, 2006; Griffin, Babin, & Attaway, 1991; Weinberger, Allen, & Dillon, 1981), decreasing purchase intentions for the affected brand (Dawar & Pillutla, 2000), and reducing the purchase or purchase price of affected brands (Pennings, Wansink, & Meulenberg, 2002; Sullivan, 1990). For example, in an early study, Weinberger et al. (1981) found that a Consumers' Union story about safety problems in Chrysler cars negatively affected beliefs and attitudes about the Chrysler brand. Empirical data regarding decreases in purchase intentions and actual purchases are also available. Dawar and Pillutla (2000) focused on the case of glass fragments that were found in containers of a European brand of instant coffee, finding a decrease in intentions to purchase the brand, especially among nonloyal versus loyal purchasers of the brand. And Sullivan (1990) found that negative publicity surrounding sudden acceleration problems in the Audi 5000 resulted in greater-than-expected levels of depreciation for used cars of the same model (Audi 5000), as well as related models (Audi 4000 and Audi Quattro).

However, research has also determined that certain factors can increase or decrease the probability of brand dilution. Among these, the way in which a firm responds to a product-harm crisis has received the most attention to date. Across studies, researchers find that failing to comment on media reports ("no comment"), simply denying that products pose a risk, or shifting blame to others are all ineffective strategies (Dean, 2004; Griffin et al., 1981; Menon, Jewell, & Unnava, 1999). In contrast, offering apologies, providing restitution, and providing strong evidence to counter negative publicity were far more effective in limiting the damage to consumer attitudes toward the affected brands (Dean, 2004; Griffin et al., 1981; Menon et al., 1999). For example, Griffin et al. (1981), studying the fallout from a hypothetical media story about salmonella poisoning at a local restaurant, found that responding to the salmonella reports by offering to redress any problems was far more successful than a firm offering a simple denial or no comment at all. Increasing advertising for the affected brand can be of additional help in responding to product-harm crises (Weinberger et al., 1981), especially for stronger rather than weaker brands (Cleeren, Dekimpe, & Helsen, 2008).

Strong brands also fare better when faced with negative publicity. For example, Dawar and Pillutla (2000) report that strong brands—characterized by favorable brand attitudes, perceptions of high quality and trust, and high purchase likelihood—are less likely to be diluted regardless of the firm's response to a product-harm crisis. Strong brands were unaffected by negative publicity, as consumers maintained their positive beliefs and attitudes toward the brand even when the firm responded in an ambiguous way. However, weak brands suffered decreases in brand beliefs and attitudes unless they responded in the most supportive way possible. Firms with positive reputations for corporate social responsibility (CSR) also receive favored treatment, as noted by Klein and Dawar (2004). In their study, firms with a positive (negative) CSR reputation were blamed less (more) for product-harm situations and, as a result, received more positive (negative) brand evaluations and purchase intentions.

Brand dilution is also lessened among consumers who are loyal and committed to a brand. For example, Ahluwalia, Burnkrant, and Unnava (2000) found that negative publicity about a running shoe that caused joint problems resulted in less favorable brand attitudes among low commitment consumers; however, high commitment consumers maintained favorable brand attitudes by generating counterarguments for the negative publicity information. Similarly, consumers who are loyal (nonloyal) to a brand are more (less) likely to maintain their purchases of the brand in light of a product-harm crisis (Dawar & Pillutla, 2000; Stockmyer, 1996).

Product Recalls

Many product-harm crises result in product recalls, which also receive a good deal of media publicity. However, in the case of product recalls, the media publicity may be a mixture of negative information (defective or dangerous products) and positive information (company is recalling and reimbursing consumers). Most of the research focuses on case studies to provide guidelines for how companies should organize and implement product recalls in the most efficacious manner.

Only a few studies speak to the issue of brand dilution, examining how product recalls influence consumer perceptions and attitudes toward recalled brands. The findings are consistent with those reported for product-harm crises. In particular, brands with strong reputations fare much better in the wake of product recalls. For example, Mowen (1980) found that a well-known brand was perceived as being less responsible for the recall than an unknown brand. Further, firms with excellent corporate social responsibility (CSR) profiles were viewed more favorably by consumers after a product recall than firms without a known CSR profile (Jolly & Mowen, 1985; Mowen, Jolly, & Nickell, 1981). With regard to impact on purchasing, van Heerde, Helsen, and Dekimpe (2007) found that a product recall of Kraft peanut butter in Australia (due to salmonella poisoning) resulted in a loss of subsequent brand sales as well as reduced effectiveness for brand marketing in subsequent time periods.

Ethical Crises

Corporate ethical violations also result in negative publicity, including those related to employment practices, environmental violations, insider trading, and accounting practices. Only a few empirical studies have addressed the impact of this type of negative publicity on consumer brand beliefs, attitudes, and purchasing behavior. The findings reveal that unethical behavior results in more negative consumer beliefs about trustworthiness, expertise, and attractiveness (Renkema & Hoeken, 1998) and more negative attitudes toward the brand (Folkes & Kamins, 1999). Negative evaluations can occur for brands with products superior to those of its competitors (Folkes & Kamins, 1999) and negative evaluations of brands can spillover to closely related brands in the same product category (Roehm & Tybout, 2006). Countering negative publicity by participating in corporate social responsibility activities (CSR) can be helpful, especially in areas totally unrelated (e.g., cancer research) to the alleged ethical violation (e.g., environmental disaster). However, CSR activities in areas related to the ethical violation can actually result in more negative consumer reactions than the negative publicity alone (Okada & Reibstein, 1998; Yoon, Gürhan-Canli, & Schwarz, 2006).

Brands can also be affected by the immoral behavior of others, including celebrity endorsers affiliated with the brand. Celebrity endorsers usually have a positive influence on brands by providing a sense of credibility, reflecting certain personality traits that are consistent with the brand's image, or increasing the visibility of the brand in a crowded marketplace. However, firms have no control over the personal lives of celebrity endorsers, who often find themselves in the midst of well-publicized scandals—including Nike's Michael Vick (charged with dog fighting), McDonald's Kobe Bryant (charged with sexual assault), Chanel's Kate Moss (photographed using cocaine), and Pepsi's Michael Jackson (charged with child molestation). Research suggests that celebrity scandals can spill over to endorsed brands. In an early study, Till and Shimp (1998) found that an endorsed brand was impacted negatively by a celebrity scandal (DUI and steroid use) when the celebrity was fictitious and unknown (Pierre Varnay), but not when the celebrity was well known and well regarded (Greg LaMond). Priester and Petty (2003) report that consumers are more vigilant about scrutinizing brand information when the brand employs a celebrity endorser (Tonya Harding, figure skater) involved in a past scandal. However, recent work by Votolato and Unnava (2006) suggests that the spillover of celebrity scandals to endorsed brands may depend on whether consumers believe that the endorsed brand had knowledge or condoned the celebrity's behavior. In this study, dilution effects for an endorsed brand were evident when consumers were told that the firm had known about immoral celebrity behavior (involving drug and alcohol use) for some time and condoned the celebrity's behavior; otherwise, the endorsed brand suffered no negative impact.

MANAGING BRAND DILUTION IN THE
FACE OF A PUBLIC HEALTH SCARE

The phrase "It's not worth peanuts" took on new relevance with the peanut contamination predicament of early 2009. As a salmonella outbreak led to a number of deaths and hundreds of illnesses in the United States and was traced to its source, the Peanut Corporation of America folded, a massive recall was instituted, and retailers large and small raced to get ahead of any possible damage to their brands.

Brand dilution in all its forms—negative changes to consumer perceptions, a drop in overall brand attitude and performance, and a decrease in financial performance—is illustrated by the tainted peanuts. Within weeks of the initial recalls, the *New York Times* reported that "Many consumers, apparently disregarding the fine print of the salmonella outbreak and food recall ... are swearing off all brands of peanut butter, driving down sales by nearly 25 percent." How, then, did savvy brands like Clif Bars, Keebler cookies, and Skippy peanut butter see their way through this crisis?

In short, by swiftly and publicly addressing the problem, recalling any products that might be affected, and distancing their brand from the outbreak's source. The J.M. Smucker Company, which owns the Jif brand, for instance, made a massive ad buy in national news outlets shortly after the first reports of contamination. The ad reassured consumers that its product did not contain nuts from the plant fingered as the outbreak's source, and featured a coupon. Soon after, the parent company of Peter Pan peanut butter, ConAgra, followed suit with a Sunday ad distancing its firm from the Peanut Corporation of America and providing its own coupon.

Six weeks from the first outbreak reports, over 2100 foods had been recalled, and products were still being pulled. *Advertising Age* reported that some spillover occurred for all peanut-related products, showing that negative evaluations can affect brands in related product categories not directly affected by the crisis. But without the swift response of some companies in distancing themselves from the crisis, the response would no doubt have been worse. It seemed that the efforts of companies to communicate with their distributors and consumers had largely stemmed the backlash against the wide variety of products featuring peanuts.

While the biggest companies, with public relations departments at the ready, were largely prepared to handle this sort of crisis deftly, small companies learned important lessons about ensuring the quality of their supply chain and weathering a storm in the face of an unexpected brand threat. Whether dealing with contaminated sparkling water, exploding cell phone batteries, or even unfounded rumors, managers need to have a recall plan in place to efficiently address problems and reassure customers. The successful handling of a brand dilution threat is precisely why, despite past problems, consumers are now happy to snack on Totino's Pizza Rolls or even take a Tylenol when the headaches of bad brand news get to be too much.

R.D.M. & L.W.P.

Unauthorized Use of Trademarks

The unauthorized use of a trademark occurs when a company uses part or all of another company's brand name, logo, slogan, package design, or other distinguishing identifier of a brand. The LEGO Group, which manufactures children's toys, regularly receives consumer complaint letters about its building block toys from consumers who purchased competitors' toys that are similar in product names (LIGO) or design elements (Zaichowsky, 2006). As this example illustrates, similarity in trademarks can lead to numerous problems for the brand that is imitated. For example, consumers may believe the imitator (*junior*) brand is manufactured by the originator (*senior*) brand, and quality associations of the junior brand may affect consumers' perceptions of the senior brand. Consumers may purchase or use the junior brand, mistakenly believing they purchased the senior brand. These concerns, regarding consumer confusion of origin, or trademark infringement, are protected by trademark law (Lanham Act, 1946). Research finds that consumers exposed to products similar to one another (primarily in package shape) are confused about product origin, as much as 25% of the time (e.g., Burgunder, 1997; Foxman, Muehling, & Berger, 1990; Howard, Kerin, & Gengler, 2000; Loken, Ross, & Hinkle, 1986).

Even in situations in which consumers are not confused about the origins of the two similar-appearing brands, negative spillover may occur from the junior to the senior brand. The Trademark Dilution Law of 2006 protects brands from this negative spillover in the form of *blurring* of a mark, which is the "gradual whittling away" of the brand's distinctive or unique associations, or *tarnishment*, which is harm to a brand's reputation or image. For example, Buick aspirin or Kodak pianos might reduce the value of these brand names by blurring or weakening the strength and distinctiveness of associations of the original brands and their product categories (Morrin, Lee, & Allenby, 2006; Peterson, Smith, & Zerrillo, 1999).

Research on trademark dilution has found that similarities in brand logos between a senior brand (e.g., Kodak film processing) and junior brand (e.g., Kodak pianos) reduce consumers' ability to retrieve from memory the product category associated with the senior brand name (Morrin et al., 2006). Consumer confusion of product origin exacerbated the amount of harm to the senior trademark. Dilution by tarnishment of a brand includes the attachment of a negative association with the brand. The Coca-Cola trademark was found to be diluted and tarnished by posters that used the phrase "Enjoy Cocaine" with font and colors identical to those of the Coca-Cola company trademarks (Taillieu, 2007).

Warlop and Alba (2004) found that when two brands were visually similar, consumers were more likely to generalize attributes from one brand to the other (also, Kapferer, 1995; Ward, Loken, Ross, & Hasapopoulos, 1986; Zaichkowsky, 2006), and consumers generally did not view the "look-alike" brand unfavorably unless the imitator appeared to have aspirations of overtaking the senior brand. Other researchers, too, have found that visual similarities between two trademarks have contributed negatively to the senior brand by weakening distinctive associations (Morrin & Jacoby, 2000; Pullig, Simmons, & Netemeyer, 2006).

Research has also found that dilution and consumer confusion due to trademark similarities is reduced when consumers have prior familiarity with the senior brand. Morrin et al. (2006) found that high familiarity with a senior trademark (relative to their familiarity with the imitator) protected the senior trademark from dilution. Foxman et al. (1990) found, too, that harm to the senior brand decreased to the extent that consumers were more familiar with the senior brand.

Below, three contexts in which trademark dilution occurs and which have received attention in recent years in the media and by marketing practitioners, are described: counterfeit goods, Internet squatting, and private label imitations.

Counterfeit Goods

The unauthorized use of trademarks is encountered by brands that are victims of counterfeit manufacturers, who produce fake products to consumers and sell them for a fraction of the cost of name brands ($10 Rolex watches or Nike shoes). The costs associated with counterfeit goods worldwide has been estimated at about $550 billion, or 5–7% of world trade (Underwriters Laboratories, 2007). Inferior inexpensive counterfeit products pose a risk to the trademark owner by encouraging consumers to buy a product they may believe is the genuine product, thus diverting purchases to counterfeit options. A more critical concern exists for products in which safety is paramount. Counterfeit drugs, for example, were sold to 25,000 cancer patients in 2002 under the brand name Procrit.

The medicine contained only one-twentieth the strength prescribed by the patient's physicians.

Purchases of counterfeited products may reduce sales of the genuine owner as well as reduce quality, prestige, and other core brand associations. The harm associated with counterfeits also may include the loss of goodwill for retailers who sell counterfeits unknowingly. One study (Gentry, Putrevu, Shultz, & Commuri, 2001) found that those who knew they were purchasing "fake" brands often did so because they liked the genuine brand but could not afford it. However, research on the effects of counterfeit goods on dilution of the brands they imitate is lacking.

Internet Squatting

As the Internet increases its reach worldwide, global brands have become increasingly concerned about Internet squatters, who incorporate similar-sounding brand names into Web site addresses to steer traffic for the trademark owner to their Internet site. These unauthorized uses not only rob the trademark owner of potential sales and exposure, but also invite consumers to add any associations they have to these Web sites or products to those of the trademark owner's brand. Internet squatters also may cause dilution of a core brand association or core brand element if the use of a brand's trademark is adopted or parodied in such a way that a brand's core association is changed or diminished. For example, the Web address www.Ballysucks.com was argued, in a trademark infringement and dilution case, to use the Bally Total Fitness federally registered trademark "Bally." The complaint by Bally's was dismissed because the Web site was a noncommercial address for consumer criticism (Samson, 1998). While the legal case for trademark dilution of Bally's was not upheld, blurred meanings of core associations of Bally's may nevertheless have occurred. These detrimental effects of Internet squatters on brands need further study.

Private-Label "Look-Alikes"

Private label brands are a special case of imitation of national brands. In the United States in 2005, private-label brands represented 20% of supermarket unit volume, and according to a 2005 ACNielsen report, over three-quarters of Americans think that private labels are a good alternative to other brands (Ridley, 2005). Private-label brands are particularly popular in several European countries, including Germany, the U.K., France, and Spain, where 50% or more of brands are private label. Many retailers in these European markets are sufficiently large and have sufficient brand equity to leverage their private labels and increase consumer acceptance (Forbes.com, 2007).

Not all private label products mimic national brands in package shape and colors. However, when imitation occurs, dilution is a threat to the national brands. Research has found that private label "look-alike" products (as compared to dissimilar-appearing products) are mistaken by consumers for national labels sufficiently often to create potential problems for the brand (Kapferer, 1995), and that distinctive associations of the national brands are transferred to the private labels (Ward et al., 1986). Private labels are less likely than competing national brands to be challenged in court for fear of retaliation by retailers, such as delisting and loss of shelf space (Collins-Dodd & Zaichkowsky, 1999).

Distribution Channel Activities

Brands are supported by firms that function as a distribution channel for goods—including distributors, retailers, and selling agents. These firms are responsible for ensuring that products are delivered to the intended selling outlets and receive appropriate marketing support. However, distribution channel members can engage in activities that run counter to this ideal, resulting in poor marketing support for the brand and potential brand dilution.

In the case of distributors, one of the most potentially harmful activities is bootlegging product shipments outside assigned geographic areas or to unauthorized retailers. Manufacturers often assign specific territories or retail outlets to their distributors to ensure desired levels of customer service and reduce undesirable competition among distributors. Bootlegging involves a violation of these agreements and its been historically viewed as being harmful to the manufacturer and its brands, disrupting customer support and eventually unraveling the distribution channel itself. Logically, consequences of this proportion should result in brand dilution, with consumers holding less positive perceptions and attitudes toward brands with less customer service and support. To date, however, there is virtually no evidence to support the idea that bootlegging is associated with brand dilution. In fact, the current state of knowledge in marketing is that a certain percentage of bootlegged distribution should be tolerated by manufacturers because such activities can profitably serve new customer segments that prefer less customer service at lower price points (Dutta, Bergen, & John, 1994).

At the retail level, activities related to pricing and merchandising take center stage. Manufacturers often suggest retail prices for their branded products, but sticking to these prices is at the discretion of the retailer. For products with a prestige image, retail prices that are lower and inconsistent with the prestige image can negatively affect consumer perceptions of the brand (cf. Kirmani, Sood, & Bridges, 1999). Retail merchandising can also negatively impact consumer perceptions. Empirical evidence suggests that brand dilution can result for high equity brands that are mixed with lower equity or unfamiliar brands in retail displays. Buchanan, Simmons, and Bickart (1999) paired a familiar and an unfamiliar brand together in a retail display that encouraged comparisons between the two brands. When the unfamiliar brand was more prominent than the familiar brand, dilution effects occurred for the familiar brand.

Consumer Backlash

Consumers' responses to brands range from loving them to hating them. A satisfied consumer is more likely to buy the brand repeatedly, be a loyal customer, and engage in positive word-of-mouth communication. A dissatisfied consumer, in contrast, is more likely to complain, engage in negative word-of-mouth (NWOM) communication, and not engage in repeat purchases of the brand. The lifetime value of a single customer loyal to a brand can be sizable (e.g., the lifetime value of the Lexus brand is about $600,000; Hoyer & MacInnis, 2007). When consumers have negative experiences with a brand, these feelings will lower purchase of those brands in the future (Bechwati & Morrin, 2003; Richins, 1983). In addition, however, consumers may express their opinions and feelings (NWOM communications) on consumer blogs, activist Web sites, or through more traditional means of complaining to family, friends, or the manufacturer. These forms of communication can serve as a way for consumers to retaliate against firms who provide poor products or services, especially when consumers attribute failures to the company itself (Curren & Folkes, 1987; Folkes, 1984; Grégoire & Fisher, 2008). In today's electronic environment, consumers' negative experiences can be conveyed to hundreds of thousands of people in minutes (Donavan, Mowen, & Chakraborty, 2001). Determining the conditions under which these forms of communication will hurt the parent brand is important for managers.

The academic literature on consumer dissatisfaction with brands is well developed and, to a large extent, concerns factors that impact whether dissatisfaction will occur in individual consumers (for reviews, see Bolton & Drew, 1991; Bechwati & Morrin, 2003; Richins, 1984; Vargo, Nagao, He, & Morgan, 2007). Research predicts and finds consumer dissatisfaction to the extent that a consumer's expectations are higher than the brand's actual performance. Only a small percentage of dissatisfied consumers will engage in complaint behavior, but such communication is important as negative word-of-mouth communication is more influential and vivid than positive word-of-mouth. To keep consumer expectations high (but not too high), prescriptive advice to companies has been to provide guarantees, warranties, and enough information about the branded products for consumers to develop realistic expectations, and to focus on communicating the firm's core competencies and strengths. To keep complaint behavior low, prescriptive advice has been to identify the source of the problem and remedy it in a speedy manner (cf. Roehm & Brady, 2007).

When many consumers experience similar problems with a brand, a more systematic and sophisticated means of communicating about the brand may be set up by individual consumers or by consumer advocacy groups (Richins, 1984). Below, we briefly discuss several outlets for systematic negative word-of-mouth communication that have become important in recent years, including (a) the use of consumer blogs, (b) the circulating of rumors about a brand, (c) consumer boycotts, and (d) broad-based consumer movements.

Consumer Blogs

A primary source of consumer backlash is through the use of Internet Web sites. While, in the past, negative word-of-mouth was a private phenomenon between family and friends, it has become a public way to voice complaints through the Internet (Ward & Ostrom, 2006). On antibrand Web sites, Nike has been associated with sweatshop labor, and Coke and Pepsi have been criticized for other overseas labor practices. Starbucks has been criticized for environmental damage and harm to local culture, which is viewed as inconsistent with Starbucks' original countercultural image as a warm, comfortable refuge for a warm beverage (Thompson, Rindfleisch, & Arael, 2006). Antibrand activists, such as Adbusters (wwwadbuster. com), alert consumers about what they perceive as consumer and environmental exploitation (Kozinets & Handelman, 2004). Some brands (e.g., Coke, Burger King, and Adidas) have used viral marketing approaches that use urban vernacular and integrate their brands into the works of arts and entertainment. The strategies are monitored by antibrand activists who do not view these campaigns as authentic and question the idea that a corporate-sponsored brand may have a sincere relationship or meet genuine emotional needs (Thompson et al., 2006).

The research on antibrand Web sites has been sparse, so the impact of these sites on consumers' perceptions of a brand is unknown. However, research does suggest that some types of brands may be more vulnerable than others to consumer backlash. For example, "emotional" brands, in which connections between consumers and brands generate warm feelings of community, sensory experiences, or strong participatory feelings, may be especially vulnerable (Thompson et al., 2006). The particular type of emotions triggered by the brand may be important as well. For example, in a different context, "sincere" brands were found to be more vulnerable to damage than "exciting" brands (Aaker, Fournier, & Brasel, 2004).

One strategy used recently by brands to promote consumer goodwill among loyal consumers and to increase the strength of brands is the establishment of brand communities (Muniz & O'Guinn, 2001). Some brand communities, such as Harley-Davidson's Harley Owners Group (HOG), are actively supported and funded by the company through participation in community events and encouraging memberships for new Harley owners. Such memberships foster strong relationships with other brand owners and strengthen brand associations that are consistent with brand community activities (e.g., Harley-Davidson and "ruggedness"). Algesheimer, Dholakia, and Herrman (2005) demonstrate that identifying with a brand community can lead to positive consequences, such as greater participation in the brand community and more favorable future purchase intentions, as long as brand users do not feel pressure to belong to the brand community.

Rumors, Urban Legends, and Innuendo

One way in which negative information about a brand can be communicated by consumers is in the form of rumors and innuendo. Rumors are word-of-mouth communications that generally lack supportive evidence for evaluating their truthfulness (Allport & Postman, 1947). Rumors pertaining to brands documented in the marketing literature have generally been false (e.g., McDonald's hamburgers containing worm meat). Urban legends are similar to rumors but are stories that have a moral twist at the end (Donavan et al., 2001). Research has found that negative urban legends were more likely to be spread than positive ones (e.g., Donavan et al., 2001), and negative rumors were spread more than positive rumors when they were about a rival than about the self (Kamins, Folkes, & Perner, 1997).

Rumors and urban legends can harm brands because once rumors are stated (e.g., "Aspirin destroys tooth enamel"), people often believe them (Skurnik, 2005). Repeatedly hearing false negative information about a brand, even from a discredited source, increases consumers' perceptions that the information is true, called the "illusion of truth" effect (cf. Hawkins & Hoch, 1992). Rumors also influence overall brand attitudes. For example, experimental research has found that those consumers who heard a rumor about McDonald's hamburgers containing worm meat held more negative attitudes toward eating at McDonald's than those not exposed to the rumor, even when they believed the rumor was false (Tybout, Calder, & Sternthal, 1981).

Researchers have also investigated "innuendo." A common form of innuendo is an implied truth in the form of either a denial or a question, such as a newspaper headline that reads "Coke products are not dangerous" or one that reads "Are Coke products dangerous?" Innuendos, whether they are communicated by word-of-mouth from consumer to consumer or as a media headline, can potentially harm a brand's image associations. When consumers receive innuendo information in the form of questions or qualification, they form negative impressions that are sometimes as damaging as receiving direct negative assertions (Wegner, 1984). Research on innuendo has primarily involved psychological, rather than brand, contexts. More research is needed to determine whether these same effects occur for brands, and if so, in which contexts.

One implication for protecting consumers from dilution due to rumors and innuendo is not to refute the negative information by restating it in marketing communications. Instead, a focus or emphasis on statements that are true is important (Skurnik, 2005). As Wegner (1984) argues, people do not have a "reset" button such that their thoughts can be cleared of false information.

Consumer Boycotts and Consumer Activism

Boycotts generally arise from advocacy groups that are protesting corporate practices. Some consumer boycotts have focused on products and brands that should be purchased, for example, urging people to buy products that are "Made in America" rather than overseas (Friedman, 1996). However, most boycotts focus on products and brands to be avoided. Recent examples of consumer boycotts have included protests over human rights violations in foreign countries (e.g., Coca-Cola, De Beers, Donna Karan), animal testing or animal rights violations (e.g., L'Oreal, Proctor & Gamble, Colgate-Palmolive, Dolce & Gabbana), and environmental concerns (e.g., Chevron-Texaco). While the number of companies and brands that consumers boycott is small, it has increased substantially over the past decade (Sen, Gürhan-Canli, & Morwitz, 2001). From a brand perspective, boycotts are important because they have the potential to impact sales, if sufficient numbers of consumers are boycotting the product. They may also have negative repercussions on more widespread consumer beliefs and attitudes if the boycott is publicized and consumers are persuaded by the negative information publicized about the brand. Furthermore, the reach of the Internet has made boycotts potentially more influential.

Most of extant academic research on boycotts has focused on consumers' motivations for boycotting, rather than the effects of boycotts on brand evaluations. However, a few studies report on the impact of actual boycotts on brands and product sales. An early study by Miller and Sturdivant (1977) found that a fast food boycott decreased sales of the fast food in the local area of the boycott, but not in surrounding areas in which the boycott was publicized. A more recent study by Klein, Smith, and John (2004) found that public opinion of a multinational firm became more negative, and retail sales dropped, following a boycott over factory closings. The negative publicity generated by a boycott of the firm was cited as a key factor for the changes. In general, higher company egregiousness scores were related to lower brand image ratings. A third boycott analyzed the American consumers' boycott of French wine in 2003 in response to France's opposition to the war in Iraq. While French wine sales in the United States dropped during the boycott (Chavis & Leslie, 2006), results may also have been due to seasonal fluctuations (Ashenfelter, Ciccarella, & Shatz, 2007). In sum, the study findings are mixed, but suggest that consumer boycotts can potentially dilute brands targeted by boycotts.

Consumer Movements

Consumer movements are forms of consumer activism that are organized around goals of resisting certain types of products or certain types of marketing or business practices (Kozinets & Handelman, 2004). For example, a number of organizations focus on tobacco control or restriction of other unsafe products, such as toys with lead components, unsafe vehicles, or unsafe food products. Consumer interest groups can also be general in scope such as Consumers Union, which publishes objective data on brand performance (in *Consumer Reports* magazine) across a wide variety of product classes. Consumer co-ops, such as credit unions or AARP (Herrmann, 1993), may focus on specific consumer issues (e.g., credit) or special populations (e.g., retirees). A more radical form of consumer movement is one in which the culture of consumerism is targeted (Kozinets & Handelman, 2004). Each of these forms of consumer movements may have macro-level effects on selected industries, specific brands, or more general attitudes toward consumerism. Future research might determine whether consumer movements dilute individual brands.

Internal Sources of Dilution

As we have seen, there are a variety of external sources of dilution that pose a risk to companies and brands. However, some of the most potentially damaging sources of dilution come from internal decisions that a firm makes about brand strategy. In this section, we identify and summarize the scholarly research on a variety of internal sources of dilution, including inconsistent marketing mix decisions and inconsistent brand leveraging strategies.

Inconsistent Marketing Mix Decisions

Strong brands are built with consistent and coordinated marketing programs. Elements of the marketing mix—including promotion, pricing, distribution, and products—must present a clear picture to the consumer in order to be effective. For example, the Godiva brand is supported by glamorous and romantic advertising images, luxurious packaging, beautiful catalogs, exclusive retail outlets, and a premium price. However, marketing mix decisions can add inconsistent elements to the overall brand strategy, and this inconsistency can be a source of brand dilution.

Despite the potential for brand dilution, little scholarly research exists to address the impact of inconsistent marketing mix decisions. Below, we offer examples of several areas where the risk for brand dilution is present, illustrated by examples and available research.

Inconsistent Distribution

Most brands are distributed through a combination of retail outlets, company-owned stores, catalogs, and Internet sites. For example, Godiva chocolate is sold through upscale department stores, Godiva boutique stores, and Godiva catalogs. When a brand is distributed through multiple channels, the mix of distribution outlets must be consistent with the brand's identity. However, this simple dictate is not always followed, especially in the case of brands that are expanding into new markets to fuel sales growth. For example, Godiva is now being sold through discount stores such as Sam's Club, which is inconsistent with the "prestige" and "exclusive" image of the brand. In a similar vein, Krispy Kreme, which is famous for selling fresh donuts served warm off the production line in Krispy Kreme stores, now sells donuts in prepackaged boxes in discount stores and gas station mini-marts.

Inconsistencies in distribution channels are especially problematic for premium brands, particularly when distribution is extended to less exclusive outlets. Although there is a lack of empirical work to substantiate the severity or nature of brand dilution in these situations, case examples exist to illustrate the potential for harm. Consider, for example, the case of Calvin Klein. Calvin Klein sued its long-time licensee, Warnaco Group, claiming that Warnaco had sold products through unauthorized mass-marketers such as Costco and B. J.'s Wholesale Club, thereby diluting the quality of the Calvin Klein brand image (*The New York Times*, June 20, 2000). Discount stores have an image that is inconsistent with an upscale brand such as Calvin Klein, and the propensity of lower-priced unknown brands stocked in these outlets presents a risk of brand dilution for high-equity brands (see Buchanan et al., 1999).

Inconsistent Price Points

Brands can be leveraged by introducing new offerings at a lower price point (downward stretch) or a higher price point (upward stretch). Upward stretches can fail because the brand lacks credibility in a more exclusive market, but downward stretches are more problematic in terms of brand dilution risk. Recently, designer brands have sold "cheap chic" fashions (e.g., Vera Wang at Kohl's), perhaps believing that the marketing for prestige and bargain brand extensions are nonoverlapping, and yet advertising messages and media reports about the extensions may reach both markets. Because downward stretches provide an offering at a lower price point (with fewer features or lower quality), they can be a source of inconsistency for a brand that has a high-price, high-quality image. Although many brands have launched successful downward stretches, such as BMW (3-Series) and Marriott (Courtyard by Marriott), the possibility exists that downward stretches can dilute the prestige and exclusive image that consumers associate with a brand. For example, Kirmani et al. (1999) found that brand owners of the prestige brand BMW reacted more positively than nonowners to an upward stretch of the brand, but responded more negatively to a downward stretch of the brand. However, brand owners of a nonprestige brand (Acura) responded less negatively to both upward and downward stretches than nonowners. Thus, although consumers with a strong attachment to prestige brands may be resistant to negative brand information in general, they may also react more negatively to information that violates their perception of the brand's prestige image, such as a downward stretch. In this research, the parent brand's image was protected by using it in combination with a new brand (Ultra by BMW) to launch downward stretches (Kirmani et al., 1999).

Inconsistent Advertising Campaigns

Advertising, whether it is placed in traditional or nontraditional media, is a key element in building and maintaining strong brands. To be most effective, advertising campaigns need to communicate the brand identity clearly and need to be consistent with the brand's desired identity. Inconsistent message content, inconsistent execution, and inconsistent media placement not only contribute to the failure of an advertising campaign, but can also lead to erosion of the associations and beliefs connected to the brand.

Although scholarly research on this topic is sparse, examples of advertising inconsistencies are not difficult to find. Celebrity endorsers provide a case in point. Celebrity endorsers can be a positive influence, which is confirmed by research showing that beliefs about a brand ("fun" or "sophisticated") can be strengthened through the use of a celeb-rity endorser who has personal attributes that fit the brand's personality (Kamins, 1990), are relevant to the product category (Batra & Homer, 2004), and enhance the advertisement's credibility (Kamins, Brand, Hoeke, & Moe, 1989). Celebrity endorsers can also increase the likelihood of con-sumers choosing the endorsed brand (Heath, McCarthy, & Mothersbaugh, 1994; Kahle & Homer, 1985). However, celebrity endorsers can also be a negative if they have personalities or lifestyles that are inconsistent with the brand's identity. For example, Jenny Craig lost points with consumers when it hired an overweight Monica Lewinsky, a former White House intern involved in an extramarital relationship with ex-President Bill Clinton, to be a spokesperson while losing 50 pounds on the Jenny Craig diet. More successful was actress Valerie Bertinelli, a middle-aged over-weight mom, who connected with the Jenny Craig consumer market. At times, the effects of celebrity endorsers can be a mixed bag of positive and negative effects. For example, Carl's Jr. produced a racy commercial for its "Spicy BBQ Dollar Burger" featuring Paris Hilton, who performed a provocative dance while soaping up a Bentley in a skimpy swimsuit. Although sales increased, so did protests from parent groups and media watchdog groups who believed the ad was inconsistent with the Carl's Jr. image as a family restaurant (CNNMoney.com, June 1, 2005).

Inconsistent Sales Promotions

Brand dilution is also a concern for sales promotions, especially those that are inconsistent with building a strong brand identity. In many cases, these promotions are more nontraditional ways of drawing attention to the brand. For example, Samuel Adams, a beer known for tradition and old-world brewing, agreed to participate in a promotion, concocted by a pair of radio shock jocks, called "Sex for Sam." The 2002 promotion offered a trip to Boston to the couple who engaged in sex in the riskiest place, which resulted in a Virginia couple being arrested while trying to win the prize in New York's St. Patrick's Cathedral. The negative publicity surround-ing the promotion and arrest in New York City resulted in considerable embarrassment for the brand (*Business Week*, September 1, 2003).

Brands can also be put at risk when the marketing mix relies too heavily on sales promotions (e.g. coupons, deals, sales) to the detriment of brand building through advertising (Srinivasan & Hanssens, 2009). Researchers have found that brand choices made on the basis of a coupon or sale price can lead to devalued brands (Dodson, Tybout, & Sternthal, 1978). Consumers may attribute their choices to the sale price rather than the brand's core benefits. Increasingly, companies are aware of the importance of building brands through repetition of core brand elements, even in sales promotions of a brand. For example, Sunday newspaper inserts (free standing inserts or FSIs) have changed from being price/coupon-based promotions to a combination of price/coupon and brand building advertising. Brand slogans are repeated, the entire family of brand offerings is pictured, and brand attribute associations are highlighted in many of the promotional pieces.

Brand Leveraging Problems

Brand leveraging, and particularly leveraging through brand extensions, has gained in popularity over the past two decades and has now become commonplace. Brand extension strategies are often viewed as beneficial because of the increased chance of a successful new product launch and lower marketing costs (Kapferer, 1994). However, brand dilution may occur as a result of unfavorable or inconsistent information received by consumers through brand leveraging. Brand extensions can diminish the important brand associations that resonate with consumers, and at times, introduce negative associations that tarnish the brand's identity. For example, the Mercedes-Benz Swatch car, which was a subcompact car incorporating the design element of Swatch watches, was inconsistent with the luxury, upscale styling, and price point associated with the Mercedes-Benz brand. Too many extensions, even if they are relatively consistent, can also cause dilution by confusing consumers about what the brand stands for or by losing its sense of exclusivity or distinctiveness. For example, commenting on the explosion of Mercedes-Benz extensions, an automobile magazine warned: "Sprinkling silver stars too liberally throughout the market will sap this brand's prestige" (Naughton, 2002). Finally, while co-branding, brand alliances, and celebrity endorsements provide leveraging opportunities to brands, some brand alliances also pose risks for the brand.

Brand Extension Failures and Inconsistent Brand Extensions

Branding experts disagree on the risks associated with brand extensions. Keller and Sood (2003) argue that parent brands are not usually vulnerable to failed brand extensions, and that a strong brand with high equity protects a brand against failed brand extensions. But other marketing experts argue that a brand's meaning can be weakened or blurred as a result of overextending a brand (e.g., Aaker, 1990; Tauber, 1985, 1988). According to Reddy and Terblanche (2005), the brand Diane von Furstenberg lost value after extending carelessly from fashion to luggage and books, and focusing on technical features rather than symbolic associations of the brand. They argue that Pierre Cardin's sales dropped, too, after extending to inconsistent extensions such as baseball caps and cigarettes.

Numerous experimental studies have found dilution of parent brand associations and parent brand attitudes whether consumers received information in the form of consumer ratings tables and/or mock advertisements (Ahluwalia & Gurlan-Canli, 2000; Chen & Chen, 2000; Drinkwater & Uncles, 2007; Gurhan-Canli & Maheswaran, 1998; John, Loken, & Joiner, 1998; Lane & Jacobson, 1997; Loken & John, 1993; Milberg, Park, & McCarthy, 1997), or in the form of actual product usage experience (Chang, 2002; Sheinin, 2000; Swaminathan, Fox, & Reddy, 2001). For example, Loken and John (1993) found that a positive core brand association was rated less favorably after consumers were exposed to negative brand information. Consumers read consumer ratings information about a new Johnson & Johnson brand extension in which the extension was rated as either low in gentleness, low in quality, or low in both gentleness and quality. When this inconsistent extension attribute information was salient to consumers, their core beliefs that Johnson & Johnson was associated with gentleness were rated lower, relative to a control group, and their core beliefs that Johnson & Johnson was associated with quality were also lower. Milberg et al. (1997), like Loken and John (1993), provided consumers with consumer ratings information about a brand extension, in this case, either a Timex or Polaroid extension. Consumers were given information about either a close brand extension (Timex clock radio, Polaroid photocopies) or a far brand extension (Timex photocopier, Polaroid clock radio), and the extension attribute information was either neutral (e.g., comes in a variety of colors, sizes, and/or options) or inconsistent with the parent brand image (poor quality; not easy to use). Dilution of the parent beliefs (quality and ease of use) was found when extension attribute information was inconsistent with the parent brand image. Parent brand attitudes (overall favorableness toward the parent brand) were also more negative as a result of inconsistent extension information.

Researchers have also found dilution of *individual products* of the brand, following exposure to negative information about a brand extension in the form of consumer ratings information (John et al., 1998) or product usage experience (Erdem, 1998, Chang, 2002). John et al. (1998) found that, when consumers were exposed to a brand extension (bath oil or bath powder) that was rated as low in gentleness, gentleness ratings of individual products of the brand (e.g., adhesive bandages, dental floss) were diluted as a result of negative gentleness ratings of a new brand extension. They also found dilution of individual products of the brand (Johnson & Johnson baby lotion, Johnson & Johnson dental floss) when consumers were exposed to information about a new brand extension (mouthwash or first aid swabs) that was rated as low in hygiene. Erdem (1998) analyzed ACNielsen scanner panel data for toothpaste and toothbrushes, and found that when the quality of a brand extension was perceived to be lower than expected, consumers were less likely to choose other products of the parent brand.

On the other hand, John et al. (1998) found that across extensions from several product categories (bath oil, baby powder, baby lotion, dental floss), and across both gentleness and hygiene beliefs, the flagship product of the brand, Johnson & Johnson Baby Shampoo, was highly resistant to brand dilution. Only negative information about a line extension (i.e., a new Johnson & Johnson Baby Shampoo with vitamin D) was capable of diluting the flagship product. The authors interpreted these findings as showing that, whereas dilution occurred to the overall parent brand and to several individual products of the brand, flagship products were more immune than nonflagship products to dilution effects. Chang (2002) found a similar resistance to dilution of the flagship product of the brand.

In addition to dilution effects on parent brand beliefs, parent brand attitudes, and individual products of the brand, negative brand extension information can also make it more difficult for a company to extend a brand in the future. For example, Swaminathan (2003) found that experience with the parent brand and a brand extension impacted purchase of a subsequent brand extension. While Keller and Aaker (1992) did not find dilution of a parent brand, they found that information about an unsuccessful brand extension of a high quality fictitious brand led consumers to report lower ratings for future extensions of the brand. Finally, even when a brand extension is successful, brand dilution can occur. Kumar (2005) found that when consumers were exposed to information about a successful brand extension (e.g., Tide dishwashing detergent) and subsequently evaluated a *counter-extension* from a competing brand (e.g., Cascade laundry detergent, introduced in the product category in which Tide was dominant), they were less likely to choose the original parent brand (Tide) in a future product decision, demonstrating an apparent retaliatory response to the original parent brand.

Research has also identified factors that mitigate brand dilution from negatively rated or inconsistent brand extensions that are introduced to consumers. One of these mitigating factors is strength of the parent brand. To the extent that consumers have trust in the brand and have extensive familiarity and/or experience with it, they will be less likely to change their core beliefs about the brand following a brand extension failure. Broniarczyk and Gershoff (2003) found that a new brand extension (down jacket) that extended along a trivial attribute (e.g., types of down fill, either goose or duck) harmed low equity brands (e.g., K-Mart, Wal-Mart) more than high equity brands (e.g., LL Bean, Eddie Bauer), especially when the attribute was disclosed as trivial. The strength of a brand's flagship product (Chang, 2002; John et al., 1998), also difficult to dilute, is another example of this effect.

Research also finds that dilution diminishes when the inconsistent or failed brand extensions are distanced from the parent brand. One of the best examples of a branding strategy with built-in distancing is what researchers refer to as *sub-branding** (e.g., Hallmark Shoebox, Courtyard by Marriott) used frequently in the marketplace. Sub-branding strategies reduce dilution effects when consumers are exposed to negative or inconsistent brand extensions (Park, McCarthy, & Milberg, 1993; Milberg et al., 2001; Janiszewski & van Osselaer, 2000; Kirmani et al., 1999; Kim, Lavack, & Smith, 2001). Further, Kumar (2005) found that a co-branded extension led to more immunity of the parent brand from retaliatory countermoves made by a competitor in response to the extension. Distancing from a brand extension failure to reduce parent brand dilution might also be accomplished by communicating that the failure is atypical of the brand (Loken & John, 1993; Gurhan-Canli and Maheswaran, 1998), or by decreasing the prominence of brand extension information (making it less accessible for consumers) and increasing the prominence of parent brand information (cf. Ahluwalia & Gürhan-Canli, 2000).

Brand Alliances That Are Unfavorable or Inconsistent

A co-branding, or brand alliance, strategy is one in which two brands partner in the marketing of a product or service. Brand alliances can include pairing of one brand with an ingredient brand (e.g., Betty Crocker Brownie Mix with Hershey's Milk Chocolate), retailer partnerships (e.g., Starbucks and T-Mobile to offer Internet connections in coffee shops), co-brands within a category (e.g., FTD florist and local florists), advertising alliances (e.g., Kellogg and Tropicana in a breakfast advertisement), and many others. To the extent that both brand names in the alliance are prominently displayed for consumers, co-branding is viewed by marketing practitioners as an effective strategy for transferring core brand associations (e.g., high quality) or distinctive product features (e.g., chocolate-flavored) from each of the individual brands to the co-branded product, and can occur within any of the marketing processes of product development, product promotion, or product distribution. Each of the two brands brings to the co-branded extension a different attribute profile.

Most academic studies of co-brands (brand alliances) have documented the favorable effects of co-brands on one or both parent brands (e.g., Park, Jun, & Shocker, 1996; Washburn, Till, & Priluck, 2004) or association transfer from the more to the less familiar brand (Simonin & Ruth, 1998; Levin & Levin, 2000). However, dilution resulting from brand alliances might result from several scenarios. First, if one of the brands is viewed less favorably than the other, consumers may transfer negative associations

---

* We adopt the sub-brand terminology used by researchers in the articles cited. However, we note that researchers such as Aaker and Joachimsthaler (2000) make a distinction between sub-brands (Hallmark Shoebox) and endorsed brands (Courtyard by Marriott).

from it to the more favorably evaluated brand. Second, inconsistencies or noncomplementarity between brands might dilute associations of one or both brands. Third, if the two partners produce a product that is viewed negatively or as inconsistent with one or both brands, dilution due to the problematic co-branded extension may occur. Finally, if during the course of the brand alliance, one of the brands receives negative publicity, as in the case of safety issues with Firestone tires on Ford Explorers, dilution may result.

Academic research on dilution in brand alliances yields mixed results, but generally finds only limited conditions in which negative spillover occurs. Perhaps this is not surprising, in view of the finding noted earlier that using sub-branding strategies mitigate dilution effects by creating distance from the brand. Some studies (Swaminathan & Reddy, 2004; Washburn et al., 2004) have found little or no negative spillover from one partner (e.g., a low-equity brand) to another partner (e.g., a high-equity brand). Van Osselaer and Janiszewski (2001) found that using an ingredient brand can dilute quality inferences due to overexpectations (and difficulty matching those expectations), and that the timing of the alliance is important as well (Janiszewski & van Osselaer, 2000). Votolato and Unnava (2006) found significant dilution when they examined brand alliances in the context of negative publicity about one of the two brands, but only when the two brands were viewed as equally to blame. Further, when one of the two brands in a supplier alliance was described as incompetent (e.g., low quality clothing), it was perceived more negatively than when it was described as immoral (e.g., mistreating plant workers). No research has addressed whether a prolonged alliance between two brands, in which one is evaluated less favorably, dilutes perceptions of the more favorably evaluated brand.

Protecting Brands from Dilution

Many sources of brand dilution exist and firms need to consider how to protect their brands from being harmed. Our discussion has suggested factors that mitigate brand dilution for individual sources, such as negative media publicity, trademark infringement, and brand leveraging strategies. These factors provide a way for firms to think about how they can protect their brands when faced with one of these sources of brand dilution.

But what if a firm is interested in more general strategies for protecting their brands across multiple sources of dilution? Looking across sources of dilution, the research findings suggest three general strategies that would be effective in protecting brands from harm. We discuss these strategies below.

Brand Monitoring and Surveillance

A natural starting point for firms is the development of brand surveillance and monitoring techniques to identify potential sources of brand dilution and respond to them in an effective manner. For example, monitoring of the external environment for negative media publicity or negative consumer blogs is a logical precursor to effectively handling problem situations. Monitoring the marketing environment can assist managers in identifying responses to product crises, product recalls, ethical crises, consumer Web sites and blogs, and consumer activism. A brand analysis might also be performed that evaluates whether consumer or media criticisms are valid and remedial action should be taken by the company, whether negative publicity is likely to escalate, and whether criticism is likely to be recognized by the general public or the brand's target consumers. Companies also need to monitor retail environments to protect their trademarks from imitators or counterfeiters, which is a precursor to effective trademark enforcement of brands. Surveillance and timely legal responses to the unauthorized use of trademarks are expected and rewarded by the courts when legal redress is sought in the United States and, increasingly, in overseas markets.

Monitoring internal sources of brand dilution can be useful for reducing inconsistencies in brand elements across product, pricing, promotion and distribution decisions. Since brand elements are often managed by different departments within a firm, brand guidelines for uses or nonuses of brand elements (e.g., brand name, logo, or slogan) help maintain consistency in core brand associations within the firm. Guidelines might also specify when sub-brands and co-brands might best be incorporated into a brand architectural plan.

Building and Maintaining Strong Brands

Across many sources of brand dilution, strong brands have been found to minimize brand dilution. Strong brands are those in which consumers have high familiarity, favorable attitudes and experiences, brand loyalty, commitment and/or trust. Our review of research on external sources of brand dilution found that consumers who were highly committed to a brand, who had trust in a brand, and who were brand loyal were less affected by negative publicity about a brand and responded less negatively to product harm crises and product recalls. Brands for which consumers had high familiarity were less likely to be harmed by trademark imitations of competing brands. And brand communities were found to build stronger connections between consumers and brands. Research on internal sources of brand dilution has also found that strong brands provided protection. When consumers trusted a brand and had high familiarity with it, they responded less negatively to brand extension failures. And flagship products of a brand, those products with particularly strong associations, were less vulnerable to dilution than non-flagship products of a brand. The common theme found in these areas of research is that when consumers have strong connections with the brand, whether through strong beliefs about the brand's core associations and/or favorable experiences with the brand, the brand is more immune from dilution effects.

While it seems clear that companies desire to build strong brands in order to leverage them and boost sales, the studies reported here demonstrate that strong brands also provide protection from negative influences both external and internal to the firm. Of course, a vast literature addresses factors that companies use to increase brand familiarity and consumer loyalty. However, in the specific context of managing decisions about numerous brand elements, a couple of considerations have been found to assist firms in building and maintaining strong brands. One consideration is that brand elements that consistently convey core brand associations—through pricing, distribution, and promotion—produce stronger brands that enjoy greater consumer acceptance and allegiance (Aaker, 1996). Building a strong brand involves identifying which of the brand's associations is core or central to the brand, and developing strategies for how these associations might be leveraged in a manner that maintains the brand's promise. Marketing choices about brand extensions, brand alliances, and other brand partnerships can increase brand strength to the extent that consistency between the brand elements is maintained.

A second consideration in building strong brands is that brands with high corporate social responsibility ratings appear to be protected from negative external influences. Researchers find that firms with high corporate social responsibility perceptions were blamed less for product harm crises, and were viewed more favorably after a product recall, than firms without a high corporate social responsibility profile. When a brand is linked with a social cause, some of the benefits accrued include enhanced company reputation (Menon & Kahn, 2003), perceptions of greater corporate citizenship (Dean, 2002), perceptions of company involvement in the community, company responsiveness to consumer needs (Javalgi, Traylor, Gross, & Lampman, 1994), and more favorable evaluations of the company (Lichtenstein, Drumwright, & Braig, 2004). Researchers have also found that a company's record of social responsibility increased consumers' attitudes toward the company and its products (Brown & Dacin, 1997; Creyer & Ross, 1997), and a company's negative reputation decreased consumers' attitudes toward the company and its products (Brown & Dacin, 1997; Goldberg & Hartwick, 1990). Company initiatives include support for minority programs, community involvement, cause marketing, sponsorship, and corporate philanthropy (Andreasen, 2003; Berger, Cunningham, & Drumwright, 2004; Hess, Rogovsky, & Dunfee, 2002; Lichtenstein et al.,

2004). The preexisting associations people have about a social cause or community event (e.g., "compassionate") may transfer to the brands that sponsor those causes. However, since so many companies are jumping on the corporate social responsibility bandwagon, such efforts might be met with cynicism by consumers when companies' efforts seem insincere (Yoon, Gurhan-Canli, & Schwarz, 2006; see also Basil & Herr, 2006 and Gürhan-Canli & Fries, Chapter 5, this volume). Research suggests that the authenticity of the sponsorship, such as integrating a CSR strategy with the core business strategy, heightens consumers' loyalty (Du, Bhattacharya, & Sen, 2007). Supporting a cause on the one hand and triggering problems associated with it on the other can make consumers suspicious of company motives and lead to consumer backlash.

Finally, it is important to note that even strong brands can be diluted, especially when negative information about a brand is particularly egregious (in the case of ethical violations) or particularly diagnostic (in the case of product failures). For example, failed brand extensions have been found to dilute strong brands, as well as individual products marketed and sold under the brand name. Extremely negative publicity about product failures can impact brand attitudes and purchase intentions even among consumers who are strongly connected and identify with the brand (Einwiller, Fedorikhin, Johnson, & Kamins, 2006). And the protective effect of a strong brand can be diminished by a firm's ineffective response to situations that have the potential for brand dilution, such as negative publicity surrounding product recalls and ethical violations.

Distancing Techniques

When the potential for brand dilution arises, firms can protect brands through the use of distancing techniques. As the name suggests, these techniques put distance between the brand and a possible source of dilution, thereby reducing the impact of any negative information on the brand. Our review suggests two different types of distancing techniques, described below.

Sub-Branding and Co-Branding Strategies

Sub-branding strategies (e.g., Syntax by Rolex), have been found to reduce dilution effects when consumers are exposed to negative or inconsistent brand extensions. Sub-brands were also found to mitigate dilution effects when downward stretches were used in introducing lower-priced extensions for prestige brands (e.g., Ultra by BMW). Co-branded extensions, like sub-branded extensions, have shown only minimal dilution effects to parent brands. And co-brands, relative to single-brands, were found to help protect parent brands from retaliatory counter-moves by a competitor in response to a new extension.

Both co-branded and sub-branded extensions create the perception that the extension is somehow different from the parent brand. As a result, sub-brands and co-brands can be used to create distance from the parent brand, while still using the original brand name in some fashion to suggest an association with the new product extension. To the extent that negative information about a brand extension, a brand alliance, or a celebrity endorser, can be attributed to non-brand factors, consumers appear to be less likely to blame the brand for the problems incurred.

Damage Control

In many cases, companies respond quickly to product problems by withdrawing failed brand extensions from the marketplace, initiating product recalls, initiating legal action against trademark infringers, dropping celebrity endorsers engaged in scandal, and countering negative publicity with restitution and acknowledgment. Distancing from product problems, such as a failed extension, through brand communications may also protect against dilution. Distancing might be generated by communicating that a brand extension failure is an "exception" or atypical of the brand. It might also be generated through communications that highlight the brand's core competencies and reduce the prominence of negative information about the brand extension. When communication of negative information is not under the control of the firm, as in the case of negative publicity from a product crisis, then speedy and effective responses by the firm (e.g., apologies and restitution) may help distance the failure from the parent brand.

Future Research

In this chapter, we have taken a broad view of brand dilution, reviewing research relevant to understanding factors both external and internal to the firm that may harm brands. Research on external sources of brand dilution has documented significant dilution effects on brands. Negative publicity about product crises and product recall has been found to dilute brand beliefs and attitudes, and has reduced purchase intentions and purchases of a brand. Ethical crises involving company policies have been found to result in more negative consumer beliefs and attitudes about brands. Research on trademark imitation by competitor brands has found evidence of harm to the original brand in the form of poorer memory of the original brand's product category, and visual similarities with imitated trademarks have been found to weaken distinctive associations of the original brand. Research on retailing variables has found that inconsistent pricing and certain types of retailer displays have negatively affected consumers' perceptions of the brand. And negative communications by consumers, such as complaints, rumors, and boycotts, were found to dilute brand associations and reduce purchases of the brand.

Nevertheless, research is absent on many topics relating to trademark misuse, problematic distribution practices, and consumer backlash. The impact of counterfeiting, Internet squatting, and meta-tagging (that misdirects consumers to competitors' Web sites) on brands is unknown. Research on channel activities, such as the effects of bootlegging of product shipments on brands, is absent. While competitors' actions have been analyzed with respect to trademark infringement and retaliatory brand extensions, more research is needed to determine competitive strategies that contribute to brand dilution. Comparative advertising, for example, can enhance attitudes for a sponsored brand under certain conditions (e.g., Pechmann and Stewart, 1990), but we know less about whether these ads harm the comparison brand. While retailer displays have been examined, researchers might also examine retailer layouts, shelf location, or other retailer variables as sources of brand dilution. Also, while antecedents of consumer dissatisfaction have been studied, research is needed on the effects of more organized consumer complaint behavior on brands, such as those found on consumer blogs, by consumer activists, and in macro-level consumerism movements. Negative word-of-mouth communications between company employers or resulting from damaged business relationships might also create dilution for a brand. Further studies are needed that extend beyond demonstrations of external sources of brand dilution and address moderating factors that increase or decrease dilution.

We have also documented numerous sources of dilution due to decisions made within the firm. Pricing and promotion decisions that are inconsistent with the brand's core image can harm a brand, although more research is needed on the effects of inconsistencies in the marketing mix on brands. Numerous studies on failed or inconsistent brand extensions have documented dilution findings that include harm to brand beliefs and attitudes, reduced sales, and negative perceptions of future extensions. When a brand was paired with another brand (co-branding), dilution effects were generally found less often. Future research might examine whether these lower dilution effects for brand pairings are the result of shared responsibility attributed to both elements of the pairing or, alternatively, whether consumers attribute primary blame for scandal, product failure, or inconsistencies to the other brand.

Research is also lacking on conceptual and methodological issues relating to dilution. Processes underlying dilution are sometimes described in single-issue dilution studies, but conceptual frameworks that take into account a broader range of dilution findings are needed. Theoretical processes, for example, that contribute to the distancing of co-brands, sub-brands, and other brand extensions are important to understand. Research might also tell us whether weakening of brand sales (e.g., decreased sales of Audi automobiles) is further along a chain reaction of dilution spillover effects than weakening of a brand association (e.g., consumers' believing that Audis have acceleration problems).

Research is also needed to understand the practical matter of how long dilution effects persist under alternative dilution scenarios. To the extent a marketing condition contributes to persistent dilution effects, the greater the harm may be done to the brand in the long run. Understanding factors that sustain dilution effects or increase their persistence over time is an important topic for future research. Further, all brands within a negatively evaluated industry (e.g., the oil industry) may be susceptible to long-term dilution effects when societal factors (e.g., the price of gas in a worsening economy) impact consumer perceptions.

In conclusion, research efforts should be broadened to include brand dilution sources beyond failed and inconsistent brand extensions. A variety of sources both external and internal to the firm have been found to harm brands. More research is needed to determine the nature of these dilution effects and strategies useful for mitigating brand dilution and protecting the brands.

References

Aaker, D.A. (1990). Brand extensions: The good, the bad, and the ugly. *Sloan Management Review, 3*, 47–56.

Aaker, D.A. (1996). *Building strong brands*. New York: Free Press.

Aaker, D.A. & Joachimsthaler, E. (2002). *Brand leadership*. Sydney: Free Press.

Aaker, J., Fournier, S., & Brasel, S.A. (2004). When good brands do bad. *Journal of Consumer Research, 31*, 1–16.

Ahluwalia, R., & Gürhan-Canli, Z. (2000). The effects of extensions on the family brand name: An accessibility-diagnosticity perspective. *Journal of Consumer Research, 27*, 371–81.

Ahluwalia, R., Burnkrant, R.E., & Unnava, H.R. (2000). Consumer response to negative publicity: The moderating role of commitment. *Journal of Marketing Research, 37*, 203–214.

Algesheimer, R., Dholakia, U.M., & Hermann, A. (2005). The social influence of brand community: Evidence from European car clubs. *Journal of Marketing, 69*, 19–34.

Allport, G.W., & Postman, L. (1947). *The psychology of rumor*. New York: Holt.

Andreasen, A.R. (2003). *Marketing for nonprofit organizations*. Upper Saddle River, NJ: Prentice Hall.

Ashenfelter, O., Ciccarella, S.M., & Shatz, H.J. (2007). French wine and the U.S. boycott of 2003: Does politics really affect commerce? *Journal of Wine Economics, 2*, 56–75.

Batra, R., & Homer, P.M. (2004). The situational impact of brand image beliefs. *Journal of Consumer Psychology, 14*, 318–330.

Bechwati, N.N., & Morin, M. (2003). Outraged consumers: Getting even at the expense of getting a good deal. *Journal of Consumer Psychology, 13*, 440–453.

Berger, I., Cunningham, P., & Drumwright, M. (2004). Social alliances: Company/nonprofit collaboration. *California Management Review, 47*, 58–90.

Bolton, R.N., & Drew, J.H. (1991). A longitudinal analysis of the impact of service changes on customer attitudes. *Journal of Marketing, 55*, 1–9.

Broniarczyk, S.M., & Gershoff, A.D. (2003). The reciprocal effects of brand equity and trivial attributes. *Journal of Marketing Research, 40*, 161–175.

Brown, T.J., & Dacin, P.A. (1997). The company and the product: Corporate associations and consumer product responses. *Journal of Marketing, 6*, 68–84.

Buchanan, L., Simmons, C.J., & Bickart, B.B. (1999). Brand equity dilution: Retailer display and context brand effects. *Journal of Marketing Research, 36*, 345–355.

Business Week (2003). Keeping the froth on Sam Adams. Accessed at http://businessweek.com/ Magazine/content/03_35/b3847069.htm.

Chang, J.W. (2002). Will a family brand image be diluted by an unfavorable brand extension? A brand trial-based approach. In S. Broniarczyk & K. Nakamoto (Eds.), *Advances in Consumer Research* (Vol. 29, pp. 299–304). Valdosta, GA: Association for Consumer Research.

Chavis, L., & Leslie, P. (2006). Consumer boycotts: The impact of the Iraq war on French wine sales in the U.S., NBER Working paper W11981.

Chen, A.C., & Chen, S.K. (2000). Brand dilution effect of extension failure – a Taiwan study. *Journal of Product and Brand Management, 9*, 243–254.

Cleeren, K., Dekimpe, M.G., & Helsen, K. (2008). Weathering product-harm crises. *Journal of the Academy of Marketing Science, 36*, 262–270.

CNNMoney.com (2005). No apologies for sexy Paris Hilton ad, June 1, 2005, accessed at http:// money.cnn.com/2005/05/24/news/newsmakers/carls_ad/index.htm.

Collins-Dodd, C., & Zaichkowsky, J.L. (1999). National brand responses to brand imitation: Retailers versus other manufacturers. *Journal of Product and Brand Management, 8*, 96–108.

Coombs, W.T., & Holladay, S.J. (2006). Unpacking the halo effect: Reputation and crisis management. *Journal of Communication Management, 10*, 123–137.

Curren, M.T., & Folkes, V.S. (1987). Attributional influences on consumers' desires to communicate about products. *Psychology & Marketing, 4*, 31–45.

Creyer, E.H., & Ross, W.T. (1997). The influence of firm behavior on purchase intention: Do consumers really care about business ethics? *Journal of Consumer Marketing, 14*, 421–432.

Dawar, N., & Pillutla, M. (2000). The impact of product–harm crises on brand equity: The moderating role of consumer expectations. *Journal of Marketing Research, 37*, 215–226.

Dean, D. (2004). Consumer reaction to negative publicity: Effects of corporate reputation, response, and responsibility for a crisis event. *Journal of Business Communication, 41*, 192–211.

Dean, D.H. (2002). Associating the corporation with a charitable event through sponsorship: Measuring the effects on corporate community relations. *Journal of Advertising, 31*, 77–87.

Dodson, J.A., Tybout, A.M., & Sternthal, B. (1978). Impact of deals and deal retraction on brand switching. *Journal of Marketing Research, 15*, 72–81.

Donavan, T.D., Mowen, J.C., & Chakraborty, G. (2001). Urban legends: Diffusion processes and the exchange of resources. *Journal of Consumer Marketing, 18*, 521–533.

Drinkwater, P., & Uncles, M. (2007). The impact of program brands on consumer evaluations of television and radio broadcaster brands. *Journal of Product & Brand Management, 16*, 178–187.

Du, S., Bhattacharya, C.B., & Sen, S. (2007). Reaping relational rewards from corporate social responsibility: The role of competitive positioning. *International Journal of Research in Marketing, 24*, 224–241.

Dutta, S., Bergen, M., & John, G. (1994). Governance of exclusive territories when dealers can bootleg. *Marketing Science, 13*, 83–99.

Einwiller, S.A., Fedorikhin, A., Johnson, A.R., & Kamins, M.A. (2006). Enough is enough! When identification no longer prevents negative corporate associations. *Journal of the Academy of Marketing Science, 34*, 185–194.

Erdem, T. (1998). An empirical analysis of umbrella branding. *Journal of Marketing Research, 35*, 339–351.

Folkes, V.S. (1984). Consumer reactions to product failure: An attributional approach. *Journal of Consumer Research, 10*, 398–409.

Folkes, V.S., & Kamins, M.A. (1999). Effects of information about firms' ethical and unethical actions on consumers' attitudes. *Journal of Consumer Psychology, 8*, 243–259.

Forbes.com (2007). Latest IRI study finds sophisticated U.S. and European private label strategies capturing market potential, accessed at http//www.forbes.com/businesswire/feeds/businesswire/2007/11/12/businesswire20071112006327r1.html

Foxman, E.R., Muehling, D.D., & Berger, P.W. (1990). An investigation of factors contributing to consumer brand confusion. *Journal of Consumer Affairs, 24*, 170–189.

Friedman, M. (1996). A positive approach to organized consumer action: The "boycott" as an alternative to the boycott. *Journal of Consumer Policy, 19*, 439–451.

Gentry, G., Putrevu, S., Shulz, C., & Commuri, S. (2001), How now Ralph Lauren? The separation of brand and product in a counterfeit culture. In M. Gilly & J. Meyers-Levy (Eds.), *Advances in consumer research* (Vol. 28, pp. 258–265). Valdosta, GA: Association for Consumer Research.

Goldberg, M.E., & Hartwick, J. (1990). The effects of advertiser reputation and extremity of advertising claim on advertising effectiveness. *Journal of Consumer Research, 17*, 172–179.

Grégoire, Y., & Fisher, R.J. (2008). Customer betrayal and retaliation: When your best customers become your worst enemies. *Journal of the Academy of Marketing Science, 36*, 247–261.

Griffin, M., Babin, B.J., & Attaway, J.S. (1991). An empirical investigation of the impact of negative public publicity on consumer attitudes and intentions. In R.H. Holman & M.R. Solomon (Eds.), *Advances in consumer research* (Volume 18, pp. 334–41). Provo, UT: Association for Consumer Research.

Gürhan-Canli, Z., & Maheswaran, D. (1998). The effects of extensions on brand name dilution and enhancement. *Journal of Marketing Research, 35,* 464–473.

Hawkins, S.A., & Hoch, S.J. (1992). Low-involvement learning: Memory without evaluation. *Journal of Consumer Research, 19,* 212–225.

Heath, T.B., McCarthy, M.S., & Mothersbaugh, D.L. (1994). Spokesperson fame and the vividness effects in the context of issue-relevant thinking: The moderating role of competitive setting. *Journal of Consumer Research, 20,* 520–534.

Herrmann, R.O. (1993). The tactics of consumer resistance: Group action and the marketplace exit. In L. McAlister & M.L. Rothschild (Eds.), *Advances in consumer research* (Vol. 20, pp. 130–134). Provo, UT: Association for Consumer Research.

Hess, D., Rogovsky, N., & Dunfee, T.W. (2002). The next wave of corporate community involvement: Corporate social initiatives. *California Management Review, 44,* 117.

Howard, D.J., Kerin, R.A., & Gengler, C.E. (2000). The effects of brand name similarity on brand source confusion: Implications for trademark infringement. *Journal of Public Policy and Marketing, 19,* 250–264.

Hoyer, W D., & MacInnis, D.J. (2007). *Consumer behavior,* 4th edition. Boston: Houghton Mifflin.

Janiszewski, C., & van Osselaer, S.M.J. (2000). A connectionist model of brand-quality associations. *Journal of Marketing Research, 37,* 331–350.

Javalgi, R.G., Traylor, M.B., Gross, A.C., & Lampman, E. (1994). Awareness of sponsorship and corporate image: An empirical investigation. *Journal of Advertising, 23,* 47–58.

John, D.R., Loken, B., & Joiner, C. (1998). The negative impact of extensions: Can flagship products be diluted? *Journal of Marketing, 62,* 19–32.

Jolly, D.W., & Mowen, J.C. (1985). Product recall communications: The effect of source, media, and social responsibility information. In E.C. Hirschman & M.B. Holbrook (Eds.), *Advances in consumer research* (Vol. 12, pp. 471–475). Provo, UT: Association for Consumer Research.

Kahle, L.R., & Homer, P.M. (1985). Physical attractiveness of the celebrity endorser: A social adaptation perspective. *Journal of Consumer Research, 11,* 954–961.

Kamins, M. (1990). An investigation into the match-up hypothesis of celebrity advertising. *Journal of Advertising, 19,* 4–13.

Kamins, M.A., Brand, M.J., Hoeke, S.A., & Moe, J.C. (1989). Two-sided versus one-sided celebrity endorsements: The impact on advertising effectiveness and credibility. *Journal of Advertising, 18,* 4–10.

Kamins, M.A., Folkes, V.S., & Perner, L. (1997). Consumer responses to rumors: Good news, bad news. *Journal of Consumer Psychology, 6,* 165–187.

Kapferer, J.N. (1994). *Strategic brand management.* New York: The Free Press.

Kapferer, J.N. (1995). Stealing brand equity: Measuring perception confusion between national brands and "copycat" own-label products. *Marketing and Research Today,* 96–103.

Keller, K.L., & Aaker, D.A. (1992). The effects of sequential introduction of brand extensions. *Journal of Marketing Research, 29,* 35–50.

Keller, K., & Sood, S. (2003). Brand equity dilution. *MIT Sloan Management Review, 45*, 12–14.

Kim, C.K., Lavack, A.M., & Smith, M. (2001). Consumer evaluation of vertical brand extensions and core brands. *Journal of Business Research, 52*(3), 211–222.

Kirmani, A., Sood, S., & Bridges, S. (1999). The ownership effect in consumer responses to brand line stretches. *Journal of Marketing, 63*, 88–101.

Klein, J., & Dawar, N. (2004). Corporate social responsibility and consumers' attributions and brand evaluations in a product-harm crisis. *International Journal of Research in Marketing, 21*, 203–217.

Klein, J.G., Smith, N.C., & John, A. (2004). Why we boycott: Consumer motivations for boycott participation. *Journal of Marketing, 68*, 92–109.

Kozinets, R.V., & Handelman, J.M. (2004). Adversaries of consumption: Consumer movements, activism, and ideology. *Journal of Consumer Research, 31*, 691–704.

Kumar, P. (2005). The impact of cobranding on customer evaluation of brand counterextensions. *Journal of Marketing, 69*, 1–18.

Lane, V., & Jacobson, R. (1997). The reciprocal impact of brand leveraging: Feedback effects from brand extension evaluation to brand evaluation. *Marketing Letters, 8*, 261–271.

Lanham Act of 1946: Act of July 5, 1946, 60 Stat. 427 (codified as amended at 15 U.S.C. 1051–1127).

Levin, I.P., & Levin, A.M. (2000). Modeling the role of brand alliances in the assimilation of product evaluations. *Journal of Consumer Psychology, 9*, 43–52.

Lichtenstein, D.R., Drumwright, M.E., & Braig, B.M. (2004). The effect of corporate social responsibility on customer donations to corporate-supported nonprofits. *Journal of Marketing, 68*, 16–33.

Loken, B., & John, D.R. (1993). Diluting brand beliefs: When do brand extensions have a negative impact? *Journal of Marketing, 57*, 71–84.

Loken, B., Ross, I., & Hinkle, R.L. (1986), Consumer confusion of origin and brand similarity perceptions. *Journal of Public Policy and Marketing, 5*, 195–211.

Menon, G., Jewell, R.D., & Unnava, H.R. (1999). When a company does not respond to negative publicity: Cognitive elaboration vs. negative affect perspective. In E.J. Arnould & L.M. Scott (Eds.), *Advances in consumer research* (Volume 26, pp. 325–329). Provo, UT: Association for Consumer Research.

Menon, S., & Kahn, B.E. (2003). Corporate sponsorships of philanthropic activities: When do they impact perception of sponsor brand? *Journal of Consumer Psychology, 13*, 316–327.

Milberg, S.J., Park, C.W., & McCarthy, M.S. (1997). Managing negative feedback effects associated with brand extensions: The impact of alternative branding strategies. *Journal of Consumer Psychology, 6*, 119–40.

Miller, K.E., & Sturdivant, F.D. (1977). Consumer responses to socially questionable corporate behavior: An empirical test. *Journal of Consumer Research, 4*, 1–7.

Morrin, M., & Jacoby, J. (2000). Trademark dilution: Empirical measures for an elusive concept. *Journal of Public Policy & Marketing, 19*, 265–276.

Morrin, M., Lee, J., & Allenby, G.M. (2006). Determinants of trademark dilution. *Journal of Consumer Research, 33*, 248–257.

Mowen, J.C. (1980). Further information on consumer perceptions of product recalls. In J.C. Olson (Ed.), *Advances in consumer research* (Volume 7, pp. 519–523). Ann Arbor, MI: Association for Consumer Research.

Mowen, J.C., Jolly, D.W., & Nickell, G.S. (1980). Factors influencing consumer response to product recalls: A regression analysis approach. In K.B. Monroe (Ed.), *Advances in consumer research* (Volume 8, pp. 405–407). Ann Arbor, MI: Association for Consumer Research.

Muniz, A.M., Jr., & O'Guinn, T.C. (2000). Brand community. *Journal of Consumer Research, 27*, 412–432.

Naughton, K. (2002). Dude where's my Benz? *Newsweek*, March 18, 2002, 40.

New York Times (2000). Calvin Klein battles maker of its jeans. June 20, 2000, p. 1 & 12.

Okada, E.M., & Reibstein, D.J. (1998). When bad stuff happens...Effects of related and unrelated positive associations on the influence of negative secondary associations. In J.W. Alba & J.W. Hutchinson (Eds.), *Advances in consumer research* (Vol. 25, pp. 349–356). Provo, UT: Association for Consumer Research.

Park, C.W., Jun, S.Y., & Shocker, A.D. (1996). Composite branding alliances: An investigation of extension and feedback effects. *Journal of Marketing Research, 33*, 453–466.

Park, C.W., McCarthy, M.S., & Milberg, S.J. (1993). The effects of direct and associative brand extension strategies on consumer responses to brand extensions. In L. McAlister & M.L. Rothschild (Eds.), *Advances in consumer research* (Vol. 20, pp. 28–33). Provo, UT: Association for Consumer Research.

Pechmann, C., & Stewart, D.W. (1990). The effects of comparative advertising on attention, memory, and purchase intentions. *Journal of Consumer Research, 17*, 180–191.

Pennings, J.M.E., Wansink, B., & Meulenberg, M.T.G. (2002). A note on modeling consumer reactions to a crisis: The case of the mad cow disease. *International Journal of Research in Marketing, 19*, 91–100.

Peterson, R.A., Smith, K.H., & Zerrillo, P.C. (1999). Trademark dilution and the practice of marketing. *Journal of the Academy of Marketing Science, 27*, 255–268.

Priester, J.R., & Petty, R.E. (2003). The influence of spokesperson trustworthiness on message elaboration, attitude strength, and advertising effectiveness. *Journal of Consumer Psychology, 13*, 408–421.

Pullig, C., Simmons, C.J., & Netemeyer, R.G. (2006). Brand dilution: When do new brands hurt existing brands? *Journal of Marketing, 70*, 52–66.

Reddy, M., & Terblanche, N. (2005). How not to extend your luxury brand. *Harvard Business Review, 83*, December, 20–24.

Renkema, J., & Hoeken, H. (1998). The influence of negative newspaper publicity on corporate image. *Netherlands' Journal of Business Communication, 35*, 521–535.

Richins, M.L. (1983). Negative word-of-mouth by dissatisfied consumers: A pilot study. *Journal of Marketing, 47*, 68–78.

Richins, M.L. (1984). Word-of-mouth communications as negative information. In T.C. Kinnear (Ed.), *Advances in consumer research* (Vol. 11, pp. 697–702). Provo, UT: Association for Consumer Research.

Ridley, K. (2005). Private label: A 'good alternative' to other brands, offering the same quality & value: ACNielsen Global Consumer Survey at http:// us.acnielsen.com/news/ 20050811.shtml.

Roehm, M.L., & Brady, M.K. (2007). Consumer responses to performance failures by high-equity brands. *Journal of Consumer Research, 34*, 537–545.

Roehm, M.L., & Tybout, A.M. (2006). When will a brand scandal spill over, and how should competitors respond? *Journal of Marketing, 43*, 366–373.

Samson, M. (1998). Bally Total Fitness Holding Corporation v. Andrew S. Faber, 29 F. Supp. 2d 1161 (C.D.Cal., Nov. 23, 1998), at www.internetlibrary.com/ cases/lib_case27.cfm.

Sen, S., Gürhan-Canli, Z., & Morwitz, V. (2001). Withholding consumption: A social dilemma perspective on consumer boycotts. *Journal of Consumer Research, 28*, 399–417.

Sheinin, D.A. (2000). The effects of experience with brand extensions on parent brand knowledge. *Journal of Business Research, 49*, 47–55.

Simonin, B.L., & Ruth, J.A. (1998). Is a company known by the company it keeps? Assessing the spillover effects of brand alliances on consumer brand attitudes. *Journal of Marketing Research, 35*, 30–42.

Skurnik, I. (2005). Special session summary: Rumors, refutations, and conflicts of interest: Problems in dealing with unreliable information. In G. Menon & A.R. Rao (Eds.), *Advances in consumer research* (Vol. 32, pp. 274–276). Duluth, MN: Association for Consumer Research.

Srinivasan, S., & Hanssens, D. (2009). Marketing and firm value. *Journal of Marketing*, forthcoming.

Stockmyer, J. (1996). Brand in crisis: Consumer help for deserving victims. In K.P. Corfman & J.G. Lynch, Jr. (Eds.), *Advances in consumer research* (Vol. 13, pp. 429–435). Provo, UT: Association for Consumer Research.

Sullivan, M.W. (1990). Measuring image spillover in umbrella-branded products. *The Journal of Business, 35*, 154–165.

Swaminathan, V. (2003). Sequential brand extensions and brand choice behavior. *Journal of Business Research, 56*, 431–442.

Swaminathan, V., Fox, R.J., & Reddy, S.K. (2001). The impact of brand extension introduction on choice. *Journal of Marketing, 65*, 1–15.

Swaminathan, V., & Reddy, S.K. (2004). Assessing the spillover effects of ingredient branded strategies. Working paper, University of Pittsburgh.

Taillieu, O.A. (2007). http://www.articles3000.com/Legal-Matters/90837/ Trademark-Dilution-Part-II.html.

Tauber, E.M. (1985). Editorial: Researching brand extensions. *Journal of Advertising Research, 16*, 6.

Tauber, E.M. (1988). Brand leverage: Strategy for growth in a cost control world. *Journal of Advertising Research, 28*, 26–30.

Thompson, C.J., Rindfleisch, A., & Arsel, Z. (2006). Emotional branding and the strategic value of the doppelganger brand image. *Journal of Marketing, 70*, 50–64.

Till, B.D., & Shimp, T.A. (1998). Endorsers in advertising: The case of negative celebrity information. *Journal of Advertising, 27*, 67–82.

Tybout, A.M., Calder, B.J., & Sternthal, B. (1981). Using information processing theory to design marketing strategies. *Journal of Marketing Research, 18*, 73–79.

Underwriters Laboratories (2007). www.ul.com/ace/counterfeiting.html.

van Osselaer, S.M.J., & Janiszewski, C. (2001). Two ways of learning brand associations. *Journal of Consumer Research, 28*, 202–223.

van Heerde, H., Helsen, K., & Dekimpe, M.G. (2007). The impact of a product-harm crisis on marketing effectiveness. *Marketing Science, 26*, 230–245.

Vargo, S.L., Nagao, K., He, Y., & Morgan, F.W. (2007). Satisfier, dissatisfiers, criticals and neutrals: A review of their effects on customer (dis)satisfaction. *Academy of Marketing Science Review, 11*(2), accessed at http/www.amsreview.org/articles/vargo2-2007.pdf.

Votolato, N., & Unnava, H.R. (2006). Spillover of negative information on brand alliances. *Journal of Consumer Psychology, 16*, 196–202.

Wall Street Journal (2007). Medtronic net slips on recall, November 20, 2007. Accessed at hppt://online.wsj.com/article/SB119550626444798293.html?mod+sphere_wd.

Ward, J., Loken, B., Ross, I., & Hasapopoulos, T. (1986). The influence of physical similarity on generalization of affect and attribute perceptions from national brands to private label brands. In T. Shimp, S. Sharma, W. Dillon, R.T. Dyer, M. Gardner, G. John, et al. (Eds.), *American Marketing Association Educator's Conference Proceedings* (Vol. 52, pp. 510–516). Chicago, IL: American Marketing Association.

Ward, J., & Ostrom, A.L. (2006). Complaining to the masses: The role of protest framing in customer-created complaint web sites. *Journal of Consumer Research, 33*, 220–230.

Warlop, L., & Alba, J.W. (2004). Sincere flattery: Trade-dress imitation and consumer choice. *Journal of Consumer Psychology, 14*, 21–27.

Washburn, J.H., Till, B.D., & Priluck, R. (2004). Brand alliance and customer based brand equity effects. *Psychology & Marketing, 21*, 487–508.

Wegner, D.M. (1984). Innuendo and damage to reputations. In T.C. Kinnear (Ed.), *Advances in Consumer Research* (Vol. 11, pp. 691–696). Provo, UT: Association for Consumer Research.

Weinberger, M.G., Allen, C.T., & Dillon, W.R. (1981). Negative information: Perspectives and research directions. In K.B. Monroe (Ed.), *Advances in Consumer Research* (Vol. 8, pp. 398–404). Ann Arbor, MI: Association for Consumer Research.

Yoon, Y., Gurhan-Canli, Z., & Schwarz, N. (2006). The effect of corporate social responsibility (CSR) activities on companies with bad reputations. *Journal of Consumer Psychology, 16*, 377–390.

Zaichkowsky, J.L. (2006). *The psychology behind trademark infringement and counterfeiting.* Mahwah, NJ: Lawrence Erlbaum Associates, Inc.

12

Brands and Trademarks: The Legal Implications of Branding*

Stephen R. Baird
Chair, Trademark and Brand Management Group
Winthrop & Weinstine, P.A.

The Relationship Between Brands and Trademarks

A common feature of brands and trademarks is that they both communicate valuable information to consumers. Although a variety of definitions exist for what may constitute a brand, a trademark essentially provides the legal framework for owning and protecting a brand. As such, trademarks are considered a form of intellectual property that can be owned, licensed, bought, sold, and used as collateral. Trademarks permit brand owners to profit from their investment in creating brands. Equally important, when respected and enforced, they also protect consumers from being confused or deceived in the marketplace. Those who sell branded goods and services have a strong interest in ensuring that no one steals or alters the message that the brand and trademark communicates, and consumers have a strong interest in being able to rely on the message that the brand and trademark represents. To this end, trademark law, a subset of unfair competition law, has developed to protect both consumers and those who sell goods and services in the marketplace.

The legal definition of a trademark is extremely broad. A "trademark" includes any word, name, symbol, or device, or any combination thereof that identifies, distinguishes, and indicates the source of goods. A "service mark" has the same broad definition, except it identifies, distinguishes,

---

* The author would like to thank Brent Lorentz, an associate attorney with Winthrop & Weinstine, P.A., for his able assistance in the preparation of this chapter.

and indicates the source of services, as opposed to goods.[1] Essentially, any subject matter perceivable by humans can qualify, so long as it identifies, distinguishes, and indicates source. Some are surprised to learn that this broad legal definition can include not only words and logos, but nontraditional marks too, such as single colors, color combinations, sounds, scents, product configurations, product containers and packaging, restaurant interiors, and building exteriors, among others.

For example, Owens Corning owns a registered trademark for the color pink used in building insulation. Corbond Corporation owns registered marks for the color lavender for building insulation. UPS has registered its ownership of the color brown for parcel transportation and delivery services. Porsche owns exclusive trademark rights for the configuration of its 911 model vehicle. Coca-Cola enjoys exclusive rights in the distinctive shape of its beverage container. NBC owns rights for its three-tone chime. Manhattan Oil owns exclusive rights for a cherry scent for motor oil. Sprint owns rights for the visual pin drop motion. Chipotle restaurant owns rights for the look and feel of its restaurant interior. White Castle enjoys exclusive rights in its distinctive building exterior. Mystic Lake Casino owns a registered service mark for the formation of light beams resembling the conical framework of a tipi emanating from a circular source of light. It is even possible that symbols perceived by the senses of taste or touch could eventually be created and registered as trademarks, although none is known to currently exist.

Trademarks Must Be Distinctive

For a word, symbol, or device to function as a trademark it must be distinctive. Trademarks exist along a spectrum of distinctiveness. This spectrum has categories ranging from the most distinctive to the least distinctive: (1) fanciful, (2) arbitrary, (3) suggestive, (4) descriptive, and (5) generic. Marks are given greater or lesser protection, depending on their classification on the distinctiveness spectrum. Further, the law recognizes fanciful, arbitrary, and suggestive marks as *inherently distinctive*, permitting them immediate protection on their first use; descriptive marks must gain *acquired distinctiveness* over time to be worthy of protection. Generic designations can never be protected as they are part of the public domain. By providing greater protection for more creative marks, trademark law rewards creativity and uniqueness.

Inherent Distinctiveness

Fanciful marks are those that have been coined for the express purpose of functioning as trademarks. They didn't exist in the English language until they were formed to be trademarks. Included within this category are completely made-up words and perhaps archaic words that have fallen out of the contemporary lexicon. Well known examples include **Kodak, Pepsi, Exxon, Xerox, Google**, and **Cingular**. Fanciful marks are entitled to the greatest protection. However, from a branding perspective, they have challenges and can be viewed as empty vessels until the owner has infused them with meaning. They are attractive to the extent that the mark owner can completely control all associations with the mark, but the costs related to solidifying a brand new word in the minds of consumers can be steep.

Arbitrary trademarks are words or symbols that are already known and in common usage, but have no connection or relationship with the associated goods. Some well known examples of arbitrary marks include **Apple** computers, **Saturn** cars, **Rainbow** grocery stores, **Camel** cigarettes, **Sun** computers, and **Sun** banks. Like fanciful marks, arbitrary marks are also entitled to strong protection. However, the level of protection is necessarily less based on the fact that the word or symbol already exists and may already be in use in a different capacity by other trademark owners. Similar to fanciful marks, arbitrary marks are also more difficult to cultivate. While they have meaning associated with them prior to adoption as a trademark, these meanings are irrelevant to the brand if the mark is truly arbitrary. For this reason, in the author's experience, when modern brand professionals are behind the creation of trademarks it is more likely that the mark will be suggestive as opposed to arbitrary.

Suggestive marks not only identify, distinguish, and indicate source, but they also communicate nonsource information about the goods or services, too. They do not, however, immediately describe the goods or services. Instead, they are inherently more subtle and creative than descriptive marks by "suggesting" or implying a characteristic or quality of the associated goods or services. In contrast to arbitrary and fanciful marks, suggestive marks have the advantage of not needing to create associations from scratch. Consumers are aware of the meanings of words that are used in suggestive marks, and the advertiser chooses the suggestive mark because of these meanings to convey not only source information, but also product or service information.

The protection afforded to suggestive marks is somewhat more limited, but as with arbitrary and fanciful marks, suggestive marks enjoy immediate protection upon their first use. The words used in these marks necessarily have common usage throughout language, and accordingly, protection is limited to the particular scope of the marks' use. Marks that have been found suggestive include **Action Slacks** pants, **Bear** outdoor clothing, **Coppertone** suntan oil, **L'eggs** womens' hosiery, **Rain Bird** irrigation sprinkler systems, **7-Eleven** food store chain, and **Wrangler** western boots and jeans.

Descriptive marks are those that immediately inform consumers of the characteristics of the product or service. They are not subtle or creative; they hit the consumer over the head with the connection between the mark and the goods or services. Because they lack any inherent source indicating capabilities, they are not immediately eligible for trademark protection. Instead, great investments of time, effort, and resources are required before exclusive rights can be obtained in descriptive marks, leaving the owners unsure of exactly when those rights come into existence. One of the dangers of descriptive marks is that if others adopt and use them, too, before exclusive rights are obtained by the first user, then exclusive rights may never be obtained. Examples of descriptive marks include **Best** computer support services, **Cheaper!** discount cigarettes, **Easyload** tape recorders, **Express** employment services, **World Book** encyclopedias, **Lotsa Suds** dishwashing liquid, **Raisin-Bran** raisin and bran cereal, and **Vision Center** optical clinic.

Generic terms are simply the names of the products themselves; thus, it is impossible for a generic term to indicate any unique source. Additionally, because generic terms are the actual generic names of the products and services, allowing them to be trademarked would take the terms out of the public domain and put the general public and competitors at a great disadvantage. This was one of the motivations in preventing Miller Brewing from owning exclusive rights to **Lite** for low calorie beer. Since **Lite** is the legal equivalent of "light" and denotes a category of beer, namely, light or low calorie beer, the courts concluded that even the misspelling was not entitled to any legal protection (outside the special script Miller Brewing uses).

Of course, just because a word is generic when applied to one type of product doesn't mean it can't be a trademark with respect to another type of product. Examples of terms generic in one setting but functioning as a trademark in another include **Apple** (generic for fruit, arbitrary for computers), **Diesel** (generic for engine, arbitrary for clothing), and **Sandals** (generic for footwear, arbitrary for resort hotels).

The generic category comprises two types of generic terms: those that started out generic, as was the case with the **Lite** beer example described above, and those that represent the end point of the tragic degeneration of a brand. Examples of generic terms that resulted from "genericide" include **Aspirin, Escalator, Cellophane, Zipper, Trampoline**, and **Linoleum**.

Acquired Distinctiveness for Descriptive Marks

Despite the fact that descriptive marks are not inherently distinctive, they can still obtain protection if they enjoy acquired distinctiveness. If a descriptive mark is used for a long period, or if the mark is aggressively promoted, the symbol will become distinctive and protectable. Acquired distinctiveness is also known as *secondary meaning*, because essentially the mark has obtained a source indicating meaning in addition to its descriptive meaning.

There are seven factors that courts typically use to evaluate whether a mark has attained secondary meaning: (1) direct consumer testimony, (2) consumer surveys, (3) exclusivity, length, and manner of use, (4) amount and manner of advertising, (5) amount of sales and number of customers, (6) established place in the market, and (7) proof of intentional copying.[2] Each of these elements has bearing on the question, at least tangentially, of whether consumers now associate a previously descriptive term with the source of particular goods or services. For example, if the person claiming ownership rights in a term is the only person using that term in association with a particular line of goods and has been doing so for an extended period of time, it is likely that consumers will recognize goods bearing that term as originating from a single source. Likewise, if the person using a term has expended a great deal of time and money promoting that term with respect to his goods or services, it is considered likely that the public has been influenced by those efforts.

Distinguishing Between Descriptive and Suggestive Marks

Distinguishing between descriptive and suggestive marks is a commonly encountered problem in trademark law, both in litigation and during the registration process. There are multiple reasons for this. First, there are no clear boundaries delineating the rather subjective borders of suggestion and description. As the great Judge Learned Hand commented, "It is quite impossible to get any rule out of the cases beyond this: That the validity of a mark ends where suggestion ends and description begins."[3] Second, whether a mark is classified as suggestive or descriptive has significant consequences for the protection of the mark. If a mark is classified as descriptive, secondary meaning must be established before the owner can gain or enforce any rights in the mark.

Courts have fashioned various tests in an effort to draw the suggestive-descriptive boundary line. The most popular of these is the "degree of imagination test," where courts consider how quickly one can leap from the mark to a characteristic of the product or service.[4] Essentially, the court looks to the train of thought that a consumer would need to follow to get from the mark to a characteristic of the goods or services; then, the court basically decides whether that particular "train" had enough railroad cars. Also, if the mark contains some incongruity, it is more likely that imagination would be necessary and that the mark is thus suggestive rather than descriptive.

Another test employed by courts is the "competitor's need test," under which a mark is more likely to be descriptive if competitors will need to use the term encompassed by the mark for advertising and promoting their own goods and services.[5] This test is a natural extension of the "degree of imagination test," since marks that require a greater degree of imagination have a lower probability of being needed by competitors.

Courts also look to other uses by competitors, the media, and dictionaries. If other sellers are currently using the proposed mark on similar goods or services, this fact weighs heavily toward a finding of descriptiveness. Trade publications and dictionaries are relevant to the descriptiveness inquiry because they indicate how the public most likely perceives the proposed mark. Additionally, if the proponent of the mark is using or has used the mark in a descriptive manner, that also weighs toward a finding of descriptiveness. In the author's experience, too often trademark owners unwittingly use their suggestive marks in a descriptive manner, perhaps as part of text on labels or ad copy in advertisements, leading courts and the U.S. Patent and Trademark Office to push them back over to the wrong side of the suggestive-descriptive line.

Despite the fact that these tests exist, it can be difficult to predict the decision that will be reached in any particular trademark dispute. In the end, the result can depend as much on experienced intuition as rigorous analysis. Indeed, any interpretation and association of a trademark necessarily depends on the particular mental state of the individual perceiving it.

Trademarks Cannot Be Functional

In order to be protectable, a trademark cannot be functional. "In general terms, a product feature is functional, and cannot serve as a trademark, if it is essential to the use or purpose of the article or if it affects the cost or quality of the article."[6] The justification for this is simple; just like generic words, functional elements of a trademark can't indicate source and they deserve to remain in the public domain for all to freely use. For example, the colors of **Dippin' Dots** ice cream could not be used to indicate the source of the ice cream because the colors are commonly used to indicate flavors. A trademark may also be functional if it provides a nonreputation based advantage over competitors. For example, **Lego** is having difficulty protecting the shapes of its toy blocks because if it could protect the shapes, competitors would be forever prohibited from making generic versions of the product. While this monopoly prospect may be attractive to the producer of **Lego**, it is not within the proper realm of trademark law. Rather, patents, another form of intellectual property, are the area for one to seek monopolies on functional elements.

The functionality issue most often arises in the case of nonconventional trademarks such as colors, product configurations, sounds, and scents.

Additionally, functionality is probably the primary reason that there are not yet any federally registered taste or touch trademarks. Some have attempted to trademark tastes, but have not yet been successful.

How Trademark Rights Are Obtained and What They Provide the Brand Owner

There are two sources of trademark rights in the United States: use and registration. These are not independent sources, but rather related and complementary sources. Initially, rights are created through the use of a mark in commerce. Then federal registration can be obtained, which enhances the rights and provides additional remedies to the mark owner.

Trademark Rights Are Created in the United States Through Use

Rights in a trademark are not established until the mark has been "used in commerce." This requires that the mark owner makes a bona fide use of the mark in the ordinary course of business.[7] Generally, this requires that the owner *actually* sells its goods or services to the public under the claimed mark; simply making a token use of the mark in an effort to reserve rights will not suffice. Additionally, the scope of the rights will depend on the extent of the actual use. For example, if a mark is only used on a particular product in Minnesota, that will be the extent of the users' rights. The owner can expand the geographic scope of the rights by expanding the use, or with a federal registration (discussed below).

Likewise, priority in an inherently distinctive mark is based on first use. For noninherently distinctive marks such as descriptive terms, colors, and product configurations, priority is established once the claimed mark acquires distinctiveness or secondary meaning. Later users' uses of a mark are subject to the rights of the user having legal priority. This characteristic is unique to the United States. Most foreign countries base priority of ownership of a mark on the first filing of an application. While the United States allows "constructive use" based on earlier filing, prior actual use by another party would defeat this constructive use.

Registration Provides Enhanced Rights

There are two different options for federally registering a mark; principal registration and supplemental registration. By far, the more relevant of these is principal registration, which provides immediate and substantial benefits to a mark owner.

Principal Registration

Requirements

For registration on the principal register, trademarks must either be inherently distinctive (fanciful, arbitrary, or suggestive) or be descriptive marks that have acquired distinctiveness (secondary meaning). Additionally, there are certain restrictions on what can constitute a federally registered trademark. Some of the most important restrictions are discussed below.

First, trademarks cannot be registered if they contain immoral, deceptive, or scandalous matter.[8] This restriction prevents the registration of such inflammatory material as profanity and racial slurs. Additionally, it prevents the registration of terms that unambiguously refer to vulgar and/or explicit sexual matter. For example, registration for a mark for Jack-Off as an adult phone conversation service was rejected.[9] However, where the term contains some ambiguity, registration typically won't be denied. Thus, **Hooters** (with an owl logo) has been permitted registration for restaurant services, despite the tight-fitting t-shirts worn by female employees, the shape and position of the owl's eyes forming the two letter Os in the logo, and the vulgar and slang meaning of the term. Similarly, registration of **Big Pecker Brand** for t-shirts bearing the image of a giant rooster was allowed.[10]

Second, trademarks cannot disparage or falsely suggest a connection with a person, living or dead, institutions, beliefs, or national symbols, or bring them into contempt or disrepute.[11] Marks that are offensive to particular subclasses of people could be considered disparaging. The mark **Dykes on Bikes** for a lesbian motorcycle group was challenged as disparaging, but was found not to be so for lack of evidence. In 1999, after a 7-year-long battle at the U.S. Patent and Trademark Office, the **Redskins** registrations owned by the professional football team located in Washington, D.C., were ordered to be cancelled as disparaging to Native Americans. That case, even after more than 17 years, was still wading its way through the appeals process.

Third, the mark cannot consist of a flag or coat of arms or other insignia of any government. This restriction is narrowly interpreted to only prevent registration of official symbols of governments. Both the Statue of Liberty and the U.S. Capitol building have successfully been used in registered trademarks.

Fourth, the mark cannot comprise a name, portrait, or signature identifying a particular living individual except by his or her written consent.

Thus, in order for **Kmart** to market the **Kathy Ireland** clothing collection or for **Nike** to provide **Tiger Woods** brand merchandise, the companies must have explicit permission from the individuals.

Benefits

There are numerous benefits associated with federal trademark registrations. First, registration on the principal register provides *constructive notice* that the mark owner has the right to use the mark throughout the entire geographic area of the United States, notwithstanding the fact that the mark is only being used in a smaller geographic area.[12] In addition, the filing date of the resulting registration is the nationwide constructive use date, such that the trademark owner is deemed to have used the mark on the goods in every corner of the country as of that date, even if that is not actually true. The only way the mark could be used legally by another person anywhere in the country would be if the other person had been using the mark prior to filing date of the resulting federal registration.

Second, registration constitutes prima facie evidence that the mark is valid, the registrant owns the mark, and the registrant has the exclusive right to use the mark in commerce.[13] This can significantly reduce some of the evidentiary burdens that need to be satisfied if a legal dispute arises. Third, after the fifth anniversary of the registration and 5 years of continuous use of the mark in commerce, the registration can become incontestable.[14] Once this occurs, defendants cannot claim that the trademark is merely descriptive, and other protections are granted the registrant, too. Fourth, the registration creates federal subject matter jurisdiction, which means the owner automatically can sue in federal court.[15] Fifth, the trademark owner may be entitled to increased statutory damages.[16] Specifically, the court may triple the amount of actual damages found, which typically occurs in cases of willful infringement. Additionally, the owner is entitled to costs of bringing the action, if successful. And sixth, the trademark owner can prevent the importation of goods containing an infringing mark.[17]

Supplemental Registration

Requirements

For the most part, registration on the supplemental register has the same restrictions as the principal register. Marks cannot be immoral, deceptive, scandalous, disparaging, etc. However, marks on the supplemental register do not yet have to be distinctive; they must only be capable of eventually becoming distinctive. This means that merely descriptive marks are registrable, but generic and functional marks are not (because they are incapable of *ever* indicating source).

Benefits

Supplemental registration is primarily for marks that are characterized as merely descriptive and have not yet acquired secondary meaning. It provides significantly fewer benefits than a principal registration. It allows access to the federal courts, the mark will appear in trademark searches, and the registrant is given the right to use the ® symbol in connection with the mark. Probably the main benefit of a supplemental registration is that it prevents others from registering confusingly similar marks while the supplemental registration owner is trying to establish secondary meaning or acquired distinctiveness in order to obtain principal registration.

Trademark Rights Are Designed to Prevent Confusion of Consumers

Perhaps the most important justification for the development of trademark law is the prevention of consumer confusion. The infringement standard itself employs terms such as "confusingly similar" and "likelihood of confusion." The obvious vagueness of these terms prohibits ready application, so courts look to various factors when determining whether marks will likely cause consumer confusion. These factors, commonly referred to as the "Polaroid factors," are (1) the strength of the mark, (2) the degree of similarity between the marks, (3) the competitive proximity of the products or services, (4) the likelihood that plaintiff will bridge the gap between the markets, (5) the existence of actual confusion, (6) the quality of defendant's product, and (7) the sophistication of the purchasers.[18]

Remedies to Trademark Owner When Rights Are Infringed

A variety of remedies are available in trademark infringement actions, but they can be broken down primarily into two categories: injunctive and monetary relief. Injunctions are used to prevent an infringer from using the mark, while monetary relief is meant to compensate mark owners for any damages they may have suffered. Infringement actions generally involve the pursuit of a combination of injunctive and monetary relief.

Injunctive Relief

Generally in legal actions, injunctive relief is limited to situations where monetary remedies are inadequate. However, because of the unique nature of trademark rights and the fact that money will rarely be enough, injunctions are ordered as a matter of course. In contrast to other types of intellectual property such as copyrights and patents, compulsory licenses are not proper because uncontrolled use of a trademark by an infringer can alter the property itself. An infringing use of a mark "place[s] the owner's reputation beyond its control."[19] As a result, nothing less than total prevention of infringing use will protect the owner.

Monetary Relief

In determining monetary relief, there are at least five ways to measure the appropriate amount of an award: (1) defendant's profits, either as a way of measuring plaintiff's loss or under an unjust enrichment theory, (2) plaintiff's actual business damages and losses caused by the wrong, (3) plaintiff's own loss of profits caused by the wrong, (4) punitive damages in addition to actual damages, for the purpose of punishing defendant, and (5) plaintiff's reasonable attorney's fees incurred in pursuing the legal action.[20] As expected from looking at these methods of computation, determining the appropriate amount of monetary relief can be extremely difficult. Adding to the complexity is the importance of the defendant's state of mind; a defendant might be willful, negligent, or innocent. Each level of culpability theoretically would justify a different level of monetary relief.

Loss of Trademark Rights

The Importance of Enforcing Trademark Rights

Once trademark rights are obtained, continuous protection of those rights is necessary. If trademark owners are not vigilant, unauthorized use can erode all value contained within a trademark. This erosion can occur both practically and legally.

Practically speaking, any unauthorized use of a mark will have at least some impact on at least some portion of the consuming public. These unauthorized uses are dangerous to a trademark owner because they have the potential to corrupt the message and goodwill that have been cultivated in the mark. Although some uses may seem insignificant, the aggregate effect over time can be substantial. Accordingly, trademark owners need to keep a keen eye out for unauthorized uses. Legally speaking, a trademark owner can lose the rights associated with a trademark. If an owner does not consistently protect his rights, courts will not protect the owner.

Potentially, the mark could be deemed abandoned or the owner could be barred from asserting his rights.

Abandonment

Because trademark law only protects marks that are presently in use and being vigorously defended by owners, it is possible that an owner can lose rights to a mark through abandonment. There are a variety of ways that abandonment can actually occur, but the primary import of each is that the mark owner has failed to provide enough protection for the mark in his own dealings. When the owner does not undertake efforts to protect the value of a mark, the court will not aid that owner.

One of the key elements of abandonment is that after ceasing use of the mark, the owner lacks an intent to resume use of the mark.[21] There are two ways that this intent may be determined: (1) the mark holder may explicitly state that he no longer intends to use the mark or (2) intent may be inferred from long periods where the mark is not used. Under the Lanham Act, 3 years of nonuse raises an inference that the mark has been abandoned.[22] Essentially, the nonuse test prevents individuals from "warehousing" marks with no actual plans for use in the future. Once 3 years of nonuse have passed, the mark owner must come forward with evidence justifying the nonuse to prevent a finding of abandonment.

The doctrine of abandonment is a legal means of accounting for the practical effects of nonuse in the marketplace. If a mark endures long periods of nonuse, goodwill slowly diminishes. If the owner does not replenish the good will through use, eventually the goodwill will evaporate completely. Once this occurs, there is no justification for providing the mark owner with further legal protection.

Genericide

As previously discussed, generic designations are those that cannot function as trademarks or indicators of source because they have come to simply name the product itself, not the source of the product. Genericide is the process whereby the public appropriates a trademark as the common name for a product, thereby depriving it of its source indicating capabilities. Once genericide occurs, the mark is lost and the owner is without remedy. The owner cannot sue the world, so to speak, and prevent the public from using the mark.

To determine if a mark has become generic, the opinion that matters is that of "the relevant public."[23] Similar to the likelihood of confusion analysis, the relevant public will consist of the population that purchases the goods and encounters the mark in the marketplace. If a majority of this population determines that the "principal significance" of the mark is nongeneric, then the mark survives. However, if the mark has become the name for the product or even a verb for using the product, the rights disappear.

Popular examples of the genericide danger can be seen in today's marketplace. Perhaps the most contemporary is **Google**'s ongoing effort to eliminate the public's use of "google" as a verb for searching the Internet. Other well-known marks that have been facing down genericide include **Xerox** for copy machines (which probably has been helped by the fact that copy machines are now only a small subset of document management technology), **Kleenex** for facial tissue, and **Rollerblade** for in-line skates.

Examples of marks that were not able to withstand the wave of genericide were **Cellophane** for plastic wrap, **Escalator** for moving staircases, **Aspirin** for salicylic acid pills, and **Thermos** for vacuum-sealed canisters. Genericide is a troublesome problem because of the fact that it is more likely to occur when a mark owner has done *too good a job* of promoting the mark and product!

To avoid this problem, companies have adopted various strategies. The most obvious is ensuring that they are using the mark in a proper manner, as an adjective, and not using it as a verb or noun. The next step is to diligently police the use of others and to provide corrective measures when necessary. Another strategy, as is frequently seen in the pharmaceutical industries, is to create both a brand name and a generic name for the product. For example, when you see a brand name for **Prilosec** with **omeprazole** listed below it, **Prilosec** is the trademark and **omeprazole** is the fanciful generic name meant to prevent genericide of the trade name.

Those who develop brands, especially for products that launch a new category, are well advised to spend considerable time and effort developing a generic term for the new product that the public will accept, so that when the category leader begins to experience competition, the consuming public has a term other than the brand to describe the product. It is the author's contention that had the generic term "in-line skates" been promoted when the **Rollerblade** brand was introduced, there would not be signs and city ordinances throughout the country forbidding in certain public areas "rollerblades" and "rollerblading" as opposed to "in-line skating."

Transfer and Licensing of Trademark Rights

As with other property rights, trademark rights can be transferred and licensed. However, because of the unique characteristics of trademarks, there are some limitations. Most importantly, assignments in gross and

TRADEMARK DEFENSE IN PRACTICE

"3M is a company that turns technology into brands, and the most valuable asset we have—beyond our employees—is our portfolio of trademarks," says Marshall Smith, senior vice president of legal affairs and general counsel for 3M. "At an estimated $20 billion, those trademarks exceed the value of our patents." This means that 3M, which sets out to create enduring franchises from its innovative technology developments, needs to begin the branding process in their labs. Once a product enters the marketplace, 3M is "extraordinarily vigorous" about enforcing trademark law, both to protect its brands from infringement and to protect consumers from imposter products.

Smith explains that 3M's integrated structure allows intellectual property lawyers and technical liaisons to work directly with its development labs. "We're always thinking about brands at every level, being sensitive to the need to secure our trademarks by working at each step along the way." By partnering its product developers and the legal affairs department to take new ideas to the marketplace, 3M hopes to stop trademark threats such as knock-off products, "genericide," and dilution before they start.

But should such a challenge arise, 3M's global legal team is prepared to respond swiftly. In one recent case, 3M filed suit against Korea's Doori Trading Company for marketing the "Post-in." Within weeks, Doori admitted its infringement and that the Post-it™ mark was, indeed, well known in Korea. As a result of the suit, Doori was forced to cease all infringement, destroy the advertising materials for the "Post-in," and surrender all of its remaining inventory and manufacturing molds to 3M. Further, the company agreed to release a public apology in a prominent Seoul newspaper.

For over 100 years, 3M has successfully established and protected its enduring brands. 3M pays careful attention to trademarks at the earliest stages of R&D, and quickly and formally respond to any infringements worldwide. "You need to jump fast," Smith concludes, "not only for the company's sake, but for the consumer's. Because of our efforts, a buyer can trust the quality of the 3M brand wherever they go."

R.D.M. & L.W.P.

naked licenses are prohibited. The prohibition of assignments in gross recognizes that a trademark separated from the business it has come to represent is of no value at all. Accordingly, assignment of the trademark can only occur with a transfer of the goodwill of the business with which the mark has been associated. The prohibition of naked licenses recognizes that the mark owner is responsible for the message that the mark represents. Therefore, a mark owner must ensure that the mark is being used in a manner consistent with that message.

An assignment in gross does not occur when the owner sells his entire business along with the trademark. When a mark owner assigns the mark with the business, the mark is still being used on the same types of goods or services and the message that the public has associated with the mark should continue to be accurate. Likewise, if a business owner transfers a specific portion of his business and the trademark that was used exclusively with that portion, there is no assignment in gross. However, if the business owner were to transfer the trademark rights, but not the underlying goodwill associated with the trademark, the assignment is invalid and risks destroying the trademark.

Naked licensing occurs when a mark owner permits another to use his mark but fails to exercise quality control over the use of the mark and the goods or services bearing the mark. The legal requirements for licensing of trademarks are premised on the notion that the owner of the mark has been responsible for developing and maintaining the goodwill of the mark. To prevent deception of the public, the mark owner must be responsible for maintaining the quality of goods or services associated with the mark. This is an affirmative duty on the trademark owner, and failure to undertake necessary steps to control the use of the mark can result in a forfeiture of rights.

There are a couple ways that a mark owner can control the quality of goods sufficiently to avoid a loss of rights. First, the mark owner can include provisions in the licensing agreement to enforce its own quality control standards. This would essentially mean that the owner retains some control over the licensee's use of the mark even after the agreement has been entered. Another manner to control quality is simply being familiar with and relying on the quality control of the licensee. Typically, for the courts to allow this reliance to be sufficient, there needs to be an extended and long-lasting relationship between the parties, such that the reliance of the mark owner was reasonable.

Contrary to assignments, marks can be licensed without a transfer of the goodwill of the business. Practically speaking, this has allowed the massive development of franchising. Despite the fact that the individual businesses are owned by numerous individuals, the fact that they license the trademarks from a central owner means that a single source is responsible for the quality of the goods marketed by the franchisees. Without licensing, trademark law would essentially be limited to the concept of one trademark, one user, and franchising would not be possible.

Famous Trademarks and Dilution

"Famous" trademarks are "widely recognized by the general consuming public of the United States as a designation of source of the goods or services of the mark's owner."[24] In addition to the protections outlined above, "famous" trademarks are afforded protection against not only likely confusion, but dilution, too. In *Polaroid Corp. v. Polaraid, Inc.*, the court summarized the basic theory of dilution:

> The gravamen of a dilution complaint is that the continuous use of a mark similar to plaintiff's works an inexorably adverse effect upon the distinctiveness of the plaintiff's mark, and that, if he is powerless to prevent such use, his mark will lose its distinctiveness entirely. This injury differs materially from that arising out of the orthodox confusion. Such confusion leads to immediate injury, while dilution is an infection which, if allowed to spread, will inevitably destroy the advertising value of the mark.[25]

Dilution is perhaps one of the most difficult doctrines of trademark law to understand; it adds an additional layer of complexity to the already existing vagueness of "likelihood of confusion." But simply stated, "dilution" is the gradual diminishment of a mark's strength or value over time. In contrast to the spontaneous nature of marketplace confusion, dilution deals with a gradual "whittling away" of a trademark's value. In contrast to infringement, dilution does not require a likelihood of confusion or that the mark be used on similar goods.

Recently, dilution law received a major overhaul by Congress. In the Trademark Dilution Revision Act of 2006,[26] Congress undertook a substantial effort to clarify the legal standards associated with dilution, and to elaborate on the definition of what constitutes a "famous" mark. Prior to this Act, various questions and disagreements had arisen in the courts regarding the proper standard for demonstrating dilution. Additionally, the concept of fame had begun drifting in a somewhat troublesome direction, where courts were starting to find fame in marks like **Panavision** and **Wawa**, marks nowhere near the notoriety of those marks Congress had previously designated worthy of such exalted protection, such as the **Dupont, Buick,** and **Kodak** trademarks.

The seminal case prior to the new Act was *Moseley v. V Secret Catalogue, Inc.*[27] There, the Supreme Court determined that a plaintiff asserting trademark dilution needed to show *actual* dilution to prevail.[28] This strict standard was troublesome for two reasons. First, the Court did not explain what evidence would be adequate to show *actual* dilution; no guidance was offered aside from saying that an actual showing of economic harm was not necessary. Second, and more importantly, the case interpreted the law such that a remedy was not available until the plaintiff had already been harmed, i.e., the trademark had already been diluted. This was clearly in contradiction of the statute's purpose, which was to provide injunctive relief before harm had occurred.

In response, Congress passed an Act containing much more specificity as to the elements involved in dilution. First, contrary to the Court's holding in *Moseley,* Congress decided that *likelihood of dilution* was the appropriate standard rather than *actual dilution.* This alone is a significant step as it has the potential to significantly decrease the burden on plaintiffs and it allows relief to be granted before damage to the trademark occurs.

Second, Congress explicitly stated that dilution could occur by either "blurring" or "tarnishment."[29] "Dilution by blurring" occurs as the result of an "association arising from similarity [in marks] that impairs the distinctiveness of the famous mark."[30] The Court can consider any relevant factors, but the six most important are (1) the degree of similarity between the marks, (2) the degree of inherent or acquired distinctiveness of the famous mark, (3) the extent to which the owner of the famous mark is engaging in substantially exclusive use of the mark, (4) the degree of recognition of the famous mark, (5) whether the user of the diluting mark intended to create an association with the famous mark, and (6) any actual association between the marks.[31] An example of dilution by blurring the famous **Polaroid** mark would be Polaraid for heating and refrigeration systems.

"Dilution by tarnishment" occurs as the result of "similarity between [marks] that harms the reputation of the famous mark."[32] When a party attaches another's trademark to negative subject matter, that negative subject matter will be recalled by the viewer every time she sees the trademark. Clearly, this affects the value of the trademark.[33] Generally, where plaintiffs have been most successful are cases where their trademark is used in an "unwholesome" or "degrading" context.[34] The most obvious examples involve adult-related industries. For example, in *Dallas Cowboys Cheerleaders, Inc. v. Pussycat Cinema, Ltd.,* an injunction was granted where pornographic movie stars were shown performing sexual acts in the distinctive uniform of the Dallas Cowboys cheerleaders.[35] In *Hasbro, Inc. v. Internet Entertainment Group, Ltd.,* the court issued a preliminary injunction where **Candy Land** was being used in a domain name for a pornographic Web site.[36] And in *Eastman Kodak Co. v. Rakow,* tarnishment was found where a crude comedic character used "Kodak" as a stage name.[37]

Another troubling development under prior dilution law (at least in the eyes of Congress) was that "niche market" and "business-to-business product" trademarks were being classified as "famous" by the courts. The legislative history of the original dilution act indicated that Congress was primarily concerned with the dilution of trademarks highly recognized by the general public. Examples of dilution found in the legislative history were **DuPont** shoes, **Buick** aspirin, and **Kodak** pianos; clearly, each of these marks had achieved exceptionally high levels of distinction. However, notwithstanding these examples, courts liberally attached the "famous" label to marks such as **Intermatic**, **Teletech**, **Nailtiques**, and **WaWa**, in most cases to remedy domain name abuses that were committed prior to the 1999 legislation specifically targeted against cybersquatting, the Anticyperpiracy Consumer Protection Act. The revisions to the Dilution Act made it clear that such "niche" fame did not satisfy the statutory requirement for "famous" marks.

The Use of Survey Evidence in Trademark Disputes

Survey evidence is often indispensable in trademark disputes. Because there is rarely any direct evidence regarding the substantive claims and defenses in trademark disputes, surveys are necessary to draw inferences and come to a resolution. Survey evidence can be used for virtually every trademark issue, including whether marks have achieved secondary meaning or fame, whether the public is likely to be confused by an allegedly infringing mark, whether a famous mark is being diluted, and whether a mark has become generic.

There are a variety of methods for obtaining trademark survey evidence including mall-intercept surveys, telephone surveys, central location surveys, and Internet surveys. The type of survey used in a particular case will depend on the goals that the survey is needed to accomplish. It will also depend largely on the amount of money that is available for conducting the survey. In some cases, the survey will be very similar to other market research that a company might undertake in the normal operation of its business.

While useful, survey evidence conducted in the course of a litigation is not without critics as a number of courts have voiced skepticism of such survey results.[38] In a fairly well-known judicial decision, Chief Judge Posner of the Seventh Circuit Court of Appeals directed heavy denigration toward the science of trademark surveys conducted by experts for litigants:

Many experts are willing for a generous (and sometimes modest) fee to bend their science in the direction from which their fee is coming. The constraints that the market in consultant services for lawyers places on this sort of behavior are weak, as shown by the fact that both experts in this case have been criticized in previous judicial opinions. The judicial constraints on tendentious expert testimony are inherently weak because judges (and even more so juries, though that is not an issue in a trademark case) lack training or experience in the relevant fields of expert knowledge.[39]

Posner further went on to characterize the defendant's survey as "three loaded questions in one Baltimore Mall" and disparaged the plaintiff's survey for containing "tricks of the survey researcher's black arts."

This potential for judicial hostility makes it important to consider some specific requirements when conducting a survey for evidentiary purposes in a trademark dispute: (1) the population should be properly defined and chosen, (2) the sample chosen should represent the population, (3) the data gathered must be accurately reported, (4) the data must be analyzed in accordance with accepted statistical principles, (5) the questions must be clear and not leading, (6) the survey must be conducted by qualified individuals following proper interview procedures, and (7) the entire process must ensure objectivity.[40] By following these requirements it is less likely that the survey will be questioned, or worse, excluded by the Court.

The most critical and difficult aspect of a survey is ensuring that the proper population is selected and sampled. Survey evidence is only helpful if the people surveyed are the ones encountering the mark in the marketplace. Consumers that are familiar with the goods and services that the mark is associated with may be able to draw distinctions that would confuse those that were less familiar. For example, the confusion of a 60-year-old man over the use of **Miss Seventeen** for women's girdles and **Seventeen** for a young women's magazine is irrelevant to the appropriate likelihood of confusion analysis, since the relevant consumers are clearly women.[41] Similarly, if a product is primarily distributed in the upper Midwest, survey evidence taken from the West Coast would not be particularly useful.

Another important component of a successful survey is that it does not contain leading questions. For example, in a case concerning possible confusion over McDonald's sponsorship of a restaurant called **McBagel's**, the surveyor simply asked (1) whether the respondent had heard of McBagel's, (2) who did the respondent believe sponsored or promoted McBagel's, (3) what made them think so, and (4) what type of business was the sponsor or promoter in.[42] Results indicated that 24.8% in the United States and 36.4% in the particular market believed that McBagel's was sponsored or promoted by McDonald's, and the court found this to be adequate evidence of actual confusion in the marketplace.[43]

Another example of a nonleading survey involved the **Swiss Army Knife**.[44] There, the surveyor provided the respondent with a catalogue page with a picture of the defendant's knife brandishing the words "Swiss Army." First, the survey asked if the respondent believed the knife to be of high quality. Second, the survey asked what led to that belief. Third, the question asked if there was anything on the knife to indicate a particular place of manufacturing. And, fourth, where was the knife manufactured?[45]

Survey evidence is also useful for determining whether a mark has become generic. Survey evidence was offered by DuPont to rebut the contention that **Teflon** had become a generic term for a nonstick coating.[46] There, the court found persuasive a survey that listed a number of words and trademarks and then simply asked whether the word was a brand name or a common name. The words were STP, Thermos, Margarine, Teflon, Jell-O, Refrigerator, Aspirin, and Coke. In the survey, 68% had indicated that Teflon was a brand name, and the court determined that this was sufficient to show that the mark had not become generic. Further, the court noted that the public seemed to be adept at distinguishing between brand names and common names based on the responses given for the other words included in the survey.

Conclusion

Branding is a critical component to the success of any business bringing goods or services to a competitive marketplace. As consumers are faced with seemingly endless options and information overload, the importance of disseminating a unique and informative message becomes increasingly important. Trademark law provides an important framework for protecting the integrity of this information exchange between sellers and buyers. Accordingly, it is in the interest of all businesses providing goods and services to consider the importance of trademark law when determining how to promote their goods and services. Hopefully, in considering trademark law and its implications, a business will find itself better positioned to deal with the rigorous requirements for selecting, creating, establishing, maintaining, and protecting an enduring brand.

Endnotes

1 15 U.S.C. § 1127 (2008). For ease, the author uses the term "trademark" interchangeably with the term "service mark" even though technically, the former indicates the source of products and the latter indicates the source of services.

2 *Echo Travel, Inc. v. Travel Associates, Inc.*, 870 F.2d 1264 (7th Cir. 1989).

3 *Franklin Knitting Mills, Inc. v. Fashionit Sweater Mills, Inc.*, 297 F. 247 (D.N.Y. 1923).

4 *E.g., Stix Products, Inc. v. United Merchants & Mfrs., Inc.*, 295 F. Supp. 479 (S.D.N.Y. 1968).

5 *E.g., Union Carbide Corp. v. Ever-Ready, Inc.*, 531 F.2d 366 (7th Cir. 1976).

6 *Qualitex Co. v. Jacobsen Prod. Co.*, 514 U.S. 159 (1995).

7 15 U.S.C. § 1127

8 15 U.S.C. § 1052(a).

9 *In re Boulevard Entertainment, Inc.*, 334 F.3d 1336 (Fed. Cir. 2003).

10 *In re Hershey*, 6 U.S.P.Q.2d 1470 (TTAB 1988).

11 15 U.S.C. § 1052(a).

12 *Id.* at §§ 1057(c), 1072.

13 *Id.* at § 1057(b).

14 *Id.* at § 1065.

15 *Id.* at § 1121(a).

16 *Id.* at § 1117

17 *Id.* at § 1124

18 These factors were initially outlined in *Polaroid v. Polarad Elecs. Corp.*, 287 F.2d 492 (2d Cir. 1961).

19 James Burrough Ltd. v. sign of Beafeater, Inc., 540 F.2nd 266 (7th Cir. 1976).

20 5J. McCarthy, *McCarthy on Trademarks & Unfair Competiton supra*, § 30:57

21 15 U.S.C. § 1127

22 Id.

23 15 U.S.C. § 1064(3).

24 Trademark Dilution Revision Act (TDRA) of 2006, Pub. L. No. 109-312, 120 Stat. 1729, 1730 (2007).

25 319 F.2d 830, 836 (7th Cir. 1963), *quoting* Callman, *The Law of Unfair Competition and Trademarks* 1643 (2d ed. 1950).

26 TDRA, *supra.*

27 537 U.S. 418 (2003).

28 *Id.* at 432-33.

29 TDRA, 120 Stat. at 1731.

30 *Id.*

31 *Id.*

32 *Id.*

33 It is important to note that just like all other speech related legislation, dilution laws are subject to fair-use exceptions. Thus, if tarnishment (and accompanying value loss) is occurring as a result of non-commercial parody or satire, it may be difficult to enjoin that use.

34 *See* 4 J. McCarthy, *McCarthy on Trademarks & Unfair Competiton* § 24:89 (4th ed. 2009).

35 467 F. Supp. 366 (S.D.N.Y. 1979).

36 1996 WL 84853, at *1 (W.D. Wash. Feb. 9, 1996).

37 739 F. Supp. 116 (W.D.N.Y. 1989).

38 *See* Joseph H. Lessem, "Consumer Surveys in Trademark Litigation: Are they Worth it?" *Corporate Counsel's Quarterly,* vol. 16, no. 2, April 2000.

39 *Indianapolis Colts, Inc. v. Metropolitan Baltimore Football Club L.P.,* 34 F.3d 410 (7th Cir. 1994).

40 David F. Herr, *Manual for Complex Litigation,* § 11.493 (4th ed. 2006).

41 *Triangle Pub's v. Rohrlich,* 167 F.2d 969, 976 n.6 (2d Cir. 1948) (Frank, J. dissenting)

42 *McDonald's Corp. v. McBagel's, Inc.,* 649 F. Supp. 1268, 1277 (S.D.N.Y. 1986).

43 *Id.*

44 *Forschner Group, Inc. v. Arrow Trading Co., Inc.,* 833 F.Supp. 385 (S.D.N.Y. 1993).

45 *Id.* at 390-91.

46 *E.I. DuPont de Nemours and Co. v. Yoshida Int'l, Inc.,* 343 F. Supp. 502 (E.D.N.Y. 1975).

Author Index

Subject Index

A

Accessibility of information, 14–15, 17–19, 31, 36, 79, 93, 94, 104–5, 201–2, 256
Accommodation, 137, 143–144
Affect, 19, 24–25, 51, 59, 66, 70–76, 83, 215, 234
Attitudes
toward brands, 16, 44, 45, 51, 54, 65, 94, 101, 103, 123, 126, 134, 234–240, 244, 247, 254, 255, 258–262
toward cause-brand alliance, 102
toward causes, 94, 99, 102, 103
toward companies, 99, 100, 101, 103
toward CSR, 94, 100
culture and, 125

B

Brand alliances; See also Co-brands, 3, 4, 12, 43–60, 101, 234–234, 253, 256, 257, 259
Brand communities, 5, 7, 71, 73, 138, 139, 140, 144, 145, 148, 246, 247, 258
Brand equity; See also Brand measurement, 3, 6, 21, 22, 54–59, 91, 125, 127, 159–185, 207–227, 243, 245, 250, 253, 255, 257
Brand extensions, 3–8, 11–37, 101, 135, 181, 213, 216, 224, 234, 235, 251, 253, 255, 256, 259–263
Brand image, 13, 14, 16, 17, 20, 24, 26, 28, 36, 44, 51, 58, 59, 83, 91, 94, 101, 120, 126, 127, 128, 207, 209, 239, 241, 244, 246, 247, 248, 250, 251, 252, 254, 262

Brand loyalty, 3–4, 7, 35, 63–84, 92, 99, 175, 196, 200, 207, 209, 213, 221, 258, 259, 260
Brand measurement of, 3, 126, 160, 167, 168, 208, 210, 214, 217, 218, 220, 221, 223, 224, 226
Brand personality, 44, 51, 72, 75, 76, 239, 252
Brand preference, 31, 51, 69, 124, 125, 129, 151
Brands; See also Attitude toward brands; Brand alliances; Brand extensions; Brand loyalty; Brand measurement; Brand personality; Brand preference; Brand equity; Brand image; Self-brand relationships
attributes of, 13, 17, 19, 20, 26, 65, 72, 83, 134, 151, 164, 166, 217, 224, 233, 242
commitment to, 14, 15, 64, 66, 74, 83, 238, 258,
corporate social responsibility and, 3, 5, 37, 91–106, 238, 239, 259, 260
dilution of, 6, 8, 24, 59, 128, 233–263
as identity, 58, 59, 71, 72, 73, 113–129, 250, 251, 252, 253
involvement with, 25, 74, 76, 118, 119
preference, 31, 51, 64, 66, 69, 124, 125, 129, 175, 194, 201, 203, 218, 220, 221, 222, 224, 234
reference groups and, 115
repositioning, 142, 147
resonance, 128, 149
social model of, 133, 135, 137
as sports teams, 166
symbolism, 5, 113–129
utility models of, 3, 6, 212,

Brand Index